# The Right to Education in India

# The Right to Education in India

## The Importance of Enforceability of a Fundamental Right

FLORIAN MATTHEY-PRAKASH

OXFORD
UNIVERSITY PRESS

OXFORD
UNIVERSITY PRESS

Oxford University Press is a department of the University of Oxford. It furthers the University's objective of excellence in research, scholarship, and education by publishing worldwide. Oxford is a registered trademark of Oxford University Press in the UK and in certain other countries.

Published in India by
Oxford University Press
22 Workspace, 2nd Floor, 1/22 Asaf Ali Road, New Delhi 110 002, India



First Edition published in 2019



ISBN-13 (print edition): 978-0-19-949428-6
ISBN-10 (print edition): 0-19-949428-2

ISBN-13 (eBook): 978-0-19-909705-0
ISBN-10 (eBook): 0-19-909705-4

Typeset in Trump Mediaeval LT Std 9.5/13
by The Graphics Solution, New Delhi 110 092
Printed in India by Replika Press Pvt. Ltd

*To my parents*
*for always supporting me*

# Contents

# Abbreviations

| | |
|---|---|
| BEO | Block Education Officer |
| BIMARU | Bihar, Madhya Pradesh, Rajasthan, Uttar Pradesh |
| CABE | Central Advisory Board on Education |
| CBSE | Central Board of Secondary Education |
| CEO | Chief Executive Officer |
| CEO-ZP | CEO of the Zila Panchayat |
| CESCR | Committee on Economic, Social and Cultural Rights |
| CRC | Convention on the Rights of the Child |
| DCPCR | Delhi Commission for the Protection of Child Rights |
| DDPI | Deputy Director of Public Instruction |
| DLERA | District Level Education Regulating Authority |
| DPEP | District Primary Education Programme |
| ECHR | European Court of Human Rights |
| ECtHR | European Convention on Human Rights |
| EFA | Education For All |
| EU | European Union |
| GDP | Gross Domestic Product |
| ICCPR | International Covenant on Civil and Political Rights |
| ICESCR | International Covenant on Economic, Social and Cultural Rights |
| ICON | International Journal of Constitutional Law |
| IMF | International Monetary Fund |

| | |
|---|---|
| JSY | Janani Suraksha Yojana |
| KSCPCR | Karnataka State Commission for Protection of Child Rights |
| MDG | Millennium Development Goals |
| NAFRE | National Alliance for Fundamental Right to Education |
| NALSA | National Legal Services Authority |
| NCPCR | National Commission for the Protection of Child Right |
| NGO | Non-Governmental Organization |
| NMBS | National Maternity Benefit Scheme |
| OBC | Other Backward Classes |
| OECD | Organisation for Economic Co-operation and Development |
| PDS | Public Distribution System |
| PIL | Public Interest Litigation |
| PISA | Programme for International Student Assessment |
| PROBE | Public Report on Basic Education in India |
| PUCL | People's Union for Civil Liberties |
| PUCLDR | People's Union of Civil Liberties and Democratic Rights |
| PUDR | People's Union for Democratic Rights |
| REPA | Right to Education Protection Authority |
| SAL | Social Action Litigation |
| SC/ST | Scheduled Castes/Scheduled Tribes |
| SCPCR | State Commission for the Protection of Child Right |
| SJC | Social Justice Committee |
| SLP | Special Leave Petitions |
| SMC | School Management Committees |
| UDHR | Universal Declaration of Human Rights |
| UNDP | United Nations Development Programme |
| UNESCO | United Nations Educational, Scientific and Cultural Organization |
| UNICEF | United Nations International Children's Emergency Fund |
| VEC | Village Education Committees |
| VSNL | Videsh Sanchar Nigam Limited |

# Acknowledgements

This book is an edited and updated version of my doctoral dissertation, which was accepted by the faculty of law at the Justus Liebig University Giessen, Germany, in early 2018.

First of all, my thanks go to Professor Philipp Dann for guiding me in the years that I was working on this book. From him, I learned to appreciate the benefits of an inter-disciplinary approach and of always following one's curiosity in all directions, especially in the early phase of research. With his encouragement, I presented my work at different forums in both India and Germany, which has allowed me to write a book that, hopefully, will appeal to an audience in India and abroad.

I would also like to thank Professor Jürgen Bast for his valuable comments on the manuscript. They, along with Philipp Dann's comments and the questions asked by Professor Marietta Auer and Professor Walter Gropp during the thesis defence at the University of Giessen, have been of great help in improving it before publication.

During my years at the University of Giessen, I benefitted greatly from being able to share and discuss my work with my colleagues. My gratitude, therefore, goes to my friends and former colleagues, Martin Wortmann, Jan Martin Vogel, Jasmin Schnitzer, Michael Riegner, and Maxim Bönnemann, as well as Tanja Herklotz, Konrad Vossen, and Aurora Sánchez Palacio, who gave valuable comments on my work on my visits to the Humboldt University of Berlin, Germany.

I am also grateful to Professor Bettina Schöndorf-Haubold for her constant support during the final two years of working on my thesis. I also extend my gratitude to Gwyneth Schulz, Carina Weitzel, and Anke Wagner for always being there to help in all administrative procedures.

While working on this book, I have learned tremendously about the Indian legal and education system. I am very grateful to all the experts for their time and patience in answering my questions, among them Jayna Kothari, Aparna Ravi, Kiran Bhatty, Archana Mehendale, Swagata Raha, Mahendra Dwivedi, Gurminder Singh, Sundeep Khare, Dattaraya Gokhale, Rama Kant Rai, Dolashree Mysoor, Malini Bhatarcharjee, Zoya Qureshi, Reena Choudhary, Hemakshi Meghani, Mamta Sahai, Professor Sarbani Sen, Professor Pritam Baruah, Professor Arun Thiruvengadam, and Professor Sudhir Krishnaswamy. I also thank my friends, Kavana Ramaswamy, Shubho Roy, Anirudh Burman, Sindhu Vasudev, Radhika Chitkara, and Protiti Roy, who were always there to offer their insights on the workings of the Indian legal system.

I would also like to thank the team at Oxford University Press, as well as Arghya Sengupta, who advised me regarding the publication process.

My special thanks go to Professor Maximilian Haedicke. While I was a student at the University of Freiburg, Germany, he made my first contact to India possible through a student exchange programme with the West Bengal National University of Juridical Sciences (NUJS) in Kolkata in 2007. That was the time when the seeds of my interest in Indian law, history, and society were sowed, which I continued to nurture. I am equally grateful to Professor M.P. Singh, who was then the vice chancellor at NUJS. He has been a guide and good friend and has stood by me through my academic pursuits for over a decade now!

I will always be grateful for the love and support of my 'Indo-German' family, Kirsten, Thomas, Juliane, and Felix Matthey, and Vibha Prakash, Om Prakash Srivastava, Bhawna, Reva, and Aastha Prakash. I dedicate this book to my parents, Kirsten and Thomas

Matthey, who have always supported me throughout the many years of my education.

During my work on the doctoral dissertation, the greatest love and support has come from my wife, Nishtha Prakash. This book would not have been possible without her.

# Introduction

When travelling around India, there is something that one can see in all parts of the country, in cities as well as in villages: advertisements for educational institutions. Articles in local newspapers praise children who have topped examinations. In smaller cities, one can actually see those children's faces on posters in the streets. At the time of 'the kids' exams', the lives of families stand still.

Educating their children is important for parents from all backgrounds. This is also not exclusive to boys. Already in 1996, 98 per cent of all parents polled in a survey stated that it was important to them that their sons be educated. Eighty-nine per cent stated that it was important for their daughters.[1] This gender-gap, although it remains, has become smaller in the last two decades, with the majority of parents now also wanting their daughters to pursue education as far as possible.[2] Many parents are willing to pay for their children's education as well. Even in rural India, the prevalence of private schools at the primary level has been growing rapidly in the past decades.[3]

[1] The PROBE Team, *Public Report on Basic Education in India* (New Delhi: Oxford University Press, 1999), 19.

[2] Anuradha De, *Probe Revisited: A Report on Elementary Education in India* (New Delhi: Oxford University Press, 2011), 50.

[3] In 2006, 34 per cent of all villages had at least one private school. In 1996, this was the case for only 21 per cent of the villages, see De, *Probe*

At first glance, the importance given to education reflects in the country's laws as well. Article 21A of the Constitution, a provision added by the Eighty-Sixth Constitutional Amendment in 2002, guarantees free and compulsory education to all children aged 6 to 14 years as a fundamental right. In 2009, Parliament passed the Right of Children to Free and Compulsory Education Act to implement this constitutional provision.

To an extent, the constitutional promise was not new. The original constitutional text of 1950 already included an obligation on the state to 'endeavour to provide free and compulsory education for all children' up to the age of 14 years. This provision was not a fundamental right, but a 'Directive Principle of State Policy', which, according to Article 37 of the Constitution, also imposes a legal obligation on the state. The decisive difference between fundamental rights and directive principles is that the former are enforceable in the Supreme Court and the high courts of the country (Articles 32 and 226), whereas the latter are not (Article 37).

This book touches upon a wide range of subjects, including the developments of the primary and secondary education systems in Independent India, the shortcomings of that system as it stands today, the relationship between fundamental rights and directive principles, general question of justiciability of socio-economic rights, the issue of access to justice, and Public Interest Litigation (PIL).

However, the central questions of the book are as follows: what has been gained from making primary education a fundamental right, as guaranteed by Article 21A of the Constitution? How do right-bearers themselves, especially children from less fortunate families, benefit from having a *right* to education? What is the legal significance of the existence of Article 21A? What has

---

*Revisited*, 39. In 2016, 30.5 per cent of all children aged 6 to 14 years in rural areas attended private schools, see ASER Centre, 'Annual Status of Education Report (Rural) 2016: Provisional' (2017), http://img.asercentre.org/docs/Publications/ASER%20Reports/ASER%202016/aser_2016.pdf, accessed on 23 February 2019, 51.

improved for them in comparison to the previous situation of it being a directive principle? What are the claims that the right confers to children against the state? Also, very importantly, by what means may they enforce it?

These questions may also be asked for other socio-economic rights that the Indian judiciary has read into Article 21 of the Constitution (the 'Right to Life') and that the Indian state has promised to its citizens by creating legislation. However, the right to education is a unique case, as it is explicitly guaranteed by the Constitution as a fundamental right: Article 21A. But surprisingly, even concerning the right to education, these questions have barely been discussed in academic or political debates, not even at the time when Article 21A was added to the Constitution or at the time when the Right to Education Act of 2009 was passed.

Scholars writing about the right to education generally summarize the two judgments that have declared it to be part of the right to life and then narrate how the right has become part of the constitutional text. However, they do not assess the significance of this additional step, which Parliament has not taken for any other socio-economic right.[4]

Generally, it appears that scholars do not believe the inclusion of Article 21A to be very significant, perhaps seeing it as more of a passing waypoint on the path towards the actual decisive step: the

[4] See, for instance, Vijayashri Sripati and Arun Thiruvengadam, 'Constitutional Amendment Making the Right to Education a Fundamental Right', *International Journal of Constitutional Law (ICON)* 2, no. 1 (2004): 148–58; Jayna Kothari, 'Social Rights Litigation in India: Developments of the Last Decade', in *Exploring Social Rights: Between Theory and Practice*, ed. Daphne Barak-Erez and Aeyal M. Gross (Oxford, Portland, Or: Hart, 2007), 186 et seq; Mahendra Pal Singh, *V.N. Shukla's Constitution of India*, 12th edition (Lucknow: Eastern Book Co., 2013), 229; Mahabir Prashad Jain, Ruma Pal, and Samaraditya Pal, *Indian Constitutional Law*, 6th edition (Gurgaon: LexisNexis Butterworths Wadhwa Nagpur, 2010), 1297 et seq; Anup Surendranath, 'Life and Personal Liberty', in *The Oxford Handbook of the Indian Constitution*, ed. Sujit Choudhry, Madhav Khosla, and Pratap B. Mehta (Oxford, New York: Oxford University Press, 2016), 768–9.

passing of the Right to Education Act. Consequently, the debate on the right to education mostly focuses on how the primary education system has been shaped by the Act.

For instance, scholars criticize the lack of provisions for improvement of quality,[5] as well as the strains the Act puts on private schools.[6] In fact, the vast majority of public attention that the Act receives concerns only one of its provisions, which obliges private schools to accept children from economically weaker parts of the society for 25 per cent of their seats. Many publications use the right to education almost synonymously with this one provision. They speak of 'right to education quota', 'right to education seats',[7] or

[5] For instance, Kingdon criticizes that '[t]he Act is completely silent on the things that really matter: teacher effort, teacher accountability and student learning outcomes' (see Geeta Kingdon, 'Schooling without Learning: How the RTE Act Destroys Private Schools and Destroys Standards in Public Schools', *Times of India*, 26 August 2015, http://blogs.timesofindia.indiatimes.com/toi-edit-page/schooling-without-learning-how-the-rte-act-destroys-private-schools-and-destroys-standards-in-public-schools/, accessed on 19 August 2018). Drèze and Sen and many others criticize that the 'no-detention rule', which the central government has recently decided to discard of, has actually led to a deterioration of quality (see Jean Drèze and Amartya Sen, *An Uncertain Glory: India and Its Contradictions* [London: Penguin Books, 2013], 138).

[6] Yuki Ohara, 'Examining the Legitimacy of Unrecognized Low-fee Private Schools in India: Comparing Different Perspectives', *Compare: A Journal of Comparative and International Education* 42, no. 1 (2012): 70; Kingdon, 'Schooling without Learning'.

[7] Purvi Jain, '70% RTE Quota Seats not Filled in MP', *Hindustan Times*, 14 October 2016, http://www.hindustantimes.com/education/70-rte-quota-seats-not-filled-in-mp/story-5S1UTCB3f1Ras3w5GaGsLI.html, accessed on 19 August 2018; Yashpal Sonkamble, 'Half-Empty RTE Seats Call for Fresh Admission Round', *Pune Mirror*, 10 October 2016, http://punemirror.indiatimes.com/pune/civic/Half-empty-RTE-seats-call-for-fresh-admission-round/articleshow/54769837.cms, accessed on 19 August 2018; Sumita Sarkari, '900 Seats Under RTE in Schools Yet to be Filled', *Times of India*, 22 September 2016, http://timesofindia.indiatimes.com/city/nashik/900-seats-under-RTE-in-schools-yet-to-be-filled/articleshow/54457478.cms, accessed on 19 August 2018.

'right to education admissions',[8] always just meaning admissions to these reserved seats in private schools. Adjudication on the Right to Education Act has, so far, also mostly focussed on the constitutional permissibility of imposing such an obligation on these schools.[9]

However, one may argue that the question concerning the significance of Article 21A is even more pressing because of the existence of the Right to Education Act. It is not the only such Act giving effect to social benefits that may be described as 'rights'. There are several other examples, like the Right to Information Act (RTI) of 2005, the National Rural Employment Guarantee Act (NREGA) of 2005, and the National Food Security Act (NFSA) of 2013. All of these Acts were passed without first adding new articles guaranteeing the right to information, the right to employment, or the right to food to the Constitution's fundamental rights catalogue. So what has been gained by taking a different route for the right to education? Failing to answer this question would mean that the first step taken in 2002 was redundant.

Generally, when observing the debate around the right to education, one may wonder to what extent the topics under discussion actually require education to be a *right*. If there were no Article 21A and the state had passed an 'Indian Education Act' rather than

[8] Milind R. Lashkari, 'Delay in RTE Admissions in Second Round Worries Parents in Indore', *Hindustan Times*, 13 October 2016, http://www.hindustantimes.com/indore/delay-in-rte-admissions-in-second-round-worries-parents-in-indore/story-JMITGZdpZbqFZEWIMS9pgL.html, accessed on 19 August 2018; *Indian Express*, 'RTE Admissions: Dismal Response Forces Authorities to Start 2nd Round of Online Applications', 9 October 2016, http://indianexpress.com/article/pune/rte-admissions-dismal-response-forces-authorities-to-start-2nd-round-of-online-applications-3072792/, accessed on 19 August 2018; *Times of India*, 'Right to Education Admissions May be Delayed Again', 21 December 2016, http://timesofindia.indiatimes.com/city/pune/RTE-admissions-may-be-delayed-again/articleshow/56091823.cms, accessed on 19 August 2018.

[9] *Society for Un-aided Private Schools of Rajasthan* v. *Union of India & Another* MANU/SC/0311/2012 (Supreme Court of India, 12 April 2012); *Pramati Educational and Cultural Trust* v. *Union of India & Ors* MANU/SC/0419/2014 (Supreme Court of India, 6 May 2014).

a 'Right to Education Act' with the same minimum standards for the education system, the course of these debates could be exactly the same. Judged by its content, a recent extensive book on the Indian lower education system, with the title *Right to Education in India: Resources, Institutions and Public Policy*, might have also been called 'Primary and Secondary Education in India: Resources, Institutions and Public Policy', as it mostly includes chapters on issues such as budgetary allocations for the education system and the utilization of funds in different parts of the country, without discussing what it means that education is a fundamental right.[10]

It appears as if education being a 'right' is perceived as having more of a political significance than a legal one. While the Constitution had always included an obligation on the state to provide free and compulsory education to children as a non-justiciable directive principle, by virtue of this obligation becoming a right, it has become more 'important' or pressing, giving society a stronger argument when calling for measures to improve and expand the education system.[11]

While an 'upgrade' in terms of political significance has value in itself, it is doubtful whether such a limited understanding of education being a 'right' is adequate, and whether it lives up to the constitutional mandate. If someone has a 'right', it implies that they have specific entitlements and claims against the state.

[10] Praveen K. Jha and P.G. Rani, eds, *Right to Education in India: Resources, Institutions and Public Policy* (Abingdon, New York: Routledge, 2016). The one chapter (out of a total of 14) on community monitoring of the right to education is the notable exception, though even in that chapter, the significance of there being a *right* is also not discussed (see Nesar Ahmad, Mahendra S. Rao, and Hariom Soni, 'Community Monitoring of Right to Education: A Case of Udaipur district', in *Right to Education in India*).

[11] One scholar and human rights advocate, in an interview with the author, stated that the significance of Article 21A was that 'it helped us get the Act'. When the idea of creating a new Article 21A emerged for the first time, Béteille criticized that '[e]conomists seek to create their utopias through planning, lawyers through legislation' (see André Béteille, 'Record of Rights: The Marie-Antoinette Solution', *Times of India*, 28 January 1999).

They must also be able to enforce these claims through effective mechanisms that must be accessible to them. Such enforceability is exactly what the Indian Constitution promises for all its fundamental rights. Unlike directive principles, they are justiciable, and every citizen has a right to claim them from the state in the higher judiciary, that is, the Supreme Court and the high courts (see Articles 32 and 226 of the Constitution).

The problem is, however, that these courts are barely accessible to those whom the right to education is primarily aimed at: the poor. In fact, almost none of the Supreme Court and high court cases dealing with the right to education were initiated by aggrieved children or their parents. Wealthier families have the luxury to choose decent quality private schools for their children. They are not dependent on the State for providing education to them or on having a right to education, but children from poor families are. Giving them an effectively enforceable claim against the state to ensure that they be provided with adequate education and ensuring that state actors fulfil their obligations is a question both of empowerment and accountability. However, if one only thinks of a right in political and not in legal terms, and if one does not create effective enforcement mechanisms and access to justice, then the constitutional promise of a right can hardly live up to the promise of *legal* accountability of bureaucrats and *legal* empowerment of citizens.

Indian courts and Indian legal academia are not unaware of the issue of lack of access to justice. However, it appears that many believe that in the Indian context there is one ultimate remedy: PIL. Adjudication of socio-economic rights has almost exclusively been initiated by socially-minded organizations and advocates acting in 'public interest', and the PIL was 'invented', in the first place, to compensate for the lack of means that the poor have to (legally) take these matters into their own hands.[12] The story of

[12] As Justice Bhagwati wrote in the *S.P. Gupta* judgment in 1981:

> [W]here a legal wrong or a legal injury is caused to a person [...] by reason of violation of any constitutional or legal right [...] and such person [...] is by reason of poverty, helplessness or disability or socially or economically disadvantaged position, unable to approach the court

adjudication of socio-economic rights by the Indian judiciary and the developments around fundamental rights and directive principles seems to be inherently linked to this judicial innovation.

In recent years, however, the image of PIL has suffered, and now it is not considered to be a tool for aiding the poor, but rather to further the interests of the relatively well-to-do.[13] Strangely, the consequence does not seem to be finding alternatives like means by which the poor may take matters into their own hands. Rather, adjudication of socio-economic rights is criticized or dismissed altogether, with some critics looking at extra-legal methods of claiming one's rights.[14]

---

> for relief, any member of the public can maintain an application for an appropriate direction, order or writ

See *S.P. Gupta* v. *Union of India and Ors* MANU/SC/0080/1981, 17 (Supreme Court of India, 30 December 1981).

[13] Shobha Aggarwal, 'The Public Interest Litigation Hoax in India: Its Adverse Impact on the Poor and Working Class', *South Asia Citizens Web*, 23 April 2015, http://sacw.net/article11105.html, accessed on 19 August 2018; Balakrishnan Rajagopal, 'Pro-Human Rights but Anti-Poor? A Critical Evaluation of the Indian Supreme Court from a Social Movement Perspective', *Human Rights Review* (2007). Shukla observes that 'from the beginnings of PIL as pro-poor and trying to effectuate rights for the exploited, it is increasingly taking a diametrically opposite direction' (see Rakesh Shukla, 'Rights of the Poor: An Overview of Supreme Court', *Economic & Political Weekly* XLI, no. 35 [2006]: 3757). Thiruvengadam agrees insofar as that 'the Indian Supreme Court has, in a process that began in the 1990s and has continued across the 2000s, transformed the nature of PIL, turning away, in several cases, from concerns it embraced in its original phase' (see Arun Thiruvengadam, 'Revisiting the Role of the Judiciary in Plural Societies [1987]. A Quarter-Century Restrospective on Public Interest Litigation and the Global South', in *Comparative Constitutionalism in South Asia*, ed. Sunil Khilnani, [New Delhi: Oxford University Press, 2013], 356). Most recently, a book by Bhuwania, which fundamentally criticizes the developments of PIL, has received a lot of attention (see Anuj Bhuwania, *Courting the People: Public Interest Litigation in Post-Emergency India,* South Asia in the Social Sciences [Cambridge: Cambridge University Press, 2017]).

[14] See Thiruvengadam, who quotes, inter alia, Krishnan, who found that only policy groups with a large amount of resources employ litigation

However, there is still a constitutional mandate to empower citizens to be able to claim their rights from the state by legal means, and particularly so for the right to education. Also, the Indian State (especially the pre-2014 UPA government, but the current NDA government has not departed from this course) has chosen to employ a 'rights-based approach', which included making education a fundamental right and passing legislation like the Right to Education Act. Consequently, it has been noted that the 'rights-based approach' by the Indian state requires additional factors, such as clear definitions of what the right actually entitles citizens to as well as enforcement mechanism that are readily available to them.[15]

The Right to Education Act itself actually defines some concrete entitlements and it also provides for enforcement mechanisms. These mechanisms are a grievance redress system within the administration, and complaint mechanisms to the states' Child

---

as a strategy—if at all, see Thiruvengadam, 'Revisiting the Role of the Judiciary in Plural Societies (1987)', 356. Krishnan, based on his interviews with civil society groups, reports that 'resource-poor policy groups commented that, even if they had a strong financial base, litigation would be the last course of action they would consider. [...] Movement leaders perceived that the government agency being sued would engage in endless delay and relentless appeals, even where the government's chance of winning was remote. Such an image seems to have documented support', see Jayanth K. Krishnan, 'Social Policy Advocacy and the Role of the Courts in India', *American Asian Review* XXI, no. 2 (2003): 112 et seq. He also mentions the example of the People's Union for Democratic Rights (PUDR), which, along with the People's Union for Civil Liberties (PUCL), is one of the two successor groups to the People's Union of Civil Liberties and Democratic Rights (PUCLDR). The PUDR believes that the PUCL relies too much on litigation, and instead itself employs a strategy (as it did in 1998 to oppose the expansion of capital punishment) of 'tactical pluralism', which also includes grass-roots measures such as 'holding vigils, public awareness meetings, and a series of protests and demonstrations', see Krishnan, 'Social Policy Advocacy and the Role of the Courts in India', 115–16.

[15] Nick Robinson, 'Closing the Implementation Gap: Grievance Redress and India's Social Welfare Programs', *Columbia Journal of Transnational Law* 53, no. 2 (2015): 351.

Rights Commissions (CRCs). However, these mechanisms are not designed to be very powerful.

Against this backdrop, in this book, it shall be argued that the state not only has a moral, but also a legal obligation to provide for access to justice. As the Constitution promises justiciability for all fundamental rights, legally, the state must provide mechanisms for citizens to effectively enforce them against the state. If this is not possible within the judicial system, then the state must create alternative mechanisms to compensate for this shortcoming. Therefore, while one may say that practical and effective enforceability is generally required to justifiably speak of 'rights', because of the existence of Article 21A, this requirement has become a constitutional necessity in the case of the right to education. In other words, while the state *should* provide for adequate enforcement mechanisms for the right to information, the right to employment, and the right to food, it *must* do so for the right to education. As the Right to Education Act does provide for some enforcement mechanisms itself, one must assess to what extent the Act lives up to this constitutional obligation in this respect.

The sole institution that can determine whether or not the state fulfils its legal obligation to provide for adequate and effective enforcement mechanisms, and to order that it must improve them if it does not, is the higher judiciary. However, the higher judiciary is the very institution whose lack of accessibility these mechanisms are supposed to compensate for. This is a dilemma. But this dilemma shows what role PIL might still play for socio-economic rights adjudication in the future. Courts, aware of their own inaccessibility, should act on PIL petitions to order that they themselves be made more accessible and/or that alternative mechanisms and institutions be strengthened. The systems created by the Right to Education Act (and similar systems created by other service delivery acts) may be a good starting point.

This book is a study of law. Still, it does not focus entirely on black-letter law. For instance, identifying whom the right to education is primarily aimed at, and to what extent these persons themselves have the means that allow them to approach the courts, cannot be deduced from the law itself.

Therefore, the approach of my study is one of 'law in context', employing a socio-legal approach.[16] It focusses on constitutional law, statutory law, and case law, but at the same time, it takes into account the socio-economic realities of India. The right to education obliges the state to create and maintain a functioning universal education system that offers a certain level of quality, and whether or not the state is fulfilling its duties in this respect can only be assessed by also taking indicators such as learning achievements of pupils into account. Also, only by identifying which groups are currently most deprived of education will one be able to assess whom the right to education is primarily aimed at and who must, therefore, be empowered to effectively claim the right from the state if it is not provided to them or if they are deprived of it. A holistic answer to the question of what has been gained from making education a fundamental right, and who may benefit from it, may only be found through this contextual approach, that is, considering both doctrinal/legal effects of the constitutional amendment as well as practical ones 'on the ground'.

Still, as this is a study of law, its arguments are primarily legal. One may identify many shortcomings in the Indian education system and the laws governing it, and may argue that the state should take certain measures to improve the system and its outcomes. But many of these arguments are political in nature. While the Indian judiciary has also been very 'political' in the past, it is difficult to predict what 'policy decisions' it will take in the future. By calling for specific actions one runs into danger of making a political argument disguised as a legal one. Therefore, the book focuses on determining what may be learned from international law (to the extent that it is applicable), doctrinal considerations, precedent,

[16] The term 'law in context' actually includes a wide variety of approaches, which especially differ concerning what the 'context' is (see William Twining, *Law in Context: Enlarging a Discipline* [Oxford: Oxford University Press, 1997], 43 et seq). Generally, 'contextualisation', in this respect, means that a study relates 'law' to 'society', and considers how socio-economic conditions influence the making and interpretation of law, and how law itself influences society (see David Nelken, 'Introduction', in *Beyond Law in Context*, ed. David Nelken [London: Routledge, 2009], xii).

and the workings of law in reality in the Indian context in order to determine the obligations imposed on the State by Article 21A. Whenever the study does go beyond this to make an argument that is not entirely 'legal', then it is explicitly identified as such.

Also, while one may question whether or not justiciability of a socio-economic right itself is desirable, the book does not entertain this question at length. The debate is not anymore relevant to the right to education in India, as the legislature (using its constitutional amending power) has decided that the right *is* justiciable by adding Article 21A to the constitutional text, whether one believes that this is a good idea or not. Therefore, the discussion will only be summarized briefly in Chapter 2 (for the Indian context) and Chapter 3 (at the international level).

The study also only focusses on elementary education, that is, the age group of 6 to 14 years that Article 21A encompasses. To make the differences in between the government and private school systems at this level clearer, the study also focusses on those schools in each category that do not stand somewhat 'in between'. Therefore, when speaking of 'government schools', it focusses on 'regular' government schools, excluding schools like *Kendriya Vidyalaya* (schools administered by the Centre) or army schools, which are somewhat independent of the regular system and are also better equipped than the ordinary government schools. When speaking of 'private schools', the study refers to private unaided schools. It also focusses on private schools that are not 'minority schools', as the Supreme Court has ordered that those must be excluded from the scope of the Right to Education Act—though the issues arising from these judgments themselves shall be discussed in several parts.

The book proceeds as follows. Chapter 1 offers an overview of the history and current status of the education system in India. It identifies those parts of the society that Article 21A is primarily aimed at and what the most pressing issues to be addressed in the field of primary and lower-secondary education are. It is quite clear that those who might profit from having a right to education are those who do not have the means to already afford quality education for themselves by obtaining it from the private market and who are, therefore, dependent on some form of state action.

Strangely, it will be shown, even after years of education being a fundamental right, decent-quality education is still not seen as a 'public good' that the state ought to provide for free but something that is supposed to be obtained from the market, with the government education system being considered as something 'meant for (very) poor children'.[17]

Chapter 2 then recounts the developments around adjudication of fundamental rights and directive principles that, as will be argued, climaxed with the inclusion of Article 21A in the constitutional text. By examining the historical background of the Eighty-Ninth Constitutional Amendment, the chapter then tries to find some answers concerning its doctrinal and practical significance. Surprisingly, as will be concluded, there was very little of a 'vision' of what the purpose of Article 21A ought to be.

Chapter 3 offers some guidance concerning the content of Article 21A. This question is approached purely legally, not politically. Therefore, the chapter does not describe what content would be *desirable*. Instead, it discusses which concrete *legal obligations* the article might impose on the state. Some clues can be found in international law and past adjudication by the Indian Supreme Court on socio-economic rights, including the right to education. Concerning many aspects, such as minimum quality standards, it will remain up to the judiciary to define them further.

This chapter then proceeds to demonstrate that Article 21A, read with Articles 32 and 226, clearly imposes an obligation on the state to provide accessible and effective enforcement mechanisms to right-bearers—whether by facilitating access to the higher judiciary, or by providing an accessible and effective alternative system. The fact that the petitioners in none of the cases concerning Article 21A decided by the Supreme Court, and in hardly any cases decided by the high courts, were aggrieved children or their parents shows that the higher judiciary is not accessible enough.

Chapter 4 deals with the issue of lack of access to justice and attempts to find reasons for the inaccessibility of the higher judiciary. While it appears to be clear to observers that the

[17] Anuradha De, *Probe Revisited: A Report on Elementary Education in India* (New Delhi: Oxford University Press, 2011).

Supreme Court and high courts are not accessible enough, surprisingly, there are actually no empirical studies that examine why this is the case. Some factors can, however, be deduced from a study dealing with the inaccessibility of district courts, that is, the lower judiciary. Based on the fact that in the previous chapter, it has been established that the state is obliged to facilitate access to justice or at least to provide alternative mechanism for enforcing the right to education, the question arises how it may do so. This chapter shows that the institution of PIL, for various reasons, cannot compensate for lack of access to justice, and that the state is not properly implementing (or not at all exploring) many other possible alternative mechanisms.

Chapter 5 examines the conceptual set-up of the grievance redress system created by the Right to Education Act and analyses studies on its performance. It will be noted that there are serious deficiencies already at the conceptual level, which becomes apparent when measuring the system against the very basic requirements for an effective independent and impartial judicial system. The different institutions that are part of the grievance redress system are either not sufficiently independent or do not have sufficient competences to enforce their 'judgments'. These deficiencies, as well as additional implementation issues, also translate into a malfunctioning system 'on the ground'.

The chapter also examines other grievance redress systems for different state services (for instance, the ones created by the Right to Information Act), highlighting that some of the deficiencies found in the right to education system are actually not universal.

Recognizing that the grievance redress system is the alternative system that the state has chosen for the right to education, the sixth and final chapter argues that it would be adequate for the judiciary, when assessing the state's measures for furthering access to justice, to focus on this system. The judiciary could then also order that it be improved in order to compensate for the current lack of access to justice. The chapter shows what alterations are necessary in order for the system to provide adequate and effective means of enforcement.

It will also be argued that the judiciary could adjudicate on the adequacy of the existing grievance redress mechanism after being approached through PIL, meaning that advocacy groups that aim to empower right-bearers should themselves raise the issue of improving enforcement mechanisms rather than just raising substantive questions of rights implementation. It shall be concluded that a system of 'micromanagement' through grievance redress at the 'bottom', with right-bearers approaching the redress bodies themselves, and 'macromanagement' of systemic deficiencies through adjudication in the higher judiciary at the 'top', with advocacy groups raising issues at that level, might actually be superior to the system that was originally conceived by the Constitution.

# 1

# History and the Current State of Elementary Education in India

The Right to Education Act of 2009 has created a new regime for elementary education (that is, education for children aged 6 to 14 years) in India. However, it did not create an education system from scratch. Instead, it built upon an existing system of state and private players. This system, in some respects, reaches back over centuries.

In this chapter, it shall be shown that a common issue in both the history of elementary education in India and the contemporary situation is that of social exclusion. Previously, this exclusion was prevalent more in terms of parameters such as caste and gender. Nowadays, it is primarily in terms of socio-economic background, with gender playing a greater role at a later stage of education.

One would expect a rights-based approach to have the aim of allowing right-bearers to overcome these factors of exclusion. Indeed, the emergence of private schools and growing demand of parents for quality education of their children (even from poorer families) shows that there is a willingness to 'take matters in their own hands'. However, as will be shown in this chapter, demands for better education are currently rarely aimed at the state, as education is generally not seen as a 'public good' that the state ought to provide, in spite of it being a fundamental right.

## History of Elementary Education in India

At the time of Indian Independence in 1947, the vast majority of Indians was untouched by organized education. Only a relatively small elite of the country could read and write, with the literacy rate being at 16.7 per cent.[1] Up until fairly recently, most Indians remained without any schooling whatsoever. To an extent, this is surprising, as Indian culture has traditionally held education as such in high regard.

### Ancient India

Teachers were very well respected in ancient Hindu tradition in Vedic times.[2] 'Gurus' taught their students in religious matters, but also such subjects as mathematics and medicine.[3] Such education mostly took place among the upper castes, with religious education, naturally, being particularly important to Brahmins (that is, the caste of priests).[4] However, it is believed that in early Vedic times, education was inclusive to some extent as far as parameters other than caste are concerned, for instance, in terms of gender.[5]

[1] 'Educating India', *The Hindu*, 4 April 2011, http://www.thehindu.com/opinion/editorial/educating-india/article1599783.ece, accessed on 19 August 2018.

[2] 2,000 BC–AD 700 (see Amita Gupta, *Early Childhood Education, Postcolonial Theory, and Teaching Practices and Policies in India: Balancing Vygotsky and the Veda*, Revised edition [New York, USA/Hampshire, UK: Palgrave Macmillan, 2013], 34).

[3] Padma Ramachandran and Vasantha Ramkumar, *Education in India*, 1st edition (New Delhi: National Book Trust, 2005), 1 et seq; Gupta, *Early Childhood Education*, 35.

[4] Gupta, *Early Childhood Education*, 36–7; Ramachandran and Ramkumar, *Education in India*, 10–12; Hartmut Scharfe, *Education in Ancient India* (Leiden, Boston, Köln: Brill, 2002), 8 et seq; F.E. Keay, *Ancient Indian Education: An Inquiry into its Origin, Development, and Ideals* (New Delhi: Cosmo Publications, 1992), 144; Jean Drèze and Amartya Kumar Sen, *India: Development and Participation*, 2nd edition (Oxford, New York: Oxford University Press, 2002), 145.

[5] Gupta, *Early Childhood Education*, 35; Keay, *Ancient Indian Education*, 81.

In the later Vedic period, that is, around 1000 BC–200 BC, education became more exclusive, with education focusing even more on religious matters and male Brahmins remaining as the sole educated class.[6]

In India's Buddhist period, religious education was common in monasteries,[7] which were, in principle, open to persons from lower castes as well. However, even here, education primarily remained an upper-caste phenomenon.[8] This time period, which lasted approximately from 600 BC to 700 AD, also witnessed the emergence of early forms of higher education, with universities being established in several cities, most notably Nalanda. These centres of learning were also held in high regard 'internationally', attracting scholars from China and even Greece.[9] While religious education played an important role here as well, these universities also taught secular subjects.[10]

## Muslim Rule

The era of Muslim rulers brought the emergence of Islamic schools such as madrasas attached to mosques.[11] These schools usually took over after children had received basic education at home and had the principal aim of preparing students for civil services and the judiciary.[12] Depending on the rulers, they were sometimes

[6] Ramachandran and Ramkumar, *Education in India*, 15; Gupta, *Early Childhood Education*, 34–5; Keay, *Ancient Indian Education*, 81.

[7] Scharfe, *Education in Ancient India*, 131 et seq; A.L. Basham, *Wonder that was India: Survey of the History and Culture of the Indian Sub-Continent before the Coming of the Muslims.* 3rd edition (London: Sidgwick & Jackson, 1967), 164.

[8] Ramachandran and Ramkumar, *Education in India*, 28 et seq.

[9] Gupta, *Early Childhood Education*, 37–8; Scharfe, *Education in Ancient India*, 144–5; Keay, *Ancient Indian Education*, 96–7.

[10] Scharfe, *Education in Ancient India*, 147; Basham, *Wonder that was India*, 165.

[11] Keay, *Ancient Indian Education*, 115.

[12] Saiyid Athar Abbas Rizvi and A.L. Basham, *The Wonder that was India*, Great civilizations series (London: Sidgwick & Jackson, 1987), 217.

open to Hindu pupils as well.[13] For instance, some Hindus learned Persian, which enabled them to work in the Muslim rulers' bureaucracy, and the synergies in between the languages of Hindus and Muslims led to the emergence of Urdu as a new language.[14] However, children from poorer and rural families remained largely excluded, and Islamic centres of learning were mostly located in towns.[15]

## British Rule

The earlier years of the British era saw very little involvement of the British (that is, the East India Trading Company, at this time) in the matters of education.[16] However, in this period, Christian missionaries[17] as well as some single individuals[18] started operating schools in the country.

As the British became more involved in actually governing India (especially after the British Crown took over the administration

[13] Most notably in the time of Emperor Akbar (1556–1605) (see Ramachandran and Ramkumar, *Education in India*, 45; Gupta, *Early Childhood Education*, 39; Keay, *Ancient Indian Education*, 121 et seq.). Other rulers were less inclusive—most notably Aurangzeb (1658–1707), who prohibited Hindu teaching even in their holy city of Benares (Varanasi) (see Keay, *Ancient Indian Education*, 130). According to Rizvi, Abbas, and Basham, however, the rulers did not have much of an influence on education, pointing out that Akbar's 'code of education regulations' were 'ignored by the *madrasas* in his empire', see Rizvi, Abbas, and Basham, *The Wonder that was India*, 218.

[14] Keay, *Ancient Indian Education*, 118.

[15] Ramachandran and Ramkumar, *Education in India*, 45; Keay, *Ancient Indian Education*, 122, 129–30, 139–40, 142.

[16] A. Biswas, *Development of Education in India: A Historical Survey of Educational Documents before and after Independence* (New Delhi: Concept Publ. Comp, 1994[1986]), 3.

[17] Gupta, *Early Childhood Education*, 40; Ramachandran and Ramkumar, *Education in India*, 50–1; Biswas, *Development of Education in India*, 3.

[18] Ramachandran and Ramkumar, *Education in India*, 50–1; Biswas, *Development of Education in India*, 3.

from the Company in 1857), their administration also started taking an interest in education. After, at first, nurturing indigenous classical education and education in India's regional languages,[19] state education was increasingly based on a Western model from the first half of the nineteenth century. English was chosen as the language of instruction after Thomas Babington Macaulay's *Minute on Indian Education* in 1835 had called for the creation of an 'anglicised class' of Indians.[20] The motives behind this were to prepare Indians to serve in the British colonial administration (as it had happened in the Moghul era with Hindus learning Persian to work in the imperial administration),[21] but also to educate the local population in 'Western values' and to 'shape their character'.[22] Another reason that was named was introducing modern science as a 'solvent of Indian religious beliefs' in order to counter 'fantastical and nonsensical explanations of the world and its functioning', which the government believed was common in the country.[23]

Indeed, Western education did create an urban English-speaking elite that was greatly influenced by Western thinking and values. This elite called for emancipation from at least some aspects of Hinduism[24] or for the reform of Hinduism inspired by Western critique of it.[25] Also, the call for English education itself had not

[19] Ramachandran and Ramkumar, *Education in India*, 62–3.

[20] Biswas, *Development of Education in India*, 4, 12 et seq., 20 et seq; Stephen Evans, 'Macaulay's Minute Revisited: Colonial Language Policy in Nineteenth-century India', *Journal of Multilingual and Multicultural Development* 23, no. 4 (2002).

[21] H.J.A Bellenoit, *Missionary Education and Empire in Late Colonial India, 1860–1920* (London: Pickering & Chatto, 2007), 1 et seq; Sanjay Seth, *Subject Lessons: The Western Education of Colonial India* (Durham, London: Duke University Press, 2007), 18; Joseph DiBona, *One Teacher, One School: The Adam Reports on Indigenous Education in 19th Century India* (New Delhi: Biblia Impex, 1983), 3.

[22] Seth, *Subject Lessons*, 17, 47; Bellenoit, *Missionary Education*, 121.

[23] Seth, *Subject Lessons*, 49. See also Bellenoit, *Missionary Education*, 139.

[24] Seth, *Subject Lessons*, 55.

[25] Which sparked religious reforms like Brahmo Samaj and Arya Samaj (see Seth, *Subject Lessons*, 63). The latter, however, was at the same time

only come from the British, but also from Indian reformists such as Raja Ram Mohan Roy.[26] However, the new state-run schools were supposed to be religiously neutral in order to find acceptance with the local population, which led to the government being less supportive of Christian missionary schools.[27]

The emergence of state-run schools coincided with the disappearance of indigenous ones. In the beginning of the nineteenth century, the British had still counted many such schools, which mostly vanished over the next 100 years.[28] While the geographical reach of the indigenous schools had been large, their popular outreach varied greatly in between different parts of the country. In many parts of the country, the literacy rates of the male

---

'anti-Christian', sometimes even working towards reconverting those who had moved to Christianity (see Sanjay Seth, 'Secular Enlightenment and Christian Conversion: Missionaries and Education in Colonial India', in *Education and Social Change in South Asia*, ed. Krishna Kumar, Amin Oesterheld [New Delhi: Orient Longman, 2007], 36). Muslims were not reached by the state's education system to a comparable degree (see Heike Liebau, '"Indianisation" and Education: Reaction from Protestant Christians of the Madras Presidency to the Lindsay Commission Report', in *Education and Social Change in South Asia*, 58; Seth, *Subject Lessons*, 110 et seq.). There are several possible explanations for this, ranging from language (that many Muslims wanted to hold on to Persian/Urdu education) to religion (that many Muslims who were used to religious education by schools attached to mosques did not favour an education based on religious neutrality) (see Seth, *Subject Lessons*, 113–14).

[26] Biswas, *Development of Education in India*, 9 et seq.

[27] Gupta, *Early childhood Education*, 40; Seth, *Subject Lessons*, 17, 48–9; Biswas, *Development of Education in India*, 32. Also, missionary schools themselves were often not very successful in spreading Christianity, as their own students tended to be very secularly inclined, seeing the missionary schools primarily as a means for better career chances (see Bellenoit, *Missionary Education*, 102–3). As Seth notes, however, there was a belief among some government officials that Western secular education would weaken many students' belief in Hinduism and might ultimately lead them to Christianity (see Seth, 'Secular Enlightenment and Christian Conversion', 34).

[28] Gupta, *Early Childhood Education*, 33.

population did not go beyond a single digit figure.[29] Also, education was mostly confined to higher castes and classes (who helped the schools survive by giving donations).[30] Education also mostly excluded girls.[31] Therefore, while the British state-run school system did put an end to an existing tradition, the reach of the latter had been quite limited in the first place.[32]

Even though the government had thus effectively taken over the education system, state spending on elementary education remained modest. The majority of Indian villages simply remained without schools.[33] Still, the British era had brought the idea of a state-run school system to India, which led to first calls for a system of *compulsory* education. These calls came at a time when the Indian Independence movement generally lobbied for more involvement in education policy:[34] Gopal Krishna Gokhale, who was an activist in the Independence movement, called for compulsory state education, hoping that this would finally help in reaching the majority of the people, an aim that the British had not given top priority to. Instead, they focused more on quality than on quantity.[35] Gokhale's bill in the Imperial Legislative Council found no majority

[29] See Scharfe, *Education in Ancient India*, 84 and Keay, *Ancient Indian Education*, 154, for an overview of findings by British scholars in the beginning of the nineteenth century.

[30] Joseph DiBona, *One Teacher, One School: The Adam Reports on Indigenous Education in 19th Century India* (New Delhi: Biblia Impex, 1983), 2, 24, 205, 209, 213. Though the Third Report on The State of Education in Bengal by William Adam did note that the (at the time, still small) number of children from lower castes was on the rise (see DiBona, *One Teacher*, 205).

[31] Keay, *Ancient Indian Education*, 145 et seq., 153; DiBona, *One Teacher*, 91.

[32] DiBona notes that the decline of the indigenous schooling system had already begun before the British introduced their state-run education system because donations from land-owners (zamindars) had decreased due to the fact that the British had started breaking up larger land holdings (see DiBona, *One Teacher*, 4).

[33] Ramachandran and Ramkumar, *Education in India*, 73–4.

[34] Biswas, *Development of Education in India*, 36 et seq.

[35] Biswas, *Development of Education in India*, 36–7.

because of budgetary concerns.[36] However, the government passed a Resolution of Education Policy in 1913, in which compulsory elementary education was named as a goal for the future.[37]

Several princely states did create acts that sought to make elementary education universal and compulsory.[38] Among them were the state of Baroda in modern-day Gujarat and the ones of Travancore and Cochin, now part of modern-day Kerala.[39] However, even with such laws being in place, actual universal attendance was not remotely achieved even in these (in this respect) progressive states.[40]

In many ways, the legacy of the British time is still alive today, even beyond the idea of the state providing education (and aiming for universal free compulsory education). As mentioned above, in 1835, English was made the language of instruction in Indian schools, which it still is for higher-quality education that the upper class receives today.[41] Also, the importance of textbooks and the practice of centralized examinations (and the resulting focus on 'rote memorization') began in the nineteenth century, and this tradition is still followed today.[42]

In spite of the introduction of state-run education and the progress that was made under British rule, the reach of elementary education remained very limited, as indicated by the literacy rates at the time of Independence. Only 16.7 per cent of all Indians could

[36] Biswas, *Development of Education in India*, 37, 40.

[37] Biswas, *Development of Education in India*, 40.

[38] Ramachandran and Ramkumar, *Education in India*, 80–1.

[39] After Independence, the state governments of Kerala were able to build upon this groundwork in order to create an educational system superior to most other states of the country (see 'Developments in Kerala' in this chapter).

[40] Philip Hartog, *Some Aspects of Indian Education Past and Present* (London: Oxford University Press, 1939), 39–40.

[41] Gupta, *Early Childhood Education*, 21 et seq. Also see 'English as the New Literacy' in this chapter.

[42] Gupta, *Early Childhood Education*, 41, 42–4. Other scholars, on the other hand, trace the tradition of rote memorization all the way back to ancient India, highlighting how learning was understood as repetition of what the teacher had previously said (see Scharfe, *Education in Ancient India*, 1–2; Bellenoit, *Missionary Education*, 97).

read and write in 1951, an increase of 11.32 percentage points as compared to 1901.[43] At the time, many children had never been reached by any schooling at all. However, in addition to that, even those who did go to school initially often dropped out even before reaching fourth class, which happened especially often with girls.[44]

## After Independence

This section shall show that in spite of loud calls for a strong education system, progress towards universalization remained quite slow in the first years following Independence. However, this section shall also explain that regionally, there was at least one positive example. This was the state of Kerala, which built on progress that had already been made in colonial times. After looking at the positive example, this section shall look at the developments in, the states of Tamil Nadu and Himachal Pradesh, which, perhaps even more importantly, made noticeable improvements even without being able to build upon a similar tradition. The fact that some states fared so much better raises the question of why this might be the case. It will be argued that the regional differences may be explained by the federal framework created by India's Constitution. Consequently, as the last portion of this section will show, there have been stronger, more centralized movements towards universal elementary education since the 1990s.

### *Early Developments*

Article 45 of the Constitution of India (in its original form), a so-called 'Directive Principle',[45] imposed a duty on the state to

[43] *The Hindu*, 'Educating India'.

[44] Hartog, *Some Aspects of Indian Education Past and Present*, 34–5. At the beginning of the twentieth century, the female literacy rate was abysmally low—below 1 per cent (see the figures of the 1901 census quoted in Drèze and Sen, *India*, 160). For more information on the exclusion of girls in colonial education, in spite of many debates on how to include them, see Seth, *Subject Lessons*, 129 et seq.

[45] For more information on the legal implications of directive principles, see Chapter 2.

achieve a state of universal free and compulsory education within 10 years, that is, by the year 1960. Considering the lack of progress in the century preceding Independence, this goal must have seemed overly ambitious. Indeed, in 1944, the Central Advisory Board on Education (CABE)[46] had already warned that actual implementation would take up to 40 years.[47] To an extent, as will be shown below, this goal has still not been achieved today (59 years after the expiry of the deadline), even though some notable progress has been made.

In the first years, and even decades following Independence, elementary education remained underfinanced in spite of pledges the freedom movement had made to make it a top priority.[48] Already in 1910, Gokhale had called the issue of compulsory elementary education the 'question of questions' for the country.[49] Article 45 is perhaps the strongest expression of that pledge, but to a large extent, it remained unheard for a long time.

There are several factors that may explain the lack of progress in the first post-Independence decades. For instance, it has been criticized that the State first employed the Gandhian philosophy of 'basic education', which may have been detrimental to advances in the education system. Most importantly, however, it appears that elementary education was just not very high on the government's list of priorities, in spite of assertions to the contrary.

The first two Five-Year Plans (1950–5 and 1956–61) expressed a belief in the Gandhian ideal of 'basic education', which argues that it is better for child development to first learn practical skills such

[46] An advisory body to the government giving non-binding recommendations that are, however, considered to be of great importance for educational policy (see Biswas, *Development of Education in India*, 72 et seq; Ramachandran and Ramkumar, *Education in India*, 156; Prachi D. Odhekar, 'India', *International Journal for Education Law and Policy* 7, no. 1 [2011]: 132).

[47] Biswas, *Development of Education in India*, 64–5.

[48] Jean Drèze and Amartya Sen, *An Uncertain Glory. India and Its Contradictions* (London: Penguin Books, 2013), 112, 130.

[49] Gokhale's Resolution of 1910, as quoted in Biswas, *Development of Education in India*, 37.

as handicrafts rather than skills like reading or writing.[50] As a consequence, regular schooling that does favour early teaching of such common primary school skills was not given a very high priority. This ideal is not followed anymore today, but as far as literacy and academic skills are concerned, a lot of time was lost in these initial years. Only in the Fourth Five-Year Plan (1969–74), whose period started right after the National Policy of Education (1968) was framed, the government itself reinforced its desire to achieve free and compulsory elementary education without hailing the ideal of basic education.[51] The National Policy of Education itself, however, did not spark great advancements in the field of elementary education. Its most important effect was that of universalizing the number of years for schooling and undergraduate studies in the country.[52]

The government was (of course) not unaware of its obligation under Article 45. However, even with the 10 year deadline indicating a higher priority over other directive principles, the issue did not seem to be as high on the agenda as one might have expected. In 1959, the chairman of the CABE stated that 'on account of lack of adequate financial resources we are compelled to cut down our immediate targets of 6 to 14 years of compulsory education

[50] See the First Five-Year Plan's chapter on education, available at http://planningcommission.nic.in/plans/planrel/fiveyr/1st/1planch33.html, at paragraph 18 et seq., accessed on 15 August 2018, as well as the same chapter in the Second Five-Year Plan, available at http://planningcommission.nic.in/plans/planrel/fiveyr/2nd/2planch23.html, at paragraphs 1, 14 et seq., accessed on 15 August 2018. Drèze and Sen criticize the idea as 'hugely romantic and rather eccentric' (see Drèze and Sen, *An Uncertain Glory*, 24). For more information on the idea of 'basic education', see, among others, Gupta, *Early Childhood Education*, 42; Biswas, *Development of Education in India*, 56 et seq., 398 et seq.

[51] See Ramachandran and Ramkumar, *Education in India*, 306. The chapter on 'Education and Manpower' of the Fourth Five-Year Plan is available at http://planningcommission.nic.in/plans/planrel/fiveyr/4th/4planch16.html., accessed on 15 August 2018. The term 'basic education' is not even mentioned.

[52] The '10+2+3' system, as it is still followed today, Odhekar, 'India', 132.

[meaning the age of children concerned] to 6 to 11 years and that too to be fulfilled by the end of the Third Five-Year Plan'.[53] Three years later, the Board called for a new time limit for Article 45, recognizing that the initial 10 year target had not been met.[54] Resolutions and further chairmen's addresses calling for greater priority for achieving this goal (but also repeatedly extending the deadline) followed in the subsequent decades, with actual on-the-ground advances remaining quite limited.[55] As far as priorities for educational policies were concerned, the central government seemed to be more focused on higher education, and that too mostly for the elites.[56] In fact, from the First to the Fifth Five-Year Plan (that is, from 1951 to 1979), the proportion of educational spending on elementary education decreased from 56 to 35 per cent, while the spending on universities increased.[57]

[53] He also warned that 'unless there is dedicated and unrelenting drive behind our efforts, even the reduced target may remain unfulfilled', as quoted in Biswas, *Development of Education in India*, 112.

[54] Resolution quoted in Biswas, *Development of Education in India*, 127.

[55] See Biswas, *Development of Education in India*, 151 et seq. In 1975, the Board recommended a new deadline of 1986 (see Biswas, *Development of Education in India*, 188). In 1983, the chairman noted that the deadline had now been moved to 1990 (which he now considered a realistic target) (see Biswas, *Development of Education in India*, 190).

[56] Ramachandra Guha, *India after Gandhi: The History of the World's Largest Democracy*, 1st Harper Perennial edition (New York, NY: Harper Perennial, 2007), 468–9; Nirmala Rao, Kai-Ming Cheng, and Kirti Narain, 'Primary Schooling in China and India: Understanding How Socio-Contextual Factors Moderate the Role of the State', *International Review of Education* 49, no. 1 and 2 (2003): 160.

[57] See the figures quoted in Rao, Cheng, and Narain, 'Primary Schooling in China and India', 162 as well as the charts in the First and Fifth Five-Year Plans at http://planningcommission.nic.in/plans/planrel/fiveyr/1st/1planch33.html and http://planningcommission.nic.in/plans/planrel/fiveyr/5th/5planch5.html, accessed on 15 August 2018. Overall spending on education (measured by their percentage as compared to the GDP) even decreased in the same period (see Rao, Cheng, and Narain, 'Primary Schooling in China and India', 162). China, on the other hand, gave higher priority to elementary education early on, which led to a

Generally, there was some progress in the decades following Independence, as the increase in literacy shows.[58] However, progress differed greatly in different states, with Kerala, and later also Tamil Nadu and Himachal Pradesh, being the most prominent success stories.

## *Developments in Kerala*

As already mentioned above, the history of a comparatively successful education system in Kerala started long before Indian Independence. In fact, it reaches back over several centuries. From sixteenth century, education started spreading to other privileged castes than just the Brahmins.[59] Already in this early period, but especially from the nineteenth century, Christian missionary schools played an important role in the spread of literacy. These

---

much faster spread of literacy in that country (see Rao, Cheng, and Narain, 'Primary Schooling in China and India', 163).

[58] Overall literacy grew from 18.33 per cent (1951) to 28.30 per cent (1961), 34.45 per cent (1971), 43.57 per cent (1981), 52.21 per cent (1991), 65.38 per cent (2001), and finally to 74.04 per cent in 2011 (see 2001 and 2011 censuses, http://indiabudget.nic.in/es2001-02/chapt2002/chap106.pdf and http://www.census2011.co.in/literacy.php, accessed on 15 August 2018). This is indeed notable progress, but the increase was much slower than in, for instance, China: there, literacy increased from around 20 per cent in the 1950s to 95.1 per cent in 2010 and 94.7 per cent in 2015 (see Rao, Cheng, and Narain, 'Primary Schooling in China and India', 156 and https://www.cia.gov/library/publications/the-world-factbook/fields/2103.html#ch, accessed on 15 August 2018). The figure given for India in 2015 in that overview is 71.2 per cent.

[59] However, non-privileged classes (as well as women) still remained largely excluded from the educational system. Tharakan believes that Gough's estimate of 50 and 25 per cent literacy for men and women for early eighteenth-century Kerala (that is, before the British) is exaggerated (see P.K. Michael Tharakan, 'Socio-Economic Factors in Educational Development. Case of Nineteenth Century Travancore', *Economic & Political Weekly* XIX, no. 10 [1984]: 1916, citing Kathleen Gough, 'Literacy in Kerala', in *Literacy in Traditional Societies*, ed. Jack Goody [Cambridge: Cambridge University Press, 1968], 151).

schools reached out also to lower classes and castes.[60] While their aim included conversion to Christianity, they also taught secular subjects.[61]

While missionary schools were run by church initiatives, they did receive support from the state of Travancore.[62] As already mentioned, the princely state's government issued a Royal Rescript in 1817 declaring state-sponsored universal compulsory education as an objective of state policy.[63] In spite of this early advance in policy, it took until the second half of the nineteenth century for the state to become involved in education on a large scale, with the government introducing a 'modern system' of education that included state-run schools (also for girls) as well as grants-in-aid for private initiatives.[64] However, traditional caste-based schools still existed simultaneously, though their numbers had diminished somewhat in the eighteenth and nineteenth centuries.[65]

In spite of all this progress, the spread of literacy still remained limited. By the end of the nineteenth century, male literacy in Travancore (which was ahead of the other states of modern-day Kerala) had not yet reached 25 per cent, and female literacy remained at a level that was even below 5 per cent.[66] Still, this limited progress was remarkable compared to other parts of India,[67] and this early progress in state-run education laid the groundwork to build upon later. Literacy started reaching lower castes on a larger scale in the 1930s, thanks to increased investments of the state aimed at expanding enrolment, as well as affirmative action through

[60] V.K. Ramachandran, 'On Kerala's Development Achievements', in Jean Drèze and Amartya Sen, *Indian Development: Selected Regional Perspectives* (Delhi, New York: Oxford University Press, 1997), 267; Tharakan, 'Socio-Economic Factors in Educational Development', 1920.

[61] Ramachandran, 'On Kerala's Development Achievements', 1920.

[62] Ramachandran, 'On Kerala's Development Achievements', 268.

[63] Ramachandran, 'On Kerala's Development Achievements', 1917.

[64] Tharakan, 'Socio-Economic Factors in Educational Development', 1921.

[65] Ramachandran, 'On Kerala's Development Achievements', 270.

[66] Tharakan, 'Socio-Economic Factors in Educational Development', 1914.

[67] Ramachandran, 'On Kerala's Development Achievements', 270.

measures like scholarships or fee concessions for lower castes. This was especially remarkable considering that caste-differences had traditionally been especially entrenched in what is now Kerala.[68] The state was also able to move far ahead of other parts of India in the twentieth century, including the state of Baroda in modern-day Gujarat (which had also fostered state education, as mentioned above), because it put a special emphasis on female literacy.[69]

After the formation of the state of Kerala in 1956, the state government managed to spread literacy to the northern part (that is, 'non-Travancore' Kerala, or former Malabar).[70] Universal literacy was then eventually reached in the early 1990s thanks to a state-wide Total Literacy Campaign which took the help of unpaid volunteers as instructors and became a role model for other parts of the country.[71]

### *Developments in Tamil Nadu and Himachal Pradesh*

While Kerala stands out also as a positive example of pre-Independence educational development, Himachal Pradesh and Tamil Nadu are perhaps even more remarkable as these states show that considerable advances in elementary education can be achieved in post-Independence India without being able to build upon previous pre-Independence groundwork.[72] Tamil Nadu is famous for

68 Ramachandran, 'On Kerala's Development Achievements', 271; C.M. Biju and Amirtha Jothi, 'The Paradigm and Practice of Pollution in Caste System in Malabar', *International Journal of Scientific & Engineering Research* 3, no. 12 (2012), http://www.ijser.org/researchpaper%5CThe-Paradigm-and-Practice-of-Pollution-in-Caste-System-in-Malabar.pdf, accessed on 19 August 2018.

69 Ramachandran, 'On Kerala's Development Achievements', 271–4; Robin Jeffrey, 'Governments and Culture: How Women Made Kerala Literate', *Pacific Affairs* 60, no. 3 (1987), http://www.jstor.org/stable/2758883, accessed on 19 August 2018.

70 Ramachandran, 'On Kerala's Development Achievements', 272.

71 Ramachandran, 'On Kerala's Development Achievements', 272 et seq.

72 Drèze and Sen note how simple measures, such as 'opening more schools, improving the infrastructure, appointing more teachers,

being the first state to introduce free mid-day meals in primary schools already in the 1960s[73] as part of a larger push for a better social infrastructure in the state.[74] Mid-day meals increased enrolment and attendance rates by a remarkable extent.[75]

The positive effects witnessed in Tamil Nadu sparked a nationwide campaign that first led to the introduction of the National Programme of Nutritional Support to Primary Education (also known as Mid-day Meal Scheme)[76] in 1995 by the central government. It also led to the Supreme Court in 2001 giving an order in the *Right to Food* case directing all state governments to introduce cooked mid-day meals in all government and government-aided elementary schools within six months.[77] Even after that, Tamil

---

simplifying the curriculum, organizing enrolment drives [and] providing free textbooks' can lead to immediate results, and that Tamil Nadu and Himachal Pradesh are positive examples of how this can be done (see Drèze and Sen, *India*, 172–3).

[73] See http://www.nihfw.org/NationalHealthProgramme/MID_DAYMEAL.html, accessed on 15 August 2018.

[74] Drèze and Sen, *An Uncertain Glory*, 78.

[75] Drèze and Kingdon have found that mid-day meals increase the likelihood of girls completing elementary education by 30 percentage points (see Jean Drèze and Geeta G. Kingdon, 'School Participation in Rural India', http://sticerd.lse.ac.uk/dps/de/dedps18.pdf, 21, accessed on 19 August 2018). The main attraction seems to be that free meals reduce the effective costs of schooling for parents, which act as a barrier especially when deciding whether or not to send a girl to school, as girls, who are often supposed to live with their 'new' family after marriage, are often seen as a liability (see Drèze and Sen, *India*, 162–3. Also see Farzana Afridi, 'The Impact of School Meals on School Participation: Evidence from Rural India', https://web.archive.org/web/20170707221925/http://www.cid.harvard.edu/neudc07/docs/neudc07_s6_p01_afridi.pdf, accessed on 19 August 2018).

[76] Reetika Khera, 'Mid-Day Meals in Primary Schools. Achievements and Challenges', *Economic & Political Weekly* XLI, no. 46 (2006).

[77] See http://www.righttofoodindia.org/orders/nov28.html, accessed on 15 August 2018. For more details on the *Right to Food* case, see Chapter 6.

Nadu still stood out as a state where the Mid-Day Meal Scheme was implemented especially successfully.[78]

The recent history of education in Himachal Pradesh is especially remarkable considering the condition that elementary education had been in just a few decades ago, before the state was formed in 1971.[79] The state's illiteracy rate among 10 to 14 year olds was as high as 61 per cent in 1971, but by 1998/1999, it had shrunk to just 4 per cent.[80] In comparison, the average illiteracy rate in that age group in all large North Indian states was at 67 per cent in 1971 (and thus, not much higher than Himachal Pradesh's at the time), but remained quite high (at 31 per cent) in 1998/1999.[81]

The expansion of education in Himachal Pradesh was rapid, in spite of a relatively difficult environment of a mountainous region, with settlements that are difficult to access, and of a local economy relying on child labour to a considerable extent.[82] These challenges were overcome by massive state involvement. Unlike in other states, private and/or missionary schools played a very limited role.[83] The government initiatives were facilitated by Himachal Pradesh becoming a separate state and by the fact that the newly formed state's government quickly invested in rural infrastructure

[78] Jean Drèze and Aparajita Goyal, 'Future of Mid-Day Meals', *Economic & Political Weekly* XXXVIII, no. 44 (2003): 4680 et seq.

[79] See The State of Himachal Pradesh Act, 1970 (Act No. 53 of 1970).

[80] See the figures at Drèze and Sen, *India*, 178.

[81] Drèze and Sen, *India*, 178.

[82] Drèze and Sen, *India*, 177.

[83] Drèze and Sen, *India*, 177. In 1994, 94.6 per cent of children were enrolled in government schools (see Abusaleh Shariff, *India, Human Development Report: A Profile of Indian States in the 1990s* [New Delhi: Oxford University Press, 1999], 120). Since the turn of the millennium, however, the percentage of children aged 6–14 years enrolled in private primary schools (in rural Himachal Pradesh) has increased to 35.2 per cent, which is actually higher than the all-Indian rural average of 30.8 per cent (see ASER Centre, 'Annual Status of Education Report [Rural] 2014: Provisional' [2015], http://img.asercentre.org/docs/Publications/ASER%20Reports/ASER%202014/fullaser2014mainreport_1.pdf, accessed on 2 March 2019, 89).

and schools, with the state's per-capita educational expenditure being twice as high as the Indian average at that time.[84]

While private schools did not play a very big role in education advances in the state, another kind of private initiative was a very important factor for expanding the education system so quickly. Importantly, the state saw a wide range of public participation, with successful cooperative action in village communities, cooperation between teachers and parents (which led to quick improvements concerning attendance), parents helping with the improvement of school infrastructure, and so on.[85] The success story of Himachal Pradesh is therefore not just a story of 'top-down' measures by a proactive state government, but also a story of 'bottom-up' implementation of the education system helped by local community participation.

## *Federal Framework*

The fact that some states managed to get far ahead of others was partly facilitated by the constitutional framework. Originally, in the federal system set up by the Constitution, education was an exclusive competence of the states. This was considered to be the optimal solution due to the vast diversity of the country, especially linguistically.[86] In 1976, a constitutional amendment[87] transferred

[84] Drèze and Sen, *India*, 183.

[85] Drèze and Sen, *India*, 180.

[86] Vijayashri Sripati and Arun Thiruvengadam, 'Constitutional Amendment Making the Right to Education a Fundamental Right', *ICON* (2004): 150. However, the issue had been debated in the Constituent Assembly, with several representatives, including India's first prime minister Jawaharlal Nehru, favouring central competence in all or most matters of education. Still, the majority decided for leaving most education subjects as a state competence (as it had been since the Government of India Act of 1935), with the exception of coordination and standards of higher education, scientific and technical institutions, and some other details (see Granville Austin, *The Indian Constitution: Cornerstone of a Nation*, Oxford India Paperbacks [Oxford, New York: Oxford University Press, 1999], 201).

[87] The Forty-Second Amendment, otherwise an infamous Act of Parliament, not because of the reform in education responsibilities, but

education to the 'concurrent' list of competences, leading to a situation in which the Centre and the states explicitly share responsibilities. Since then, the Centre has been competent to formulate educational policies that the states have to follow.[88] However, it took another decade until the central government actually started focussing more on the field of elementary education.[89] Actual tangible advances followed even later. With education being a 'concurrent' subject, it was possible to set standards at the central level while at the same time employing an approach of decentralized implementation.

One decade after the constitutional amendment, through the central government's National Policy on Education and Programme of Action of 1986, the implementation framework started becoming more decentralized down to the block (a rural administration division) and village level. A larger focus was put on areas of the country that had remained more 'backward'.[90] The Policy set the aim of achieving the goal of universal free and compulsory education for children up until the age of 14 years by 1995 (that is, 35 years after the expiry of the deadline set by Article 45). However, once again, it did not set a clear agenda of policy changes to facilitate an achievement of this goal in time.[91]

---

for generally transferring more powers to the central government during Indira Gandhi's Emergency (see Henry C. Hart, 'The Indian Constitution: Political Development and Decay', *Asian Survey* 20, no. 4 [1980]).

[88] Ramachandran and Ramkumar, *Education in India*, 129; Odhekar, 'India', 133–4.

[89] Problematically, even as the central spending on elementary education increased, the states' expenditure decreased relative to the state domestic product (and in some states, even in absolute terms) in the 1990s. This happened in part because of increased reliance on centre-sponsored schemes and also because of an increasing tendency to rely on (at least sometimes questionable) low-cost arrangements for the expansion of schooling (see Drèze and Sen, *India*, 168–72). For the phenomenon of low-cost 'contract teachers' in particular, see 'Teacher Performance' in this chapter.

[90] Rao, Cheng, and Narain, 'Primary Schooling in China and India', 163 et seq.

[91] Drèze and Sen, *India*, 165.

Around the same time (1987), 'Operation Blackboard', which called for more government involvement at all levels (Centre, states, local bodies, voluntary agencies, and individuals), was started by the central Ministry of Human Resource Development (the central ministry responsible for education).[92] This 'operation' did bring at least some concrete results. These included transferring teachers from large to small schools (and thus turning the latter from one-teacher into at least two-teacher schools), which did not work as well as it was intended, but brought an increase in elementary school completion rates for girls and children of poorer parents.[93]

The emphasis on elementary education in the National Policy was further underlined by its modification in 1992, which again highlighted the importance of elementary education and the goal of making it universal for children up to 14 years of age.[94] Again, the Policy did not give a concrete outline of how this goal should be achieved[95] but instead expressed a belief that Indian tradition, freed from foreign influences, would somehow automatically bring education to all parts of the society.[96] While this view, unsurprisingly, did not remain without criticism,[97] the education system

92 Odhekar, 'India', 134.

93 Aimee Chin, 'Can Redistributing Teachers Across Schools Raise Educational Attainment? Evidence from Operation Blackboard in India', *Journal of Development Economics* 78, no. 2 (2005).

94 Odhekar, 'India', 134.

95 Drèze and Sen, *India*, 165; Rao, Cheng, and Narain, 'Primary Schooling in China and India', 163.

96 The Policy states that Indian tradition nurtures both 'the base and the top of the pyramid' of education and that 'the skew set in with foreign domination and influence', and that therefore given the tradition, 'we are bound to succeed in achieving our objectives' (see Government of India, *National Policy on Education, 1986. [As modified in 1992]* [1992], http://mhrd.gov.in/sites/upload_files/mhrd/files/document-reports/NPE86-mod92.pdf, accessed on 19 August 2018, 37).

97 Rao criticizes it as an example of 'a bureaucratic attitude of devising policies without thinking too much about their practical implementation', 'the belief that things would straighten out by themselves' and 'a tendency to blame British colonial rule for the conditions even four decades after

did advance to a certain extent in the following years, even though progress was not as fast as one might have hoped.

## *Developments since the 1990s*

In fact, the largest amount of progress up until today has been made since the 1990s.[98] Literacy has increased at an unprecedented speed since that time,[99] which is partly thanks to government initiatives like the District Primary Education Programme (1994), the Total Literacy Campaign (1989), and the National Programme of Nutritional Support to Primary Education (or Mid-Day Meal Scheme), as well as initiatives at the state level.[100] Generally, government initiatives since the 1990s have put a larger focus on not just building schools, but also on ensuring that children actually attend schools, with several states, for instance, introducing mid-day meals.[101] The increase in literacy is also thanks to the fact that since the 1990s public demand for education has grown,[102] which also brought a large increase in the number of private elementary

---

independence' (see Rao, Cheng, and Narain, 'Primary Schooling in China and India', 163).

[98] Odhekar, 'India', 131, 134; Drèze and Sen, *India*, 151.

[99] Geeta G. Kingdon, 'The Progress of School Education in India', Global Poverty Research Group, https://web.archive.org/web/20130421051641/http://economics.ouls.ox.ac.uk/12991/1/gprg-wps-071.pdf, accessed on 19 August 2018, 10–11. See note 58 for an overview of the development of literacy rates.

[100] See Drèze and Sen, *India*, 151.

[101] Rao, Cheng, and Narain, 'Primary Schooling in China and India', 161–2.

[102] Drèze and Sen, *India*, 168. Public demand has also been increased by initiatives that the state was involved in itself, like the Total Literacy Campaign which 'buil[t] a social consensus about the centrality of elementary education for every child's upbringing' (see Drèze and Sen, *India*, 155). The Total Literacy Campaign was part of the National Literacy Mission, which the central government started in 1988 (see Nitya Rao, 'Total Literacy Campaigns: A Field Report', *Economic & Political Weekly* XXVIII, no. 19 [1993]: 914).

schools.[103] Also in the 1990s, the Supreme Court picked up the issue of elementary education in two landmark decisions.[104] In those judgments, the Court declared that the state's duty to provide free and compulsory education, as defined in Article 45 of the Constitution, was part of the fundamental right to (dignified) life (Article 21). The implications of these decisions shall be looked at in depth in the following chapters.

This, as well as the educational aspect of the Millennium Development Goals (MDG) that India prescribed to,[105] led to even more decisive developments in the next decade. The government started the *Sarva Shiksha Abhiyan* (Education for All Movement) in 2000.[106] It once again set the goal of providing all children aged 6 to 14 with eight years of decent-quality education, this time aiming to achieve it by 2010.[107] However, unlike many other initiatives, it went beyond mere written pledges. It also outlined a framework of how this could be made a reality. The framework, for instance, defined how many primary schools ought to exist in the country (one within 1 kilometre of every hamlet, village, or urban community), what the teacher–pupil ratio ought to be (1:40), that textbooks and school uniforms should be available for free, and so on.[108] The programme is implemented as a partnership of the central and state governments, with the Ministry of Human Resource Development's Elementary Education Bureau acting as a monitoring institution.[109]

Significantly, the programme has not only set out goals and identified state bodies that ought to implement them, but it also

[103] Kingdon, 'The Progress of School Education in India', 6–7, 21–2.

[104] *Miss Mohini Jain* v. *State of Karnataka and Ors* MANU/SC/0357/1992 (Supreme Court of India, 30 July 1992); *Unni Krishnan, J.P. and Ors* v. *State of Andhra Pradesh and Ors* MANU/SC/0333/1993 (Supreme Court of India, 4 February 1993).

[105] The importance of international obligations for India's legal educational framework shall be dealt with in Chapter 3.

[106] See http://www.ssa.nic.in/about_ssa.html, accessed on 7 August 2018.

[107] See Michael Ward, 'Aid to Education: the Case of Sarva Shiksha Abhiyan in India and the Role of Development Partners', *Journal of Education Policy* 26, no. 4 (2011): 544.

[108] http://www.ssa.nic.in/about_ssa.html, accessed on 7 August 2018; Ward, 'Aid to Education', 545.

[109] Ward, 'Aid to Education', 546.

includes substantial funding in addition to the education expenses that were already in existence.[110] The financial responsibilities in between the Centre and the states were to be shared at a ratio of 85:15 initially, with the state's responsibility set to progressively increase to 50 per cent by 2016.[111] Some of the funds came from foreign donors,[112] who also gave technical assistance.[113]

Another decisive development in the 2000s was the creation of a new fundamental right, added to the constitutional text by the Eighty-Sixth Constitutional Amendment in 2002. The newly included Article 21A transformed the contents of Article 45 into a justiciable right.[114] Based on this new article, Parliament passed the Right of Children to Free and Compulsory Education Act in 2009 as an implementation measure for the fundamental right to education. This central Act created a new legal framework for elementary education that the states had to build upon. It shall be looked at in detail below, as well as in the following chapters.

## Problems Concerning Elementary Education in India Today

The developments in the last few decades, especially since the turn of the century, have led to some remarkable achievements.

[110] Ward, 'Aid to Education', 547; Kingdon, 'The Progress of School Education in India', 24–5.

[111] Deepa Sankar, 'Financing Elementary Education in India through Sarva Shiksha Abhiyan: Challenges in recent times', The World Bank, http://siteresources.worldbank.org/INTINDIA/2132853-1191444019328/21507645/SankarFinancingEducation.pdf, accessed on 19 August 2018; India, *Eleventh Five Year Plan, 2007–2012: Volume II. Social Sector* (New Delhi: Oxford University Press, 2008), http://planningcommission.nic.in/plans/planrel/fiveyr/11th/11_v2/11th_vol2.pdf, accessed on 19 August 2018, 10; India, *Twelfth Five Year Plan (2012–2017): Volume III. Social Sectors* (New Delhi: SAGE, 2013), http://planningcommission.gov.in/plans/planrel/fiveyr/12th/pdf/12fyp_vol3.pdf, accessed on 19 August 2018, 65.

[112] Ward, 'Aid to Education', 547.

[113] Ward, 'Aid to Education', 552.

[114] With one limitation being that this new right only addresses children in the age group of 6 to 14, rather than all children up to the age of 14.

Sarva Shiksha Abhiyan, Supreme Court orders, and the Right to Education Act are said to be responsible for a significant increase in the enrolment rate at the primary level.[115] Thus, today, there are relatively few children who have remained entirely untouched by education, except for those living in remote areas.[116] Even for those areas, the State's outreach has improved due to the creation of new schools and residential schools with hostels in remote areas such as the ones inhabited by 'Scheduled Tribes',[117] or offering schooling for children speaking minority languages in different parts of the country.[118]

However, this does not mean that the problems concerning elementary education are solved, or that a state of universal free and compulsory elementary education has been achieved, unless one defines this goal as a state in which most children are enrolled in schools but nothing more. The fact that a child is enrolled in a school does not necessarily mean that they actually receive education, and even if they do, it does not mean that this education lives up to the minimum standards that one would expect from a functional educational system (or that a right to education would call for, as will be shown in Chapter 3).

## Infrastructure

At first glance, perhaps the most noticeable deficiencies concern the infrastructure of schools, though some progress has been made in this respect. The *Public Report on Basic Education in India* (PROBE) *Report* of 1999 highlighted serious infrastructural problems across the country. For instance, only 11 per cent of all the rural schools visited had functioning toilets, and 84 per cent

115 Drèze and Sen, *An Uncertain Glory*, 118.

116 Ward, 'Aid to Education', 554.

117 That is, tribal population recognized by the Constitution's Schedule.

118 Government of India: Ministry of Women and Child Development, 'India: Third and Fourth Combined Periodic Report on the Convention on the Rights of the Child', New Delhi, 2011, http://www.utsahassam.org/pdf/resource/INDIA-periodic-Report-CRC.pdf, accessed on 2 March 2019, 359.

had no toilets at all.[119] Furthermore, only 41 per cent had available drinking water, and 26 per cent of the schools were without a (functional) blackboard in every classroom.[120] Since then, the situation has improved considerably. For instance, already in 2006, 82 per cent of rural primary schools had drinking water, and 32 per cent of all schools had toilets for both boys and girls.[121] This progress came, at least to a considerable extent, thanks to additional funds provided through Sarva Shiksha Abhiyan and its predecessor programme, the District Primary Education Programme (DPEP).[122] However, as most recent reports show, there is still a lot of progress to be made. In 2016, only 60.4 per cent of all rural schools had a boundary wall, 25.9 per cent still did not offer clean drinking water, 31.3 still had no (usable) toilets, and only 61.9 per cent of all rural schools had separate (available) toilets for boys and girls.[123]

The Right to Education Act aims to address these issues by setting minimum standards that primary schools have to adhere to. Section 19 requires that all schools established and recognized (that is, established by private parties and recognized by the state) fulfil all the requirements named in the Act's Schedule, while Sections 8(g) and 9(h) require the state governments and local authorities to 'ensure good quality elementary education conforming to the standards and norms specified in the Schedule'.[124] The Schedule's

[119] The PROBE Team, *Public Report on Basic Education in India* (New Delhi: Oxford University Press, 1999), 42.

[120] The PROBE Team, *Public Report on Basic Education in India*, 42.

[121] Anuradha De, *Probe Revisited: A Report on Elementary Education in India* (New Delhi: Oxford University Press, 2011), 14.

[122] Kingdon, 'The Progress of School Education in India', 16.

[123] ASER Centre, 'Annual Status of Education Report (Rural) 2016: Provisional', 2017, http://img.asercentre.org/docs/Publications/ASER%20Reports/ASER%202016/aser_2016.pdf, accessed on 23 February 2019, 59.

[124] One may argue that only private schools have to fulfil the minimum standards defined by the Schedule, as only they are threatened with a loss of recognition (and, therefore, with being shut down by the state [see Section 18(1, 4) of the Act]) if they do not do so. Bhattacharjee and Mysoor speak of an 'implicit understanding' to this effect (see Malini Bhattacharjee and Dolashree Mysoor, '"Unredressed" Grievances under

infrastructure provisions concern the school building (2) which (i) is supposed to have one classroom per teacher as well as an additional room, (ii) should provide barrier-free access, (iii) should have separate toilets for boys and girls, (iv) should offer adequate drinking water as well as a kitchen for mid-day meals, (v) should have a playground, and (vi) be secured by a boundary wall or fence. Also, every school shall provide 'learning equipment' (5.) (though the Act does not state what this includes), have a library providing 'newspapers, magazines and books on all subjects, including story-books' (6.), and shall provide 'play material, games and sports equipment' (7.).

What is remarkable is how much the Right to Education Act focuses on such provisions concerning infrastructure, setting relatively detailed, concrete, and strict minimum standards, but that the Act is at the same time very vague concerning other parameters, especially learning outcomes and quality.[125] What is also

---

RTE: Navigating the State Labyrinth', *Governance: An International Journal of Policy, Administration, and Institutions* 29, no. 1 [2016]: 42). Consequently, the NGO 'Independent Thought' believes that government schools should also seek recognition under Section 18 of the Act (and cease operations without such recognition). It filed a PIL petition in the Delhi High Court challenging Section 18 as unconstitutional in this regard (see http://www.ithought.in/a/in_img/IndependentThought2015.pdf, accessed on 15 August 2018). In response to this (still pending) petition, the central government has stated that schools in the country were adhering to the norms of the schedule and that the government monitors schools to ensure compliance (see *India Today*, 'Schools Follow RTE Act: Says MHRD', 25 October 2016, http://indiatoday.intoday.in/education/story/schools-follows-rte-act-says-mhrd/1/794821.html, accessed on 19 August 2018; *Indian Express*, 'Government Schools Adhering to RTE Act Norms: Centre to HC', 24 October 2016, http://indianexpress.com/article/education/government-schools-adhering-to-rte-act-norms-centre-to-hc-3100815/, accessed on 19 August 2018). In any case, the wording of Sections 8, 9, and 19 shows that, at the very least, it shall be the state's goal to have its schools adhere to those standards. This question shall be discussed further in Chapter 6.

[125] Kingdon criticizes that '[t]he Act is completely silent on the things that really matter: teacher effort, teacher accountability and student

remarkable is that not adhering to the infrastructure provisions has far-reaching consequences for private schools. They will lose their recognition (Section 19(1), (3)) and will thus not be allowed to operate at all in the future (Section 18(1) forbids any school to function without recognition). Apart from infrastructure issues, the only other violation of the Right to Education Act that will lead to de-recognition concerns the pupil–teacher ratio and teachers' working hours in these schools.[126]

This raises the question whether or not focusing on this one (albeit broad) aspect of infrastructural standards is justified. A decent infrastructure is obviously important, and improving it leads to decisive positive effects that go beyond mere convenience. For instance, many studies show that having a separate toilet for girls (or at least any toilet in the school) helps in ensuring that girls continue going to school, especially once they reach puberty.[127] Also, teaching is obviously more difficult without teaching material like blackboards or textbooks, though it is not impossible.[128]

---

learning outcomes' (see Geeta Kingdon, 'Schooling without Learning: How the RTE Act Destroys Private Schools and Destroys Standards in Public Schools', *Times of India*, 26 August 2015, http://blogs.timesofindia.indiatimes.com/toi-edit-page/schooling-without-learning-how-the-rte-act-destroys-private-schools-and-destroys-standards-in-public-schools/, accessed on 19 August 2018).

126 Sec Section 19(1) read with the Schedule (at 1.: 'Number of teachers', at 3., 4.: 'Minimum number of working days/instructional hours in an academic year', 'Minimum number of working hours per week for the teacher').

127 Drèze and Sen, *India*, 182; Madhur Tankha, 'Lack of Toilets Keeps Girls Away from Schools', *The Hindu*, 12 October 2013, http://www.thehindu.com/todays-paper/tp-national/tp-newdelhi/lack-of-toilets-keeps-girls-away-from-schools/article5227297.ece, accessed on 19 August 2018.

128 Bhatty notes that,

> [i]t is quite conceivable that a dedicated teacher could impart the three Rs and much more to a bunch of pupils under a tree. Equally an indifferent teacher not concerned about what the pupils learn or do not learn, trough teaching in a proper classroom with running water in the toilet, can still cause half of them to drop out and the rest to stagnate or learn little.

While having a library in every school is surely desirable, a school with able, motivated teachers without a library will surely benefit students more than a school with a library that is lacking in teaching quality. However, of course, better infrastructure may also have indirect positive effects on quality, which the Right to Education Act may recognize by speaking of 'good quality elementary education' when referring to the standards set by the Schedule.[129]

Interestingly, it appears that private schools with bad infrastructure still lead to better learning achievements than government schools with similarly inferior facilities.[130] This shows that other factors might be as important, if not more important, for quality education. Based on studies in India's largest (and problem-ridden) state, Uttar Pradesh, performed in the late 1990s, it has been argued that the availability of infrastructure is sometimes not the biggest problem, but rather the fact that the existing infrastructure is not used.[131]

It is certainly positive if a classroom has a blackboard, but if the teacher is not competent to teach, or does not effectively teach at all, children will not gain much from such a facility. On the other hand, an able teacher might still be quite successful at imparting skills and knowledge even without a blackboard. Therefore, the question of teaching quality and learning outcomes seems to be more decisive. Still, it appears that the current legal framework for education neglects this aspect. However, the central government

See Kiran Bhatty, 'Educational Deprivation in India. A Survey of Field Investigations', *Economic & Political Weekly* XXXIII, no. 27 (1998): 1738.

[129] Bhatty believes that 'given the motivation of the teacher [...] and basic academic qualifications, infrastructure becomes important specially if the number of students in a class is large and there is multigrade teaching. Infrastructure is also important to keep the teacher motivated' (see Bhatty, 'Educational Deprivation in India', 1738).

[130] Karthik Muralidharan, 'Public-Private Partnerships for Quality Education in India', Seminar, no. 565 (2006): 3–4, 10–11, http://econweb.ucsd.edu/~kamurali/papers/Other%20Writing/public%20private%20partnerships%20for%20quality%20education%20in%20india.pdf, accessed on 19 August 2018.

[131] Jean Drèze and Haris Gazdar, 'Uttar Pradesh: The Burden of Inertia', in Drèze and Sen, *Indian Development*, 76–7.

now pledges to increase its focus on quality of education in budgetary allocations.[132]

## Teacher and Student Absence

The absolute minimum expected of a teacher should be that they are regularly present and teaching. However, in India, situations in which teachers are either entirely absent or present but not engaged in any form of teaching are not uncommon. A study of teacher absence in government primary schools in India in 2005 has shown that teacher absence rates compared to other countries were very high. Twenty-five per cent of all teachers who should have been present at the time of inspection were absent, with the absence rate being as high as 41.9 per cent in one state (Jharkhand) and higher than 30 per cent in several others (Chhattisgarh, Uttaranchal, Assam, Punjab, and Bihar).[133] Moreover, on average, only 45 per cent of the teachers who were present were 'actively engaged in teaching' at the time of inspection, with the rate being as low as 20 to 25 per cent in some states.[134] Teacher absence (or lack of teacher activity) are obviously especially grave if schools are run by only one teacher, which is still not entirely uncommon in rural areas.[135]

More recent surveys show that this problem persists today, though perhaps not to the same extent. The Annual Status of Education Report for Rural India of 2016 (ASER 2016) reported a teacher absence rate of 15.3 per cent in classes one to eight. This is a much lower figure than the one Kremer et al. found in 2005. However, it is actually higher than the figure that ASER

[132] See https://www.indiabudget.gov.in/ub2018-19/bs/bs.pdf (at points 47 et seq.), accessed on 12 August 2018.

[133] Michael Kremer, Karthik Muralidharan, Nazmul Chaudhury, Jeffrey Hammer, and F. Halsey Rogers, 'Teacher Absence in India: A Snapshot', *Journal of the European Economic Association* 3, no. 2–3 (2005): 659–60.

[134] Kremer, Muralidharan, Chaudhury, Hammer, and Rogers, 'Teacher Absence in India', 659–60.

[135] Both in 1996 and 2006, 12 per cent of all primary schools were single-teacher schools (see De, *Probe Revisited*, 37).

had reported in 2010 (13.6 per cent).[136] In any case, the number of teachers who are not *regularly* present still seems to be considerable. Also, there is no evidence that the problem of lack of teaching activity while being physically present is solved. At least, there has been little progress in this regard in the (relatively) recent past:[137] in both the PROBE Reports of 1999 and 2006, there was practically no teaching activity in half of the schools that the investigators visited.[138]

In addition to teacher absence, student absence is also a problem. The ASER report of 2016 found that on the day of the unannounced visits, 26.8 per cent of children were absent. As compared to the 2010 figures, this percentage has increased slightly, from 26.6 per cent (though it has decreased from 28.9 per cent in 2014).[139]

One of the factors which keep parents from sending their children to school is the cost of schooling. Tuition fees have been more or less negligible for a long time, but additional costs like expenses for uniforms, textbooks, and so on, are considerable for low-income families,[140] and are still in existence today in some areas, even though Sarva Shiksha Abhiyan aimed to provide them to all children for free.[141] There is still a gender disparity as far as school enrolment is concerned, with a (nowadays: slightly) higher percentage of girls who are out of school than boys who are out of school. This is especially the case as children grow older, with

[136] ASER Centre, 'Annual Status of Education Report (Rural) 2016', 56.

[137] The ASER reports do not offer numbers for this issue.

[138] The PROBE Team, *Public Report on Basic Education in India*, 47; De, *Probe Revisited*, 35.

[139] ASER Centre, 'Annual Status of Education Report (Rural) 2016', 56.

[140] The PROBE Team, *Public Report on Basic Education in India*, 16–17.

[141] Rajesh Moudgil, 'Lapses in SSA: Long Delays in Providing Books, Uniforms', *Hindustan Times*, 16 July 2014, https://www.hindustantimes.com/chandigarh/lapses-in-ssa-long-delays-in-providing-books-uniforms/story-6APSM3tSw7HaOf3PptFyiM.html, accessed on 19 August 2018; Shruti Sharma, 'An Assessment of Girls Education under Sarva Shiksha Abhiyaan', *Mainstream Weekly*, 21 June 2014, http://www.mainstreamweekly.net/article5000.html, accessed on 19 August 2018.

more girls than boys dropping out after a few years.[142] While most parents send their boys to school so that their job opportunities increase, enabling girls to earn money is apparently not as much of a priority.[143] For some parents, educating a girl 'too much' is actually seen as a burden, as this might lessen her chances to find an 'adequate' groom later on in life.[144]

Generally, however, if good, affordable education is available in the vicinity, studies show that parents do show interest in sending their children to school. This is the case both for boys and girls. However, if local schools perform very badly, parents' motivation is accordingly low.[145] Child labour, on the other hand, is not as great a factor as is often believed. Studies show that on average, out-of-school children do little work,[146] and that if they do work, the

[142] See the figures in ASER Centre, 'Annual Status of Education Report (Rural) 2014', 85. 5.7 per cent of girls and 4.4 per cent of boys aged 11 to 14 years were out of school (that is, not enrolled in any school) at the time of the study in rural India. In the age group of 15 to 16 years, the figures increased to 17.3 per cent for girls and 15.9 per cent for boys. A report by the Ministry of Women and Child Development speaks of a 63.5 per cent dropout rate of adolescent girls, which suggests that the educational deprivation of girls is a lot higher, at least at a later level (see Ministry of Women and Child Development, 'Report of the Working Group on Child Rights for the 12th Five-Year Plan (2012–2017)', https://web.archive.org/web/20140922134717/http://wcd.nic.in/reportwgdtd01032012.pdf, accessed on 19 August 2018, 20). De reports that while 69 per cent of parents say that their boys should be educated 'as far [i.e. as long] as possible', the same figure is as low as 52 per cent for girls (see De, *Probe Revisited*, 102).

[143] The PROBE Team in 1999 found that while 87 per cent of all parents believe that education is important for their boys because of employment opportunities, only 40 per cent said the same about girls. The most important factor for girls (at 50 per cent) was so that they could 'help to write letter and keep accounts' for the family (see The PROBE Team, *Public Report on Basic Education in India*, 19). This discrepancy still exists, though the gender gap seems to be closing: De's findings show that the eagerness to have daughters educated has increased in recent years (see De, *Probe Revisited*, 48, 50).

[144] Drèze and Sen, *India*, 162.

[145] Drèze and Sen, *India*, 154–5.

[146] The PROBE Team, *Public Report on Basic Education in India*, 16.

reason why they (or their parents) prefer that they work over going to school is often also connected to the bad quality of education.[147]

Ultimately, it appears that whenever quality of education is improved, the problem of child absence at least becomes considerably smaller almost automatically. However, some parents might still decide against sending their children to school. This leads to the issue of *compulsory* education. Both the constitutional provisions as well as the Right to Education Act explicitly speak of 'compulsory education', and the Act defines 'compulsory education' as an 'obligation of the appropriate government to [...] provide free elementary education [...] and [...] ensure compulsory admission, attendance and completion of elementary education' (Section 8(a)). The wording 'compulsory admission and attendance' means that there is a legal obligation for parents to send their children to school, meaning that there ought to be repercussions if they do not do so. However, one may question to what extent this is actually desirable in the Indian context, as shall be discussed in Chapter 3.

The idea of compulsory education, as mentioned above, dates back to the colonial era. Also, in the early decades following Independence, acts attempting to make elementary education compulsory were passed at the state level.[148] However, this compulsion was not enforced effectively.[149] Under the current legal regime, it is unclear how it could be enforced at all, as the Right

[147] Drèze and Sen, *India*, 156. The authors therefore conclude: 'There is some overlap between the two problems—child labour and school exclusion—but no congruence' (see Drèze and Sen, *India*, 157). Bhatty, already in 1998, noted that parents may have their children work 'as a deterrent to idling, rather than as an economic necessity' and that '[i]f child labour were the main reason for dropping out, we would not expect dropping out to be concentrated in the early grades. This is because [...] child labour is relatively unimportant at young ages' (see Bhatty, 'Educational Deprivation in India. A Survey of Field Investigations', 1734–5).

[148] See the Delhi Primary Education Act of 1960, the Punjab Compulsory Education Act of 1960, and similar acts passed in 1962 in Andhra Pradesh, Gujarat, Madhya Pradesh, and Mysore.

[149] See some statistics on coercive measures (or lack thereof) in Ojha, Pandit Gopesh Kumar, *Progress of Compulsory Education in India* (Delhi: Universal Book & Stationary Co., 1966), 78.

to Education Act remains entirely mum on possible consequences for parents not sending their children to school. It merely reiterates in Section 10 the fact that it is the parents' constitutional duty (a 'fundamental duty', see Article 51A(k)) to do so. However, it is clear that today, with more than one fourth of all children in classes one to eight not actually regularly attending school, the State is not fulfilling its duty to ensure attendance, if necessary even against the parents' will.

The problems caused by lack of attendance become especially apparent when combining the figures concerning teacher and student attendance and teacher (in)activity. Based on various education reports, and taking all these factors into account, it has been observed that the average child in the country is only taught for 25 per cent of the ideal amount of teaching time.[150] While this figure is not based on most up-to-date data, it shows that there is a huge discrepancy between enrolment rate (which, as noted above, is now almost universal) and the amount of time that children are actually taught. This only becomes apparent in its entirety when taking both teacher and student attendance and activity into account. If one takes the goal of 'free and compulsory education' seriously, then the amount of education that children receive, and not just the percentage of mere enrolment, must be a decisive figure.

## Learning Achievements

As may be expected from an elementary education system where a significant number of children are not properly taught, learning achievements among Indian children are quite low. When two Indian states participated in the Programme for International Student Assessment (PISA) Plus survey in 2009, they ranked at the bottom of the 74 participating countries in almost all categories, even though the two states that participated (Tamil Nadu and Himachal Pradesh) are among the most successful in India as far as learning achievements are concerned.[151] Generally, there are few comparative

[150] Drèze and Sen, *An Uncertain Glory*, 120.

[151] Maurice Walker, 'PISA 2009 Plus Results: Performance of 15-Year-Olds in Reading, Mathematics and Science for 10 Additional

studies of learning achievements in India and other countries, but when such comparisons are made, India usually fares quite badly.[152] This is also the case when comparing India to other South Asian countries, including those that are considerably poorer.[153]

What is especially worrisome is the fact that there is evidence that learning achievements have deteriorated in the last few years. For instance, ASER 2016 found that only 41.6 per cent of children in class V in rural government schools were able to read texts written for children in class II.[154] In 2010, this figure was at 50.7 per cent.[155] Also, the percentage of class III children in rural government schools who were able to perform subtraction tasks has decreased from 33.2 in 2010 to 20.2 in 2016; the percentage of class V children who were able to divide has decreased from 33.9 to 21.1 in the same time period.[156]

It is not quite clear how the deterioration in learning achievements can be explained. Enrolment has increased in this time period, which means that there are more children to cater to, but the most major achievements in enrolment were made in the years before 2009. Today, enrolment is almost universal, at 95.9 per cent for children aged 6 to 14 years in 2016, and it had been close to this figure in 2009 already.[157] Therefore, the increase in

---

Participants', ACER Press, http://research.acer.edu.au/cgi/viewcontent.cgi?article=1000&context=pisa, accessed on 19 August 2018, 11–12, 18–20, 42, 44, 53, 55, 68–71.

[152] Kingdon, 'The Progress of School Education in India', 5.

[153] For instance, Sri Lanka is far ahead of India in terms of literacy, and even Bangladesh's literacy rates have been growing more quickly than India's in recent years (see Drèze and Sen, *An Uncertain Glory*, 48 et seq., 58 et seq., 65 et seq., 112 et seq.).

[154] ASER Centre, 'Annual Status of Education Report (Rural) 2016', 52.

[155] ASER Centre, 'Annual Status of Education Report (Rural) 2016', 52.

[156] ASER Centre, 'Annual Status of Education Report (Rural) 2016', 53.

[157] At 90.8 per cent according to World Bank figures (see http://data.worldbank.org/indicator/SE.PRM.NENR?page=1, accessed on 15 August 2018). Also see the figures at ASER Centre, 'Annual Status of Education Report (Rural) 2013', ASER Centre, New Delhi, 2013, 69; ASER Centre, 'Annual Status of Education Report (Rural) 2016', 51.

enrolment cannot be the only factor to explain the deterioration in quality.

Another factor could be negative development concerning the student–teacher ratio. More children in the schooling system creates a necessity to hire more teachers, especially in order to adhere to the student–teacher ratio that the Right to Education Act prescribes. The student–teacher ratio still lags behind the Act's requirements, with only 53 per cent of schools in rural India having met the goal set by the Act in 2016.[158] However, the situation has still improved in recent years, meaning that the student–teacher ratio cannot be responsible for deterioration in learning achievements.[159]

Interestingly, some provisions of the Right to Education Act might not be particularly beneficial but actually detrimental to learning achievements. For instance, for several years, Section 16 prescribed that no child may be held back in any class until the completion of elementary education, even if their learning achievements do not progress as desired. At the same time, every teacher has a duty to 'assess the learning ability of each child and accordingly supplement additional instructions, if any, as required', according to Section 24(1)(d). If teachers were able to give such an intense amount of attention to every child requiring it then such care may be an adequate alternative to holding children back if they fail a year. However, with the pupil–teacher ratio still remaining high in many schools, such individual care may not be feasible. Therefore, children whose abilities do not progress at the desired speed are often just passed on to the next year without any special help offered to them to make up for their deficiencies. Based on the figures offered by ASER, it has been observed that because of the 'no-detention rule', children's 'conceptual lag keeps getting wider with each successive grade'.[160] As a consequence,

[158] ASER Centre, 'Annual Status of Education Report (Rural) 2016', 58.

[159] Only 38.9 per cent of all rural schools had achieved the Act's goal in 2010 (see ASER Centre, 'Annual Status of Education Report (Rural) 2016', 58).

[160] Disha Nawani, 'Reflections on "Annual Status of Educational Research 2012"', *Economic & Political Weekly* XLVIII, no. 12 (2013): 20.

in an effort to improve quality of education, in 2016 the Central Advisory Board of Education has reached a consensus with state and central ministers of Human Resource Development recommending a policy change that would allow state governments to modify or entirely omit the 'no detention' rule.[161] Parliament eventually scrapped the no-detention rule in 2018, with Section 16 of the Right to Education Act now prescribing regular examination in classes V and VIII. State governments are allowed to prescribe that a child be held back for a year if they fail those examinations as well as re-examinations that follow two months after the regular examinations.[162] The National Council of Educational Research and Training, on the other hand, had warned that scrapping the rule would lead to an increase in the numbers of children dropping out of school.[163]

One more issue limiting learning achievements is the fact that progress, or lack thereof, is hardly monitored. The Right to Education Act, in Section 30(1), states that no child shall be required to pass any board examination until the completion of elementary education (that is, class VIII). Board examinations,

[161] Abhishek Choudharil, 'States, UTs may be Allowed to Formulate Their Own No-Detention Policy Soon', *Times of India*, 26 October 2016, http://timesofindia.indiatimes.com/city/nagpur/States-UTs-may-be-allowed-to-formulate-their-own-no-detention-policy-soon/articleshow/55058260.cms, accessed on 19 August 2018; Prashant K. Nanda, 'CBSE Class X Board Exam to Return, No-Fail Policy to Go', *Live Mint*, 25 October 2016, http://www.livemint.com/Education/SR6AToBI1jzo4Vaffn2YWO/Govt-may-bring-back-CBSE-Class-X-board-exam-amend-nofail-p.html, accessed on 19 August 2018.

[162] See the contents of the Right of Children to Free and Compulsory Education (Amendment) Bill, 2018, as passed by the Lok Sabha on 18 July 2018 http://164.100.47.4/BillsTexts/LSBillTexts/PassedLoksabha/166_C_2017_LS_Eng.pdf, accessed on 12 August 2018.

[163] Introduction of the rule is said to have lowered the drop-out rates (see Anubhuti Vishnoi, 'NCERT Asks Government Not to Scrap "No Detention"', *Economic Times*, 10 October 2016, http://economictimes.indiatimes.com/news/politics-and-nation/ncert-asks-government-not-to-scrap-no-detention/articleshow/54770835.cms, accessed on 19 August 2018).

administered by both central and state boards, are usually conducted in India only after class X or XII, that is, much later than the lower limit that the Act imposes (class VIII). The Act does call for 'comprehensive and continuous evaluation of [a] child's understanding of knowledge and his or her ability to provide the same' in Section 29(2)(h), without elaborating further on how this process shall be designed in detail. Reportedly, this results in no evaluation taking place at all in government schools in most states.[164]

Therefore, apparently, it is difficult to assess how individual children perform in school. At the same time, while the no-detention rule was in place, children progressed from class to class, even if they are far behind of what is expected by the curriculum. Then, once the children reach a level beyond elementary education (if they do study beyond that), they are 'sent for slaughter in the Board Examination'.[165]

Another factor that may explain the lack of quality (though not the deterioration in the more recent past) are general teaching methods that have been employed in India for a long time. As mentioned above (at least) since the British period, children have been required to employ the learning method of rote memorization, with creative and critical thinking not being nurtured.[166] Consequently, there is a common practice of 'mindless rote learning, including repetition – typically without comprehension – of what has been read, and endless chanting of multiplication and other tables'.[167]

[164] 'States Criticise the "No-Detention" and "Continuous Evaluation" Provisions of RTE', *Economic Times*, 7 June 2012, https://economictimes.indiatimes.com/industry/services/education/states-criticise-the-no-detention-and-continuous-evaluation-provisions-of-rte/articleshow/13885701.cms, accessed on 19 August 2018.

[165] Drèze and Sen, *An Uncertain Glory*, 138.

[166] Rao, Cheng, and Narain explain that, both in India and China, '[t]he teacher has typically been a transmitter of knowledge rather than a facilitator of learning' (see Rao, Cheng, and Narain, 'Primary Schooling in China and India', 169).

[167] Drèze and Sen, *An Uncertain Glory*, 120.

The deterioration of learning achievements in government schools has been observed for several years. While there are no signs of a reversal of this trend, it seems to have slowed down at least according to the ASER numbers. According to those figures, the largest drop in learning achievements occurred before 2012.[168] Indeed, after having focused on universalization of education with Sarva Shiksha Abhiyan and the Right to Education Act, the Indian State does seem to slowly shift its focus to quality and learning outcomes. Politicians and government reports both by the previous and the current governments highlight such measures rather than the mere expansion of the system in recent years.[169]

168 See the charts in ASER Centre, 'Annual Status of Education Report (Rural) 2014', 87, 88.

169 The previous government announced a desire to focus on quality shortly before the last election (see *Times of India*, 'With RTE a Success, Govt to Shift Focus to Quality of Education', 15 January 2014, http://timesofindia.indiatimes.com/india/With-RTE-a-success-govt-to-shift-focus-to-quality-of-education/articleshow/28811588.cms, accessed on 19 August 2018). The current government pledged to focus on quality with the most recent budget announcements (as mentioned above) (see http://indiabudget.nic.in/ub2016-17/bh/bh1.pdf and https://www.indiabudget.gov.in/ub2018-19/bs/bs.pdf, accessed on 12 August 2018). It also names 'Quality Issues' as one of the 'Key Challenges in Education Sector', stating that '[t]he biggest challenge facing school education relates to unsatisfactory levels of student learning', in its 'Inputs' for a new National Education Policy, Government of India: Ministry of Human Resource Development, 'Some Inputs for Draft National Education Policy 2016', New Delhi, 2016, http://mhrd.gov.in/sites/upload_files/mhrd/files/Inputs_Draft_NEP_2016_1.pdf, accessed on 2 March 2019, 7–8. An August 2014 (that is, shortly after the last Lok Sabha election) report by the Ministry of Human Resources Development set the goal of 'quality with equity' (see Government of India: Ministry of Human Resource Development, 'Education for All. Towards Quality with Equity', 1st edition, New Delhi, 2014, http://mhrd.gov.in/sites/upload_files/mhrd/files/upload_document/EFA-Review-Report-final.pdf, accessed on 2 March 2019). India's 2011 Report on the Convention on the Rights of the Child already named several programmes on improvement of quality in different states, but remained somewhat superficial (see Government of India: Ministry of Women and Child Development, 'India', 322 et seq.).

It remains to be seen whether or not measures employed by the State will be able to close the gap in between private and government schools. Notably, the Aam Aadmi Party government of the National Capital Territory of Delhi has recently pushed for improving the government schools that it is responsible for. Those schools seem to now perform better than the average private schools, with the passing percentage of Delhi's government schools in the class XII centralized board examinations being slightly higher in 2018 than the passing percentage of Delhi's private schools.[170]

## Teacher Performance

Another aspect that may be responsible for low learning outcomes is lack of teacher performance. As mentioned above, teachers are not only frequently absent, to a considerable degree, they also tend to not actually teach even when they are physically present in the classroom. This behaviour is often without any noticeable consequences for the teachers.

Government school teachers directly employed by the states are in very secure jobs, and their salaries are not in any way linked to their performance.[171] There are certain standards that these teachers have to meet as far as qualifications are concerned (most of the time being a Bachelor of Elementary Education degree or teacher training for class XII graduates) in order to be employed.[172] But once they are employed, there is very little monitoring done on their performance.[173] What often happens is that teaching becomes

[170] *Financial Express*, 'How Delhi Government Schools Performed Better than Private Schools in CBSE 12th Exams', 28 March 2018, https://www.financialexpress.com/india-news/how-delhi-government-schools-performed-better-than-private-schools-in-cbse-12th-exams/1183001/, accessed on 12 August 2018.

[171] Drèze and Sen, *An Uncertain Glory*, 351, note 26.

[172] See 'Notification F. No. 61-03/20/2010/NCTE/(N&S)', National Council for Teacher Education, https://web.archive.org/web/20150412072603/http://www.ncte-india.org:80/Norms/RTE-3.pdf, accessed on 19 August 2018.

[173] *Drèze* and *Sen* observe a lack of accountability for the entire schooling systems, but also teachers in particular (see Drèze and Sen, *An Uncertain Glory*, 140–1).

a 'plum [job] that attract[s] anyone with the required qualifications – including those who have no interest whatsoever in teaching'.[174]

Generally, there is a big accountability problem with Indian State employees, partly amplified by legal provisions. For instance, public servants are very well protected against prosecution in case of corruption. The Prevention of Corruption Act, 1988, states that a violation by a state servant can be determined only with previous sanction of the concerned government.[175] Such a provision can also be found in the Right to Education Act in Section 36, which states that prosecution for public offences punishable under the Act shall only be instituted 'with the previous sanction of an officer authorised in this behalf by the appropriate Government'.

Corruption works at many levels in the education system, also in the education administration. School inspections, which at first sight appears to be an effective means to limit teacher absence and to improve accountability, have been found to be detrimental to educational advances because of corrupt inspectors.[176] Being harassed by such state officials is one reason why teachers and teachers' unions have resisted stronger accountability measures in the past.[177]

Teacher accountability in particular is no exception. Even with the recent education reforms, little has been done to improve it. For instance, the School Management Committee created by the Right to Education Act (a board that is supposed to take over the running of government schools with the majority of members being parents) is usually headed by the head teacher of the school rather than a more impartial person. The committee has no

[174] Drèze and Sen, *An Uncertain Glory*, 132.

[175] Section 19 of the Prevention of Corruption Act. Drèze and Sen call it an 'outrageous piece of bureaucratic safeguard that demands immediate repeal' (see Drèze and Sen, *An Uncertain Glory*, 99). Noorani notes that there is 'no other democracy' with comparable immunity provisions (see Abdul G.A.M. Noorani, 'How the Political Class has Looted India', *The Hindu*, 30 July 2012, http://www.thehindu.com/opinion/lead/how-the-political-class-has-looted-india/article3700211.ece, accessed on 19 August 2018).

[176] Drèze and Sen, *India*, 173–4.

[177] Drèze and Sen, *India*, 173–4.

disciplinary powers, even though such had originally been considered in the Right to Education Bill of 2015.[178] School inspections by the concerned government are not very common and they are not prescribed by the Right to Education Act.[179] This is surprising, as studies have shown that such inspections, even without sanctions, do improve teacher performance, particularly as far as attendance is concerned (provided, of course, that the inspectors are not corrupt and do not misuse their competences).[180]

In spite of lack of performance, state-employed government teachers are actually paid quite well. Their salaries are determined by (legally non-binding, but usually adopted)[181] recommendations of Pay Commissions, whose members are state servants themselves.[182] Also, teachers and teachers' unions are quite powerful

[178] Section 22(4)(iv) of the Right to Education Bill of 2005 aimed to empower School Management Committees to 'disburse salary to teachers [...] and to deduct payment of salary for the period of unauthorised absence'. The text of the Bill is available at https://web.archive.org/web/20160808001155/http://planipolis.iiep.unesco.org/upload/India/India_RighttoEducationBill2005.pdf, accessed on 15 August 2018. For more information on School Management Committees, see Florian Matthey-Prakash, 'School Management Committees as a Means for Bottom-Up Implementation of the Right to Education in India', *Law and Politics in Africa, Asia, Latin America (VRU)* 49, no. 2 (2016), https://www.nomos-elibrary.de/10.5771/0506-7286-2016-2-193/school-management-committees-as-a-means-for-bottom-up-implementation-of-the-right-to-education-in-india-jahrgang-49-2016-heft-2?page=1, accessed on 19 August 2018.

[179] An omission that Drèze and Sen criticize (see Drèze and Sen, *An Uncertain Glory*, 141).

[180] Kremer, Muralidharan, Chaudhury, Hammer, and Rogers, 'Teacher Absence in India', 664.

[181] See Drèze and Sen, *An Uncertain Glory*, 134.

[182] See Drèze and Sen, *An Uncertain Glory*, 134. The most recent 7th Pay Commission Report is available at https://web.archive.org/web/20171118051909/http://7cpc.india.gov.in/pdf/sevencpcreport.pdf, accessed on 15 August 2018. Pay Commission Reports are released once every decade (see https://web.archive.org/web/20171228141444/http://7cpc.india.gov.in/about_us.html, accessed on 15 August 2018). The 7th report recommended an average 23.55 increase in government

politically. Their most common demand is that of higher salaries, and not a raise in general education expenditures from which students might benefit as well.[183] The teacher-salary-to-Gross Domestic Product (GDP) ratio in India has grown considerably in the last few years to a level that is far higher than in most countries,[184]

---

employee salaries, and it appears that the central and state governments are once again accepting the recommendations (see *Indian Express*, '7th Pay Commission: Govt "By and Large" Accepts Recommendations, Minimum Salary Raised to Rs 18,000', 30 June 2016, http://indianexpress.com/article/business/business-others/7th-pay-commission-cabinet-meeting-latest-updates-today-2882835/, accessed on 19 August 2018; *New Indian Express*, 'State Govt to Implement 7th Pay Commission Recommendations', 28 October 2016, http://www.newindianexpress.com/states/odisha/2016/oct/28/state-govt-to-implement-7th-pay-commission-recommendations-1532809.html, accessed on 19 August 2018; Sukhbir Siwachi, 'Haryana to Implement 7th Pay Commission Report Soon', *Times of India*, 3 October 2016, http://timesofindia.indiatimes.com/city/chandigarh/Haryana-to-implement-7th-pay-commission-report-soon/articleshow/54662265.cms, accessed on 19 August 2018; *DNA India*, 'Maharashtra to Raise Government Staffers' Salaries, Pensions', 30 June 2016, http://www.dnaindia.com/mumbai/report-maharashtra-to-raise-government-staffers-salaries-pensions-2229526, accessed on 19 August 2018; 'Gujarat Government to Implement 7th Pay Commission from August 1', *Indian Express*, 31 July 2016, http://indianexpress.com/article/business/7th-pay-commission-gujarat-government-to-implement-7th-pay-commission-from-august-1-2946531/, accessed on 19 August 2018). For statistics on the development of government employee remuneration, also measured against figures like the overall union budget and GDP, see Samarth Bansal, 'What does the 7th Pay Panel Mean for Govt. Employees?,' *The Hindu*, 30 June 2016, http://www.thehindu.com/news/national/7th-pay-commission-benefits-to-government-employees/article8791800.ece, accessed on 19 August 2018.

[183] Kingdon points out that the percentage of education expenditure spent on teacher salaries has increased significantly (see Geeta G. Kingdon and Mohd Muzammil, 'A Political Economy of Education in India–II: The Case of UP', *Economic & Political Weekly* XXXVI, no. 33 [2001]: 3184).

[184] Drèze and Sen note that the primary school teacher salary to GDP per capita ratio in India in 2013 was around five or six, whereas the Organisation for Economic Co-operation and Development (OECD)

even though research suggests that higher teacher salaries do not significantly improve student achievements.[185]

The biggest problem arising from comparatively high teacher salaries is the fact that it makes expanding the education system to a universal system with appropriate teacher–pupil ratios extremely expensive. The number of children in the education system is growing while (according to the Right to Education Act) the teacher–pupil ratio needs to be improved, which means a lot more teachers need to be employed in the near future. Because of this, goals set out in the Right to Education Act will be difficult to achieve even if education expenditures rise to 6 per cent of the GDP, an already relatively high target that the government has been aiming for, but one that it has still not achieved.[186] Unless the state relies on public–private partnerships in elementary education to an even larger extent than it currently does,[187] or finds other inexpensive solutions, achieving an appropriate teacher–pupil ratio will be very difficult.

In the past, the problem of high teacher salaries has been circumvented by hiring so-called 'contract teachers' or 'para-teachers'

---

average had been around 1.2 in between 2000 and 2009. The authors point out that such high salaries are also problematic because they increase the social divide in between parents and teachers (in addition to making the expansion of education extremely expensive) (see Drèze and Sen, *An Uncertain Glory*, 131 et seq.).

185 Kingdon and Muzammil, 'A Political Economy of Education in India–II', 3182.

186 See Bharatiya Janata Party, 'Ek Bharat Shreshtha Bharat. Election Manifesto 2014' (2014), http://www.bjp.org/images/pdf_2014/full_manifesto_english_07.04.2014.pdf, accessed on 23 February 2019, 23. In 2012, education expenditure constituted 3.3 per cent of the GDP (see http://hdr.undp.org/en/content/expenditure-education-public-gdp, accessed on 15 August 2018). The '6 per cent aim' was originally set by the Kothari Commission report already in 1966 (see Drèze and Sen, *India*, 166).

187 Pankaj S. Jain and Ravindra H. Dholakia, 'Feasibility of Implementation of Right to Education Act', *Economic & Political Weekly* XLIV, no. 25 (2009); Pankaj S. Jain and Ravindra H. Dholakia, 'Right to Education Act and Public-Private Partnership', *Economic & Political Weekly* XLV, no. 8 (2010).

for government schools. Such teachers do not have the job security that state-employed teachers have, and have considerably smaller salaries.[188] Also, many of these teachers are not properly trained, or have only received training through 'dubious' correspondence courses.[189] Interestingly, their performance still seems to be comparable to the well-paid state teachers, even though their qualifications are, on average, lower.[190]

Having two 'categories' of teachers with similar responsibilities and, apparently, similar performance levels but with a considerable difference in salaries is questionable in itself. However, under the Right to Education Act, it is also not permissible anymore, as the Act requires teachers to meet minimum qualifications as defined by the government, that is, usually a Bachelor of Elementary Education degree or a Senior Secondary (that is, class XII) degree with additional teacher training.[191] Different Indian states are trying different solutions to find a way to integrate contract teachers without infringing the Act's provisions but also without going way beyond their own financial means.[192]

## Private Schools

One way to reach the goals set out by the Right to Education Act without having to excessively raise state expenditures (mainly on teacher salaries) would be to increase the number of private

188 Drèze and Sen, *An Uncertain Glory*, 119.

189 Drèze and Sen, *An Uncertain Glory*, 135.

190 Drèze and Sen, *An Uncertain Glory*, 135; Kingdon, 'The Progress of School Education in India', 26.

191 Section 23 of the Right to Education Act. Section 23(2) only allows a relaxation of minimum qualifications by the central government in case a state does not have adequate institutions offering courses or teacher trainings, and even this relaxation must not extend beyond five years, a time period in which teachers must 'acquire such minimum qualifications', Section 23(2). The minimum qualifications have been defined by the National Council for Teacher Education by Notification, available at http://www.education.kerala.gov.in/Downloads2011/rte/national_council.pdf, accessed on 15 August 2018.

192 Drèze and Sen, *An Uncertain Glory*, 136.

schools. Indeed, the State is relying on private schools at least to a certain extent, as private schools play a decisive role under the Right to Education Act's regime. Section 12(1)(c) obliges private un-aided schools to deliver free and compulsory education to children from 'economically weaker sections' living in their neighbourhood to the extent that these children fill at least 25 per cent of each of these schools' seats. The State reimburses the schools for delivering free education to these children, though the reimbursement will not go beyond what a government school receives for each child (Section 12(2)).[193]

Even before the Act was passed, the reach of private schooling at an elementary level had been growing quite quickly, particularly since the 1990s.[194] This coincided with the era of economic liberalization, which brought a higher demand for education and an increase (at least perceived) in upward social mobility.[195] Today, in rural India, more than 30 per cent of all children in the age group of 6 to 14 are enrolled in private schools,[196] reflecting an increase of more than 10.3 percentage points since 2006.[197] In urban areas, the percentage is even higher.[198]

193 Which, in the case of more expensive private schools, means that they receive considerably less money for these seats.

194 Kingdon, 'The Progress of School Education in India', 21–2; IDFC Foundation, 'India Infrastructure Report 2012: Private Sector in Education' (2013), http://www.idfc.com/pdf/report/iir-2012.pdf, accessed on 2 March 2019, 84.

195 Kingdon, 'The Progress of School Education in India', 6–7; The PROBE Team, *Public Report on Basic Education in India*, 19, 102 et seq; Drèze and Sen, *India*, 172.

196 30.5 per cent according to the (most recent) 2016 figures at ASER Centre, 'Annual Status of Education Report (Rural) 2016', 51.

197 ASER Centre, 'Annual Status of Education Report (Rural) 2013', 65.

198 Odhekar, 'India', 135–6; Anne O. Krueger, *Economic Policy Reforms and the Indian Economy* (Chicago: University of Chicago Press, 2002), 316. For instance, Mehendale, Mukhopadyay, and Namala note that in Karnataka, 48.9 per cent of all urban schools are private unaided schools, with an additional 12.3 per cent being private aided schools (see Archana Mehendale, Rahul Mukhopadyay, and Annie Namala, 'Right to Education and Inclusion in Private Unaided Schools. An Exploratory Study

Interestingly, according to national assessments of learning outcomes, the performance levels of private schools are considerably higher than those of government schools, and the gap is widening. This is not only true for elite urban private schools, but also for average rural private schools. The ASER report of 2016 has found that 62.9 per cent of children in rural private schools in class V were able to read class II level texts (compared to 41.6 per cent in government schools, as mentioned above)[199] and 44 per cent of children in class III were able to perform subtraction tasks (as compared to 20.2 per cent in government schools).[200] The performance of children has decreased even in private schools in recent years, but to a much smaller degree than in government schools, which means that the government/private gap has increased as far as learning achievements are concerned.[201] Some studies suggest that such a gap also exists when taking the socioeconomic backgrounds of pupils into account, meaning that poor parents' children enrolled in inexpensive private schools do better on average than similarly situated children in government schools.[202]

---

in Bengaluru and Delhi', *Economic & Political Weekly* L, no. 7 [2015]: 44). In rural areas of Karnataka, however, 85 per cent of all schools are government schools (2013 figures). A 2011 report by the Ministry of Women and Child Development shows that 'per-capita out-of-pocket expenditure' on elementary education is almost 10 times higher among the richest 20 per cent of the population than among the poorest 20 per cent in urban areas, but less than five times higher in rural areas (see Government of India: Ministry of Women and Child Development, 'India', 364).

[199] ASER Centre, 'Annual Status of Education Report (Rural) 2016', 52.

[200] ASER Centre, 'Annual Status of Education Report (Rural) 2016', 53.

[201] ASER Centre, 'Annual Status of Education Report (Rural) 2016', 52, 53.

[202] See, for instance, Sangeeta Goyal and Priyanka Pandey, 'How Do Government and Private Schools Differ?', *Economic & Political Weekly* XLVII, no. 22 (2012). However, the author notes that some of this difference may also be explained by factors like 'better'/abler pupils visiting private schools more often.

Rural private schools are especially common in such villages where government school teachers are frequently absent.[203] These villages are typically located in poorer areas, which is also reflected in the observation that a higher per capita income of a particular area means that the percentage of children in private schools is typically lower.[204] In other words, the phenomenon of children attending private schools is far from being one that only occurs in richer parts of the society. To some extent, the contrary is the case. For instance, in the relatively wealthy states of Gujarat and Maharashtra, teacher absence is relatively low and rural private schools are relatively uncommon.[205] Therefore, private schools seem to be particularly successful if the government school system is deficient, even if the local population is relatively poor.

In order to be accessible to the poor, many private schools are relatively inexpensive and inferior to government schools according to some indicators. Many are lacking in terms of infrastructure and teacher qualifications. Still, such schools' performance appears to be superior as far as learning outcomes are concerned.[206] Considering this, it appears even more questionable to focus on infrastructure, rather than on other performance aspects. It also puts the common requirements for teacher qualifications in perspective. Rural private school teachers are often not specifically trained as teachers, and they often do not have a teaching certificate. Instead, they are young, but still relatively educated.

[203] Muralidharan, 'Public-Private Partnerships for Quality Education in India', 2–3.

[204] Karthik Muralidharan and Michael Kremer, 'Public and Private Schools in Rural India', 2007, http://scholar.harvard.edu/files/kremer/files/public_and_private_schools_in_rural_india_final_pre-publication.pdf, accessed on 19 August 2018, 7–10.

[205] Muralidharan and Kremer, 'Public and Private Schools in Rural India', 7–10.

[206] Muralidharan, 'Public-Private Partnerships for Quality Education in India', 3–4; Muralidharan and Kremer, 'Public and Private Schools in Rural India', 15.

On average, they are 10 years younger and more likely to have a college degree (just not in teaching) than government school teachers. They are also often from the same village that they teach in, and often see the teaching profession as a temporary solution until they can find higher-paid jobs elsewhere.[207] Like contract teachers in government schools, their salaries are much lower than those of state-employed teachers.[208] Still, it appears that these teachers are more motivated, even if they do not see teaching as a permanent profession.

As the indicators mentioned above suggest, private schools appear to deliver better results at considerably lower costs.[209] Still, according to the Right to Education Act, many such schools would need to cease operation in the near future. Section 18(5) of the Act forbids running private schools without obtaining previous recognition by the state. Many of the private schools, however, are unrecognized. This is especially the case for such schools with low tuition fees, which are mostly accessed by poor children in relatively large numbers.[210]

According to the Right to Education Act, no school shall be recognized unless it fulfils the norms and standards as specified

[207] Muralidharan and Kremer, 'Public and Private Schools in Rural India', 13–14.

[208] Muralidharan and Kremer note that private school teachers are on average paid one fifth of what teachers earn in government schools, with the salary sometimes being as low as one tenth (see Muralidharan and Kremer, 'Public and Private Schools in Rural India', 4). Ohara notes that the teachers in her study of Delhi were indeed paid less than one tenth of the salary prescribed for teachers in recognized schools (see Yuki Ohara, 'Examining the Legitimacy of Unrecognised Low-Fee Private Schools in India: Comparing Different Perspectives', *Compare: A Journal of Comparative and International Education* 42, no. 1 [2012]: 80).

[209] See Muralidharan, 'Public-Private Partnerships for Quality Education in India', 3; Muralidharan and Kremer, 'Public and Private Schools in Rural India', 2–3; Goyal and Pandey, 'How Do Government and Private Schools Differ?'.

[210] 51 per cent of all rural private schools were unrecognised in 2006 (see Muralidharan and Kremer, 'Public and Private Schools in Rural India', 6). More recent figures do not seem to be available.

in the schedule of the Act (see Section 18(1)). Unrecognized schools, as mentioned above, were supposed to cease operation under the Act's regime within three years after the Act came into force, that is, by 2013 (Section 19(2) and 19(3)). The provisions in the Act's schedule lay down minimum standards for schools' infrastructure and also prescribe a student–teacher ratio as well as minimum working hours for teachers. Many of the unrecognized schools do not have the financial means to adhere to the standards because of the low fees that they charge.[211] Consequently, they would have had to shut already in 2013. However, in some cases, the state governments chose to temporarily relax the Right to Education Act provisions so that the schools can continue operation.[212] While there have been reports of some schools having to cease operations,[213] there seems to be no widespread effort to effectively enforce the rules: there are reports that unrecognized private schools continue operation

211 Ohara, 'Examining the Legitimacy of Unrecognised Low-Fee Private Schools in India', 70.

212 See the example of Delhi: Gaurav V. Bhatnager, 'Norms for Delhi Schools Relaxed', *The Hindu*, 27 March 2013, http://www.thehindu.com/news/cities/Delhi/norms-for-delhi-schools-relaxed/article4554032.ece, accessed on 19 August 2018; Shikha Sharma, 'Again, Govt Extends Provisional Recognition of Schools', *Indian Express*, 7 January 2015, http://indianexpress.com/article/cities/delhi/again-govt-extends-provisional-recognition-of-schools/, accessed on 19 August 2018; *Business Standard*, 'Govt Extends Provisional Recognition to Pvt Schools for 5th Time', 28 April 2016, http://www.business-standard.com/article/pti-stories/govt-extends-provisional-recognition-to-pvt-schools-for-5th-time-116042801191_1.html, accessed on 19 August 2018.

213 Alys Francis, 'Why India's Landmark Education Law is Shutting Down Schools', *BBC*, 6 March 2014, http://www.bbc.com/news/world-asia-india-26333713, accessed on 19 August 2018. In 2018, the government of the National Capital Territory of Delhi increased the pressure on unrecognized schools, threatening that they would be closed from the academic session 2018–19 (see *Indian Express*, 'Unrecognised Delhi Schools Face Threat of Closure', 8 February 2018, https://indianexpress.com/article/education/unrecognised-delhi-schools-face-threat-of-closure-5055594/, accessed on 12 August 2018).

even after losing recognition,[214] and of schools 'buying' recognition by paying bribes.[215]

Before the Act came into force, the schools' unrecognized status was, to a large extent, tolerated.[216] In practice, not being recognized meant that such schools could not offer official certificates, including 'certificates' that would allow their pupils to continue

[214] Aneesha Bedi, 'Denied Recognition, Several Schools Continue to Function', *Hindustan Times*, 23 September 2015, http://www.hindustantimes.com/chandigarh/denied-recognition-several-schools-continue-to-function/story-FaxqCjuGMvXW68qYsj1i1I.html, accessed on 19 August 2018; *Hans India*, '105 Unrecognised Schools Continue to Exist in Krishna', 12 January 2016, http://www.thehansindia.com/posts/index/Andhra-Pradesh/2016-06-12/105-unrecognised-schools-continue-to-exist-in-Krishna/234588, accessed on 19 August 2018; Payal Dhawan, 'RTE: "Closed" Schools Function without Problem', *Times of India*, 31 January 2014, http://timesofindia.indiatimes.com/city/ludhiana/RTE-Closed-schools-function-without-problem/articleshow/29622330.cms, accessed on 19 August 2018.

[215] *Times of India*, 'Time to Roll Back Licence Raj in Education', 18 October 2016, http://timesofindia.indiatimes.com/city/hyderabad/Time-to-roll-back-licence-raj-in education/articleshow/54908232.cms, accessed on 19 August 2018.

[216] With one exception being a petition in Delhi, the legitimacy of unrecognised schools had been questioned even before the Right to Education Act was passed, with the Delhi High Court in 2008 ordering the local authorities to inspect such schools and grant recognition to those schools that fulfil the requirements, with the possibility of them being closed down if they do not (see *Social Jurist* v. *GNCT and Ors* MANU/DE/0203/2008, 34 [Delhi High Court, 8 February 2008]). A non-governmental organization (NGO) had brought the case to the court arguing that such schools were 'sub-standard teaching shops' that were merely exploiting children, parents, and teachers, and that they needed to be closed down (see Ohara, 'Examining the Legitimacy of Unrecognised Low-Fee Private Schools in India', 75). The schools appealed to the Supreme Court, which stayed the High Court order, but did call for government regulation of the matter (which then followed with the Right to Education Act) (see Ohara, 'Examining the Legitimacy of Unrecognised Low-Fee Private Schools in India', 77; *Social Jurist a Civil Rights Group* v. *Govt. of NCT of Delhi and Ors* MANU/DE/1647/2015 [Delhi High Court, 7 May 2015]).

their education in recognized schools. Most importantly, admission into class IX was only possible after completion of class VIII in a recognized school or by passing public examination.[217] However, many parents first had their children attend unrecognized schools for a few years, they then enrolled them in recognized schools, or they obtained transfer certificates through 'unofficial' channels (another example of corrupt practices by government officials involved in the education system).[218] Others double-enrolled their children in government schools and unrecognized schools to receive the benefits they saw in unrecognized schools, while at the same time making sure that their children's education was recognized, even though the children did not actually attend classes in the government schools.[219]

The reason why parents enroll their children in such schools is that they expect better outcomes than from government schools.[220] Higher-cost recognized private schools are usually out of the question for them. A decisive factor for those parents is the fact that these schools are (at least on paper) bilingual from the start, teaching both in the local language as well as in English.[221]

[217] Ohara, 'Examining the Legitimacy of Unrecognised Low-Fee Private Schools in India', 78. See the admission rules of the Central Board of Secondary Education (Rule 7.2), http://www.cbse.nic.in/examin~1/admissionmt.htm, accessed on 15 August 2018.

[218] Ohara, 'Examining the Legitimacy of Unrecognised Low-Fee Private Schools in India', 83–4.

[219] Ohara, 'Examining the Legitimacy of Unrecognised Low-Fee Private Schools in India', 85.

[220] Ohara, 'Examining the Legitimacy of Unrecognised Low-Fee Private Schools in India', 75–7; Renu Singh and Sudipa Sarkar, 'Teaching Quality Counts: How Student Outcomes Relate to Quality of Teaching in Private and Public Schools in India', Young Lives, http://www.younglives.org.uk/files/working-papers/wp91-singh-sarkar, accessed on 19 August 2018, 12.

[221] T. Raphael, 'The Problem of Horizontal Effect', *European Human Rights Law Review* (2000): 21; Ohara, 'Examining the Legitimacy of Unrecognised Low-Fee Private Schools in India', 78. However, in a study performed in Delhi, the language of instruction was in fact Hindi even when it was supposed to be English (see Ohara, 'Examining the Legitimacy of Unrecognised Low-Fee Private Schools in India', 80).

Even though such a belief in higher quality services might not entirely reflect in the actual performance of these schools, it does appear that their achievements are at least not inferior to government schools.[222] Considering that they often compensate for a deficiency in the availability of state-run schools,[223] it might be detrimental for the overall performance of education in the country if they ceased operations at once.[224]

Still, in spite of indicators suggesting that private schools are a cheaper and at the same time a more effective solution to improve education, there are voices that are critical of increasingly relying on the private sector. In fact, the figures themselves, or at least the direct conclusions being drawn from them, have been questioned. Pratham, the NGO behind ASER, has been described as an organization which favours privatization, public–private partnership, education vouchers, and 'the NGO-ization of school education',[225] and also as one which selectively refrains from highlighting that learning outcomes are also lacking in private schools.[226] Members of education advocacy groups point to the fact that many of Pratham's supporters are multinational corporations and their foundations.[227]

[222] Rather, they appear to be higher even in these schools (see United Nations Educational, Scientific and Cultural Organization [UNESCO], *Teaching and Learning: Achieving Quality for All*, Education For All [EFA] global monitoring report 2013/4 (2014), 272–3; Singh and Sarkar, 'Teaching Quality Counts'; IDFC Foundation, 'India Infrastructure Report 2012', 85).

[223] Which is reflected in the fact that in rural areas, they are mostly found where government schools are not operating properly (see above).

[224] Kingdon therefore strongly criticizes the effect the Right to Education Act has on private schools, arguing that closing affected private schools 'depriv[es] children of their right to education', and that the Act 'destroy[s] the autonomy of private schools' (see Kingdon, 'Schooling without Learning').

[225] Vikas Gupta, 'Politics of the Guarded Agenda of National Education Policy 2015–16', *Economic & Political Weekly* LI, no. 42 (2016): 69.

[226] Gupta, 'Politics of the Guarded Agenda of National Education Policy 2015–16', 62.

[227] See http://www.pratham.org/about-us/supporters, accessed on 15 August 2018. These apprehensions were mentioned by several educationalists in interviews with the author.

However, there are no other studies that are as up-to-date and that have a coverage as wide as ASER. Furthermore, even the critics appear to criticize the conclusions being drawn from the figures more than the figures themselves (for instance, by criticizing the 'selective highlighting' mentioned above). Therefore, while it would be desirable to have a wider range of sources of data on the 'public/private divide' in learning outcomes, alternative data at a comparable scale is currently not available.

However, other data collected at a smaller scale does seem to confirm that there is a public/private divide in terms of quality, even when considering only low-cost private schools.[228] Still, even if that is the case, that does not necessarily mean that privatization is the ideal solution. The State could also improve the quality of government schools to a degree that they are at par with private schools, to an extent that they might end up being more attractive to parents.

While even low-cost private schools may perform better than government schools, the learning outcomes of children in the average private school are also not very high.[229] Problematically, some private schools also ask for very high (by poor parents' standards) tuition fees, and the children's parents, who are themselves often uneducated, are not able to assess whether the fees are justified in terms of quality.[230] The providers of private education and parents, therefore, do not meet at an even level, meaning that market forces of offer and demand cannot work fairly. In rural areas, this situation is worsened by the fact that there is often a lack of competition, as there may be only one private primary school in the area.[231]

For these reasons, it has been argued that a system of education vouchers would not work as desired. Such systems have also not worked very well in some other countries, with the exception

[228] Muralidharan, 'Public-Private Partnerships for Quality Education in India'; Muralidharan and Kremer, 'Public and Private Schools in Rural India'.

[229] Drèze and Sen, *An Uncertain Glory*, 126.

[230] Drèze and Sen, *An Uncertain Glory*, 136–7.

[231] Drèze and Sen, *An Uncertain Glory*, 137.

being Chile, which, however, based its system on a superior administrative framework (as compared to India), and created it as a supplement for an already well-functioning system of state-run schools,[232] which is not currently found in India.

Importantly, education is a 'public good', meaning that it is foremost the state's responsibility to provide for it.[233] Similarly, relying on low-cost private schools and private tuitions to improve children's learning outcomes would 'ensure and legitimise social inequalities at a low cost', while the actual aim of the education system should be to provide 'uniform, equitable quality education to all children irrespective of differences in background'. This may be achieved by, inter alia, making government schools more accountable and engaging better qualified and well-trained teachers.[234]

Importantly, as it was the case even in Chile, advances in (elementary) education and literacy were state-driven in most other countries 'across the world', notably also in East Asian countries that are often named as positive examples of development through economic liberalization.[235] It is therefore 'difficult to see how India can achieve the same educational results without a similar level

[232] Drèze and Sen, *An Uncertain Glory*, 352, note 31. Still, the Right to Education Act, by requiring 25 per cent of all private school seats to be filled with children from economically backwards families (Section 12(1)(c)), decided to create a system that is similar to a voucher system insofar as it also allows parents to choose one private school for their children (to the extent that seats are available) without having to pay tuition fees. Shah describes the provision as the 'world's largest voucher programme' (see Parth J. Shah, 'Where Private and Public Co-Exist', *Pragati*, 1 March 2010, http://pragati.nationalinterest.in/2010/03/where-private-and-public-co-exist/, accessed on 19 August 2018).

[233] Drèze and Sen, *An Uncertain Glory*, 137.

[234] Nawani, 'Reflections on "Annual Status of Educational Research 2012"', 22.

[235] Drèze and Sen, *An Uncertain Glory*, 130. Jha argues similarly, pointing out that only 10 per cent of all students in OECD countries attend private schools (see Praveen K. Jha, *Public Provisioning for Elementary Education in India* [New Delhi, India, Thousand Oaks, Calif.: SAGE, 2008], 36 et seq.).

of commitment and effort by the state'.[236] Since the 1990s, however, the Indian State seems to be willing to increasingly rely on private schools. In the last few years, with Section 12 of the Right to Education Act being in place, this reliance has even increased.

One additional point is the fact that the very parents who choose to have their children 'exit' the government school system, or to not have them be part of it in the first place, tend to be the same ones who would otherwise most vocally call for improvements to be made to public education. Such calls would, in the end, make state schools 'more responsible and accountable'.[237] Reliance on private schools gives more prosperous and more vocal parents 'a way out', which can cause further deterioration, or at least stagnation, of the state system,[238] and might end up entrenching the 'compartmentalization' of the Indian education environment.[239] The chances of the government school system improving would be a lot higher if those parents who are willing to invest at least some time and money into better education for their children could instead be motivated to focus their efforts on institutions through which they could improve the government school system, namely, School Management Committees or the grievance redress system described in Chapters 5 and 6.

Such a development would improve the education system as a whole: not just the government education system, but also private schools, because private schools tend to be of better quality in areas that have well-functioning government schools, with the latter being a benchmark for the private schools in terms of quality.[240] Generally, the fragmentation of the school system into 'very good' (some of the private ones) schools and 'bad' schools (government,

[236] Which makes them wonder why many 'development thinkers' in India still call for a reliance on private schools (see Drèze and Sen, *An Uncertain Glory*, 130).

[237] Drèze and Sen, *An Uncertain Glory*, 137–8.

[238] Drèze and Sen, *An Uncertain Glory*, 137–8.

[239] Drèze and Sen, *India*, 172.

[240] Kiran Bhatty, 'Hobsons (School) Choice', *Indian Express*, 28 May 2009, http://indianexpress.com/article/opinion/columns/hobsons-school-choice/, accessed on 19 August 2018.

but also many of them private) causes a solidification of social differences and limits opportunities for social mobility.[241]

To an extent, the state's privatization strategy in itself might include some measures to counter the extent to which the stratification and polarization of children's education achievements correlate with their socio-economic backgrounds. Section 12(1)(c), as mentioned above, aims to ensure that children 'belonging to weaker section and disadvantaged group in the neighbourhood' constitute at least a fourth of every private un-aided school, meaning that even elite urban private schools will have to accept children from poorer and otherwise disadvantaged parts of the society.[242]

The Model Rules for the Right to Education Act further[243] define that children accepted from these parts 'shall not be segregated from the other children in the classrooms nor shall their classes be held at places and timings different from the classes held for other children' (Rule 7(1)). Also, such children 'shall not be discriminated from the rest of the children in any manner pertaining

[241] Drèze and Sen, *India*, 172.

[242] It is up to the states to further define which children belong to a 'weaker section' or 'disadvantaged group' and how the seats are to be assigned. As far as family income is concerned, some rules name a concrete figure of parents' income, such as 60,000, 100,000, or even 200,000 rupees, or refer to the 'Below Poverty Line' definition. For this, see the notifications by different state governments available at http://mhrd.gov.in/rte_dws, on 15 August 2018. The 'one lakh (100,000) rupees per annum' definition was used, for example, by Delhi, Bihar, and Maharashtra. Tamil Nadu includes all children whose parents have an annual income below 200,000 rupees. Andhra Pradesh's and Kerala's definition is 60,000 rupees, Gujarat's 36,000 for urban and 27,000 rupees for rural areas. The seats are usually assigned through a lottery system. For this, see the 'RTE Matrix' document available at http://righttoeducation.in/resources/rte-matrix, accessed on 6 November 2016.

[243] The Model Rules were created by the central government as a 'model' for rules that Section 38 empowers state governments to make. While state governments are empowered to draft entirely different rules, most of them copied extensive parts of the Model Rules without many alterations. For an overview of the state rules, see http://mhrd.gov.in/rte_state_rules, accessed on 15 August 2018.

to entitlements and facilities such as text books, uniforms, library and ICT [Information and Communication Technology] facilities, extra-curricular and sports' (Rule 7(2)). Therefore, from class I onwards, even elite, expensive schools shall educate children from poor families in the same manner as they educate their 'regular' children, meaning that at least a part of the urban poor shall receive the same high-quality education that the children from rich, urban upper-class families receive. However, in 2012 and 2014, the Supreme Court ruled that Section 12 (as well as, in fact, all other provisions of the Right to Education Act) does not apply to 'minority schools', as they enjoy an elevated degree of constitutional protection as far as their right to establish and administer educational institutions is concerned (most importantly, Article 30(1)).[244] The Supreme Court verdicts went as far as declaring that such schools were not even obliged to accept children from weaker sections of the society from the respective minority community.[245] Problematically, there is no established definition of what constitutes a 'minority school', especially no definition that applies nationally.[246] The Supreme Court verdicts led to a 'sudden rush to seek minority status' by private schools.[247]

[244] *Society for Un-aided Private Schools of Rajasthan* v. *Union of India & Another* MANU/SC/0311/2012 (Supreme Court of India, 12 April 2012); *Pramati Educational & Cultural Trust* v. *Union of India & Ors* MANU/SC/0419/2014 (Supreme Court of India, 6 May 2014).

[245] See the criticism by K.V. Reddy, 'Minority Educational Institutions', in *The Oxford Handbook of the Indian Constitution*, ed. Sujit Choudhry, Madhav Khosla, and Pratap B. Mehta (Oxford, New York: Oxford University Press, 2016), 928.

[246] Therefore, it is currently up to the state governments to define what a 'minority school' is, as the Karnataka government has done (see *The Hindu*, 'Cabinet Defines What Is a Minority Institution', 7 July 2012, http://www.thehindu.com/news/national/karnataka/cabinet-defines-what-is-a-minority-institution/article3610611.ece, accessed on 19 August 2018).

[247] Mehendale, Mukhopadyay, and Namala, 'Right to Education and Inclusion in Private Unaided Schools', 49. Also see Mridula Chari, 'Why Bangalore Schools are Rushing for Minority Certificates', *Scroll.in*, 19 May 2014, http://scroll.in/article/664538/why-bangalore-schools-are-rushing-for-minority-certificates, accessed on 19 August 2018.

A clear, nationally applicable definition of what a 'minority school' is might limit the number of schools that will actually benefit from this exemption. Only then will Section 12 really help in reducing segregation in education. Until then, the uncertainty brought by the Supreme Court verdicts may considerably delay progress in this regard. Even in Karnataka, where the state government has defined 'minority school' quite narrowly (a school that has 75 per cent minority students),[248] at least one prominent group of schools has been accused of forging documents to prove its own minority status.[249] Today, nine years after the Right to Education Act has come into force, there are still many media reports about 'RTE quota seats' remaining unfilled in some states and cities, sometimes even a large majority of them.[250] Furthermore, if

[248] *The Hindu*, 'Cabinet Defines What Is a Minority Institution'.

[249] *New Indian Express*, 'CBSE Disaffiliates Six National Public Schools in Karnataka', 7 September 2016, http://www.newindianexpress.com/states/karnataka/CBSE-disaffiliates-six-National-Public-Schools-in-Karnataka/2016/09/07/article3614785.ece, accessed on 19 August 2018. On this, also see Chapter 6.

[250] 70 per cent of the seats in Madhya Pradesh in 2016 (see Purvi Jain, '70% RTE Quota Seats Not Filled in MP', *Hindustan Times*, 14 October 2016, http://www.hindustantimes.com/education/70-rte-quota-seats-not-filled-in-mp/story-5S1UTCB3f1Ras3w5GaGsLI.html, accessed on 19 August 2018), more than 50 per cent of the seats in Pune in 2016, reportedly because of both lack of awareness and schools refusing to cooperate (see Yashpal Sonkamble, 'Half-Empty RTE Seats Call for Fresh Admission Round', *Pune Mirror*, 10 October 2016, http://punemirror.indiatimes.com/pune/civic/Half-empty-RTE-seats-call-for-fresh-admission-round/articleshow/54769837.cms, accessed on 19 August 2018), around 64 per cent of the seats in Mumbai in 2017 (see Puja Pednekar, '4.8K RTE Seats Vacant in Marathi Schools as Parents Opt for Popular English Institutes', *Hindustan Times*, 22 April 2017, https://www.hindustantimes.com/mumbai-news/4-8k-rte-seats-vacant-in-marathi-schools-as-parents-opt-for-popular-english-institutes/story-kOxZV6zUSxgaYqjSbpsGzH.html, accessed on 12 August 2018), around 21 per cent of the seats in Karnataka for the school year 2018–19 (see *New Indian Express*, 'RTE Seat Vacancies on the Rise in Karnataka', 6 August 2018, http://www.newindianexpress.com/states/karnataka/2018/aug/06/rte-seat-vacancies-on-the-rise-in-karnataka-1853905.html, accessed on 12 August 2018).

a considerable percentage of private schools ends up being considered as 'minority schools', then the state would lose a great amount of the control over private schools that it sought to receive with the Act's provisions. Consequently, the government has been criticized for not planning to clarify the situation.[251]

## English as the New Literacy

As mentioned above, one reason why parents choose to send their children to private schools is the fact that many of those are, at least on paper, either bilingual or entirely 'English-medium'. The fact that this is of such importance to parents is not surprising. English has been of high significance for career options in India for decades, and its importance is increasing in a globalized modern world. This is the case for India to a larger extent than for most other countries, including those in the West. For the urban elite, English is like a mother tongue, and most of their work life is conducted in that language, irrespective of their indigenous mother tongue.[252] Learning English is a sensible 'investment', considering that merely knowing some English brings a 13 per cent increase in hourly wage for the average Indian man compared to not knowing any English at all, and knowing fluent English brings a 34 per cent increase.[253] Also, university courses at elite institutions like National Law Schools or Indian Institutes of Technology are exclusively in English. Generally, academia works mostly in English, court proceedings in high courts and the Supreme Court, as well as their judgments, are entirely in English, the leading quality national newspapers and academic books are in English, and so on.[254] Those

[251] Gupta, 'Politics of the Guarded Agenda of National Education Policy 2015–16', 66; Jayna Kothari and Aparna Ravi, 'A Battle of Rights: The Right to Education of Children Versus Rights of Minority Schools', *Oxford University Commonwealth Law Journal* 16, no. 2 (2017).

[252] Rita Kothari, *Translating India* (Hoboken: Taylor and Francis, 2014), 32; Guha, *India after Gandhi*, 762–4.

[253] Mehtabul Azam, Aimee Chin, and Nishith Prakash, 'The Returns to English-Language Skills in India', April 2011, http://www.uh.edu/~achin/research/azam_chin_prakash.pdf, accessed on 2 March 2019, 3.

[254] See Guha, *India after Gandhi*, 762–4.

who do not speak English fluently are practically excluded from university courses and jobs above a certain level and also from everyday life in elite social groups. It will be very difficult (if not practically impossible, in many cases) for them to catch up to those who have grown up bilingually or those who have at least experienced bilingual schooling from an early age.

The importance of knowing English for social mobility is not a new phenomenon. Ram Manohar Lohia, an Indian Independence activist who lived until 1967, is quoted as having said that 'high-caste, wealth, and knowledge of English are the three requisites, with anyone possessing two of these belonging to the ruling class'.[255] This still holds true today, with caste perhaps being a smaller, but English being a bigger factor.[256]

To some extent, one could say that English, today, is the 'new literacy'. Nowadays, most children are at least enrolled in school and learn how to read and write. The country has moved a lot closer to universal literacy in the past couple of decades, at least as far as its youth is concerned.[257] Therefore, the decisive barrier between a small elite and the vast majority of people is not literacy anymore, as it was at the time of Independence. Now, it is proficiency in the English language. The percentage of Indians who can speak English fluently is very low, around 4 per cent.[258] This

[255] As quoted by Drèze and Sen as well as other sources (see Drèze and Sen, *An Uncertain Glory*, 216). The quote itself is undated.

[256] Still, upper castes are overrepresented in higher positions in society (see Drèze and Sen, *An Uncertain Glory*, 220–1). However, educational achievements of lower castes are more widespread than at the time of Independence, partly thanks to affirmative action (see Sonalde Desai and Veena Kulkarni, 'Changing Educational Inequalities in India in the Context of Affirmative Action', *Demography* 45, no. 2 [2008]: 245 et seq, http://www.ncbi.nlm.nih.gov/pmc/articles/PMC2474466/, accessed on 19 August 2018).

[257] Enrolment in the age group of 6 to 14 is now at 95.6 per cent (see ASER Centre, 'Annual Status of Education Report [Rural] 2016', 51); youth (ages 15 to 24) literacy was at 86.15 per cent in 2011 (see https://data.worldbank.org/indicator/SE.ADT.1524.LT.ZS?end=2011&locations=IN&start=2011&view=bar, accessed on 12 August 2018).

[258] See the figures quoted in Rema Nagarajan, 'Those Who Speak English Fluently Earn Up to 34% More Than Others: Study', *Economic*

number is dramatic when considering the absolute importance that English has for most of the better-paying jobs, and the fact that English proficiency is seen as a given for the highly educated part of the society.

Considering all of this, it is not surprising that parents who choose private schools are primarily motivated by the hope that their children will learn English (as well as the hope that there will be other qualitative advantages, such as a lower level of teacher absence).[259] Wealthier parents, of course, almost exclusively enroll their children in English-medium schools.[260] To a large extent, sending one's children to an 'English school' has also become a status symbol.[261] For instance, in Mumbai in 2017, many of the seats in private schools reserved for children from poorer families remained vacant because those schools were not 'English medium', meaning that the language of instruction is Marathi.[262]

Still, Section 29(2)(f) of the Right to Education Act defines instruction in the mother tongue of each child as a desirable goal for the elementary education curriculum. This is understandable insofar as it is important to ensure that children are able to understand what is taught. Also, language is a sensitive issue in India as far as regional identities are concerned.[263] On the other hand,

---

*Times*, 5 January 2014, http://economictimes.indiatimes.com/jobs/those-who-speak-english-fluently-earn-up-to-34-more-than-others-study/articleshow/28426329.cms, accessed on 19 August 2018.

[259] Muralidharan and Kremer, 'Public and Private Schools in Rural India', 12.

[260] Geeta B. Nambissan, 'The Indian Middle Classes and Educational Advantage. Family Strategies and Practices', in *The Routledge International Handbook of the Sociology of Education*, ed. Michael W. Apple, (London: Routledge, 2009), 286 et seq.

[261] Chaise LaDousa, *Hindi is Our Ground, English is Our Sky: Education, Language, and Social Class in Contemporary India* (New York: Berghahn Books, 2014), 183 et seq.

[262] Pednekar, '4.8K RTE Seats Vacant in Marathi Schools'.

[263] For the importance that language plays for regional identities (having in the past sparked violent riots and movements for separate states), see Guha, *India after Gandhi*, 189 et seq. The tradition of purposely not teaching English at the early primary level dates back to the time of

such regional identities and sentiments are also the reason why no Indian language has ever become the national language to the extent that it was envisaged for Hindi at the time of Independence. This paved the way for English to become the single most important professional language in the country among the upper classes.[264] Ultimately, with parents increasingly demanding English-medium instruction for their children[265] and the elite being taught almost exclusively in English, single-language government schools will not seem very appealing to many parents, even in lower-wealth social groups. The social divide between the privileged English-speaking few and the majority without proficiency in English will not be overcome until teaching English to the masses becomes a priority.

## Media and Public Opinion

Considering that India is a relatively well-functioning and established democracy, it is a bit surprising that the large majority of people whose children do not enjoy good-quality education are not calling for improvements to be made to the education system more loudly or actively. Politicians also do not seem to be very eager to put the issue on their agenda, even though it affects such a large number of potential voters. In fact, children's issues in general do not receive much attention in the political field.[266] It has

---

Independence: in the resolution of the first conference of provincial education ministers in 1949, it was decided that English should be taught at the secondary and the university stage, but should *not* be introduced earlier than in class IV, as quoted in Biswas, *Development of Education in India*, 205.

264 See Guha, *India after Gandhi*, 118–20, 391 et seq., 762–4.

265 'The institutional distinction [in between Hindi and English schools in North India] has grown in importance in the era of economic liberalization [...] because educational pursuits and credentials are linked to future employment plans for more people than ever before', LaDousa, *Hindi is Our Ground, English is Our Sky*, 183.

266 Drèze and Sen, *An Uncertain Glory*, 144, 162 et seq.; Drèze and Sen, *India*, 145, 186 et seq.

been noted that 'there is little in the citizens' experience of the Indian state that leads them to believe that the state will be a credible provider of social services [...] because the state has not in the past been an effective provider of health and education, the voters at large do not hold it to account on that score'.[267]

To a large extent, the political agenda is set by the media, which also does not take as much interest in the subject as one may expect, considering its importance for a large part of the society. A sample study of the local edition of a national newspaper in Mumbai conducted in 2008 and 2009 (that is, at the time when the Right to Education Act was passed) showed that only 1.6 per cent of the news stories concerned education and only 3 per cent of those stories concerned rural areas.[268] The majority of the news stories on education were about issues that interested the English-speaking urban middle class, for example, admission to junior colleges (that is, classes XI and XII), quality of private schools, and so on.[269] As far as the Right to Education Act was concerned, there was 'no substantial discussion of the Act, its provisions or the implementation'.[270]

This study concerned just one newspaper in one (major) Indian city but it appears that the findings are in line with a general trend. The media across the country focuses on issues that the relatively well-to-do are interested in, while topics relevant to rural areas are grossly underrepresented.[271] 'Rural topics' constitute about 2 per cent of the total news coverage,[272] even though India's rural population makes up two thirds of the country's total population.[273] If the media writes about issues of the *aam admi* (ordinary man),

[267] Pratap Bhanu Mehta, *The Burden of Democracy* (New Delhi, New York: Penguin Books, 2003), 138.

[268] Vidya K.S. and Padma M. Sarangapani, 'Is Education News?', *Economic & Political Weekly* XLVI, no. 42 (2011).

[269] K.S. and Sarangapani, 'Is Education News?', 72.

[270] K.S. and Sarangapani, 'Is Education News?', 73.

[271] Drèze and Sen, *An Uncertain Glory*, 264 et seq.

[272] Drèze and Sen, *An Uncertain Glory*, 266.

[273] http://www.tradingeconomics.com/india/rural-population-per-cent-of-total-population-wb-data.html, accessed on 15 August 2018.

they usually actually mean a relatively privileged part of the population.[274] One reason for this discrepancy might be the fact that media is so dependent on advertisement. The actually underprivileged do not have much purchasing power, so targeting them as readers does not promise high financial returns.[275]

The poor, to an extent, seem to 'live precariously with such deprivations, and keep, rather fatalistically, a low profile'.[276] They also remain relatively unorganized.[277] This leads to an 'asymmetry of power and influence' between parents and teachers, as well as parents and administrators.[278] It is, therefore, argued that improvements in accountability in the education system should focus more on action 'from below', as top-down accountability measures give even more power to few persons in the administration.[279] A bottom-up approach, on the other hand, would empower those persons who themselves have a personal interest in actual systemic improvements.[280] Examples of bottom-up measures implemented in several Indian states have shown that they do lead to better results.[281] Chapters 5 and 6 shall show how existing systems may provide measures for 'bottom-up implementation' (in addition to democratic elections), while Chapter 3 shall explain why this is not only desirable politically, but also is a constitutional necessity.

[274] Drèze and Sen argue that 'tycoons, at one end, to educated ordinary people, at the other' have created a 'social universe of their own' (see Drèze and Sen, *An Uncertain Glory*, 286).

[275] Drèze and Sen, *An Uncertain Glory*, 265.

[276] Drèze and Sen, *An Uncertain Glory*, 190.

[277] Drèze and Sen, *India*, 174.

[278] Drèze and Sen, *India*, 174.

[279] Drèze and Sen, *India*, 175 et seq.

[280] Drèze and Sen, *India*, 175.

[281] Drèze and Sen name the examples of Karnataka, where early (1980s) experiments with *panchayati raj* (self-administration of the village community) have reduced teacher absenteeism, and of Tamil Nadu, where empowering parents has improved pre-school education and the implementation of mid-day meals (see Drèze and Sen, *India*, 175). Decentralization without 'democratisation' (by empowering the public), on the other hand, did not lead to similar results, as the experience with Village Education Committees (VEC) has shown, the authors argue.Coressit ventis aut

* * *

Looking back at the decades since Independence, it is clear that much has been achieved, particularly since the 1990s. However, many problems remain, and some have been replaced by others. Previously, many children used to be completely out of school, and only the privileged received any education. Today, on the other hand, the majority receives education, but very bad education, while the privileged few can afford sending their children to good private schools. While the majority of the country used to be illiterate, today, most children can at least read and write, but their abilities do not extend much beyond that. English proficiency is the new decisive boundary that is difficult to cross.

There is obviously some political will to improve the situation, as the last quarter of a century has shown, particularly the last few years that brought a new fundamental right as well as the Right to Education Act. A rights-based approach seems sensible considering that experience with 'bottom-up implementation' has been positive, but political agitation through conventional democratic means is not working as well as it should.

However, clarification is required concerning the question of what legal and practical implications a right to education actually has and to what extent the people who are targeted by it can actually profit from it. The next chapter shall examine why Parliament may have turned elementary education into a fundamental right, and summarize what developments have led to this remarkable decision.

# 2

# From a Directive Principle to a Fundamental Right

What implications does the existence of the fundamental right to education have for the right-bearers themselves? Some answers might be found in the history behind the 'creation' of the right. This chapter shall show that the developments around education becoming an explicitly justiciable fundamental right is closely linked to the ones around socio-economic rights in India in general, and how some of them have been 'transformed' from non-justiciable 'Directive Principles of State Policy' into 'Fundamental Rights'. It shall then be explained that even though the creation of Article 21A is somewhat of a climax of this development, it has received surprisingly little scholarly attention. Paradoxically, it is in fact almost impossible to ascertain what the aim of adding the new fundamental right to the constitutional text might have been.

## Directive Principles and Fundamental Rights: Historical Background

The words 'right to education' had always been part of the Constitution, whose Article 41 reads as follows:

> Right to work, to education and to public assistance in certain cases.

> The State shall, within the limits of its economic capacity and development, make effective provision for securing the right to work, to education and to public assistance in cases of unemployment, old age, sickness and disablement, and in other cases of undeserved want.

Article 45 (in its original form) reads as follows:

> Provision for free and compulsory education for children.
>
> The State shall endeavour to provide, within a period of ten years from the commencement of this Constitution, for free and compulsory education for all children until they complete the age of fourteen years.

Article 21A, which Parliament included in the Constitution by passing the Eighty-Sixth Constitutional Amendment in 2002, reads as follows:

> Right to education.
>
> The State shall provide free and compulsory education to all children of the age of six to fourteen years in such manner as the State may, by law, determine.

When reading the original Article 45 and Article 21A in isolation, their legal effects appear to be almost identical. Both declare that the State is under an obligation to provide for free and compulsory education to children up to the age of 14 years. Article 21A's obligation appears to be stronger ('shall provide' instead of 'shall endeavour to provide'), though its actual scope, in direct comparison, is also limited (aiming at children ages 6 to 14 instead from birth until age 14). Also, Article 21A does not include a time limit within which it shall be implemented.

What really differentiates the two articles is the position that they take in the constitutional framework. Article 21A is found in Part III, the catalogue of fundamental rights. Article 45 (as well as Article 41) is positioned in Part IV, which lists the 'Directive

Principles of State Policy'. Part IV includes several provisions that can be classified as 'socio-economic rights', including the right to education, the right to work and public assistance (Article 41, as quoted above), welfare of the people (Article 38), the right to adequate means of livelihood, equal pay for equal work for men and women, health and strength of workers, healthy and dignified development for children (all Article 39), equal justice and free legal aid (Article 39A), adequate living wage (Article 43), participation of workers in management of industries (Article 43A), promotion of educational and economic interests of 'Scheduled Castes' and 'Scheduled Tribes' (Article 46),[1] promotion of public health (Article 47), and so on. However, it also contains other provisions which do not fit into the 'socio-economic rights' category.[2] The directive principles, therefore, call for a wide range of state measures that include, but are not restricted to, the protection and promotion of socio-economic rights.

The Constitution's fundamental rights catalogue, on the other hand, mostly lists what are conventionally known as civil and political rights, such as equality before the law (Article 14), freedom of speech and expression, the right to assemble peaceably, the right to form associations or unions, the right to move freely throughout India, the right to practise a profession (all Article 19), freedom of religion (Article 25), and so on.

Thus, the Constitution differentiates relatively clearly between civil and political and socio-economic rights, or 'negative' and 'positive' rights, as they are also called. However, as shall be discussed in the next chapter, it is not always easy, and perhaps not even possible, to draw a clear line between those two 'categories' of

[1] That is, communities listed in the Schedule to the Constitution, for whom the State has created numerous affirmative action measures.

[2] Such as Article 40, which obliges the State to create village councils (panchayat) at a lower administration level, Article 44, which states that the State shall create a uniform civil code for all citizens (irrespective of religion), Article 48, which calls for the welfare (and prohibition of slaughter of) 'cows and calves and other milch and draught cattle', and Article 47, which also includes a provision to prohibit the consumption 'of intoxicating drinks'.

rights.[3] Consequently, the terminology of 'negative' and 'positive' rights is usually not used anymore, but shall be used in this chapter when describing the debates in the Constituent Assembly and the first years of rights adjudication under the Indian Constitution.

The provisions that actually create the decisive difference between Parts III and IV are Articles 13, 32, 37 and 226. Article 13(2) provides that all laws made by the State that 'take away or abridge' fundamental rights shall be void. Articles 32 and 226 confer the right to move high courts and the Supreme Court for the enforcement of fundamental rights. Article 37, on the other hand, states that directive principles 'shall not be enforceable by any court', but that the principles are 'nevertheless fundamental in the governance of the country and it shall be the duty of the State to apply these principles in making laws'.

In other words, the Constitution states that if the state violates someone's fundamental right, that person is entitled to move the courts against the violation. If, however, the State is not fulfilling its duty under a directive principle, aggrieved persons cannot move the court against this infringement.

However, it is unclear whether 'enforceable' in Article 37 only relates to the situation of someone actively trying to move the courts for enforcement of a directive principle, or whether Article 37 means to say that courts must not base any judgment on the provisions of Part IV, and that they must not consider the contents of Part IV when adjudicating any matter. Also, considering that there are situations in which promotion of a directive principle might affect someone's fundamental rights, or in which exercising that fundamental right might be in contravention with the

[3] Some provisions in the fundamental rights catalogue do not fit the categorization of socio-economic and civil and political rights even from a 'classical' point of view. For instance, several articles in Part III impose duties both on the State as well as private individuals. Article 15 prohibits discrimination on grounds of religion, race, caste, sex, or place of birth, also by private individuals in some cases. Article 17 prohibits the discriminatory practice of 'untouchability' (unequivocally for private parties as well as the State); Articles 23 and 24 prohibit traffic in human beings, forced labour, and employment of children in factories; and, of course, since 2002, there is Article 21A.

goal of a directive principle, the question arises how these provisions relate to one another in cases of conflict, that is, how such a conflict might be resolved, and whether it can be resolved by the courts.

The answer to these questions may help in explaining the significance of the 'transformation' of the State's duty to provide elementary education from a directive principle to a fundamental right. The questions themselves have been a cause of heated debates and power struggles ever since the time at which the Constitution was originally drafted, and they are still not fully answered.

## Relationship Envisioned by the Constituent Assembly

Before Independence, British India's 'Constitution' did not have a fundamental right catalogue. The Government of India Act of 1935, which acted as a blueprint for many of the later Constitution's provisions,[4] did not include a Bill of Rights.[5] The Indian Independence movement, however, had called for fundamental rights already in the late nineteenth and early twentieth centuries. In as early as 1895, leaders of the movement created a Constitution of India Bill. This Bill, in Article 16, included several rights. According to the classical understanding, those were mainly civil and political rights. But the catalogue also included the right to free education.[6] Several resolutions by the Indian National Congress followed

[4] See, for instance, Granville Austin, *The Indian Constitution: Cornerstone of a Nation* (Oxford, New York: Oxford University Press, 1999), 33 et seq; Mithi Mukherjee, *India in the Shadows of Empire: A Legal and Political History; 1774–1950*, 3rd edition (New Delhi: Oxford University Press, 2011), 203 et seq.

[5] Though it did contain one article (Article 298) proclaiming equality of all 'subjects of His Majesty' irrespective of 'religion, place of birth, descent [or] colour' when accessing office under the crown, acquiring property, and so on (see Kalyani Ramnath, '"We the People": Seamless Webs and Social Revolution in India's Constituent Assembly Debates', *South Asia Research* 32 [2012]: 62).

[6] See Austin, *The Indian Constitution*, 52–3.

in the early twentieth century. Those, however, were primarily restricted to civil and political rights.[7]

In 1925, the Indian National Congress drafted a Commonwealth of India Bill under the direction of the then Congress president Annie Besant, which was introduced in the British Parliament by the Labour politician (and later Labour Party leader) George Lansbury.[8] This Bill, which envisaged a parliamentary democracy for India, included several civil and political rights like freedom of expression, equality before the law, and freedom of assembly, but also one socio-economic right. Again, this was the right to free elementary education, which was to become enforceable as soon as the State would have created necessary educational facilities.[9] In 1928, an All-Party Conference set up the 'Nehru Committee' (named after Motilal Nehru, the father of India's first prime minister, Jawaharlal Nehru), whose task was to outline a desired constitutional status within the Commonwealth.[10] Its 'Nehru Report' featured a Bill of Rights which also included a right to free education (Article 4 (v)). This right was also to become justiciable as soon as infrastructural prerequisites would be in place.[11] In 1931, a Congress Session at Karachi adopted a 'Resolution on Fundamental Rights and Economic and Social Change', which included an extensive catalogue of social and economic rights. This catalogue is considered to be the 'root' or 'antecedent' of the directive principles.[12] Interestingly, the resolution called for 'suitable legislation' to make these socio-economic rights a reality, indicating that they were aimed at the legislature, rather than at the judiciary.[13]

[7] See Austin, *The Indian Constitution*, 53.

[8] Austin, *The Indian Constitution*, 39.

[9] Austin, *The Indian Constitution*, 54.

[10] See Mukherjee, *India in the Shadows of Empire*, 136; Jona Aravind Dohrmann, *Directive Principles of State Policy in der indischen Verfassung unter Berücksichtigung der Staatszielbestimmungen des deutschen Grundgesetzes* (Würzburg: Ergon, 2002), 19.

[11] See Austin, *The Indian Constitution*, 55; Dohrmann, *Directive Principles of State Policy*, 19.

[12] Austin, *The Indian Constitution*, 56; Dohrmann, *Directive Principles of State Policy*, 21.

[13] See Austin, *The Indian Constitution*, 56.

In the Constituent Assembly, India's colonial background led to a desire to include both civil and political rights as well as social and economic rights in the Constitution. Civil and political rights, or 'negative rights', 'expressed a desire for civil liberty in reaction to the political subservience', while the 'positive rights', imposing a duty on the State to act by providing services to its citizens, 'represented the casting off of the economic inferiority of colonial status'.[14] In addition to that, including socio-economic rights in a constitution was an expression of the idea that the State was responsible for the welfare of the people, which had gained traction globally in the decades preceding Indian Independence.[15]

For Congress, the dominating party in the Assembly, a 'social revolution' is said to have been as important as India's Independence and its transition into a liberal democracy.[16] In fact, the social revolution might have been even more important.[17] India's first prime minister Jawaharlal Nehru had already written in 1938 that freedom was 'a means to an end, that end being the raising of the people [...] to higher levels'.[18]

The Constituent Assembly created an Advisory Committee for fundamental rights, which compiled a list that included both 'negative' and 'positive rights'.[19] It was clear that civil and political or 'negative rights' should be justiciable; there was not much debate about this issue.[20] As far as 'positive rights' were concerned,

[14] Austin, *The Indian Constitution*, 60.

[15] The idea was also influenced by the fundamental rights catalogue (especially the socio-economic rights conferred by Article 165) of the German Weimar Constitution (see Austin, *The Indian Constitution*, 60; Dohrmann, *Directive Principles of State Policy*, 21).

[16] See Austin, *The Indian Constitution*, 26 et seq.

[17] Mukherjee believes that the Indian Constitution stands in 'sharp contrast' to Western constitutions insofar as 'the category of justice' (meaning social justice) is supposed to be 'the sovereign legislative principle'. To illustrate this, she points to the Constitution's preamble, which names 'justice, social, economic and political' before 'liberty' and 'equality' (see Mukherjee, *India in the Shadows of Empire*, 188).

[18] Quoted in Austin, *The Indian Constitution*, 26.

[19] See Austin, *The Indian Constitution*, 62–3.

[20] See Austin, *The Indian Constitution*, 63.

several members of the Constituent Assembly believed that they should be justiciable as well.[21]

However, the majority of the Constituent Assembly spoke out against making 'positive rights' justiciable. They mainly raised monetary concerns, as implementing such rights requires considerable budgetary allocations.[22] Assembly member Benegal Narsing Rau, one of the key figures in drafting the Constitution, did however suggest that a provision should be added to clarify that non-justiciability did not mean that the principles are less important or inferior to the fundamental rights. His idea was to have the Constitution declare that 'no law made and no action taken by the state in the discharge of its duties under [the Directive Principles] [...] shall be invalid merely by reason of its contravening the provisions of [the chapter on Fundamental Rights]'.[23] However, a provision of this kind was not added to the final version of the Constitution.[24] Assembly member K.T. Shah, on the other hand, suggested that there ought to be a time limit, after whose expiry all directive principles should become justiciable.[25] Such a provision was not added to the final Constitution either. The only time limit included in the catalogue of directive principles is the one in Article 45, calling for free and compulsory elementary education to become a reality within 10 years. However, that article also did not state any consequences that would follow after the expiry of its time limit.

The Assembly's sub-committee concerned with rights opted for a 'split' between justiciable and non-justiciable rights already at an early stage of the Assembly's tenure: on 31 March 1947.[26] After this decisive step was made, the Assembly focused on details concerning rights in each of the two categories. Interestingly, the right

[21] See Austin, *The Indian Constitution*, 78.

[22] Austin, *The Indian Constitution*, 80.

[23] As quoted in Austin, *The Indian Constitution*, 77–8.

[24] It was, however, 'resurrected' by the Twenty-Fifth and Forty-Second Amendment Acts of 1972 and 1976 as Article 31C (discussed later in the chapter).

[25] See Austin, *The Indian Constitution*, 79.

[26] See Austin, *The Indian Constitution*, 79–80..

to free elementary education was initially part of the catalogue of justiciable rights, while the right to equality before the law was supposed to be non-justiciable. Their positions were eventually reversed, leaving elementary education as a non-justiciable directive principle.[27]

In spite of the Constituent Assembly deciding to draw a clear difference between fundamental rights and directive principles, it appears that the majority did not consider the principles' position to be necessarily inferior as a consequence,[28] though some members did voice an opinion to this effect. One believed that the directive principles were a 'veritable dustbin of sentiment [...] sufficiently resilient as to permit any individual of this House to ride his hobby horse into it'.[29] Another stated that without a time limit, the principles would remain mere 'pious wishes'.[30] Bhimrao Ramji Ambedkar, independent India's first law minister and perhaps the most influential figure in the constitutional drafting process, pointed out that the principles would bind future governments who (in the event of them not fulfilling their duty) would not have to answer to the judiciary, but to the electorate,[31] which somewhat put the *legal* quality of the principles into perspective.

Still, the directive principles may be seen as the primary expression of Congress' sentiment that (social and economic) justice was

[27] See Austin, *The Indian Constitution*, 79.

[28] Shankar, Tyagi, as well as Singh believe that the sentiment at the time was that both categories of rights are equally important, and that the distinction concerning justiciability was mainly made for practical considerations, considering the directive principles unsuitable for enforcement in courts (see Uday Shankar and Divya Tyagi, 'Socio-Economic Rights in India: Democracy Taking Roots', *Law and Politics in Africa, Asia, Latin America (VRU)* 42, no. 4 [2009]: 536, https://www.nomos-elibrary.de/10.5771/0506-7286-2009-4-527/socio-economic-rights-in-india-democracy-taking-roots-jahrgang-42-2009-heft-4?page=0, accessed on 19 August 2018; Mahendra P. Singh, 'The Statics and the Dynamics of the Fundamental Rights and the Directive Principles—A Human Right Perspective', *Supreme Court Cases (Journal)*, no. 5 [2003]: 4–5).

[29] As quoted in Austin, *The Indian Constitution*, 75–6.

[30] As quoted in Austin, *The Indian Constitution*, 79.

[31] As quoted in Austin, *The Indian Constitution*, 78.

the *primary* goal of the state, perhaps even at a higher position than liberty, which is protected by the fundamental rights. The fact that the directive principles are not justiciable only shows that the Congress (which dominated the Constituent Assembly) believed that '[j]ustice itself—as it appeared in the Indian Constitution—was not a law; it was the law of all laws; the source and measure of all laws. Justice, in other words, constituted the ontology and the teleology of law'.[32] Even though this may have been the intention, the developments of the following decades pointed in a very different direction.

## Early Adjudication: Primacy of Fundamental Rights

Perhaps the clearest indication towards a belief that the directive principles are not supposed to be inferior to fundamental rights is how actively the first government and parliament of the Indian Republic (which, like the Constituent Assembly, were dominated by members of the Congress party) tried to further their goals of land reform in spite of conflicts with landowners' fundamental rights. This started a long struggle between the legislature and the judiciary.

This struggle brought a long list of judgments and subsequent constitutional amendments. Again, considering the fact that there was a certain amount of congruency between the drafters of the Constitution and members of Parliament throughout the 1950s,[33] the amendments may be seen as a clue in determining

[32] Mukherjee, *India in the Shadows of Empire*, 189.

[33] In the 1951–2 general election, the Indian National Congress won 364 of 489 seats in the Lok Sabha (see https://web.archive.org/web/20180614194711/http://eci.nic.in/eci_main/StatisticalReports/LS_1951/VOL_1_51_LS.PDF, accessed on 15 August 2018, 41). The Constituent Assembly included 208 members of the Indian National Congress, out of a total of 389 seats (later 299 seats, after new elections in the states of West Bengal and Punjab [see https://web.archive.org/web/20180131014107/http://parliamentofindia.nic.in:80/ls/debates/facts.htm, accessed on 15 August 2018]). Of the 302 members of the Constituent Assembly listed at https://web.archive.org/web/20180210214023/http://www.parliamentofindia.nic.in:80/ls/debates/members.htm, accessed on

the Constituent Assembly's members' 'original intent' for the relationship between fundamental rights and directive principles. This is especially the case for the First Amendment, which was passed in 1951. At that time, before the first Lok Sabha elections, the same individuals who had previously constituted both Parliament and the Constituent Assembly were still members of Parliament.[34]

Shortly after the commencement of the Constitution, the judiciary passed initial judgments on fundamental rights that also concerned their relationship with the directive principles. The first such Supreme Court judgment came in the case of *Champakam Dorairajan*.[35] In *Dorairajan*, two prospective medicine and engineering college students in the state of Madras challenged state orders (which had been in force even before Independence) that allotted seats to applicants based on their caste—Brahmin (that is, the highest caste) and non-Brahmins—and their religion (Hindus,

---

15 August 2018, at least 91 were also members of the first elected Lok Sabha (compare with the names of elected members available at https://web.archive.org/web/20180614194711/http://eci.nic.in/eci_main/StatisticalReports/LS_1951/VOL_1_51_LS.PDF, accessed on 15 August 2018, 9 et seq.).

[34] From 1950, the commencement of the Constitution, until 1952, Parliament was identical to the Constituent Assembly as far as its members were concerned, as Nehru pointed out when arguing in favour of the First Constitutional Amendment (see Granville Austin, *Working a Democratic Constitution: A History of the Indian Experience* [Delhi, Oxford: Oxford University Press, 2003], 87). The Amendment was passed in this period (1951) by a vast majority of the members present at the time of voting (228 to 20) (see Austin, *Working a Democratic Constitution*, 49). Singh points out how this is a good indication of the Constituent Assembly's vision of the relationship between fundamental rights and directive principles (see Mahendra P. Singh, 'Constitutionalization and Realization of Human Rights in India', in *Human Rights, Justice, and Constitutional Empowerment*, ed. C.R. Kumar, K. Chockalingam, and V.R. Krishna Iyer, 2nd edition [New Delhi: Oxford University Press, 2010], 32–3).

[35] *State of Madras* v. *Champakam Dorairajan*, and *The State of Madras* v. *C.R. Srinivasan* MANU/SC/0007/1951 (Supreme Court of India, 9 April 1951).

Christians, and Muslims). The petitioners were not able to secure seats, as they were Brahmins for whom only two out of 14 seats were allotted. The Madras High Court held the state orders as unconstitutional, which led to an appeal by the state of Madras to the Supreme Court.

The petitioners argued that the order violated their fundamental rights under Article 15(1) and Article 29(2) of the Constitution. Article 15(1) forbids the state to discriminate 'against any citizen on grounds only of [...] religion [...] [or] caste' and Article 29(2) states that '[n]o citizen shall be denied admission into any educational institution maintained by the State [...] on grounds only of [...] religion [...] [or] caste'.[36] The state order had the effect of facilitating entry into colleges for members of castes lower than Brahmins, giving six out of 14 seats to non-Brahmins, additional two seats to *Harijan*s (the 'untouchable' caste, nowadays usually called Dalits), and another two seats to 'Backward Hindus'. But neither Article 15 nor Article 29 contained any sub-clause justifying any discrimination to benefit members of lower castes or of different religions.

However, the state of Madras argued that the encroachment on these rights was justified by Article 46, a directive principle, which states that '[t]he State shall promote [...] the educational and economic interests of the weaker sections of the people, in particular, the Scheduled Castes and the Scheduled tribes'. In other words, the state of Madras believed that the state was justified in limiting the scope of a fundamental right if that limitation was a result of performing its duties under the directive principles, or that limitations to fundamental rights could be found in other parts of the Constitution, specifically Part IV.

The Supreme Court rejected this view. Without even entertaining the question of whether or not the order was suitable for the furtherance of the goal defined by Article 46, it stated that 'the directive principles [...] which by article 37 are expressly made unenforceable by a Court, cannot override the provisions found in Part III [i.e. the Fundamental Rights] which [...] are expressly made

[36] The other grounds listed in the articles are race and sex (both articles), place of birth (Article 15(1)), and language (Article 29(2)).

enforceable'.[37] It further declared that the fundamental rights are 'sacrosanct' and that legislative or executive acts or orders could only legally abridge them 'to the extent provided in the appropriate article in Part III'.[38] The principles therefore had to 'conform to and run as subsidiary' to the fundamental rights.[39]

Only two months after the *Dorairajan* judgment, Parliament passed the Constitution (First Amendment Act) of 1951. In the Statement of Objects and Reasons, Prime Minister Jawaharlal Nehru wrote about 'certain difficulties brought to light by judicial decisions', especially concerning fundamental rights.[40] Nehru cited Article 46 and suggested that in order to ensure that the State can follow its duty to implement that directive principle, Article 15(3) should be 'suitably amplified' so that advances in this direction 'may not be challenged on the ground of being discriminatory'.[41] In a speech in Parliament, Nehru pointed out that the 'Directive Principles [...] represent a dynamic move towards a certain objective. The fundamental rights represent something static, to preserve certain rights which exist. *Both again are right.*

[37] Note 35, 10.

[38] Note 35, 10.

[39] Note 35, 10. To substantiate this view, the Supreme Court pointed at Article 16. This provision guarantees 'equality of opportunity in matters of public employment', with sub-clauses (1) and (2) giving, like Articles 15(1) and 29(2) do, specific grounds on which discrimination is not permissible. Interestingly, however, Article 16(4) declares that the State shall not be prevented 'from making any provision for the reservation of appointments or posts in favour of any backward class of citizens' if members of that class are 'not adequately represented in the services under the State'. The Court argued that if Article 46 justified such 'positive discrimination' and therefore an abridgement of equality rights, 'then clause (4) of article 16 would have been wholly unnecessary and redundant'. The fact that Article 29 did not contain a similar clause, but that Article 16 did, showed, according to the Court, that such reservations were not supposed to be permissible in matters of access to educational institutions.

[40] Quoted in H.M. Seervai, *Constitutional Law of India: A Critical Commentary*, 4th edition, 3 vols (Mumbai, Delhi: N.M. Tripathi; F.H. Seervai; Distributors, Universal Law Pub. Co, 1991–6), 1983.

[41] Quoted in Seervai, *Constitutional Law of India*, 1983.

But somehow and sometime it might so happen that that dynamic movement and that static standstill do not quite fit into each other' (emphasis added).[42] Nehru spoke of a 'contradiction' that had arisen between fundamental rights and directive principles, and that it is up to Parliament 'to remove this contradiction and *make the Fundamental Rights subserve the Directive Principles*' (emphasis added).[43]

The Amendment Act added a new sub-section (4) to Article 15, which declared that 'nothing in this article' or in Article 29(2) 'shall prevent the State from making any special provision for the advancement' of backward classes, Scheduled Castes, and Scheduled Tribes. Thus, the content of Article 46 was explicitly added to Article 15, and indirectly to Article 29. This, however, did not clarify the relationship between fundamental rights and directive principles in general. Instead, its effect was somewhat confusing. By reacting to the *Dorairajan* judgment with a Constitutional Amendment in the first place, Parliament (whose members were at the time still the same as those in the Constituent Assembly) expressed the view that the goals defined by the directive principles ought to be able to act as a limitation to the fundamental rights. However, taking the content of one of the principles and adding it to the constitutional text as a new sub-section of a fundamental right article sent the message that without such explicit limitations within Part III, encroachments on the fundamental rights were not permissible.[44]

42 Quoted in Seervai, *Constitutional Law of India*, 1983.

43 Quoted in Austin, *The Indian Constitution*, 101.

44 Parliament could have given more force to its view on the relationship between the two parts by creating a new provision that would generally define how conflicts might be resolved, rather than just limiting the scope of isolated provisions within the fundamental rights catalogue. Creating such a provision could have also avoided another, much more far-reaching change that the First Amendment brought. In addition to the alterations just mentioned, the Amendment also added Articles 31A and 31B. Article 31A declared that no law providing for the acquisition of any estate by the State 'shall be deemed void on the ground that it is inconsistent with, or takes away or abridges any of the rights conferred by, any provision of [Part III]' as long as the law received presidential assent.

The struggle between the Supreme Court and Parliament continued in the following years, with the Supreme Court repeatedly invalidating laws (mainly concerning land acquisition) and Parliament repeatedly reacting with constitutional amendments.[45] As far as the judiciary's stance on the general relationship between fundamental rights and directive principles is concerned, the cases of *Buddhu* and *Kameshwar Singh* (both 1952) are worth mentioning.[46] These judgments, at first sight, appear to point in the opposite direction of *Dorairajan*, as the courts (the Allahabad High Court and the Supreme Court, respectively) did refer to the directive principles to justify state actions. However, the courts only invoked directive principles when interpreting provisions defining limitations within Part III. The right to carry an occupation may be limited by laws 'in the interest of the general public' (Article 19(6)), and expropriation, according to Article 31(2), could only be permissible for a 'public purpose'. When interpreting the legal terms 'interest of the public' and 'public purpose', the

---

Article 31B, on the other hand, refers to the Ninth Schedule, which the Amendment added to the Constitution. Article 31B states that none of the acts listed in the Ninth Schedule 'shall be deemed void, or ever to have become void' for infringing on or being inconsistent with any fundamental right. 'Notwithstanding any judgment, decree or order of any court or tribunal', the acts listed in the Ninth Schedule shall continue in force. In other words, all acts listed in that schedule were deemed as constitutional by virtue of being added to it, and no court was supposed to be able to rule on its validity, at least as far as fundamental rights were concerned. Unlike Article 15(4) or Article 31A, the scope of Article 31B was not limited to acts concerning positive discrimination or land reform, or to state action promoting directive principles. At least on the face of it, any act on any matter could now be deemed as constitutional by adding it to the Ninth Schedule through constitutional amendments.

[45] For an overview of these judgments and amendments, see Austin, *Working a Democratic Constitution*, 99 et seq.

[46] *Buddhu* v. *Municipal Board and Ors* MANU/UP/0297/1952 (Allahabad High Court, 18 March 1952); *The State of Bihar* v. *Maharajadhiraja Sir Kameshwar Singh* MANU/SC/0019/1952 (Supreme Court of India, 2 May 1952).

Court used directive principles as a guidance. These terms, however, were parts of explicit limitations in the fundamental rights catalogue. Had they not been there, the Court would (most likely) not have referred to directive principles as possible limitations to fundamental rights.[47]

One famous case also concerned Article 45, the core directive principle concerned with elementary education. In the case of *The Kerala Education Bill*,[48] the Supreme Court was asked by the president[49] to test the constitutional validity of the Kerala Education Bill of 1957. The Bill, which was passed by the Kerala Legislative Assembly shortly after the Communist Party had won the state election, aimed for education to be provided free of cost in all elementary schools, including private schools. Private schools in Kerala were traditionally operated by Christian communities to a large extent, as described in Chapter 1. The Supreme Court ruled that the Bill, if it became an act, would violate Article 30(1), which gives religious and linguistic minorities a right to establish and administer educational institutions. The Court rejected the argument that the Bill's encroachment on Article 30(1) may be justified by Article 45.[50] Even though the Court spoke of 'two conflicting interests' and the goal 'to give effect to both if that is possible and bring about a synthesis between the two' (and that the court should 'adopt the principle of harmonious construction'), it then immediately went on to say that 'the directive principles cannot

47 Dohrmann, *Directive Principles of State Policy*, 60–1.

48 In *Re: The Kerala Education Bill* MANU/SC/0029/1958 (Supreme Court of India, 22 May 1958).

49 Article 143(1) and (2) of the Constitution gives the president (who acts based on the advice of his or her government) the power to refer 'questions of law' to the Supreme Court. Article 143(2) specifically concerns disputes between the central government and the states or in between states, as described in Article 131. In the case of the Kerala Education Bill of 1957, the governor of Kerala had referred the Bill to the president for his assent (which he was empowered to do by Article 200).

50 Importantly, Article 30 does not include limitation clauses referring to the 'common good' or 'public purpose', which might be defined with the help of directive principles.

ignore or override the fundamental rights but must, as we have said, subserve the fundamental rights'.[51] The Court thus remained of the opinion that whenever there is a conflict between directive principles and fundamental rights that cannot be solved by interpretation of limitation clauses within the fundamental rights, the latter will prevail.

In the late 1960s and 1970s, the tensions between the judiciary and the government (now led by Nehru's daughter Indira Gandhi as the prime minister) worsened. The government increasingly saw the judiciary as an obstacle in pursuing the 'social revolution'. The Twenty-Fourth and Twenty-Fifth Constitutional Amendments were part of a larger strategy aimed at weakening the courts vis-à-vis the government and legislature.[52] However, at least for a while, the judiciary still asserted itself against the other branches of power.

In the case of *Golaknath*,[53] another land acquisition case, the Supreme Court defined the meaning of 'law' in Article 13(2). That Article states that the State 'shall not make any law which takes away or abridges the rights conferred by this Part [i.e. by the fundamental rights]' and that 'any law made in contravention of this clause shall [...] be void'. The Supreme Court held that 'law' also includes constitutional amendments, meaning that Parliament would henceforth (the judgment did not have retrospective effect) not be able to impose any limitation on fundamental rights, neither by statutory law nor by constitutional amendments, unless it is expressly enabled to do so by a clause already existing in Part III.[54]

[51] Note 48, 46.

[52] The transfer of judges was another part of the strategy. To ensure that the judiciary would be more in line with the government's point of view, high court judges who had decided 'against the government' were transferred to other high courts as 'punishments', and Supreme Court judges who would have been next in line to become Chief Justice of India (by convention, the government had always chosen the senior-most judge for this position) were superseded (see Austin, *Working a Democratic Constitution*, 278 et seq., 344 et seq.).

[53] *I.C. Golak Nath* v. *State of Punjab* MANU/SC/0029/1967 (Supreme Court of India, 27 February 1967).

[54] Note 53, 34 et seq.

Parliament duly reacted to this judgment by passing the Twenty-Fourth Constitutional Amendment of 1971. This created a new sub-section (4) for Article 13, which declared that '[n]othing in this article shall apply to any amendment of this Constitution made under article 368'. Correspondingly, a new sub-section (3) was added to Article 368, the Article prescribing the procedure for constitutional amendment. Article 368(3) declares that '[n]othing in Article 13 shall apply to any amendment made under this article'. The Twenty-Fourth Amendment sought to completely reverse the effect of *Golaknath*. According to the Supreme Court's new, extensive interpretation of Article 13(2), the amendment itself would be unconstitutional.

The Twenty-Fifth Constitutional Amendment of 1971, on the other hand, introduced a new Article 31C, which stated that 'no law giving effect to [...] the principles specified in cl. (b) or cl. (c) of Article 39 shall be deemed to be void on the ground that it is inconsistent with [...] any of the rights conferred by Article 14, Article 19 or Article 31'. In addition to this, the new article also stated that if any law contained a declaration that its purpose is to give effect to Article 39(b) or (c), it shall not be 'called in question in any court on the ground that it does not give effect to such policy'. In other words, the legislature was to be empowered to be able to completely ignore Articles 14, 19, and 31 by merely *declaring* that it is following its duty under Article 39(b) and (c).

The next episode in the power struggle came in *Kesavananda Bharati*, also known as the 'Fundamental Rights case', in which the petitioner challenged both the Twenty-Fourth and Twenty-Fifth Amendments.[55] Overruling its own 'extreme' *Golaknath*

[55] *Kesavananda Bharati* v. *State of Kerala* MANU/SC/0445/1973 (Supreme Court of India, 24 April 1973). Austin describes how the Supreme Court decided under considerable time pressure because the approaching retirement of the Chief Justice was about to change the power balance in the Court in favour of the government (see Austin, *Working a Democratic Constitution*, 272–3). The decision has also been described as 'the case that saved Indian democracy' (see Arvind P. Datar, 'The Case that saved Indian Democracy', *The Hindu*, 24 April 2013, http://www.thehindu.com/opinion/op-ed/the-case-that-saved-indian-democracy/article4647800.ece, accessed on 19 August 2018).

precedent, the Supreme Court famously created the 'basic structure doctrine'.[56] The Court argued that while the power of a Constituent Assembly in creating a new constitution was unlimited, the power to amend a constitution through a process defined in that constitution was not. According to the Court, the amending power could never extend so far that the institution holding that power would alter the 'basic structure' of the Constitution, that is, creating what would ultimately be an entirely new constitution through amendments. Thus, in principle, there is no limitation to Parliament's amending power, as long as the amendments alter the constitution's basic structure. This also meant that 'law' in Article 13 does not include constitutional amendments.

As far as the amendments challenged in *Kesavananda Bharati* were concerned, sub-section (4) of Article 13 and sub-section (3) of Article 368 were held to be constitutional. The fact that Article 31C gave Article 39(b) and (c) primacy over fundamental rights was also held constitutional. However, the Article's provision excluding any law that claims to act in furtherance of these directive principles from the discretion of the courts was deemed unconstitutional. The Supreme Court, therefore, wanted to reserve the right to assess whether a law was made in favour of those principles for the judiciary, and argued that giving unchecked powers to the legislature concerning this aspect would violate the basic structure.

Shortly after *Kesavananda Bharati*, Indira Gandhi's government declared the infamous 'Emergency'.[57] In this time period,

[56] On the basic structure doctrine, see Sudhir Krishnaswamy, *Democracy and Constitutionalism in India: A Study of the Basic Structure Doctrine* (New Delhi: Oxford University Press, 2009). For the role that the German jurist Dieter Conrad's essay, 'Limitation of Amendment Procedures and the Constituent Power', in *Zwischen den Traditionen: Probleme des Verfassungsrechts und der Rechtskultur in Indien und Pakistan gesammelte Aufsätze aus den Jahren 1970–1990*, ed. Dieter Conrad (Stuttgart: Steiner, 1999), 47–85, might have played for this development, see Austin, *Working a Democratic Constitution*, 201, 261.

[57] As a measure against 'internal disturbance', see Article 352(1) in its original form. For more details on the Emergency, see Katherine Frank, *Indira: The Life of Indira Nehru Gandhi* (New Delhi: HarperCollins,

Parliament passed the Forty-Second Amendment, which sought to give priority to *all* directive principles over Articles 14, 19, and 31. Leading politicians stated that an un-amendable 'basic structure' of the Constitution did not exist.[58] This view was also expressed by the changes to the Constitution themselves. The amendment added two new sub-clauses to Article 368 concerning the amendment power of Parliament. Article 368(4) read that '[n]o amendment to this Constitution (including the provisions of Part III) [...] shall be called in question in any court on any ground'. Article 368(5) stated '*[f]or the removal of doubts*, it is hereby declared that there shall be *no limitation whatever* on the constituent power of Parliament to amend [...] this Constitution under this article' (emphasis added).

By this time, it also looked like the government had succeeded in ensuring that the judiciary would be loyal to its course. In the *Habeas Corpus* decision,[59] the Supreme Court upheld the suspension of the fundamental right of *habeas corpus* as part of the right to life and personal liberty (Article 21) under the Emergency. This case is said to demonstrate that the judiciary would henceforth act in the government's favour.[60] It is also said that it severely damaged the Supreme Court's reputation,[61] and that the judicial

---

2005), 371 et seq; Austin, *Working a Democratic Constitution*, 293 et seq; Ramachandra Guha, *India after Gandhi: The History of the World's Largest Democracy*, 1st Harper Perennial edition (New York: Harper Perennial, 2008, c2007), 493.

58 Austin, *Working a Democratic Constitution*, 381–2.

59 *Additional District Magistrate, Jabalpur* v. *Shiv Kant Shukla Etc.* MANU/SC/0062/1976 (Supreme Court of India, 28 April 1976). On this case, also see Austin, *Working a Democratic Constitution*, 334 et seq.

60 'The common view has been that the four judges were protecting the institution from an ill-intentioned government or protecting their personal futures or both' (see Austin, *Working a Democratic Constitution*, 342).

61 Dieter Conrad, 'Die Zukunft des indischen Rechtsstaates', in *Zwischen den Traditionen: Probleme des Verfassungsrechts und der Rechtskultur in Indien und Pakistan gesammelte Aufsätze aus den Jahren 1970–1990*, ed. Dieter Conrad (Stuttgart: Steiner, 1999), 142; Burt Neuborne, 'The Supreme Court of India', *ICON* 1 (2003): 494.

activism that would follow in the following decades was the Court's attempt to compensate for the damage it had done by this judgment—first by extending the scope of civil and political rights, but then later also by 'creating' socio-economic fundamental rights.[62]

## Later Adjudication: 'Harmony' Between Fundamental Rights and Directive Principles

The Emergency ended with a defeat of Indira Gandhi's government in the 1977 general election. The newly elected government led by the Janta Party introduced several constitutional amendment bills into Parliament to undo changes that the previous government had made, and to protect the country from abuses of power in the future. Most notably, the Forty-Fourth Constitutional Amendment brought a major change in the fundamental rights catalogue. The Janta government decided that it would be best to omit the fundamental right to property from Part III of the Constitution, and to instead turn it into a 'constitutional right', now guaranteed by Article 300A. The idea behind this was to delete the fundamental right that had caused the largest amount of tension between the government, legislature, and judiciary, believing that completely removing the basis for these

[62] Neuborne, 'The Supreme Court of India', 494. Robinson notes that the initial expansion of the scope of Article 21 concerned civil and political rights, which may have been a reaction to the government's *civil* rights abuses during the Emergency. The 'urban middle class', which had been targeted during the Emergency, 'desired to see a strong independent judiciary to check the state's power' once it was over. The court itself was 'caught up in the post-Emergency euphoria' and 'embraced [a] more populist direction in part to regain the legitimacy it had lost during the Emergency and in its early decisions, which often sided with property owners'. A shift from these early decisions meant that the Court would be more 'pro-poor', which may explain the shift towards adjudicating socio-economic rights (see Nick Robinson, 'Expanding Judiciaries: India and the Rise of the Good Governance Court', *Washington University Global Studies Law Review* 8, no. 1 [2009]: 42).

tensions would protect other fundamental rights from further attacks by future governments.[63]

Also after the Emergency, the Supreme Court ruled once more on the relationship between directive principles and fundamental rights in 1980.[64] The case of *Minerva Mills*[65] concerned the nationalization of a private textile company that had occurred in 1974. The petitioners challenged the validity of the nationalization act,[66] which itself stated that it was giving effect to Article 39(b).[67] As mentioned above, the provision included in Article 31C that stated that an act, by such a declaration, can save itself from judicial scrutiny had already been ruled as unconstitutional in *Kesavananda Bharati*. In *Minerva Mills*, the Supreme Court tested the validity of the changes the Forty-Second Amendment had made in that Article and in Article 368.

The Court unanimously decided that Article 368(4) and (5) were unconstitutional. It reiterated the view that there is an unchangeable basic structure of the Constitution, which these provisions explicitly denied. As a consequence, they could only be unconstitutional.[68] Furthermore, four out of five judges decided that the

[63] See the Statement of Objects and Reasons of the Constitution (Forty-Fourth Amendment Act), 1978: '*In view of the special position sought to be given to fundamental rights*, the right to *property, which has been the occasion for more than one amendment of the Constitution*, would cease to be a fundamental right and become only a legal right.' (emphasis added). On the right to property, also see Gopal Sankaranarayanan, 'The Fading Right to Property in India', *Law and Politics in Africa, Asia, Latin America (VRU)* 44, no. 2 (2011), https://www.nomos-elibrary.de/10.5771/0506-7286-2011-2-220/the-fading-right-to-property-in-india-jahrgang-44-2011-heft-2?page=0, accessed on 19 August 2018.

[64] The case had been pending in the courts since 1976, that is, at a time when property was still a fundamental right (see Austin, *Working a Democratic Constitution*, 498).

[65] *Minerva Mills Ltd. & Ors* v. *Union of India & Ors* MANU/SC/0075/1980 (Supreme Court of India, 9 May 1980, 31 July 1980).

[66] The Sick Textile Undertakings (Nationalisation) Act, 1974.

[67] Section 39 of the Act.

[68] Note 65, 21 et seq.

alteration the Forty-Second Amendment had made in Article 31C was unconstitutional, declaring that all laws giving effect to *any* of the directive principles, according to the majority, was in violation of the basic structure.[69] Declaring this portion of the Forty-Second Amendment as unconstitutional meant that Article 31C once again let Article 39(b) and (c) prevail over Articles 14 and 19 in case of conflict, but no other directive principles. As Justice Bhagwati pointed out in his concurring (but separately written and, concerning this detail, dissenting) opinion, this distinction is not very convincing, as the Constitution does not imply any 'hierarchy' within the catalogue of directive principles. Instead, Article 37 declares them all to be 'fundamental'.[70]

As far as the position of fundamental rights and directive principles in the constitutional framework is concerned, the majority opinion states that the two parts created by the Constituent Assembly were in spirit 'parts of an integral, indivisible scheme [...] To destroy the guarantees given by Part III in order purportedly to achieve the goals of Part IV is plainly to subvert the Constitution by destroying its basic structure'.[71] Together, the Court says, Parts III and IV are 'like two wheels of a chariot' (quoting Austin), and 'to give absolute primacy to one over the other is to disturb the harmony of the Constitution. This *harmony and balance between fundamental rights and directive principles is an essential feature of the basic structure* of the Constitution' (emphasis added).[72]

Apparently, the Court wanted to clarify that it did not believe that the fundamental rights were more important or stronger than the directive principles or vice versa. However, evoking a 'harmony' between the two parts of the Constitution still did not really clarify how the parts should be applied in case of conflict.

[69] Note 65, 29 et seq., 63 et seq., 79.

[70] 'If the exclusion of the Fundamental Rights embodied in Articles 14 and 19 could be legitimately made for giving effect to the Directive Principles set out in clauses (b) and (c) of Article 39 without affecting the basic structure, I fail to see why these Fundamental Rights cannot be excluded for giving effect to the other Directive Principles,' see Note 65, 118.

[71] Note 65, 59.

[72] Note 65, 61.

## Reading Directive Principles into Fundamental Rights

In the following years, however, this question was not raised as much as it had been in the decades following Independence. Perhaps this may be explained by the fact that property was not a fundamental right anymore, meaning that the Janta government's promise had been fulfilled.

Instead, directive principles and fundamental rights have now entered into a somewhat complementary relationship that might be seen as an expression of the 'harmony' that the Supreme Court had called for. Some of the directive principles have been read into a fundamental right (the right to life and personal liberty as guaranteed by Article 21). Several judgments paved the way for this, beginning with the case of *Maneka Gandhi* in the late 1970s.

### *The Case of* Maneka Gandhi

Reading the content of directive principles into Article 21 was made possible through an extensive reading of Article 21 that started with the case of *Maneka Gandhi*.[73] After the Janta Party took over the government in 1977, the government took several measures directly against the Nehru–Gandhi family, partly as a reaction to the Emergency and the abuse of power by some members of the family.[74] One of the measures was to impound several family members' passports, including the one by Indira Gandhi's daughter-in-law Maneka Gandhi.[75] She challenged this decision in a writ petition filed in the Supreme Court.

The petitioner's passport had been impounded without a prior hearing, which was in line with the procedure prescribed by statutory law. The Passports Act of 1967 in Section 10(3)(c) stated that a passport could be impounded 'in public interest'. Section

[73] *Maneka Gandhi* v. *Union of India* MANU/SC/0133/1978 (Supreme Court of India, 25 January 1978).

[74] In particular Indira Gandhi's son Sanjay Gandhi, who at the time of the Emergency did not hold any official political office, but exerted (and abused) a great amount of power (see Frank, *Indira*, 390 et seq.).

[75] Frank, *Indira*, 417.

10(5) stated that the passport holder may apply to receive a copy of the statements of reasons for impounding the passport. However, according to that provision, this statement may be withheld by the State 'in the interest of the general public'. Based on this reasoning, the regional passport officer informed Maneka Gandhi that she could not receive such a copy.

In the petition, Gandhi argued (inter alia) that her right under Article 21 to life and personal liberty had been violated. She believed that the Passports Act lacked sound procedural requirements. The procedure that the Act did provide were, according to the petitioner, arbitrary, as they did not prescribe any prior hearing.[76]

The Supreme Court had already decided in *Satwant Singh* that the right to personal liberty includes the right to travel abroad, meaning that impounding a citizen's passport instituted an encroachment on that right.[77] Therefore, as Article 21 states, a passport must only be impounded 'according to procedure established by law'. In *Satwant Singh*, the authorities had impounded the petitioner's passports without any procedure prescribed by any law. There was no Passports Act or similar law in force at the time. Consequently, the court ruled that the petitioner's right under Article 21 had been violated.[78] Parliament reacted to this judgment by passing the Passports Act of 1967.

Now that this Act was in place, the crucial question in *Maneka Gandhi* was whether the limitation 'according to procedure established by law' in Article 21 merely meant that the legislature could prescribe *any* kind of procedure for the executive to follow when encroaching on a person's right to personal liberty. On the other hand, the limitation clause could also be read as referring to a 'procedure established by *just/fair* law', meaning that the constitutional validity of the statutory limitation itself would need to be assessed.

[76] *Maneka Gandhi* v. *Union of India* MANU/SC/0133/1978 at 39.

[77] *Satwant Singh Sawhney* v. *D. Ramarathnam, Assistant Passport Officer* MANU/SC/0040/1967 (Supreme Court of India, 10 April 1967).

[78] Note 77, 57 et seq.

The wording of the constitutional text does not explicitly state that the 'law' itself should be tested for its constitutionality. In fact, the Constituent Assembly had consciously decided against extending the scope of Article 21 to this extent. Several members had suggested choosing a wording that would bring the provision in line with the 'due process' clause of the Fifth and Fourteenth Amendments of the US Constitution,[79] which declares that 'no person [...] shall be deprived of life, liberty, or property, without due process of law'.[80] However, in the end, all suggestions in favour of a wording similar to the 'due process' clause were rejected, meaning that the Constituent Assembly arguably did not intend for statutory laws to be assessed against Article 21, and instead opted for 'parliamentary supremacy'.[81]

Still, the question whether or not 'law' in Article 21 might mean something more than any law enacted by Parliament was raised in Court already in 1950 in *A.K. Gopalan*.[82] In this case, the petitioner challenged the constitutionality of the Preventive Detention Act of 1950, arguing that it violated Article 21, as well as several other fundamental rights. However, the Court affirmed the decision taken by the Constituent Assembly. Thus, as far as

[79] Austin, *The Indian Constitution*, 102. For an analysis of the discussion in the Constituent Assembly, also see Ajay K. Mehra, '"Due Process" or "Procedure Established by Law"?', in *The Supreme Court Versus the Constitution: A Challenge to Federalism*, ed. Pran Chopra (New Delhi, Thousand Oaks, Calif: Sage Publications, 2006).

[80] Wording of the Fifth Amendment. The Fourteenth Amendment reads 'nor shall any State deprive any person of life, liberty, or property, without due process of law'. Constituent Assembly member Benegal Narsing Rau had travelled to the USA to speak with Supreme Court justice Felix Frankfurter about a possible inclusion of such a clause. Frankfurter voiced apprehensions, stating that the 'due process' clause gives the judiciary too much leverage against a democratically elected legislative, and that it can also be burdensome for the judiciary (see Austin, *The Indian Constitution*, 103).

[81] On this, also see Madhav Khosla, *The Indian Constitution* (New Delhi: Oxford University Press, 2012), 107–8.

[82] *A.K. Gopalan* v. *The State of Madras* MANU/SC/0012/1950 (Supreme Court of India, 19 May 1950).

the scope of the right to life and personal liberty was concerned, the Court saw an unlimited discretion given to the legislature. Only the executive was bound by the article insofar as it was only allowed to encroach on the right when acting based on a statutory law, like the Passports Act of 1967.

While the judgments of *A.K. Gopalan* and *Satwant Singh* only meant that the State must create a statutory law before impounding a person's passport, the judgment in *Maneka Gandhi* brought much more extensive prerequisites, thus laying the groundwork for future extensive adjudication of Article 21. The Court declared that the 'procedure established by law' as prescribed by Article 21 needed to be just and fair. Chief Justice Beg, concurring with the majority opinion given by Justice Bhagwati, evoked principles of natural law or 'natural law rights' which 'were meant to be converted into our constitutionally recognised fundamental rights' and stated that 'a divorce between natural law and our constitutional law would be disastrous. It would defeat one of the basic purposes of the Constitution'.[83] Justice Bhagwati himself declared that 'obviously' the 'procedure' as per Article 21 called for 'cannot be arbitrary, unfair or unreasonable'.[84] He based this argument on Article 14, the right to equality before the law: 'Equality and arbitrariness are sworn enemies [...] Article 14 strikes at arbitrariness in State action and ensures fairness and equality of treatment. [...] [T]he procedure contemplated by Article 21 must answer the test of reasonableness in order to be in conformity with Article 14'.[85]

Therefore, according to the judgment, even if it is not expressly provided by the Passports Act, 'as soon as the order impounding the Passport is made, an opportunity of hearing, remedial in aim, should be given to [the passport holder] so that he may present his case [...] and point out why his passport should not be impounded'.[86] Additionally, in the given case, the Central Government 'was wholly unjustified in withholding the reasons for impounding the passport'.[87]

[83] *Maneka Gandhi* v. *Union of India* MANU/SC/0133/1978 at 21.
[84] Note 83, 54.
[85] Note 83, 56.
[86] Note 83, 65.
[87] Note 83, 66.

The Court also declared that the rights conferred by Article 19 were part of Article 21. Justice Bhagwati declared that '[t]he expression "personal liberty" in Article 21 is of the widest amplitude and covers a variety of rights which go to constitute the personal liberty of man and some of them have been raised to the status of distinct fundamental rights and given additional protection under Article 19(1)'.[88] The door to reading other rights into the right to life had been opened.

## *The Right to Dignified Life*

The case of *Maneka Gandhi* was just the beginning of a progressively more and more extensive reading of Article 21 by the Supreme Court. This extensive reading was one important part of the 'judicial activism' that commenced in the late 1970s, with the invention of PIL (as a procedural innovation facilitating these substantial developments) being the other. PIL shall be dealt with more extensively in Chapters 4 and 6.

In *Francis Coralie Mullin*,[89] Justice Bhagwati once again spoke out in favour of an extensive reading of fundamental rights in general, and Article 21 as the 'most precious right' in particular.[90] It was decided that right to life must mean more than 'mere animal existence. It means something much more than just physical survival'.[91] This declaration was another decisive step towards

[88] Note 83, 54.

[89] *Francis Coralie Mullin* v. *The Administrator, Union Territory of Delhi and Others* MANU/SC/0492/1981 (Supreme Court of India, 13 January 1981).

[90] 'A constitutional provision must be construed, not in a narrow and constricted sense, but a wide and liberal manner so as to anticipate and take account of changing conditions and purposes [...] The fundamental right to life which is the most precious human right and which forms the ark of all other rights must therefore be interpreted in a broad and expansive spirit' (see Note 89, 6).

[91] Note 89, 7. By evoking 'more than mere animal existence', the Court was using the same language that was found in a passage in the American Supreme Court's case of *Munn* v. *Illinois*, 94 U.S. 113 (1876), 142 (US Supreme Court, 1 March 1877). This passage had already been quoted in *Kharak Singh* v. *The State of U. P. & Others* MANU/SC/0085/1962,

being able to read socio-economic rights into the right to life, as the Court stated that 'the right to life includes the right to live with human dignity and all that goes along with it, namely, the bare necessaries of life'.[92]

## *Directive Principles and the Right to Life*

With this wide interpretation of Article 21 ('personal liberty' including any liberties of the individual, not just ones of physical movement, 'life' meaning 'dignified life', and 'procedure established by law' meaning 'procedure established by fair/just/reasonable law' or 'due process of law'), the Supreme Court had enabled itself to extend the article to such an extent that it allowed for the creation of 'new' fundamental rights. This could also include socio-economic rights, as dignified life was not only understood in a way that the State is not allowed to actively encroach on an individual's dignity, but that it has a duty to protect it, and potentially also to provide means for a dignified living.

Ever since the 1980s, many socio-economic rights have been read into the right to life and personal liberty. The courts have declared that the right includes, among others, the right to livelihood; the right to medical care; the right to prevention of sexual harassment or abuse; the right to privacy; the right of agriculturalists to cultivation; the right to one's home being accessible by road when living in remote settlements in hilly areas; the right to an unpolluted environment and the preservation and protection of nature's gifts; the right to protection of wildlife, forests, lakes, ancient monuments, and flora and fauna; the right to protection from noise, air, and water pollution; the right to maintenance of

---

13 (Supreme Court of India, 18 December 1962). That American judgment extended the scope to 'all those limbs and faculties by which life is enjoyed', stating that the right also prohibits 'mutilation of the body'—meaning that the scope was still limited to protection against physical encroachments, *Munn* v. *Illinois*, 142.

[92] *Francis Coralie Mullin* v. *The Administrator, Union Territory of Delhi and Others* MANU/SC/0492/1981, 8.

ecological balance and sustainable development; the right to protection of tradition, culture, and heritage; the right to a reasonable accommodation to live in; the right to (clean drinking) water; the right to self-preservation; the right to reputation; the right to sleep undisturbed; and so on.[93]

In many judgments on socio-economic rights, the courts relied on directive principles that have thus extended the scope of Article 21. For instance, in *Madhav Hayawadanrao Hoskot*, the Court evoked Article 39A when reading free legal aid into Article 21.[94] In the famous case of *Olga Tellis*, the Supreme Court cited Articles 39(a) and 41 when reading the right to livelihood and shelter into Article 21. The Court noted that even though Article 37 states that directive principles shall be unenforceable in court, the said articles 'must be regarded as equally fundamental in the understanding and interpretation of the meaning and content of fundamental rights. If there is an obligation on the State [...] it would be sheer pedantry to exclude the right to livelihood from the content of the right to life'.[95]

## Status of Directive Principles Today

After decades of adjudication on the matter of fundamental rights and directive principles, the question arises how their relationship

[93] This list has been compiled based on the judgments mentioned by Singh and Jain (see Mahendra Pal Singh, *V.N. Shukla's Constitution of India*, 12th edition [Lucknow: Eastern Book Co., 2013], 209–10, as well as Mahabir Prashad Jain, Ruma Pal, and Samaraditya Pal, *Indian Constitutional Law*, 6th edition [Gurgaon: LexisNexis Butterworths Wadhwa Nagpur, 2010], 1227 et seq.). One may argue that in many of those cases, the courts merely solemnly declared that such rights exist, without actually giving them extensive content or providing strong remedies. On this argument, see Chapter 3.

[94] *Madhav Hayawadanrao Hoskot* v. *State of Maharashtra* MANU/SC/0119/1978, 22 et seq, (Supreme Court of India, 17 August 1978).

[95] *Olga Tellis and Others* v. *Bombay Municipal Corporation and Others* MANU/SC/0039/1985, 33 (Supreme Court of India, 10 July 1985). This case (and the criticism brought against it) shall be discussed in more detail in the next chapter.

may be described today. One may summarize that the Constituent Assembly did not intend that fundamental rights be superior to directive principles. The Assembly also did not intend for the former to necessarily prevail in a case of conflict, even though it purposely refrained from including a provision in the Constitution that would make this clear.

Still, the high courts and the Supreme Court are the highest authority in interpreting the Constitution. Considering that they saw supremacy of the fundamental rights over the directive principles, there was some justification to describe the relationship between the two Parts as drastically as Seervai did. He was of the opinion that directive principles are, in spite of being part of the Constitution, 'not law at all'.[96] He argued that it would not have made any difference (legally) if the directive principles had been struck out of the Constitution. The fact that Article 37 stated that they shall not be enforceable in court meant that they 'impose no legal obligation on Parliament or the State Legislatures to make laws complying [with them]'.[97] This lack of means of enforcement, in his opinion, meant that they could not be considered to be 'law' at all.[98]

However, already in the early years following Independence, other scholars argued that such a strict hierarchy between

[96] Seervai, *Constitutional Law of India*, 1923.

[97] Seervai, *Constitutional Law of India*, 1923.

[98] Seervai also believed that not making these provisions law was justified. Taking Article 45—elementary education—as an example, he points out that giving a parent of every child under 14 a legally enforceable right against the state 'was not practicable immediately, or even after 10 years [from the commencement of the Constitution]', and that this was the reason why the Constituent Assembly decided to place this provision in Part IV of the Constitution (see Seervai, *Constitutional Law of India*, 1928). However, as Singh points out, this would also mean that several other provisions of the Constitution that the courts cannot enforce are not 'law'. See, for instance, Article 74(2), which states that whether the president acts on advice of the cabinet 'shall not be inquired into in any court' (see Singh, 'The Statics and the Dynamics of the Fundamental Rights and the Directive Principles', footnote 28). This demonstrates that Seervai's definition is problematically narrow.

fundamental rights and directive principles was not justified. The directive principles were described as a limitation to the exercise of fundamental rights, meaning that the rights needed to be interpreted in light of the principles.[99] It was also argued that lack of sanctions in case of an infringement does not mean that a provision is not law.[100] Baxi differentiates between some directive principles, which he calls '"social revolution" directives' and others, which he calls 'compromise directives'. For the latter, Baxi considers the 'dustbin of sentiment' assessment quoted above[101] to be apt. The directives he considers to be 'social revolution' ones are, for instance, Articles 38 and 39 (promoting welfare of the people by securing and protecting a just social order and the modalities to attain this goal). The 'compromise' or 'dustbin' ones contain, for instance, Articles 42, 46, 47, and 49 (maternity relief, prohibition of liquor, prohibition of cow-slaughter, and protection of monuments).[102] While Baxi believes that it would have been more favourable to not include the 'dustbin directives' at all, he believes that even those are still law. Not considering them to be 'law' would only be possible if one only understood 'law' in the sense

99 'Just as the fundamental rights were proclaimed to free man from the personal shackles perpetrated by a feudal system, so, the directive principles were acknowledged and posited to protect man from the antipode of economic enslavement in which the capitalistic system would inevitably plunge him through an unrealistic and blind emphasis on the fundamental rights themselves. Coming as they do, chronologically, after the fundamental rights the directive principles are meant to solve the very problems created by the fundamental rights: they set the limits to the application of the fundamental rights: they define those "rights" anew, in the light of news experiences and in terms of new needs' (see P.K. Tripathi, *Spotlights on Constitutional Interpretation* [Bombay: N.M. Tripathi, 1972], 296).

100 Upendra Baxi, 'Directive Principles and Sociology of Indian Law: A Reply to Dr. Jagat Narain', *Journal of the Indian Law Institute* 11, no. 3 (1969): 255.

101 See 'Relationship Envisioned by the Constituent Assembly' in this chapter.

102 Upendra Baxi, '"The Little Done, the Vast Undone"—Some Reflections on Reading Granville Austin's "The Indian Constitution"', *Journal of the Indian Law Institute* 9, no. 3 (1967): 344.

of 'legal rules'. But if 'law' is understood as containing 'rules, principles, conceptions, doctrines, and standards', then the directive principles are 'law' and they can thus be considered by the courts when interpreting other provisions.[103] Furthermore, according to Baxi, '[n]on-enforceability [as prescribed by Article 37] has [...] not meant judicial non-cognizability'.[104]

This point is crucial: not being able to enforce a provision containing a right in court does mean that the beneficiary of that provision cannot claim that right against the state or a third person. But it does not necessarily mean that the court must ignore that provision altogether. The judiciary seems to have taken this stand in later judgments by stating that fundamental rights and directive principles ought to be interpreted 'harmoniously'.

By reading the content of directive principles into Article 21, the courts then ended up going one step further. Interpreting the right to life and personal liberty so broadly meant that the directive principles were ultimately enforceable. In a way, this development has strengthened the directive principles enormously. However, it also means that the courts still seem to believe that they are inferior to fundamental rights. As Singh points out, these judgments meant that only if the principles are transformed into fundamental rights, only if they are read into Article 21, do they gain this strength.[105] Therefore, ultimately, even though the relationship between fundamental rights and directive principles has sparked a lot of debate and controversial judgments over the last few decades, their relationship is still not entirely clear.

## The Right to Education as a Fundamental Right

Singh also sees the inclusion of Article 21A in the Constitution as problematic: '[T]his selective transfer of important Directive Principles to the Fundamental Rights implies not only primacy of the Fundamental Rights [...] but also further weakens the position

[103] Baxi, 'Directive Principles and Sociology of Indian Law', 258 et seq.

[104] Baxi, 'Directive Principles and Sociology of Indian Law', 250.

[105] Singh, 'The Statics and the Dynamics of the Fundamental Rights and the Directive Principles', 2.

of Directive Principles.'[106] So far, however, the right to elementary education has remained the only directive principle that has been added to the fundamental rights catalogue. Somewhat bizarrely, it is unclear what the legislature actually meant to achieve with this constitutional amendment, as the following summary of its genesis shall demonstrate.

## The Right to Education as Part of the Right to Life

The Supreme Court decided in two cases that the right to education was part of the right to life and personal liberty, and that its contents were to be defined by the directive principles found in Articles 41 and 45. Those were the cases of *Mohini Jain* and *Unni Krishnan*.

### *The Case of* Mohini Jain

In 1992, the Supreme Court for the first time stated that the right to life also includes the right to education. In the case of *Mohini Jain*,[107] the petitioner challenged a notification by the Karnataka state government regulating tuition fees and other fees for private medical colleges in the state. Jain had been refused admission into a course because she was unable to pay the high tuition fees (60,000 rupees for the first year, plus additional fees). The decisive question was whether the fact that the state allowed such high financial thresholds for admission (known as 'capitation fees' in India) in government-recognized private colleges should be deemed unconstitutional because of an infringement of the right to life and personal liberty.

The Court ruled that '[t]he right to life under Article 21 and the dignity of an individual cannot be assured unless it is accompanied by the right to education', and, in this context, also used the language of Article 45: 'The State Government is under an

[106] Singh, 'The Statics and the Dynamics of the Fundamental Rights and the Directive Principles', 2–3.

[107] *Miss Mohini Jain* v. *State of Karnataka and Ors* MANU/SC/0357/1992 (Supreme Court of India, 30 July 1992).

obligation to [...] endeavour to provide educational facilities at all levels to its citizens.'[108] The argument was that education was a prerequisite for dignified living: 'An individual cannot be assured of human dignity unless his personality is developed and the only way to do that is to educate him.'[109] The Court also highlighted the State's duty to provide education to its citizens as prescribed by the directive principles in Articles 41 and 45. However, it did not further elaborate on their contents. Instead, it limited its judgment to the decision that capitation fees were unconstitutional: 'Capitation fee is nothing but a price for selling education. The concept of "teaching shops" is contrary to the educational scheme and is wholly abhorrent to the Indian culture and heritage. [...] The State action in permitting capitation fee [...] is wholly arbitrary and as such violative of Article 14.'[110]

Thus, in *Mohini Jain*, the Supreme Court had, for the first time, declared the right to education to be a part of Article 21. This meant that the state not only has a duty to provide education to its people but also that citizens could claim it from the state as part of their right to life and personal liberty. The Court had not, however, delineated the contents or the limitations of that right. Instead, it appeared that there was no personal limitation to that right, meaning that even adults had a fundamental right to education. After all, the case of *Mohini Jain* concerned admission into a private institution of higher education.

## *The Case of* Unni Krishnan

A clearer definition of the content of the 'new' right followed in the subsequent case of *Unni Krishnan*.[111] In *Unni Krishnan*, the Supreme Court relied on Articles 41 and 45 more strongly. In

[108] Note 107, 12.

[109] Note 107, 8.

[110] Note 107, 18.

[111] *Unni Krishnan, J.P. and Ors* v. *State of Andhra Pradesh and Ors* MANU/SC/0333/1993 (Supreme Court of India, 4 February 1993). The case was decided by a bench of five judges, larger than the bench of two judges in *Mohini Jain*, which means that that case could be overruled.

this case, private education institutions from several states challenged the *Mohini Jain* decision, arguing that outlawing 'capitation fees' altogether constituted a violation of their right to carry on any occupation, trade, or business under Article 19(1)(g). The Court reiterated that Article 21 contains a fundamental right to education but that this was 'not an absolute right': 'Its contents and parameters have to be determined in the light of Articles 45 and 41.'[112]

Therefore, the Court did not see an unlimited right to education (meaning that the State must provide all levels of education to all its citizens), but rather that every citizen has a right to free education until completion of the age of 14 years, as it was prescribed as a directive principle by Article 45 in its original form.[113] The Court went on to state that 'after a child/citizen completes 14 years, his right to education is circumscribed by the limits of the economic capacity of the State and its development'.[114] Once again, the Court was relying on directive principles to define the content of a new fundamental right read into Article 21. This time, the directive principle was used to limit the right's content, but also to confirm the existence of the right. In doing so, the Court pointed out that Article 45 contained the only directive principle with a time limit, which meant that '[t]he State should honour the command of Article 45. It must be made a reality'.[115]

As far as the significance of such an interpretation for the relationship in between fundamental rights and directive principles was concerned, the Court pointed out that 'by saying so, we are not transferring Article 41 from Part IV to Part III[;] we are merely relying upon Article 41 to illustrate the content of the right to education flowing from Article 21'.[116] The judges also took the opportunity to reprimand the government for not having fulfilled its duty under Article 45 within the time limit, or even the decades following its expiry: 'Can the State flout the

[112] Note 111, 1.
[113] Note 111, 32, 145.
[114] Note 111, 145.
[115] Note 111, 145.
[116] Note 111, 148.

said direction even after 44 years on the ground that the article merely calls upon it to "endeavour and provide" the same and on the further ground that the said article is not enforceable by virtue of the declaration in Article 37.'[117] The Court seems to see the expiration of the time limit as an addition justification to declare that its content be a fundamental right: 'Does not the passage of 44 years [...] convert the obligation created by the article into an enforceable right?'[118]

As far as the relevance of private educational institutions is concerned, the Court in *Unni Krishnan* declared that the obligation to provide education to citizens need not be fulfilled by the State alone. 'It can also be done by permitting, recognising and aiding voluntary nongovernmental organisations', and 'unaided private schools [...] too [...] have a role to play. They meet the demand of that segment of the population who may not wish to have their children educated in State-run schools'.[119] As the State was unable to meet the demand of the citizen, particularly for medical and technical education, it is 'not possible to do without [private educational institutions]'.[120] While State-aided educational institutions, the Court declared, shall not be entitled to charge higher fees than government institutions,[121] there must be a limitation for un-aided institutions as well: '[C]ommercialisation of education cannot and should not be permitted. [...] Both in the light of our tradition and [from] the stand-point of interest of [the] public commercialisation is positively harmful.'[122] Therefore, the occupation of running private education institutions could not be considered to be 'a trade, business, or profession' according to Article 19(1)(g): 'Trade or business normally connotes an activity carried out with a profit motive. Education has never been a commerce in this country. Making it one is opposed to the ethos, tradition and sensibilities of this nation. The argument to the contrary has an

[117] Note 111, 145.
[118] Note 111, 145.
[119] Note 111, 146.
[120] Note 111, 160.
[121] Note 111, 162.
[122] Note 111, 163.

unholy ring to it.'[123] Therefore, outlawing capitation fees remained permissible as it did not constitute a violation of Article 19(1)(g).

The fact that elementary education came into the picture can be explained by the fact that the Court in *Unni Krishnan* needed to clarify that there could not be a right to free education (irrespective of the state's economic capacity!)[124] at all levels, but that such a right was limited to the scope as defined by Article 45. Insofar, citing Articles 41 and 45 was relevant to the case. However, the passages relating to the importance of elementary education and the passing of Article 45's deadline allowing a conversion of the directive principle into an enforceable right were obiter dicta, as access to or the provision of elementary education was not actually the question at hand either in *Mohini Jain* or in *Unni Krishnan*. Still, *Mohini Jain* and especially *Unni Krishnan* did bring the declaration that there is a right to free elementary education as part of the right to life and personal liberty, which paved the way for the inclusion of Article 21A in the Constitution.

## The Eighty-Sixth Constitutional Amendment

Many rights that have been read into the right to life and personal liberty have remained just that: part of Article 21. The right to education, however, stands out as the one socio-economic right that was added to the catalogue of Part III of the Constitution. The right was 'elevated' to this status by the Eighty-Sixth Constitutional Amendment in 2002.

As mentioned above, the idea that elementary education could be a justiciable fundamental right had already been entertained by the Constituent Assembly. Several decades later (a couple of years before the Supreme Court passed its judgment in *Mohini Jain*), the Committee for Review of the National Policy on Education (1986) (also known as the Acharya Ramamurti Committee, established in 1990) recommended that an inclusion of a right to education in the constitutional fundamental rights catalogue should

[123] Note 111, 164.

[124] Note 111, 1, 35, 42, 136, 145, 148, 149.

be considered.[125] At the time, however, the recommendation was ignored by policymakers.[126] It is unclear whether the judges concerned with the cases of *Mohini Jain* and *Unni Krishnan* were aware of this recommendation, though it is quite possible that they were not. Mehendale believes that the *Unni Krishnan* judgment was 'purely an accident' that 'no one from the field of elementary education' had expected.[127] She notes that Justice Jeevan Reddy, one of the judges in *Unni Krishnan*, stated in an interview that the court had performed 'purely an application of law by reading Article 45 into Article 21'.[128] Thus, it appears that the Court was not entirely aware of educational debates at the time.

Whatever the case may be, the idea of amending the Constitution in this respect remained dormant for a few years after the Supreme Court judgments. The issue only returned to the political agenda in 1997, when the idea of adding the right to education as a new Article 21A was first introduced in Parliament. After the 1996 election, the United Front Government led by the Janata Dal party gave itself a 'Common Minimum Programme' which included the creation of a fundamental right to education.[129] Also in 1996, a Committee of State Education Ministers (also known as the Saikia

[125] 'The Right to Education should be examined for inclusion amongst the fundamental rights guaranteed under the Constitution of India. All the socio-ecomonic measures, without which realisation of this right will not be possible, should be taken' (see Committee for the Review of National Policy on Education, 'Report of the Committee for the Review of National Policy on Education, 1986', 26 December 1990, https://web.archive.org/web/20120131104621/http://www.education.nic.in/cd50years/g/t/v/Toc.htm, accessed on 19 August 2018, at Universalisation of Elementary Education).

[126] Archana Mehendale, 'Right to Education and Constitutional Amendment: A Case of India', currently not available online. On file with the author, 14.

[127] Mehendale, 'Right to Education and Constitutional Amendment', 17.

[128] Mehendale, 'Right to Education and Constitutional Amendment', 17.

[129] Mehendale, 'Right to Education and Constitutional Amendment', 19.

Committee) was formed,[130] which, in January 1997, concluded with a recommendation to add a fundamental right to elementary education to the Constitution.[131]

In July 1997, the Constitution (Eighty-Third) Amendment Bill was introduced in the Rajya Sabha (the Indian Upper House of Parliament).[132] The new Article 21A that it proposed was similar to the one that was finally included in the Constitution five years later. For instance, its scope was also limited to children in the age group of 6 to 14 years. However, it explicitly excluded private educational institutions.[133] Article 45, the Bill stated, should be omitted entirely. The Bill was referred to the Parliamentary Standing Committee which invited suggestions for amendments to the Bill, though it only gave a period of one month to submit these suggestions, which proved to be too short for civil society organizations to adequately respond.[134] Then the United Front Government collapsed, which led to dissolution of the Lok Sabha (the Lower House of Parliament) in November 1997. However, the fact that the Bill had been introduced in the Rajya Sabha meant that it remained on the parliamentary agenda, as India's Upper House cannot be dissolved.[135]

A couple of years after the BJP-led National Democratic Alliance had won the 1999 election, the government introduced a new bill (The Constitution [Ninety-Third Amendment] Bill, 2001), this

[130] Praveen K. Jha, *Public Provisioning for Elementary Education in India* (New Delhi, Thousand Oaks: SAGE, 2008), 259.

[131] See https://web.archive.org/web/20160804045032/http://www.teindia.nic.in/mhrd/50yrsedu/x/7C/HA/7CHA0101.htm, accessed on 15 August 2018.

[132] Bill Number XXXIX of 1997 (see https://web.archive.org/web/20140725112306/http://www.educationforallinindia.com/page144.html, accessed on 15 August 2018).

[133] 'The State shall not make any law, for free and compulsory education under clause (2), in relation to the educational institutions not maintained by the State or not receiving aid out of State funds.'

[134] Mehendale, 'Right to Education and Constitutional Amendment', 20.

[135] Mehendale, 'Right to Education and Constitutional Amendment', 19–20.

time in the Lok Sabha.[136] This bill differed from the Eighty-Third Amendment Bill insofar as it did not exclude private schools from the reach of Article 21A and did not provide that Article 45 should be struck. Instead, Article 45 was to be altered to now prescribe a duty of the state to provide for pre-elementary education.[137] Like the earlier bill, the Ninety-Third Amendment Bill also sought to create a new fundamental duty on parents and guardians to provide opportunities for education for their children (Article 51A(k)). The Bill was finally adopted in the Lok Sabha (unanimously!) on 28 November 2001 and became the Constitution (Eighty-Sixth Amendment) Act of 2002.[138]

Even though elementary education was now explicitly a fundamental right, and even though the Bill had been passed unanimously, the amendment faced strong criticism. The issue of the amendment's age limitation was probably the point of criticism that was raised most vocally.[139] While Article 45 had called for free and compulsory education for all children up to the age of 14, the scope of Article 21A is limited to children in the age group of 6 to 14. Therefore, to an extent, the amendment meant a step back compared to the effect of *Unni Krishnan*. After that judgment, there had been a fundamental right to education without this age limitation at the lower end as part of the right to life and personal liberty.

[136] The previous Eighty-Third Amendment Bill, still pending in the Rajya Sabha, was withdrawn (see Mehendale, 'Right to Education and Constitutional Amendment', 25).

[137] Article 45 now reads: 'Provision for early childhood care and education to children below the age of six years: The State shall endeavour to provide early childhood care and education for all children until they complete the age of six years.'

[138] Lok Sabha Debate, Discussion on the Constitution (Ninety-Third Amendment) Bill, 2001—346 votes in favour, 0 in opposition.

[139] See, for instance, P.P. Rao, 'Fundamental Right to Education', *Journal of the Indian Law Institute* 50, no. 4 (2008): 588; Vijayashri Sripati and Arun Thiruvengadam, 'Constitutional Amendment Making the Right to Education a Fundamental Right', *ICON*, 2004, 154 et seq; Anil Sadgopal, 'Right to Education vs. Right to Education Act', *Social Scientist* 38, no. 9 and 12 (2010): 28; Jha, *Public Provisioning for Elementary Education in India*, 59.

Some observers even go as far as stating that this could mean that the amendment was invalid, as the right to life and personal liberty may be part of the basic structure of the Constitution.[140] This view, however, is not convincing. Parliament's power to amend the Constitution is only limited by its basic structure, as mentioned above. The Supreme Court had never stated that every detail of its interpretation of the right to life and personal liberty (or any *particular* fundamental right, for that matter) were part of the basic structure of the Constitution. On the contrary, the 'basic structure' judgments have been quite vague, declaring, for instance, that the institution of judicial review, democracy, free and fair elections, secularism, rule of law, or the harmony and balance between fundamental rights and directive principles were parts of the basic structure.[141] Therefore, 'undoing' part of a Supreme Court judgment interpreting the Constitution by passing a constitutional amendment is in itself permissible.

Less criticism was expressed concerning the upper age limit of the fundamental right, that is, 14 years of age. Children older than 14 years had previously also been excluded by Article 45, which might be one reason why not including them was not seen as an omission. However, one should note that at the time that the Constitution (and therefore, Article 45 in its original form) was drafted, children received a formal education certificate after class VII, while today (and also in 2002), there is no formal certification before completion of class X.[142] In other words, the limitation in Article 21A meant that children would be guaranteed free education up until they are 14 years old, but not that free schools would allow them to graduate with a degree.

Another point of criticism does not concern Article 21A itself, but rather the inclusion of Article 51A(k), that is, the fundamental duty on parents and guardians to send their children to school.

[140] See Rao, 'Fundamental Right to Education', 588–9.

[141] Singh, *V.N. Shukla's Constitution of India*, 1086–7.

[142] Philip Alston and Nehal Bhuta, 'Human Rights and Public Goods: Education as a Fundamental Right in India', in *Human Rights and Development: Towards Mutual Reinforcement*, ed. Philip Alston (Oxford: Oxford University Press, 2005), 254.

Some observers believe that this is an attempt by the State to shift the responsibility for providing education to children from itself to the parents.[143] However, Article 21A (like the original Article 45 had) calls for *compulsory* education. Elementary education is only compulsory if the parents have such a duty, and it is then the State's responsibility to ensure that parents have their children attend school regularly. For this, legally prescribed enforcement measures as well as sanctions (in case parents do not fulfil their duty) would be necessary. Merely creating a constitutional provision stating so without implementing it through such legislation (which has not happened until today)[144] is not enough to truly make elementary education compulsory. But that does not mean that the constitutional provision itself has any negative effect, or that the State is necessarily giving up on its duty. It is therefore more apt to criticize that the 'division of the domain of responsibility' in between State and parents is not made clear, and that the fact that a majority of Indian parents lives close to or below the poverty level makes it questionable to what extent a responsibility should be given to them.[145] This argument shall be assessed more in-depth in Chapter 3.

Furthermore, several observers object to the portion of Article 21A stating that free elementary education shall be provided 'in such a manner as the State may, by law, determine'.[146] They believe that this wording means that the contents of the fundamental right may be entirely defined by the State through regular legislation, that is, that once the State would have created legislation implementing Article 21A (which it did in 2009 by passing the Right to Education Act), the fundamental right would cease to have a meaning of its own. For instance, Sadgopal warns that this phrase '[gives] the State the instrumentality to arbitrarily restrict, dilute and distort the Fundamental Right'.[147]

143 Rao, 'Fundamental Right to Education', 588.

144 See Chapter 1 and Chapter 3.

145 Jha, *Public Provisioning for Elementary Education in India*, 59.

146 See Mehendale, 'Right to Education and Constitutional Amendment', 31.

147 He sees this as part of the measures in which the State allowed 'neo-liberal policies to distort the notion of Fundamental Right emerging

Whether or not this criticism is justified depends entirely on how that element of Article 21A is to be read. Sadgopal points out that there is no other fundamental right that is 'tied to such a pre-condition'.[148] However, this comparison does not take into account the fact that Article 21A is, as of now, the only social and economic right included in the fundamental rights catalogue. Social and economic rights require more positive State action than civil and political rights. While every citizen can exercise their right to free speech save for State intervention, State intervention is required to make a right to free and compulsory education a reality.[149] Schools need to be built, teachers need to be trained and employed, attendance of children has to be ensured, a curriculum has to be formulated, funds have to be allocated, and so on. In a rule-of-law system, the State ought to act based on legislation, which is why a legal framework is desirable for the fulfilment of duties prescribed by social and economic rights. The words in Article 21A may therefore mean nothing else but that the State ought to create an implementation act, and not that the act will define and limit the contents of the right. Rather, it is still possible for courts to measure that act against the constitutional mandate. Therefore, the phrase can be read as an expression of this requirement for the implementation of a social and economic right. As a provision as short as Article 21A, but encompassing such a broad field as a state education system, can hardly be 'self-executing', this might also be considered a given. In this respect, the wording of Article 21A may rather be compared to that of the directive principles, which need to be applied by the State 'in making laws' (Article 37). As shall be demonstrated in Chapter 3, the provision actually has to be read in a way that it does not yield entirely to the legislature concerning the definition of the contents of the right.

---

from the Unnikrishnan Judgment' (see Sadgopal, 'Right to Education vs. Right to Education Act', 27, 28).

[148] Sadgopal, 'Right to Education vs. Right to Education Act', 29.

[149] This is a simplification for the sake of argument; the relationship between social and economic rights and civil and political rights shall be looked at more in-depth in Chapter 3.

Interestingly, one can find very little criticism about adding the fundamental right to education to the fundamental rights catalogue in the first place, or, rather, very few voices that question the benefits of such a step. To many, it seems to be a given that the inclusion of the right is positive. The Eighty-Sixth Amendment is described by some as a 'milestone in the direction of children's right to education'.[150] The Government of India itself speaks of having moved to a 'rights based framework that casts a legal obligation on the Central and State Governments to implement this fundamental child right'.[151] Many observers merely state that education is 'now a fundamental right' or 'clearly […] a justiciable social right' without investigating what the (legal and practical) consequences of the inclusion may be.[152] Similarly, Kothari, writing in 2007, also saw the Amendment positively, but also wrote only opaquely about its legal implications: 'While Article 45 constantly acted as an ideal for the state to strive for, the insertion of Article 21A into Part III of the

[150] Jai S. Singh, 'Expanding Horizons of Human Right to Education: Perspectives on Indian and International Vision', *Journal of the Indian Law Institute* 52, no. 1 (2010): 19–20. The PROBE team speaks of 'only one more milestone on the long road to universal elementary education', but considers it a 'very important' one (see The PROBE Team, *Public Report on Basic Education in India* [New Delhi: Oxford University Press, 1999], 141).

[151] Government of India: Ministry of Human Resource Development, Department of School Education & Literacy, 'Sarva Shiksha Abhiyan—Framework for Implementation: Based on the Right of Children to Free and Compulsory Education Act, 2009', http://mhrd.gov.in/sites/upload_files/mhrd/files/upload_document/SSA-Frame-work.pdf, accessed on 19 August 2018, 2.

[152] Padma Ramachandran and Vasantha Ramkumar, *Education in India*, 1st edition (New Delhi: National Book Trust, India, 2005), 327; Parmanand Singh, 'Promises and Perils of Public Interest Litigation in India', *Journal of the Indian Law Institute* 52, no. 2 (2010): 175; Jayna Kothari, 'Social Rights Litigation in India: Developments of the Last Decade', in *Exploring Social Rights: Between Theory and Practice*, ed. Daphne Barak-Erez and Aeyal M. Gross (Oxford, Portland, Or: Hart, 2007), 190.

Constitution clearly makes the right to free elementary education a justiciable social right.'[153]

In fact, the question concerning legal and practical consequences may also be raised in regard to the effects of the previous Supreme Court judgments. Concerning these, it had been said that giving every child the ability to approach a court with a writ of mandamus (that is, petitioning for a judicial order to a government authority) 'was a powerful weapon',[154] and that the 'courts are willing to enforce the realisation of social rights by directing financial and other resources to areas that have been identified in the Constitution', and that the government was 'forced [...] to live up to its constitutional obligations'.[155] But questions like how children may use their 'powerful weapon', what they may achieve by using them, and to what extent courts can be expected to further the implementation of the right remain unanswered. In fact, Kothari had also pointed out that in those early 'right to education decisions', the Supreme Court, after it had 'made a glorious declaration of the right to education', did not specify what measures of enforcement would make the right a reality.[156] She also notes that follow-up litigation before the constitutional amendment was only with regard to professional education and fees,[157] as *Mohini Jain* and *Unni Krishnan* had been in the first place. This is not surprising, as it is not very realistic for those children who should benefit from the right (represented by their parents) to actually approach the higher judiciary, as shall be shown in Chapter 4.

Concerning this lack of clarity, there were some critical voices, like in the PROBE Report of 1999. While the authors believe

153 At the same time, she was cautious about being optimistic about the effects of the amendment, stating that it remained to be seen 'whether the state machinery is put to work' to implement the right (see Kothari, 'Social Rights Litigation in India', 190).

154 Sripati and Thiruvengadam, 'Constitutional Amendment Making the Right to Education a Fundamental Right', 153.

155 Fons Coomans, 'Justiciability of the Right to Education', *Erasmus Law Review* 2, no. 4 (2009): 431.

156 Jayna Kothari, 'Social Rights and the Indian Constitution', *Social Justice & Global Development Journal*, no. 8 (2004).

157 Kothari, 'Social Rights and the Indian Constitution'.

that the Eighty-Sixth Amendment is important 'if only because the notion of a fundamental right has great value in overcoming the objections and excuses that are constantly invoked to continue postponing the goal of universal elementary education', they also note that a constitutional amendment '*alone* cannot make the fundamental right to education a reality. With or without the amendment, attempts to dilute the right [...] are likely to continue'.[158] Generally, though, their assessment of the effects of the amendment also seems to be more political than legal.

Dam, consequently, expressed scepticism, raising the question of how the situation of the right to education being part of the right to life and personal liberty and being a new article in the Constitution differed: 'Though novel, the essence of this explicit guarantee had already been recognised a decade earlier, when the Supreme Court declared the right to education as "implicit in" the right to "life or personal liberty".'[159] He believes that Parliament's decision to create a new article may be a sign of a 'dialogic' in between the legislature and the judiciary, but highlights that this phenomenon 'remains undertheorised' in India.[160]

Therefore, generally, the questions of how the right-bearers may benefit from their right having become a fundamental right, or how they may realistically claim it from the State, and what legal effect the constitutional amendment may have, remain open questions. However, these questions are decisive. There had already been a constitutional duty on the State to provide for free and compulsory education defined by Article 45, meaning that this aspect of Article 21A (the State's duty) is actually not a novelty. It appears that this is not clear to many observers. A significant number of policy-makers, researchers, advocacy coalitions, and NGOs and donor agencies believed that the constitutional amendment was 'a first step towards placing a legal obligation on the State'.[161]

[158] The PROBE Team, *Public Report on Basic Education in India*, 141.

[159] Shubhankar Dam, 'Right to Education in India: Horizontal Implications', *The Law Quarterly Review* 128, Part 4 (2012): 507.

[160] Dam, 'Right to Education in India', 507.

[161] See the survey of Mehendale, 'Right to Education and Constitutional Amendment', 31.

However, if one does recognize that directive principles are law, then the novelty of reading the right to education into Article 21 or creating Article 21A was that this right became justiciable, not that it constituted a duty of the State to act. If there were no benefits following from justiciability, then these steps would have been entirely unnecessary, at least from a legal point of view.

Dam, when writing about Article 21A, notes that what the article meant for children deprived of education 'was far from clear'.[162] He does, however, believe that some answers were given by the creation of the Right to Education Act that 'define[d] the substance of the right more clearly'.[163] But this leads to another open question: what would have happened if Parliament had passed legislation implementing the right to elementary education, like the Right to Education Act of 2009, without taking a first step of adding a new Article 21A. After all, this is what the State did concerning the right to food by passing the National Food Security Act of 2013. Would the situation have been any different to what it is today? If not, then one could argue that almost a decade was lost unnecessarily by first amending the Constitution in 2002 and then having the implementing act come into force only in 2010. When asked what the role was that Article 21A played, when viewed from this perspective, Kothari, speaking from the point of view of civil society groups, responded that one benefit might have been that 'it helped us get the [Right to Education] Act'.[164] This underlines the *political* significance that the constitutional amendment had, meaning that it helped the civil society to be heard with calls for new national elementary legislation. Legally, however, one may still get the impression that first creating Article 21A was unnecessary.

Still, Parliament did see a need to add the new article before drafting a Right to Education Act. Curiously, there appears to be hardly any examination of the legislature's possible motivation for passing the constitutional amendment, except for a study

[162] Dam, 'Right to Education in India', 507.

[163] Dam, 'Right to Education in India', 507.

[164] *Jayna Kothari* (Centre for Law and Policy Research, Bengaluru) in an interview with the author (October 2014).

performed by Mehendale.[165] She interviewed the former union minister for Human Resource Development, S.R. Bommai, who had been the government's driving force in introducing the 1997 bill. Bommai named his experiences in travelling the country and seeing the impacts of literacy on development, 'particularly in the state of Kerala', as one of the reasons.[166] But this only answers why he believed the State needed to focus more on education, not why elementary education needed to become a fundamental right.

Additionally, Bommai wanted to give permanence to the *Unni Krishnan* verdict.[167] As a larger bench of the Supreme Court could have later overruled *Unni Krishnan* or limited the scope of the right to education as read into the right to life and personal liberty, this is indeed one effect that the amendment had. But this does not answer the question of the practical and realistic application of a justiciable fundamental right. Interestingly, in the short period of time that the government allowed for submissions from civil society organizations and researchers concerning the 1997 bill, researchers from the University of Delhi did question why a constitutional amendment was necessary after elementary education had already been read into Article 21.[168]

Mehendale believes that 'pressure' from several directions might be responsible to a considerable extent, at least for the passage of the Eighty-Sixth Amendment in 2002, if not for introducing the 1997 bill.[169] As examples for 'pressure from the top',

[165] Mehendale, 'Right to Education and Constitutional Amendment'.

[166] Mehendale, 'Right to Education and Constitutional Amendment', 19.

[167] Mehendale, 'Right to Education and Constitutional Amendment', 19.

[168] They also suggested, among other things, that *quality* of education should become part of the justiciable fundamental right (see Mehendale, 'Right to Education and Constitutional Amendment', 21).

[169] She does note that civil society organizations and networks of NGOs—most notably the National Alliance for Fundamental Right to Education (NAFRE)—had lobbied for the 1997 Constitutional Amendment Bill in the late 1990s (see Mehendale, 'Right to Education and Constitutional Amendment', 23).

she mentions an enquiry by the UN Committee on Rights of the Child on India's education policies in 2000, a 'Children's Code Bill' prepared in 2000 by United Nations International Children's Emergency Fund (UNICEF), and the 2000 Dakar Conference on Education for All.[170] Additionally, there was pressure on the government within the country by several committees and commissions that released their reports shortly before the introduction of the bill.[171] 'Pressure from below', according to Mehendale, came from several civil society organizations, NGO networks, advocacy coalitions, and so on, that did not, however, call for any amendment to the Constitution, but for one that would enlarge the scope of *Unni Krishnan*, for instance, by extending the scope to all children from ages 0 to 18 years.[172] When it became clear that such alterations would not be made to the amendment, advocacy groups tried to urge parliamentarians to not allow the constitutional amendment to pass as it stood.[173]

To an extent, it appears that the amendment was passed in order to 'appease' the organizations and institutions exerting pressure on Indian politics. Perhaps, it was to be done quickly, so that pressure for an amendment with a larger scope would not grow.[174] One could see this as an example of a phenomenon that Conrad once described about Indian politics and its legal system. He sees a 'traditional Indian tendency' to 'consider a verbally formulated ideal to be a reality'.[175] An example he cites for this is Article 17, which

[170] Mehendale, 'Right to Education and Constitutional Amendment', 25.

[171] Mehendale, 'Right to Education and Constitutional Amendment', 24–5.

[172] Mehendale, 'Right to Education and Constitutional Amendment', 24–5.

[173] Mehendale, 'Right to Education and Constitutional Amendment', 26.

[174] See Mehendale, 'Right to Education and Constitutional Amendment', 32 et seq.

[175] '[Eine] traditionell ausgeprägte indische Neigung, das sprachliche Ideal für Wirklichkeit zu halten' (see Conrad, 'Zukunft des indischen Rechtsstaates', 136).

states that '"Untouchability" is abolished'. According to him, in India, one often hears that this phenomenon of caste-based discrimination is truly abolished in reality because the Constitution states that it is.[176]

Conrad's assessment is somewhat exaggerated, as it is questionable whether one can really speak of a 'traditional Indian tendency' to this effect in such general terms. Still, scholars' assessment of Article 21A and the Right to Education Act does show a similar line of reasoning. Concerning the right to education, scholars note that the right 'has *become a reality* by the Right to Free and Compulsory Education Act, 2009' (emphasis added), or that education has 'become a fundamental right',[177] without answering, and most of the time not even discussing, the question of how this duty may be enforced in practice, and what obligation the State has to provide measures of enforcement. Perhaps this sentiment also explains why Article 21A, unlike the original Article 45, does not include a time limit. It declares that elementary education 'is now a fundamental right', so a time frame for it to become effective is no longer required. According to this understanding, it already *is* effective, whatever that actually means in practice.

In 1999, the Indian sociologist Béteille commented on the proposal of the constitutional amendment by stating that in India, '[e]conomists seek to create their utopias through planning, lawyers through legislation'.[178] According to him, in the early decades following Independence, policy-makers believed that the transformation of society would be possible through economic planning, while '[n]ow the spotlight is on "rights" rather than "models", and judges, advocates and jurists are joined by social scientists and

[176] 'Bekanntestes Beispiel dieser Neigung ist die in Indien häufig gehörte Behauptung, die Unberührbarkeit sei abgeschafft—weil die Verfassung [...] diese Abschaffung [...] dekretiert' (see Conrad, 'Die Zukunft des indischen Rechtsstaates', 136).

[177] See, for instance, Ramachandran and Ramkumar, *Education in India*, 327; Singh, 'Promises and Perils of Public Interest Litigation in India', 175; Kothari, 'Social Rights Litigation in India', 190.

[178] André Béteille, 'Record of Rights: The Marie-Antoinette Solution', *Times of India*, 28 January 1999.

activists who all demand the creation and expansion of rights'.[179] Their belief, Béteille warns, 'may turn out no less deluding' than the one in planning.[180] He points out that children who are in practice deprived of education will find 'small consolation' in the fact that they have a right to education, and that judges and jurists should argue that rights must not be created unless they are enforced.[181] Otherwise, he writes, the State will merely show a similar attitude as the one expressed by the 'They don't have bread? Let them eat cake' comment that is often ascribed to Marie Antoinette.[182] Consequently, he names the inclusion of rights into the Constitution the 'Marie Antoinette solution'.

Still, the fundamental right to elementary education is now part of the constitutional text, and the fact that there is one explicitly justiciable socio-economic right might have a significance that goes beyond mere symbolism. Whatever the motivation for including Article 21A in the constitutional text may have been (even if the intention was only to symbolically declare that the State takes the matter of elementary education seriously, or to appease groups calling for State action), the provision is now part of the constitutional text, and the judiciary is called upon to adjudicate on it when it is approached. Consequently, the Constitution gives a promise to the people that they may effectively claim their right (for their children) from the State.

The following chapters shall analyse what the contents of Article 21A may be, and how that promise may be fulfilled.

179 Béteille, 'Record of Rights'.
180 Béteille, 'Record of Rights'.
181 Béteille, 'Record of Rights'.
182 Béteille, 'Record of Rights'.

# 3

# Article 21A

## Clues for Its Content in International Law and Socio-Economic Rights Adjudication in India

The present chapter shall assess what the contents of the right to education in India may be. It shall also consider some clues for what legal effects the courts may give to the right in practice. So far, there has been comparatively little adjudication on Article 21A and the Right to Education Act. Therefore, the international discussion on the right to education, as well as socio-economic rights in general, may offer some guidance. As far as socio-economic rights in general are concerned, the experience with and discussion around adjudication in India will also be considered.

The aim of this chapter is to show different parameters that function as waypoints for what the content of the right to education may be. Based on this, one could ascertain how Indian courts in particular may be expected to adjudicate the right. However, this chapter shall show that without the courts having developed more basic precedent or case law, it is difficult to ascertain what the contents of Article 21A are. Based on the issues mentioned in Chapter 1, one may easily identify measures that one may find politically desirable. But it is difficult to ascertain to what extent

Article 21A creates a constitutional obligation on the State to take these measures.

Ultimately, it is up to the executive and legislature to decide which measures shall be taken. Whenever appropriate measures are not taken, it is the judiciary's task to decide to what extent it is competent to give specific orders to the other branches of power for such measures.

However, there is one specific obligation that Article 21A imposes on the State. The fact that the article is placed in Part III of the Constitution requires that the right be *justiciable*, meaning that the State must provide the right-bearers with means to enforce their right against the State. This realization shall be the foundation for the following chapters (Chapters 4, 5, and 6), in which the possibilities for effective adjudication and the potential results thereof shall be looked at in more detail.

Before coming to this conclusion, this chapter shall examine international human rights obligations and what contents for the right to education may be deduced from them.

The next part of this chapter shall summarize the discussion around the adjudication of socio-economic rights in India in general. In doing so, that part will also examine recent arguments stating that the remedies that the courts have given are actually a lot less far-reaching than commonly believed. It shall be shown that such judicial restraint is not permissible when adjudicating the right to education. The existence of Article 21A obliges the courts to award more extensive remedies than they have done with other socio-economic rights (which are not part of the Constitution's fundamental rights catalogue) in the past.

Finally, this part shall also show that the content of the right is not merely defined by the Right to Education Act, as Article 21A itself includes certain benchmarks against which the Act must be measured. Importantly, as private education has become increasingly significant in India in the last few decades, the question arises whether or not and to what extent Article 21A may have 'horizontal' implications as well. This question will be dealt with in the last section of this part.

The chapter goes on to discuss that while there has already been some adjudication on Article 21A since its inclusion in the constitutional text, this has only provided few answers concerning its content. Still, it is ultimately the courts' task to determine the content of the right.

However, in order for the judiciary to fulfil this task, it has to be approached to provide remedies for possible violations of the right in the first place. As the final part of this chapter shall show, the fact that Article 21A allows right-bearers to approach the courts for its implementation is actually the single most important aspect that can be determined without further development of precedent concerning the other parts of its content.

## International Obligations

India is a signatory state to several international human rights treaties, also ones that include the right to education.[1] Since the era of economic liberalization has begun in the 1990s, international law has become of additional importance. This is also due to the fact that international donors, such as the International Monetary Fund (IMF) and the World Bank, have exerted pressure for India to adhere to international provisions, also as far as 'good governance' is concerned.[2] One may specifically note the Millennium Development Goals (MDG) which, as mentioned in Chapter 1, have also played an important role for India's education policy, including the creation of the Sarva Shiksha Abhiyan, which was notably financed by the World Bank, among other international donors.[3]

[1] India has signed and ratified the International Covenant on Civil and Political Rights (ICCPR), the International Covenant on Economic, Social and Cultural Rights (ICESCR), the Convention on the Rights of the Child, the International Convention on the Elimination of All Forms of Racial Discrimination, as well as several other human rights treaties (see http://indicators.ohchr.org, accessed on 15 August 2018).

[2] See Adrian Leftwich, 'Governance, Democracy and Development in the Third World', *Third World Quarterly* 14, no. 3 (2007); Michel Chossudovsky, 'India under IMF Rule', *Economic & Political Weekly* 28, no. 10 (1993).

[3] See Ellie Meleisea, *Promising EFA Practices in the Asia-Pacific Region: Sarva Shiksha Abhiyan Case Study* (Paris: The United Nations

For a long time, the international debate focused on whether or not the obligations imposed on the signatory states differed according to the kind of right or 'category' that the given right belongs to. It was argued that the category had implications for how strongly states should be bound by these rights. This differentiation was also the guiding philosophy behind the creation of the two separate catalogues of fundamental rights and directive principles in the Indian Constitution, as described in Chapter 2. The right to education is generally seen as a 'socio-economic right'.

Internationally as well as nationally,[4] the previously dominant view on civil and political rights and socio-economic rights was that while civil and political (or 'first-generation') rights ought to be justiciable, socio-economic rights should not, or perhaps even cannot be. Socio-economic rights were therefore seen as policy directives rather than 'hard' legal rights.[5] At an international level,

---

Educational, Scientific and Cultural Organization, 2015); http://web.worldbank.org/archive/website01291/WEB/0__CO-49.HTM, accessed on 12 August 2018.

[4] Up until the middle of the twentieth century, justiciable social and economic rights were not part of national constitutions. Early examples of constitutions that listed them as non-justiciable rights are the German Weimar Constitution of 1919 (see, for instance, the State duty to provide welfare for mothers and families with multiple children, Article 119, the duty to provide free education, Articles 143, 145, the duty to provide a health insurance system, Article 161, and so on), and the Constitution of Ireland of 1937 with its catalogue of directive principles of Social Policy (Article 45 et seq.), which were also explicitly not justiciable. It was a commonly held belief in the earlier post-World War II period that socio-economic rights ought not to be enforced by the courts, which was perhaps most famously expressed by Isaiah Berlin in his 1958 lecture 'Two Concepts of Liberty', in which he argued that '[y]ou lack political liberty or freedom only if you are prevented from attaining a goal by human beings. Mere incapacity to attain a goal is not lack of political freedom' (see Isaiah Berlin, *Four Essays on Liberty* [London, New York: Oxford University Press, 1969], 122).

[5] Notably, however, Article 2 of Protocol No. 1 to the European Convention of Human Rights guarantees the right to education. Other rights of that Protocol are 'classic' civil and political rights, that is, the right

the fact that human rights are most prominently listed in two separate treaties, the International Covenant on Civil and Political Rights (ICCPR) and the International Covenant on Economic, Social and Cultural Rights (ICESCR), and the fact that the latter declares that states have a duty to 'achieve progressively' the realization of the Covenant's rights (Article 2(1)), rather than speaking of an immediate realization, is often seen as an expression of this view.[6] The ICCPR does not have any provision that declares such a limitation.[7] This would also mean that the right to education,

---

to property (Article 1) and the right to free elections (Article 3). However, this Article is worded 'negatively' ('no person shall be denied the right to education'). Also, the European Court of Human Rights generally interprets the right as one giving equal/non-discriminatory *access* to *existing* educational institutions, not a right against the State obliging the latter to create new educational institutions (see Klaus Dieter Beiter, *The Protection of the Right to Education by International Law: Including a Systematic Analysis of Article 13 of the International Covenant on Economic, Social, and Cultural Rights* [Leiden, Boston: Martinus Nijhoff Publishers, 2006], 163).

[6] Vierdag argued that 'only enforceable rights will be considered as "real", legal, rights', and uses Article 2 of the ICESCR to illustrate that this qualification cannot (yet) be given to the ICESCR rights: 'It appears from the instrument as a whole that "recognition" [of rights] is exactly what this word means, and nothing more; that an eventual "assurance" and "guarantee" *are dependent on steps that must first be taken*' (see E.W. Vierdag, 'The Legal Nature of the Rights Granted by the International Covenant on Economic, Social and Cultural Rights', *Netherlands Yearbook of International Law*, 1978, 76–7, 80).

[7] However, as the CESCR General Comment No. 3 notes, there still are immediate obligations arising from the ICESCR: '[I]t also imposes various obligations which are of immediate effect. [...] One of these [...] is the "undertaking to guarantee" that relevant rights "will be exercised without discrimination..." [...] The other is the undertaking in article 2 (1) "to take steps", which in itself, is not qualified or limited by other considerations' (see 'CESCR General Comment No. 3: The Nature of States Parties' Obligations [Art. 2, Para. 1, of the Covenant]', Office of the High Commissioner for Human Rights, 1990, http://www.refworld.org/docid/4538838e10.html, accessed on 23 February 2019, 1, 2). Also see paragraph 21 of the Limburg Principles, available at Committee on

which is part of the ICESCR, would impose no immediate obligations on states parties.

There were various reasons for understanding civil and political rights and socio-economic rights as two separate 'concepts' or 'categories' of rights, and for arguing that the latter category ought to be non-justiciable.[8] One argument is that adjudicating socio-economic rights means that courts would effectively make policy decisions that should be left to the discretion of the legislative power, especially considering the higher democratic legitimacy that legislatures have.[9] Socio-economic rights, it is argued, are too unspecific, which means that legislation is required to define the scope and the manners in which the State should implement the right.[10] Another aspect is the fact that implementing

---

Economic, Social and Cultural Rights, 'Substantive Issues Arising in the Implementation of the International Covenant on Economic, Social and Cultural Rights: Day of General Discussion Organized in Cooperation with the World Intellectual Property Organization (WIPO)', 2000, https://web.archive.org/web/20151004182847/http://www.unhchr.ch/tbs/doc.nsf/898586b1dc7b4043c1256a450044f331/6b748989d76d2bb8c12569970 0500e17/$FILE/G0044704.pdf accessed on 19 August 2018, which states that '[u]nder no circumstances shall this be interpreted as implying for States the right to defer indefinitely efforts to ensure full realization. On the contrary all States parties have the obligation to begin immediately to take steps to fulfil their obligations under the Covenant'.

[8] For an overview of the development of the debate, see Henry J. Steiner, Philip Alston, and Ryan Goodman, *International Human Rights in Context: Law, Politics, Morals; Text and Materials*, 3rd edition (Oxford: Oxford University Press, 2008), 263 et seq.

[9] For instance, Vierdag argued that '[t]he expenditure necessary for every addition is essentially a matter of economic, social and cultural priorities. Consequently, the implementation of these provisions is a political matter, not a matter of law, and hence not a matter of rights' (see Vierdag, 'The Legal Nature of the Rights Granted', 103).

[10] Cross writes that '[w]hile all language is somewhat ambiguous, positive rights would suffer from particular indeterminacy. The reason for this indeterminacy is that such rights are consequentialist, requiring the judiciary to create a program that achieves a given result' (see Frank B. Cross, 'The Error of Positive Rights', *UCLA Law Review* 48 [2001]: 901).

socio-economic rights requires that a substantial amount of funds be allocated for the implementation process. Money is needed so that schools can be built, so that housing or food can be supplied, and so on. As funds are naturally limited—especially in economically developing countries—implementation of socio-economic rights requires that decisions be made as far as priorities are concerned. Therefore, it is argued that these decisions cannot (and should not) be made by courts that decide on a case-by-case basis without previously making broader policy decisions as far as priorities are concerned.[11]

Finally, it is argued that even if one does believe that giving so much discretion to courts is justified, then the judiciary will still be ineffective in fulfilling the promises of socio-economic rights, as they lack the capacity to design greater implementation policies and/or to supervise their execution.[12]

However, counterarguments have been made against these points of criticism.[13] For instance, as far as the point that socio-economic rights are too 'vague' is concerned, one may argue that this is not an exclusive feature of socio-economic rights. Rather, this point could be raised against the justiciability of all rights,

[11] For instance, Cross points out that courts, unlike legislatures, can only take up issues that are brought before them by plaintiffs (which, he notes, will also mainly benefit those who can afford approaching the courts) (see Cross, 'The Error of Positive Rights', 901: 880 et seq.). Ackerman states that '[e]ven if a constitutional court were disposed to take such textual guarantees seriously, the judges would lack the remedial capacity to order the big budgetary appropriations necessary to transform "positive rights" into social realities', and also warns that 'the judges' failure to enforce positive rights may demoralize their efforts to protect more traditional rights'. He then, however, discusses the possibility of a 'distributive justice branch' of government (see Bruce Ackerman, 'The New Separation of Powers', *Harvard Law Review* 113, no. 3 [2000]: 721–3).

[12] See, for instance, Lon L. Fuller, 'The Forms and Limits of Adjudication', *Harvard Law Review* 92, no. 2 (1978): 393 et seq.

[13] See Malcolm Langford, 'The Justiciability of Social Rights: From Practice to Theory', in Langford, *Social Rights Jurisprudence: Emerging Trends in International and Comparative Law*. Cambridge, New York: Cambridge University Press, 2008, 30 et seq. for an overview.

or even against law in general.[14] One may also fundamentally question the categorization of socio-economic rights as 'positive rights' (to be provided by the State) and civil and political rights as 'negative rights' (meaning that individuals may defend themselves against intrusions by the State).[15]

Rights—both civil and political and social ones—it is argued, can have a negative as well as a positive scope. For instance, there can be an obligation on the State to not interfere with resources belonging to a collective like indigenous populations, meaning that this right of the indigenous people to such resources, commonly understood as a socio-economic right, has a negative scope in this regard.[16] On the other hand, the right to life, commonly understood as a civil and political right, may call for 'positive' State intervention in cases of high child mortality because of malnutrition, and the right to equal access to justice—as part of the right to equality, or also the right to a fair trial—may require that the State provide legal aid.[17] The 'institution' of civil and political rights in

[14] Endicott argues that '[l]aw is necessarily vague' (see Timothy A.O. Endicott, 'The Impossibility of the Rule of Law', *Oxford Journal of Legal Studies* 19, no. 1 [1999]: 6).

[15] Eide believes that this is a 'common misunderstanding' (see Asbjørn Eide, 'Economic, Social and Cultural Rights as Human Rights', in Asbjørn Eide, Catarina Krause, and Allan Rosas, *Economic, Social and Cultural Rights A Textbook*. 2nd edition [Dordrecht: Martinus Nijhoff, 2001], 23). A very clear distinction between negative and positive rights was attempted, for instance, by Fried (see Charles Fried, *Right and Wrong* [Cambridge, Mass.: Harvard University Press, 1978], 110 et seq.). Fabre holds on to the distinction, but argues that this does not mean that one needs to reject social rights as 'rights' (see Cécile Fabre, *Social Rights under the Constitution: Government and the Decent Life* [Oxford, New York: Clarendon Press; Oxford University Press, 2000], 41 et seq.). Fredman argues that 'all rights can be seen to give rise to a range of duties, including both duties of restraint and positive duties' (see Sandra Fredman, *Human Rights Transformed: Positive Rights and Positive Duties* [Oxford, New York: Oxford University Press, 2008], 65 et seq.).

[16] Eide, 'Economic, Social and Cultural Rights as Human Rights', in Eide, Krause, and Rosas, *Economic, Social and Cultural Rights*, 24.

[17] Eide, 'Economic, Social and Cultural Rights as Human Rights', in Eide, Krause, and Rosas, *Economic, Social and Cultural Rights*, 24. Holmes

general may often require some sort of 'positive' State intervention, and, therefore, involve policy decisions concerning priorities and allocation of funds. In order for citizens to enjoy these rights, the State needs to 'establish a system of courts, to train police and other public officials, and to establish a system of safeguards against potential abuses of rights by state officials themselves'.[18]

Therefore, at the very least, the distinction between 'first and second-generation rights' cannot be drawn as clearly as critics have often suggested, and at least some of the arguments against justiciability of socio-economic rights could also be raised against first-generation rights. Consequently, it is now more common to see all categories or generations of human rights as 'indivisible'.[19]

---

and Sunstein provide similar arguments and come to the conclusion that 'all rights are positive' (see Stephen Holmes and Cass R. Sunstein, *The Cost of Rights: Why Liberty Depends on Taxes*, 1st edition [New York: W.W. Norton, 1999], 35–48). Scheinin speaks of a 'social dimension' of the right to a free trial, and cites the European Court of Human Rights (ECHR) case of *Case of Airey* v. *Ireland* (European Court of Human Rights, 9 October 1979), http://hudoc.echr.coe.int/eng?i=001-57420#{"itemid":["001-57420"6]}, accessed on 19 August 2018, as an example (see Martin Scheinin, 'Economic and Social Rights as Legal Rights', in Eide, Krause, and Rosas, *Economic, Social and Cultural Rights*, 34).

[18] Philip Alston, 'Development and the Rule of Law: Prevention Versus Cure as a Human Strategy', Development, *Human Rights and the Rule of Law*, Vol. 31 (1981): 33–108, at p. 51.

[19] Scott and Scheinin argue that because of the interdependence of both 'categories' or rights, civil and political rights need to be interpreted extensively in order to incorporate socio-economic rights into them, such as into the right to life, as it has happened in India (see Craig Scott, 'Interdependence and Permeability of Human Rights Norms: Towards a Partial Fusion of the International Covenants on Human Rights', *Osgoode Hall Law Journal* 27, no. 3 [1989], http://digitalcommons.osgoode.yorku.ca/cgi/viewcontent.cgi?article=1791&context=ohlj, accessed on 19 August 2018, and Scheinin, 'Economic and Social Rights as Legal Rights', in Eide, Krause, and Rosas, *Economic, Social and Cultural Rights*, 40–1). Steiner, Alston, and Goodman also name the developments in India as an example for how content may be given to socio-economic rights (see Henry J. Steiner, Philip Alston, and Ryan Goodman, *International Human*

The right to education actually illustrates this rather well. As General Comment 11 of the Committee on Economic, Social and Cultural Rights dealing with the right to education notes, it may be understood as an economic, as a social and a cultural right, and as a civil and political right all at the same time, 'since it is central to the full and effective realization of those [other] rights as well. In this respect, the right to education epitomizes the indivisibility and interdependence of all human rights'.[20]

More recent human rights treaties like the Convention on the Rights of the Child (CRC) show that international law does not clearly differentiate between 'first and second-generation rights' anymore. The CRC includes civil and political as well as socio-economic rights side by side,[21] without defining them as separate categories,[22] and it also does not contain a 'progressive realization' for socio-economic rights clause as the ICESCR does.[23] Also, as there is now a fair amount of experience with adjudicating socio-economic rights, there are relatively few voices that argue against the possibility of their justiciability in its entirety. The focus of the discussion now is rather to what degree they should and can be justiciable.[24]

This question shall thus also be the focus of this part. After naming the treaties and provisions that concern the right to education,

---

*Rights in Context: Law, Politics, Morals; Text and Materials*, 3rd edition [Oxford: Oxford University Press, 2008], 321 et seq.).

[20] Committee on Economic, Social and Cultural Rights, 'General Comment 11: Plans of Action for Primary Education (Twentieth session, 1999)', U.N. Doc.E/1992/23 (1999), 2.

[21] See, for instance, Articles 6(1) (right to life), 13 (inter alia, freedom of expression), 24 (right to health), 28 (right to education).

[22] See Eide, 'Economic, Social and Cultural Rights as Human Rights', in Eide, Krause, and Rosas, *Economic, Social and Cultural Rights*, 11.

[23] See Eide, 'Economic, Social and Cultural Rights as Human Rights', in Eide, Krause, and Rosas, *Economic, Social and Cultural Rights*, 22.

[24] See Langford, 'The Justiciability of Social Rights', 29 et seq; Martin Scheinin, 'Justiciability and the Indivisibility of Human Rights', in *The Road to a Remedy: Current Issues in the Litigation of Economic, Social, and Cultural Rights*, ed. John Squires, Malcolm Langford, and Bret Thiele (Sydney, NSW, Geneva, Switzerland: Australian Human Rights Centre, University of New South Wales; Centre for Housing Rights and Evictions, 2005).

the different doctrines that have been developed in order to ascertain the contents of (socio-economic) rights shall be introduced briefly. Then, the focus shall be on the contents the right to education may have in particular, with the emphasis being on elementary education. The final part will illustrate whether or not the current state of elementary education in India, as described in Chapter 1, may be measured against those international human rights standards and to what extent it does or does not live up to them.

## Relevant Treaties

There are several international declarations and treaties that refer to and/or are relevant to the right to education. The (not legally binding) Universal Declaration of Human Rights (UDHR) in Article 26 states that everyone has the right to education, that education 'shall be free, at least in the elementary and fundamental stages' and that it shall be 'directed to the full development of the human personality and to the strengthening of respect for human rights and fundamental freedoms'. Also, parents shall 'have a prior right to choose the kind of education that shall be given to their children'.

The CRC mentions education in several provisions. Most importantly, Article 28 states that 'States Parties recognize the right of the child to education [...] they shall, in particular [...] [m]ake primary education compulsory and available free to all'. Article 29 describes what goals education shall have; inter alia '[t]he development of the child's personality, talents and mental and physical abilities to their fullest potential; [...] [t]he development of respect for human rights and fundamental freedoms', and so on. Furthermore, the International Convention on the Elimination of All Forms of Racial Discrimination in Article 5(v) states that everyone shall have '[t]he right to education and training' without discrimination.

The most comprehensive protection of the right to education, however, is given by the ICESCR.[25] Article 13 declares that

[25] This assessment is expressed by Kalantry, Getgen, and Koh (see Sital Kalantry, Jocelyn E. Getgen, and Steven A. Koh, 'Enhancing Enforcement of Economic, Social, and Cultural Rights Using Indicators: A Focus on

the states parties 'recognize the right of everyone to education'. Articles 2(2) and 3 of the ICESCR state that 'rights enunciated in the present Covenant will be exercised without discrimination', meaning that education must be accessible to all citizens in a non-discriminatory manner. Article 13 also sets some standards for the contents of education. For instance, it shall be 'directed to the full development of the human personality and the sense of its dignity'. More specifically, it states that '[p]rimary education shall be compulsory and available free to all' (Article 13(2)(a)). Article 14 creates an obligation on each state party that has not been able to secure free and compulsory primary education to create a 'detailed plan of action for the progressive implementation'.

## International Doctrines Facilitating Definitions of the Content of Rights

As it is commonly the case with bills of rights, the international provisions on the right to education are worded quite unspecifically. As the Optional Protocol to the ICESCR, which creates complaint and inquiry mechanisms for the Covenant,[26] has only entered into force quite recently (in 2013), and as it has only been ratified by relatively few countries[27] (with India not being one of the signatories), there is not yet any 'case law' on the right to education under the ICESCR. Thus, its contents may best be assessed with the help of doctrines that have been developed for social rights in general.

---

the Right to Education in the ICESCR', *Human Rights Quarterly* 32, no. 2 [2010]: 261). Also see Beiter, who writes that Articles 13 and 14 of the ICESCR constitute 'a codification of the right to education in international law', and that Article 13 'may arguably be viewed as the most important formulation of the right to education in an international agreement' (see Beiter, *The Protection of the Right to Education by International Law*, 86, 341).

[26] Article 2 allows 'individuals or groups of individuals [...] claiming to be victims of a violation' to submit communications to the Committee on Economic, Social and Cultural Rights.

[27] 23 State Parties and 26 Signatories as of 15 August 2018 (see http://indicators.ohchr.org, accessed on 15 August 2018).

## *Respect, Protect, Fulfil*

Scholars describe that rights create obligations on states 'to respect, protect and fulfil'.[28] States must *respect* an individual's resources and their freedom to find means to accumulate those resources. They must also *protect* the freedom of action and the use of resources 'against other, more assertive or aggressive subjects'. Finally, states also have the obligation to *fulfil* socio-economic rights 'by way of facilitation or direct provision'.[29]

The UN Committee on Economic, Social and Cultural Rights (CESCR) has adopted this idea in its General Comment No. 12 on the ICESCR, as well as in subsequent comments.[30] In Comment

[28] Eide describes how that idea has evolved (see Asbjørn Eide, 'State Obligations Revisited', in *Food and Human Rights in Development*, ed. Wenche B. Eide [Antwerpen: Intersentia, 2007], 146).

[29] Eide, 'Economic, Social and Cultural Rights as Human Rights', in Eide, Krause, and Rosas, *Economic, Social and Cultural Rights*, 23–4.

[30] Committee on Economic, Social and Cultural Rights, 'General Comment 12, Right to Adequate Food (Twentieth session, 1999)' U.N. Doc. E/C.12/1999/5 (1999), 15. General Comments are issued 'with a view to assisting the States parties in fulfilling their reporting obligations', that is, they are supposed to inform states how they should assess their own rights implementation when reporting on the status of the rights to the Committee (see United Nations, Committee on Economic Social and Cultural Rights, 'Report on the Forty Second and Forty Third Sessions [4–22 May 2009, 2–20 November 2009]' [2010], 16). The Comments are not legally binding, but do have 'considerable legal weight' (Beiter, *The Protection of the Right to Education by International Law*, 365), as they interpret provisions and formulate the obligations flowing from them similar to how a judiciary would: Craven speaks of a practice that 'would be more closely associated with bodies that exercise quasi-judicial functions than with ones concerned merely with the provision of advice and assistance' (see Matthew Craven, 'Towards an Unofficial Petition Procedure: A Review on the Role of the UN Committee on Economic, Social and Cultural Rights', in *Social Rights as Human Rights: A European Challenge*, ed. Krzysztof Drzewicki, Catarina Krause, and Allan Rosas [Turku/Åbo, Finland: Institute for Human Rights, Åbo Akademi University, 1994], 101). Also, the fact that states parties participate in the supervisory process of the ICESCR may be seen as a reflection of a 'state

No. 12, which deals with the contents of the right to food, the Committee writes that the obligation to *respect* means that states should not take measures that result in preventing access to adequate food.[31] The obligation to *fulfil* (or *facilitate*), on the other hand, means that states must strengthen 'access to and utilization of resources and means to ensure their livelihood', and that states may 'have the obligation to *fulfil* (*provide*) that right directly' if an individual or group is unable to provide themselves with adequate food by using the means available to them.[32]

## *Obligations of Conduct and of Result*

Another doctrine developed at the international level is to differentiate between 'obligations of conduct' and 'of result': one may take the view that rights only impose an obligation on a state to achieve a certain situation or result, irrespective of what means it uses for that end.[33] Therefore, Article 2(1) of the ICESCR may be read in a way that the states parties have full discretion to choose

---

practice' defining international law, as described by Article 31(3)(b) of the Vienna Convention on the Law of Treaties. For this argument concerning the role of General Comments, see Beiter, *The Protection of the Right to Education by International Law*, 365.

[31] Committee on Economic, Social and Cultural Rights, 'General Comment 12 (Twentieth session, 1999)', 15.

[32] Committee on Economic, Social and Cultural Rights, 'General Comment 12 (Twentieth session, 1999)', 15.

[33] In 1977, the International Law Commission set out to draft general rules on state responsibilities for internationally wrongful acts. In its report on its Twenty-Ninth Session, it described, when discussing the draft Article 21, the idea of an obligation of 'result', noting that such obligations are 'much more common in international law than in internal law': 'obligations "of result" [...] do not require a particular course of conduct on the part of the State, or, in other words, a course of conduct on the part of specified State organs', International Law Commission, 'Report of the International Law Commission on Its Twenty Ninth Session: Yearbook of the International Law Commission', Vol. 2, International Law Commission, 1977, 19.

the measures they employ in order to achieve the result of each of the rights of the Covenant.[34] However, this view is especially problematic concerning the positive scope of socio-economic rights. The ICESCR states that the 'result' of each right is supposed to be 'achieved progressively'. If states then are entirely free concerning the choice of means to achieve these ends, there would be 'little basis upon which to judge whether or not they were acting in good faith'.[35]

Therefore, it appears more adequate that the ICESCR should be read in a way that it also includes obligations of conduct. Hence, it gives directions to states parties concerning what methods they may employ for achieving the results, at least to a certain extent.

Consequently, the CESCR has clarified in General Comment 3 that states' obligations include both obligations of conduct as well as obligations of result.[36] The Comment clarifies that the term 'tak[ing] steps' in Article 2(1) of the ICESCR is to be understood in a way that 'steps should be deliberate, concrete and targeted as clearly as possible towards meeting the obligations recognized in the Covenant'. Legislation 'is highly desirable and in some cases even indispensable', with the case of education being one of

[34] Consequently, on those articles, the International Law Commission writes:

> There can be no doubt that, in these cases, legislative means are expressly indicated [...] as being the most normal and appropriate for achieving the purposes on the Covenant [...] though recourse to such means is not specifically or exclusively required. The State is free to employ some other means if it so desires, provided that those means also enable it to achieve *in concreto* the full realization of the individual rights.

See International Law Commission, 'Report of the International Law Commission on Its Twenty Ninth Session', 20–1.

[35] Matthew C.R. Craven, *The International Covenant on Economic, Social, and Cultural Rights: A Perspective on its Development* (Oxford: Clarendon Press, 1995), 107.

[36] Committee on Economic, Social and Cultural Rights, 'General Comment 3, The Nature of States Parties' Obligations (Fifth session, 1990)' U.N. Doc. E/1991/23, 1.

those instances.[37] As Article 2(1) speaks of 'all appropriate means', the 'obligation of conduct' also includes other measures in addition to legislation, and the Committee believes that it has the authority to assess the appropriateness of the measures taken.[38] Among measures that may be taken in addition to legislation, the Comment also explicitly names 'the provision of judicial remedies with respects to rights which may, in accordance with the national legal system, be considered justiciable'.[39]

Even with the Committee having clarified its view, subsequently, there has been confusion considering the distinction between the two categories of obligations in both scholarly work and reports.[40] Therefore, one may argue that it might be sensible to give up the distinction altogether and to recognize that the rights of the Covenant are ultimately '"hybrids" of both kinds of obligations'.[41] The Committee has, in fact, itself not made the distinction in its comments after General Comment No. 3.[42]

[37] The right to education is named explicitly as an example for this view in Committee on Economic, Social and Cultural Rights, 'General Comment 3 (Fifth session, 1990)', 2, 3.

[38] '[T]he phrase "by all appropriate means" must be given its full and natural meaning. While each State party must decide for itself which means are the most appropriate [...] the "appropriateness" of the means chosen will not always be self-evident. It is therefore desirable that States parties' reports should indicate [...] also the basis on which [the measures] are considered to be the most "appropriate" [...] The ultimate determination as to whether all appropriate measures have been taken remains one for the Committee to make' (see Committee on Economic, Social and Cultural Rights, 'General Comment 3 [Fifth session, 1990]', 8).

[39] Committee on Economic, Social and Cultural Rights, 'General Comment 3 (Fifth session, 1990)', 5.

[40] See Malcolm Langford and Jeff A. King, 'Committee on Economic, Social and Cultural Rights', in Langford, *Social Rights Jurisprudence*, 483.

[41] M. Magdalena Sepúlveda Carmona, *The Nature of the Obligations under the International Covenant on Economic, Social, and Cultural Rights*, Vol. 18 (Antwerpen, New York: Intersentia, 2003), 195.

[42] Sepúlveda Carmona, *The Nature of the Obligations*, 195. The idea of 'hybrid' obligations was first raised by Alston and Quinn, who argue that if the text of a rights provision is 'silent on the concrete steps to be taken', then the rights' obligations are 'obligations of result in the sense

Whether the distinction is made or not, it is clear that the rights are meant to be understood in a way that the signatory states have to strive towards a certain goal for each right, and that the 'steps' that they take for their 'progressive achievement' may be scrutinized as well when assessing whether or not a state is fulfilling its duties under the Covenant.

### *Principles of Progressive Realization and Non-Retrogression*

Another doctrine is the one of 'progressive realization' of rights. General Comment 3 clarifies that the obligation to 'undertake to take steps [...] to the maximum of its available resources [...] by all appropriate means' includes an obligation on the states to act *immediately.*[43] This follows from the wording '*to undertake to take* steps'

---

that states must match their performance with their objective capabilities. They are loose obligations of conduct in the sense that states are obliged to take active, though largely unspecified, steps towards their satisfaction'. The rights are necessarily hybrids

> due to the fact that the concept of 'progressive achievement' mandates the existence of an ongoing process of development the adequacy of which is loosely controlled by norms deduced from a state's objectives capabilities. The existence of such a process or course of conducts is, in other words, a necessary but not a sufficient element of the full satisfaction of state obligations under the Covenant.

See Philip Alston and Gerard Quinn, 'The Nature and Scope of States Parties' Obligations under the International Covenant on Economic, Social and Cultural Rights', *Human Rights Quarterly* 9, no. 2 (1987): 185. Similarly, Craven notes that even if obligations primarily following from the ICESCR are obligations of results, there is still an immediate duty for states parties to take immediate steps towards those results, and these immediate steps in themselves are an obligation of conduct: 'In cases of obligations of conduct, there will often be an objective towards which that conduct is aimed. Similarly, obligations of results will invariably require a specific course of action' (see Craven, *The International Covenant on Economic, Social, and Cultural Rights*, 107).

[43] Committee on Economic, Social and Cultural Rights, 'General Comment 3 (Fifth session, 1990)', 1.

in Article 2(1), which means that some sort of action must be taken immediately, even though 'the full realization of the relevant rights may be achieved progressively'.[44] In other words, states parties are under 'an obligation to move as expeditiously and effectively as possible' towards full realization of the rights in question.[45]

What measures must be taken immediately and what measures can follow is, of course, the next question that may be up for debate. In General Comment 12 on the right to adequate food, the Committee acknowledges that the Covenant obliges states to take some measures immediately while others are 'more of a long-term character'.[46] Problematically, because of this 'dichotomy', states may find excuses to refrain from taking immediate action altogether.[47] However, even if a state may not be required 'to realise the *full entitlement*' of a right immediately, 'in neither case is it entitled to not act at all'.[48] If one combines the principle of progressive realization with the 'respect, protect, fulfil' doctrine, then one may argue that such duties that follow from the obligations to respect and protect call for immediate action.[49]

As far as adoption of legislation is concerned, one may argue that this should be considered to be an immediate obligation,[50] as

[44] Committee on Economic, Social and Cultural Rights, 'General Comment 3 (Fifth session, 1990)', 2.

[45] Committee on Economic, Social and Cultural Rights, 'General Comment 3 (Fifth session, 1990)', 9.

[46] Committee on Economic, Social and Cultural Rights, 'General Comment 12 (Twentieth session, 1999)', 16.

[47] Langford and King, 'Committee on Economic, Social and Cultural Rights', 487.

[48] Langford and King, 'Committee on Economic, Social and Cultural Rights', 487.

[49] Langford and King, 'Committee on Economic, Social and Cultural Rights', 487.

[50] Langford and King, 'Committee on Economic, Social and Cultural Rights', 487. They also cite Sepúlveda Carmona, who argues that there is an immediate obligation to pass legislation to eradicate child labour and to establish a minimum age for work, to protect the right to form and join trade unions and the right to strike, and to pass anti-discrimination legislation to protect women (citing articles 10(3), 8, 2(2) and 3 of the ICESCR) (see Sepúlveda Carmona, *The Nature of the Obligations*, 180).

the feasibility of creating legislation is not restricted by financial resources. Therefore, the Committee has, in the past, called for specific states to pass specific legislation.[51] Another measure that has been called for to be undertaken immediately is the creation of a plan of action, and also to identify indicators and benchmarks for progress (or lack thereof) of rights implementation.[52]

Thus, there is a duty on every state to continuously move forward towards the goal of full realization of each right, with some steps having to be taken immediately and some as soon as it is possible for the respective state to do so. Consequently, states are also generally not allowed to move *backwards* concerning the fulfilment of a right.[53]

### *Non-Discrimination and Equal Treatment*

One example for an *immediate* obligation is that parties to the Covenant must provide the rights without discrimination. Articles 2(2) and 3 of the ICESCR state that 'rights enunciated in the present Covenant will be exercised without discrimination' and that the states parties 'undertake to ensure the equal right of men and women to the enjoyment' of all rights included in the Covenant. In General Comment 13, the Committee clarifies that this prohibition against discrimination applies fully and immediately without being subject to progressive realization or the availability of resources.[54] This principle thus further defines the principle of

[51] See Langford and King, 'Committee on Economic, Social and Cultural Rights', 488.

[52] See Langford and King, 'Committee on Economic, Social and Cultural Rights', 488–9.

[53] The Committee states in General Comment 3 that 'any deliberately retrogressive measures in that regard would require the most careful consideration and would need to be fully justified by reference to the totality of the rights provided for in the Covenant and in the context of the full use of the maximum available resources' (see Committee on Economic, Social and Cultural Rights, 'General Comment 3 [Fifth session, 1990]', 9).

[54] Committee on Economic, Social and Cultural Rights, 'General Comment 13, The Right to Education (Twenty-first session, 1999)' U.N. Doc. E/C.12/1999/10 (1999) (1999), 31.

progressive realization. Whatever steps states take when providing for a right, they must do so without discrimination.

## *Minimum Core*

In both international human rights law as well as national constitutional law, the 'minimum core' doctrine has become a common guideline in defining the content of state duties to a certain extent. This is especially the case for 'positive' duties concerning the duty to *fulfil*. The doctrine was explicitly adopted by the CESCR in General Comment 3 of 1990.[55]

Generally, according to Article 2(1) of the Covenant, a state has to take steps for the fulfilment of the Covenant's rights 'to the maximum of its available resources'. Concerning 'minimum core' obligations, according to the General Comment 3, this provision has to be read even more strictly. A state must then use 'all resources that are at its disposition' and prioritize those obligations.[56] Therefore, as long as *some* resources are available, the state must immediately use them to provide the minimum core of every Covenant right.

However, declaring that a minimum core must be provided without delay does not answer the question as to what the 'minimum core' of a right contains. One could focus on 'basic rights' that are a prerequisite for other rights, that is, such rights that enable rights-bearers to enjoy other rights, or to continuously

[55] '[A] minimum core obligation to ensure the satisfaction of, at the very least, minimum essential levels of each of the rights is incumbent upon every State party. Thus, for example, a State party in which any significant number of individuals is deprived of essential foodstuffs, of essential primary health care, of basic shelter and housing, or of the most basic forms of education is, prima facie, failing to discharge its obligations under the Covenant. If the Covenant were to be read in such a way as not to establish such a minimum core obligation, it would be largely deprived of its raison d'être' (see Committee on Economic, Social and Cultural Rights, 'General Comment 3 [Fifth session, 1990]', 10).

[56] Committee on Economic, Social and Cultural Rights, 'General Comment 3 (Fifth session, 1990)', 10.

enjoy that same right.[57] For instance, a minimum amount of nutrition is important for a farmer to be able to grow and harvest crops and thus, to acquire food security for themselves by their own means.[58] However, this would mean that only the core of some rights would be the 'minimum core' of ICESCR rights in general, which does not really help in finding common rules for the definition of a minimum core of each one of the rights.

In order to define such common rules, one may identify two degrees of urgency or 'thresholds' for rights fulfilment. For instance, concerning the right to housing, states must provide, at the very least, such minimal amounts of shelter so that citizens can retain health and survive, as the 'most urgent interest' or first threshold is 'being free from general threats to one's survival'.[59] The second threshold in the case of right to housing would be for human beings to 'live in an environment that does not impair their development but enables them to be in a position to flourish and achieve their goals'.[60] Similar distinctions may be drawn for other rights as well, but with more difficulty concerning such rights whose contents are not a prerequisite for physical survival.

## Contents of the Right to Education in Particular

The international obligations on states imposed by the right to education, as guaranteed by international treaties, are not yet very clearly defined also because of the fact that there is a lack of 'case law', as already mentioned above. However, General Comments as well as scholarly work do offer some guidance.

[57] Bård-Anders Andreassen, Alan G. Smith, and Hugo Stokke, 'Compliance with Economic and Social Human Rights: Realistic Evaluations and Monitoring in the Light of Immediate Obligations', in *Human Rights in Perspective: A Global Assessment*, ed. Asbjørn Eide, Reprint (Oxford: Blackwell Business, 1993[1992]), 258 et seq.

[58] Andreassen, Smith, and Stokke, 'Compliance with Economic and Social Human Rights', 261.

[59] David Bilchitz, *Poverty and Fundamental Rights: The Justification and Enforcement of Socio-Economic Rights* (Oxford, New York: Oxford University Press, 2007), 187–8.

[60] Bilchitz, *Poverty and Fundamental Rights*, 188.

## *General Comments 3, 11, and 13*

General Comment 3 states that the minimum core of socio-economic rights in general is not provided for if 'any significant number of individuals' is deprived of the 'most basic forms of education', without giving more information of what 'the most basic forms of education' may be.[61] General Comment 13 offers some more concrete parameters concerning how the fulfilment of the right may be assessed. The Comment states that education 'shall exhibit' four 'interrelated and essential features': availability, accessibility, acceptability, and adaptability.[62]

'Availability' means, inter alia, that education facilities need to be available in sufficient quantity and offer a certain amount of infrastructural standards.[63] States must *respect* the availability of education 'by not closing private schools', and *fulfil/facilitate* the availability 'by taking positive measures to ensure that education is culturally appropriate [...] and of good quality for all'. States must also *fulfil/provide* 'by designing and providing resources for curricula which reflect the contemporary needs of students in a changing world [...] and [...] by actively developing a system of schools, including building classrooms, delivering programmes, providing teaching materials, training teachers and paying them domestically competitive salaries'.[64]

Tomaševski, then special rapporteur on the right to education, also notes that the 'availability' of schools should not only be measured with the common indicator 'enrolment', as this 'does not capture what a real-life school may look like'.[65] For this reason,

[61] Committee on Economic, Social and Cultural Rights, 'General Comment 3 (Fifth session, 1990)', 10.

[62] Committee on Economic, Social and Cultural Rights, 'General Comment 13 (Twenty-first session, 1999)', 6.

[63] Committee on Economic, Social and Cultural Rights, 'General Comment 13, (Twenty-first session, 1999)', 6(a).

[64] Committee on Economic, Social and Cultural Rights, 'General Comment 13 (Twenty-first session, 1999)', 50.

[65] United Nations: Economic and Social Council, 'Preliminary report of the Special Rapporteur on the right to education, Ms Katarina Tomasevski, submitted in accordance with Commission on Human Rights resolution

looking at infrastructural standards is also important. Factors such as the availability of electricity or piped water or the provision of textbooks in a child's mother tongue may decide whether or not parents see benefit for their children from schooling. Non-availability, on the other hand, may lead to children '"voting with their feet" and opting out of school'.[66] Special attention should also be given whether or not schools are, in practice, available to girls.[67]

'Accessibility' means non-discriminatory physical and economic access to education.[68] Challenges lie in providing practically accessible education, particularly when considering accessibility for refugee children or children with disabilities (who might have access legally but might be restricted physically).[69] As far as education being accessible for girls is concerned, states should create a demand for girls' education by providing economic incentives to parents so that they are willing to invest in their daughters' education.[70]

Furthermore, the education system should be designed in a way that children may still be able to perform household chores and aid in food production or family life, as poor families often rely on help of each member of the family and may refrain from sending children to school if they cannot help at home because of their education.[71] Making education accessible for girls does not only

---

1998/33: Commission on Human Rights. Fifty-fifth session. Item 10 of the provisional agenda', E/CN.4/1999/49 (1999), 52.

66 United Nations: Economic and Social Council, 'Preliminary report of the Special Rapporteur on the right to education', 52.

67 United Nations: Economic and Social Council, 'Preliminary report of the Special Rapporteur on the right to education', 53–5.

68 Committee on Economic, Social and Cultural Rights, 'General Comment 13 (Twenty-first session, 1999)', 6(b).

69 United Nations: Economic and Social Council, 'Preliminary report of the Special Rapporteur on the right to education', 58.

70 United Nations: Economic and Social Council, 'Preliminary report of the Special Rapporteur on the right to education', 60.

71 United Nations: Economic and Social Council, 'Preliminary report of the Special Rapporteur on the right to education', 60.

mean that primary education must be free. Other factors that may prevent girls from attending school need to be regarded as well, for example, early marriage and childbearing. States should therefore work towards 'overcoming the denials of access to school for pregnant girls and very young mothers', also by working towards changing social norms in this respect.[72]

'Acceptability' means that 'the form and substance of education' have to be acceptable, which includes curricula and teaching methods that ensure a certain amount of quality.[73] States are obliged to ensure that all schools conform to some minimum criteria developed by the States themselves, regardless of whether a State leans towards providing education primarily by itself or by relying on private education to a large extent.[74]

Acceptability also means that States need to respect parents' freedom to have their children educated 'in conformity with their religious moral or philosophical convictions', that children may be taught in minority languages, and that minority schools can exist.[75] Education should also be 'child-friendly', meaning, for instance, that it should nurture every individual child's curiosity.[76]

'Adaptability' calls for a flexible education system that can 'adapt to the needs of changing societies and communities'.[77]

[72] United Nations: Economic and Social Council, 'Preliminary report of the Special Rapporteur on the right to education', 61.

[73] Committee on Economic, Social and Cultural Rights, 'General Comment 13 (Twenty-first session, 1999)', 6(c).

[74] United Nations: Economic and Social Council, 'Preliminary report of the Special Rapporteur on the right to education', 62.

[75] United Nations: Economic and Social Council, 'Preliminary report of the Special Rapporteur on the right to education', 63–6.

[76] Such a goal, however, may be difficult to realize in a short amount of time, as it 'clashes with the reality of schools that may be grappling with the lack of running water and sanitation, with the incompatibility of the school timetable with family and community life, or with violence against and among children' (see United Nations: Economic and Social Council, 'Preliminary Report of the Special Rapporteur on the Right to Education', 67).

[77] Committee on Economic, Social and Cultural Rights, 'General Comment 13 (Twenty-first session, 1999)' 6(d).

This means that the best interests of the individual child need to be kept in mind according to what those interests may be at a given time.[78] Also, an education system should be ready to adapt itself to future developments of globalization and localization.[79] It should also include human rights education, including awareness of discrimination.[80] Consequently, curricula and textbooks that might be discriminatory should be revised.[81] As part of the 'adaptability' of education, the attempt towards gender equality should, for instance, also aim at having more male teachers at the level of primary education.[82]

The General Comment also clarifies which obligations shall be of immediate effect. According to the Comment, education must immediately be provided 'without discrimination of any kind', and States must immediately take steps towards the fulfilment of the right (which follows from the wording Article 2 of the Covenant, interpreted as described above).[83] In addition to that, however, providing free compulsory education to all children is in itself named as an obligation that has immediate effect.[84] Introducing free and compulsory primary education is, therefore, an immediate duty that is not limited by fiscal constraints,[85] which may suggest that

[78] United Nations: Economic and Social Council, 'Preliminary report of the Special Rapporteur on the right to education', 70.

[79] United Nations: Economic and Social Council, 'Preliminary report of the Special Rapporteur on the right to education', 71–2.

[80] United Nations: Economic and Social Council, 'Preliminary report of the Special Rapporteur on the right to education', 72.

[81] United Nations: Economic and Social Council, 'Preliminary report of the Special Rapporteur on the right to education', 72.

[82] United Nations: Economic and Social Council, 'Preliminary report of the Special Rapporteur on the right to education', 74.

[83] Committee on Economic, Social and Cultural Rights, 'General Comment 13 (Twenty-first session, 1999)', 43.

[84] Committee on Economic, Social and Cultural Rights, 'General Comment 13 (Twenty-first session, 1999)', 51.

[85] For the other 'levels' of education, on the other hand, the states parties have to '"take steps" [...] towards the realization [...] At a minimum, the State party is required to adopt and implement a national educational strategy' (see Committee on Economic, Social and Cultural Rights, 'General Comment 13 [Twenty-first session, 1999]', 52).

primary education in itself constitutes part of the minimum core of the right.

Still, the obligation to act immediately is somewhat limited by provisions in the ICESCR itself. The ICESCR calls for a 'detailed plan of action' to be adopted within two years by states parties that do not yet provide free and compulsory education in all of their territories. This suggests that states' immediate obligation is to plan taking action, rather than a necessity to immediately take action itself.

General Comment 11 defines what such plans of action shall contain; for example, that they must highlight how primary education shall be compulsory in practice (meaning that 'neither parents, nor guardians, nor the State are entitled to treat as optional the decision as to whether the child should have access to primary education').[86] It must also explain how the State plans to provide primary education free of charge (meaning that there must be no fees or any hidden costs).[87] The plan must also be aimed at securing the progressive implementation of the right 'within a reasonable number of years', that is, it must set several targets for the progressive implementation of the plan and dates at which these goals shall be achieved.[88] This somewhat elevates the right to free and compulsory primary education, as Article 2(1) of the Covenant does not prescribe specific time limits for the implementation of other rights.

## *Scholarly Work*

In addition to the General Comments, scholars have also made attempts to define the contents of the right to education.

For instance, there have been attempts to identify different kinds of obligations concerning the right to education according to

[86] Committee on Economic, Social and Cultural Rights, 'General Comment 11 (Twentieth session, 1999)', 6.

[87] Committee on Economic, Social and Cultural Rights, 'General Comment 11 (Twentieth session, 1999)', 7.

[88] Committee on Economic, Social and Cultural Rights, 'General Comment 11 (Twentieth session, 1999)', 10.

the 'respect/protect/fulfil' distinction. Article 13(3) of the ICESCR itself states that states must *respect* parents' choice for private or public schools for their children, and their choice that the religious and moral education of the children is in conformity with the parents' conviction.[89] Also, they must *respect* the right by not discriminating based on sex or other grounds when admitting children to schools, and by not tolerating or practicing corporal punishment in schools.[90]

States must *protect* the right by preventing 'other individuals, groups or private institutions from violating this right'. For instance, the State must protect right-bearers against discriminatory admission practices and corporal punishment by private schools.[91]

Obligations to *fulfil* are said to be the 'most important' aspect of the right to education.[92] One may further differentiate between obligations of conduct and result within the group of '*fulfil* obligations'. The adoption of a plan for primary education as called for by Article 14 of the ICESCR is an example for an obligation of conduct.[93] Obligations of result, however, are said to be more important. The goals that states must work towards are, for instance, that primary education shall be free and compulsory for all and that 'illiteracy and ignorance' should be 'eliminated', also by means of international cooperation.[94]

[89] Manfred Nowak, 'The Right to Education: Its Meaning, Significance and Limitations', *Netherlands Quarterly of Human Rights* 9, no. 4 (1991): 421.

[90] Nowak notes this point, citing the UNESCO Convention against Discrimination in Education and the ECHR judgment of *Campell and Cosans* v. *The United Kingdom* (European Court of Human Rights, 25 February 1982) (see Nowak, 'The Right to Education', 421–2). Beiter also argues that preventing corporal punishment in schools is an obligation to be fulfilled immediately (see Beiter, *The Protection of the Right to Education by International Law*, 649).

[91] Nowak, 'The Right to Education', 422.

[92] Nowak, 'The Right to Education', 422.

[93] Nowak, 'The Right to Education', 422.

[94] Nowak, 'The Right to Education', 422–3.

It is argued that providing primary education is so fundamental that primary education in itself constitutes part of the minimum core of the right to education.[95] In other words, there cannot be much of a compromise in providing universal free and compulsory *primary* education. Therefore, absence of legislation requiring primary education to be compulsory is said to constitute an infringement of the right to education.[96] Primary education also needs to be prioritized in budgetary choices, meaning that investing high amounts of resources in higher education at the expense of primary education would constitute a violation of the right.[97]

[95] Beiter argues that '[p]rimary education is so important for the development of the individual's abilities that it must be considered to form part of the core content of the right to education' (see Beiter, *The Protection of the Right to Education by International Law*, 644). Similarly, Coomans argues that elementary education is 'so fundamental for the development of a person's ability that it can be rightfully defined as a minimum claim' (see Fons Coomans, 'Identifying the Key Elements of the Right to Education: A Focus on Its Core Content', 2007, http://webcache.googleusercontent.com/search?q=cache:bn6IL1_TKCgJ:www.crin.org/en/docs/Coomans-CoreContent Right%2520to%2520EducationCRC.pdf+&cd=1&hl=en&ct=clnk&gl=de&client=safari, accessed on 23 February 2019, 4). He also identifies four aspects as the core content of the right to education, with free and compulsory elementary education in itself being one of them: (i) That no one must be denied access to education, (ii) that compulsory and free elementary education must be available, (iii) that religious and philosophical beliefs must be respected when choosing education, and (iv) a right of every person to be educated in their mother tongue (see Coomans, 'Identifying the Key Elements of the Right to Education', 3–4, 7–8, quoted/summarized in Beiter, *The Protection of the Right to Education by International Law*, 644).

[96] Beiter, *The Protection of the Right to Education by International Law*, 644–5.

[97] Beiter, *The Protection of the Right to Education by International Law*, 645. Furthermore, he believes that lower secondary education should be compulsory and free, as these years of development of an individual's abilities are equally crucial, a view which he sees confirmed by the fact that international law sets the minimum working age at not less than 15 years. For similar reasons, education for adults that replace primary or lower secondary education should be considered to be part of the 'core' of

The State's duty to 'fulfil progressively' and especially to provide the 'minimum core' of a right also persists during times of economic crisis, as '[i]n these circumstances, vulnerable members of society need special protection'.[98] Furthermore, the State is not only obliged to refrain from actively discriminating against certain groups itself, but should also take positive steps for 'substantive equality', for instance, by taking measures addressing 'static' discrimination in societies, for example, against prioritization of boys' education over girls'.[99]

---

the right. While upper secondary, higher, and other forms of adult education are not part of the core content, 'the duty to adopt and implement a national educational strategy' that also encompasses these forms of education is part of that core content (see Beiter, *The Protection of the Right to Education by International Law*, 645).

[98] Beiter, *The Protection of the Right to Education by International Law*, 401.

[99] Beiter, *The Protection of the Right to Education by International Law*, 403–4, 644. He notes that several provisions of the ICESCR 'embody the idea of substantive equality', for example, Article 3, which provides the 'equal right' of men and women to enjoy the rights of the Covenant, and which, according to the *travaux préparatoires* of the Covenant, was meant to 'increase factual equality between men and women'. He also refers to Article 7(c), which provides that equal opportunity must be promoted 'for everyone [...] in his employment'. The wording of Article 13(2)(c), which calls for higher education to 'be made equally accessible to all [...] by every appropriate means', shows, he argues, that there is 'a direction to states parties to establish substantive equality as regards access to higher education'. He comes to the conclusion that Article 13 'as a whole embodies the idea of substantive equality in the educational sphere' (see Beiter, *The Protection of the Right to Education by International Law*, 404). He further notes that comments by the CESCR support a reading of Article 2(2) according to which substantive equality is 'implicit' in Article 2(2) (see Beiter, *The Protection of the Right to Education by International Law*, 405). For instance, General Comment 1 calls for 'special attention' to be given 'to any specific groups or subgroups which appear to be particularly vulnerable or disadvantaged' when drafting state reports (see Committee on Economic, Social and Cultural Rights, 'General Comment 1, Reporting by States Parties [Third session, 1989]' U.N. Doc. E/1989/22, 3), and General Comment 13 states that 'states parties must closely

Furthermore, a violation may be identified if the education system only provides an infrastructure that is seriously lacking. For instance, poorly equipped school buildings and/or buildings that are too remote from children's homes, a lack of textbooks, unqualified teachers, an unacceptable student–teacher ratio, a failure to enact laws against child labour, or, of course, charging school fees for primary education may constitute a violation.[100] Also, it is argued that the right to education must be understood as a right to quality education, at least to a certain degree, 'otherwise attending classes would be meaningless'.[101]

As mentioned above, passing legislation may be considered an obligation to be fulfilled immediately by all states' parties to the ICESCR. However, further measures will need to be taken *within* the framework created by legislation, for instance, formulating fiscal, social, and cultural policies, developing programmes to help disadvantaged parts of the society (for instance, organizing transport to schools for children from families who cannot afford transport), and also raising rights awareness among the people, and so on.[102]

Article 2(2) is said to include an obligation on states' parties to ensure that private parties—especially, of course, private schools—do not discriminate in the field of education. This can, for instance, be deduced from Article 13(4), which calls for education 'given [by private institutions] […] [to] conform to such minimum standards as may be laid down by the State'.[103]

At the same time, states may be required to support private initiatives in primary education. When considering the 'availability' of resources (see Article 2(1) of the ICESCR), one should also

---

monitor education […] so as to identify and take measures to redress any de facto discrimination' (see Committee on Economic, Social and Cultural Rights, 'General Comment 13 [Twenty-First session, 1999]', 37).

[100] Beiter, *The Protection of the Right to Education by International Law*, 644–5.

[101] Coomans, 'Identifying the Key Elements of the Right to Education', 7.

[102] Beiter, *The Protection of the Right to Education by International Law*, 393–4.

[103] Beiter, *The Protection of the Right to Education by International Law*, 412–13.

consider allowing private initiatives in the country, including private schools. For those, the state should not put up educational or administrative requirements that are too high.[104]

General Comment 3 states that the right to free and compulsory education as guaranteed by Article 13(2)(a) can be justiciable.[105] Concerning justiciability, one may differentiate between a situation in which a state has already created an education infrastructure (for instance, through legislation) and a situation in which it has not; if an educational infrastructure exists, 'the concepts "compulsory" and "free" are sufficiently precise to be susceptible to judicial determination'.[106] Other aspects that may be easily justiciable are the prohibition of discrimination under Article 2(2) and the guarantee to equality prescribed by Article 3 read with Article 13.[107] However, it is more difficult for a court to order that such infrastructure be set up in the first place, as this would require 'extensive legislative and administrative measures' and policy decisions.[108] Therefore, in the case that infrastructure does not exist, one may argue that Article 13(2)(a) is primarily addressed at the legislature and administration, rather than at the judiciary.[109]

104 Beiter, *The Protection of the Right to Education by International Law*, 383–4. The author also argues that, in addition to private initiatives, states should, for instance, also consider resources that may be available through international cooperation.

105 Committee on Economic, Social and Cultural Rights, 'General Comment 3 (Fifth session, 1990)', 5.

106 Beiter, *The Protection of the Right to Education by International Law*, 399.

107 Beiter, *The Protection of the Right to Education by International Law*, 400, noting that the right of access to educational institutions without discrimination has been declared justiciable for Article 2 of the First Protocol to the European Convention on Human Rights (ECtHR) (which protects the right to education) by the ECHR in the *Belgian Linguistic Case* (see 'Relating to Certain Aspects of the Laws on the Use of Languages in Education in Belgium'. For the obligation [European Court of Human Rights, 9 February 1967].)

108 Beiter, *The Protection of the Right to Education by International Law*, 399.

109 Beiter, *The Protection of the Right to Education by International Law*, 399.

However, a court could direct the government 'to take "appropriate" steps within a reasonable period of time',[110] which would especially be imperative in the case of primary education.[111]

Of course, it is still difficult to ascertain what a 'reasonable amount of time' may be. Article 14 of the ICESCR itself only speaks of a 'reasonable number of years' to be stipulated in a plan to make free and compulsory primary education a reality. Scholars have struggled to recognize when a violation may be identified, with one of them saying that such a violation may occur in the case of non-realization of free and compulsory primary education 'within let's say 10 years' after ratification.[112] Recognizing this opaqueness, the author calls for 'reliable and objective indicators' that may help in identifying violations in a more concrete manner.[113]

The ICESCR itself does not name specific indicators for the right to education.[114] However, Kalantry, Getgen, and Koh have suggested what such indicators may be, noting that there has been comparatively little work on finding measures to monitor and enforce compliance concerning the right to education.[115] The authors categorize their indicators using the '4-A Framework' (availability, acceptability, accessibility, and adaptability) and further subcategorize them into 'structure, process, and outcome'.[116] These categories had previously been used by the UN special rapporteur Hunt for the right to health.[117]

[110] Beiter, *The Protection of the Right to Education by International Law*, 399–400.

[111] Beiter, *The Protection of the Right to Education by International Law*, 399.

[112] Nowak, 'The Right to Education', 423.

[113] Nowak, 'The Right to Education', 424.

[114] Kalantry, Getgen, and Koh, 'Enhancing Enforcement of Economic, Social, and Cultural Rights Using Indicators', 260.

[115] Kalantry, Getgen, and Koh, 'Enhancing Enforcement of Economic, Social, and Cultural Rights Using Indicators', 260.

[116] Kalantry, Getgen, and Koh, 'Enhancing Enforcement of Economic, Social, and Cultural Rights Using Indicators', 281.

[117] United Nations: Economic and Social Council, 'Report of the Special Rapporteur on the Right of Everyone to the Enjoyment of the

Structural indicators concern the question whether or not 'key structures and mechanisms' for the realization of the right are put in place, for example, whether legislation has been passed or regulatory agencies have been created.[118] Process indicators measure state effort, that is, 'programmes, activities, and interventions'.[119] For the right to health, such indicators may be the proportion of births attended by skilled personnel, the percentage of people provided with health information, and so on.[120] Outcome indicators 'measure the impact of programmes, activities, and interventions'. For the right to health, this includes indicators such as child and maternal mortality, HIV prevalence, or knowledge among women about contraceptive methods.[121]

Kalantry, Getgen, and Koh argue that in order to delineate structural and process indicators more clearly structural indicators should be limited 'to monitoring whether the State's laws reflect, incorporate, and implement its international treaty obligations'. Process indicators, on the other hand, should account for whether or not the State has created 'appropriate institutions' and taken additional implementation measures for fulfilling its obligations. That way, these indicators may measure the effectiveness of the design of a State's laws and policies for working towards the realization of the right.[122] In sum, structural indicators shall

---

Highest Attainable Standard of Physical and Mental Health, Paul Hunt', Commission on Human Rights. Sixty-second session. Item 10 of the provisional agenda, E/CN.4/2006/48 (2006), 54–6, quoted in Kalantry, Getgen, and Koh, 'Enhancing Enforcement of Economic, Social, and Cultural Rights Using Indicators', 281.

118 United Nations: Economic and Social Council, 'Report of the Special Rapporteur', 54.

119 United Nations: Economic and Social Council, 'Report of the Special Rapporteur', 55.

120 United Nations: Economic and Social Council, 'Report of the Special Rapporteur', 55.

121 United Nations: Economic and Social Council, 'Report of the Special Rapporteur', 56.

122 Kalantry, Getgen, and Koh, 'Enhancing Enforcement of Economic, Social, and Cultural Rights Using Indicators', 282.

measure domestic laws against international treaty obligations, while process indicators measure the implementation of the laws that exist in a state.[123]

The authors note that while the respect–protect–fulfil framework helps in identifying positive and negative obligations, the distinction between structure, process, and outcome indicators helps in identifying obligations of conduct and obligations of result. The distinction also clarifies how much control states have over particular obligations.[124] As states have a higher degree of control over obligations of conduct than over obligations of result, structure and process indicators measuring obligations of conduct will help identifying state failures more easily.[125]

Generally, the authors believe that, when trying to identify violations, one should differentiate according to the level of state control, as 'it adds legitimacy, reasonableness, and fairness to the evaluation process'.[126] They also argue that indicators should be both quantitative and qualitative, as quantitative indicators alone cannot measure the provision of quality education. To illustrate, the authors cite the example of low-quality or outdated textbooks provided to schools.[127]

As far as data sources for right to education indicators are concerned, Kalantry, Getgen, and Koh argue for using events-based data ('what happened, when it happened, and who was involved',

[123] Kalantry, Getgen, and Koh, 'Enhancing Enforcement of Economic, Social, and Cultural Rights Using Indicators', 282.

[124] Kalantry, Getgen, and Koh, 'Enhancing Enforcement of Economic, Social, and Cultural Rights Using Indicators', 283.

[125] Kalantry, Getgen, and Koh, 'Enhancing Enforcement of Economic, Social, and Cultural Rights Using Indicators', 283–4.

[126] Kalantry, Getgen, and Koh, 'Enhancing Enforcement of Economic, Social, and Cultural Rights Using Indicators', 284.

[127] Kalantry, Getgen, and Koh, 'Enhancing Enforcement of Economic, Social, and Cultural Rights Using Indicators', 286, quoting Beeckman, who notes that generally the importance given to quantitative indicators is too high as far as the right to education is concerned (see Katrien Beeckman, 'Measuring the Implementation of the Right to Education: Educational Versus Human Rights Indicators', *The International Journal of Children's Rights* 12, no. 1 [2004]: 71 et seq.).

such as 'a girl who becomes pregnant is expelled from school on account of her pregnancy'), socio-economic and administrative statistics, household perception and opinion surveys, and expert judgments. In this list, socio-economic statistics, which include data like net enrolment in schools, are considered to be most relevant for measuring progressive realization of the right.[128] Events-based data that only identifies singular events is less likely to facilitate measuring progressive realization, but it can be useful for identifying violations concerning obligations that states must realize immediately, for example, when discrimination occurs, as with the 'pregnant girl example' cited just now.[129] Household and perception surveys, on the other hand, may provide context for certain socio-economic statistics.[130]

As far as structural indicators are concerned, the authors cite the Maastricht Guidelines,[131] which see a violation of ICESCR if a state adopts legislation inconsistent with the Covenant 'or fails to amend or repeal existing laws that are inconsistent with the obligations under the ICESCR'. This principle applies regardless of whether it is an immediate, minimum core, or progressive obligation.[132] With process indicators, one may recognize a prima facie violation by identifying if policies or plans 'deliberately retard or halt' progressive realization of the right to education. In such an instance, the State will have to justify these measures such as showing that they were 'introduced after the most careful considerations' or that the State was still using the maximum of its

[128] Kalantry, Getgen, and Koh, 'Enhancing Enforcement of Economic, Social, and Cultural Rights Using Indicators', 286–7.

[129] Kalantry, Getgen, and Koh, 'Enhancing Enforcement of Economic, Social, and Cultural Rights Using Indicators', 288.

[130] Kalantry, Getgen, and Koh, 'Enhancing Enforcement of Economic, Social, and Cultural Rights Using Indicators', 288.

[131] 'Maastricht Guidelines on Violations of Economic, Social and Cultural Rights: Maastricht, January 22–26, 1997', https://www1.umn.edu/humanrts/instree/Maastrichtguidelines_.html, accessed on 19 August 2018.

[132] Kalantry, Getgen, and Koh, 'Enhancing Enforcement of Economic, Social, and Cultural Rights Using Indicators', 295–6.

available resources.[133] For the obligation of progressive realization, the authors also suggest that states should commit (for instance, to the CESCR) to benchmarks that they want to achieve in a certain period of time.[134] A prima facie violation will then occur if the state fails to meet these benchmarks.[135]

Concerning obligations to be realized immediately, there are 'no justifications' if a state fails in doing so.[136] Concerning minimum core obligations, a State must demonstrate that is has made every effort to use all its available resources.[137] If outcome indicators suggest that a minimum core obligation is not fulfilled (such as providing 'the most basic forms of education', as described in the CESCR's General Comment 3), this will constitute a prima facie violation that may only be justified in exceptional circumstances.[138] Outcome indicators that measure such obligations that need to be realized immediately may help in ascertaining violations quite quickly. For instance, if fewer girls than boys are enrolled in schools in a State, this itself may constitute a violation of the ICESCR, as the State would not have ensured equality and non-discrimination.[139] The authors also name the example of indicators showing that there is no universal enrolment in primary schools, which 'suggest[s] that education is not free, not compulsory, or both'.[140]

[133] Kalantry, Getgen, and Koh, 'Enhancing Enforcement of Economic, Social, and Cultural Rights Using Indicators', 301–2.

[134] Kalantry, Getgen, and Koh, 'Enhancing Enforcement of Economic, Social, and Cultural Rights Using Indicators', 297.

[135] Kalantry, Getgen, and Koh, 'Enhancing Enforcement of Economic, Social, and Cultural Rights Using Indicators', 302.

[136] Kalantry, Getgen, and Koh, 'Enhancing Enforcement of Economic, Social, and Cultural Rights Using Indicators', 296.

[137] Kalantry, Getgen, and Koh, 'Enhancing Enforcement of Economic, Social, and Cultural Rights Using Indicators', 296.

[138] Kalantry, Getgen, and Koh, 'Enhancing Enforcement of Economic, Social, and Cultural Rights Using Indicators', 298.

[139] Kalantry, Getgen, and Koh, 'Enhancing Enforcement of Economic, Social, and Cultural Rights Using Indicators', 298.

[140] Kalantry, Getgen, and Koh, 'Enhancing Enforcement of Economic, Social, and Cultural Rights Using Indicators', 299.

## *Conclusion*

If one tries to ascertain violations of the right to education concerning primary or elementary education in particular, the problem with the guidelines given by the ICESCR, official comments by the Committee, and scholarly opinions is that none of them give clear benchmarks to identify when a state of 'compulsory and free primary education' is achieved. Does it suffice for all children to be formally enrolled in a school? Or is the 'core content' of the right only fulfilled if the state also ensures that they attend regularly? The fact that primary education may otherwise barely be called 'compulsory' suggests that mere enrolment does not suffice. However, if children attend regularly, what are the minimum quality standards and how can it be determined if they have been reached? What amount of teacher absence and teacher inactivity may be tolerated before recognizing a violation of the core content of the right? To what extent can these benchmarks differ in different countries and surroundings? Further, even though it may now be a consensus that the non-provision of the 'most basic forms of education' constitutes a violation of the minimum core of the right, it does not answer the question of what the 'most basic forms of education' may be.

These questions have not been answered conclusively as of now. The interpretations of international treaties by UN institutions and scholars have so far only provided some guidelines on how to answer some fundamental questions, such as what the minimum standard of education should be, what rights children have against parents and teachers, whether the right has horizontal effect, where the limits of state responsibility for and state interference with private schools are, and so on.[141]

Indicators help in assessing progress and are a necessity in order to determine if minimum standards are fulfilled, but those have to be defined in the first place, which can perhaps only be done through 'case law', both at an international as well as a national level. As long as the content of the obligations is not clearly defined, it is impossible to identify violations even with the help of indicators, apart from relatively clear cases.

[141] Nowak, 'The Right to Education', 268.

## Adoption of International Doctrines in Indian Constitutional Law and Adjudication

While Indian courts often refrain from explicitly naming the international human rights doctrines for adjudicating socio-economic rights described above, they do effectively apply them in their rights adjudication. The courts also recognize international obligations as such in their judgments on national constitutional law by explicitly referring to international treaties in their arguments. Indian courts have, in the past, repeatedly referred to international human rights treaties and also to the ICESCR in particular.[142]

In such cases, the courts have effectively ruled that the legislative and executive powers are bound by these international treaties. This is surprising considering that formally Indian constitutional law employs a dualistic approach. The idea of dualism (unlike the idea of monism) means that international and municipal law are two separate entities, and that therefore, international treaties' effect in domestic law is dependent on them being implemented by accordingly creating statutory provisions.[143] The Indian Constitution itself does not explicitly prescribe to dualism or monism. Article 51 (a directive principle) merely obliges the State to 'foster respect for international law and treaty obligations in the dealings of organized peoples with one another'. However, the Supreme Court has clarified that provisions in international treaties have to be implemented by creating domestic law in order to be applicable in the domestic legal system.[144]

[142] For direct references to the ICESCR see, for instance, *Mohd. Ahmed (Minor)* v. *Union of India* MANU/DE/0915/2014, 51 (Delhi High Court, 17 April 2014); *Unni Krishnan, J.P. and Ors* v. *State of Andhra Pradesh and Ors* MANU/SC/0333/1993, 47 (Supreme Court of India, 4 February 1993). For reference to several other human rights treaties, see, for instance, *Vishaka & Ors* v. *State of Rajasthan & Ors* MANU/SC/0786/1997, 7 et seq (Supreme Court of India, 13 August 1997).

[143] Malcolm N. Shaw, *International Law*, 8th edition (Cambridge, United Kingdom, New York, NY, Port Melbourne, VIC, Delhi, Singapore: Cambridge University Press, 2017), 96 et seq.

[144] *Jolly George Varghese and Ors* v. *The Bank of Cochin* MANU/SC/0014/1980, 13 (Supreme Court of India, 4 February 1980).

Nevertheless, if one takes the reality of rights adjudication by the Supreme Court into account, one may conclude that India follows a system of 'formal dualism' but 'functional monism'.[145] While the Supreme Court still holds that international provisions have to be implemented by domestic legislation, it does not refrain from applying international provisions directly in adjudication. Therefore, concerning the right to education (as well as other rights), one may expect the judiciary to refer to international human rights treaties and the internationally recognized doctrines for rights interpretation in the future as well.

The principle of progressive realization, for instance, is even embedded in the constitutional text itself: Article 37 of the Indian Constitution imposes a similar obligation on the Indian State concerning the directive principles, declaring that the principles are 'fundamental in the governance of the country' and that the State has a duty 'to apply these principles in making laws'. The wording of Article 21A goes in a similar direction, also calling for implementation through legislation.

Neither of these articles explicitly speaks of 'taking steps' or of 'progressive realization'. However, the directive principles are to be understood that way, which is expressed by several articles in this part of the Constitution (Article 38(1): 'The State shall strive to promote'; Article 41: 'The State shall, within the limits of its economic capacity [...], make effective provision'; Articles 40 and 43A: 'The State shall take steps'; Articles 43 and 45: 'The State shall endeavour to secure' and 'to provide', and so on). The full realization of these principles is therefore a goal or an ideal that the State shall strive for, particularly by, but not limited to, legislation. This must also apply for those directive principles that have been read into Article 21, and especially for the one directive principle that has even been transformed into an explicitly justiciable right, that is, Article 21A, the right to education.

Furthermore, it appears that Indian courts are aware of the 'minimum core' doctrine and that they do follow it to a certain

[145] Aparna Chandra, 'India and International Law: Formal Dualism, Functional Monism', *Indian Journal of International Law* 57, no. 1–2 (2017).

extent, even though they rarely use that term. Notable exceptions in which the judiciary explicitly refers to the doctrine are the Delhi High Court cases of *Mohd. Ahmed*,[146] which will be discussed in more detail below, and of *Laxmi Mandal*.[147]

The Supreme Court has applied the doctrine in practice without speaking of a 'minimum core' in several cases.[148] In *Paschim Banga Khet Mazdoorsamity*, the Court declared that non-availability for emergency treatment of serious injuries in government hospitals resulted in a denial of the right to life (Article 21). Taking the example of the provision of free legal aid to a poor accused, and arguing that this would apply 'with equal, if not greater, force in the [...] constitutional obligation [...] to provide medical aid to preserve human life', the Court held that the State could 'not avoid its constitutional obligation in that regard on account of financial constraints'.[149] In the case of the *People's Union for Civil Liberties'* petition concerning the right to food, the Supreme Court gave an interim order[150] creating a scheme for provision of

146 The Court states that it is 'of the view that core obligations under the right to health are non-derogable. This minimum core is not easy to define, but includes at least the minimum decencies of life consistent with human dignity' (see *Mohd. Ahmed (Minor)* v. *Union of India* MANU/DE/0915/2014, 66).

147 In this case, the Court states that '[i]n effect, the Supreme Court has spelt out what the "minimum core" of the right to health and food is, and also spelt out, consistent with international human rights law, the "obligations of conduct" and the "obligations of result" of the Union of India, the States and the UTs [Union Territories]' (see *Laxmi Mandal* v. *Deen Dayal Harinagar Hospital* MANU/DE/1268/2010, 27 [Delhi High Court, 4 June 2010]).

148 Müller aptly names these two cases as examples for an application of the minimum core doctrine (see Amrei Müller, *The Relationship between Economic, Social and Cultural Rights and International Humanitarian Law: An Analysis of Health-Related Issues in Non-International Armed Conflicts* [Leiden, Boston: Martinus Nijhoff Publishers, 2013], 93).

149 *Paschim Banga Khet Mazdoor Samity* v. *State of West Bengal* MANU/SC/0611/1996, 16 (Supreme Court of India, 6 May 1996).

150 *People's Union for Civil Liberties* v. *Union of India and Others* (Supreme Court of India, The Supreme Court Order of 28 November 2001 is available at http://www.righttofoodindia.org/orders/nov28.html,

food as mid-day meals for school children, and also named concrete minimum amounts of nutrition that need to be supplied. In this case, the Court effectively acted as a legislative and executive power, arguing that otherwise 'the very existence of life of those [...] below the poverty line' would 'come under danger'.[151]

Therefore, one can expect that Indian courts will consider international norms when adjudicating the right to education, meaning that the current state of primary education may be measured by international human rights standards.

## Measuring the State of Primary Education in India by International Standards

As the parameters for indicators and State's obligations under international law, as described above, have not yet been defined very clearly, it is difficult to apply them to the legal and factual situation of primary education in India. Still, some conclusions can be drawn.

When comparing Indian constitutional law to international obligations, one may see some parallels. Article 21A makes free and compulsory education a fundamental right, without naming any limitation to this provision as far as budgetary or other constraints are concerned. The scope of Article 21A is actually broader than the international standards for primary education, as it targets all children aged 6 to 14 years, that is, the period that is understood as 'elementary education' in India. Therefore, it includes some years of what is understood as lower secondary education internationally. Pre-elementary education remains a directive principle (Article 45 in its current form), while higher secondary and higher education is encompassed by the broader Article 41, which calls for the State 'within the limits of its economic capacity' to 'make effective provision for securing the right [...] to education'. This

---

accessed on 15 August 2018). For a more detailed assessment of the Right to Food Adjudication in India, see Chapter 6.

[151] Supreme Court Order of 2 May 2003, available at http://www.righttofoodindia.org/orders/may203.html, accessed on 15 August 2018.

limitation by economic constraints is in line with the international norms, particularly Article 13(2)(b, c) of the ICESCR.

Obviously, merely calling for free and compulsory elementary education in constitutional law is not sufficient. Consequently, Article 21A explicitly calls for legislation to govern the education system and infrastructure. India's states had provided a framework for its elementary education system through legislation even prior to the creation of Article 21A. After the constitutional amendment, the education system was given a new central framework with the Right to Education Act of 2009. The (in)adequacy of legislation concerning a certain issue is, as mentioned above, a structural indicator. Based on the parameters mentioned above, inadequate legislation concerning some issues (for instance, compulsory education) may in itself be a violation of the international obligation.

On the other hand, the statistics concerning the Indian elementary education system mentioned in Chapter 1 may be used as process as well as outcome indicators. The process and/or outcome indicators identifying the most important problems mentioned in that chapter may be summarized here as follows: elementary education is now free (there are no tuition fees anymore), and the issue of 'hidden' costs appears to be a lot more limited than it used to be. For several years now, there has been close to universal enrolment in the age group of 6 to 14. Still, enrolment is not entirely universal, as data concerning some remote areas shows.

Importantly, the problem of widespread absence of children (meaning that they enrol in school, but do not attend regularly) persists. Teacher absence, or lack of actual teaching performed by teachers even if they are present, remains common as well. Furthermore, the amount of training many teachers have received (especially 'contract teachers') is very limited. These factors, among others, lead to a situation in which the amount of (quality) teaching that children actually receive is quite limited, which leads to (on average) very low learning outcomes. This is especially the case concerning English proficiency, even though it has become so important for children's later career opportunities. The quality of elementary education as a whole is therefore quite low, and recent studies suggest that it has actually been deteriorating in the past few years. Additional problems include infrastructural issues that have improved in the past years, but are still very widespread.

The Right to Education Act is the core piece of legislation that is meant to be a decisive step towards implementation of the right to education. Measuring State action with structural indicators would therefore, in this case, mean that the State has fulfilled its obligation under the ICESCR to provide a legislative framework for primary education. However, there are several shortcomings in the Act that fail to address the shortcomings that may be measured by the outcome indicators mentioned just now.

The question is whether these omissions or inadequacies in the Act already constitute a (prima facie) violation. The definition for a violation identified with structural indicators given by the Maastricht Guidelines, as mentioned above, states that a violation occurs if a state has 'failed to amend existing laws' inconsistent with the ICESCR obligations. In order to identify a violation with these parameters, one must obviously also consider legislation 'below' the Act, especially the rules passed by the Indian states. Also, one would first have to ascertain whether a specific field in which the system is lacking needs to necessarily be addressed with more specific legislation, or if there are other means by which the State could act. If it could, but has failed to do so, then these failures may more adequately be identified by employing process or outcome indicators. Only if one identifies a necessity to regulate a certain aspect by legislation in order to facilitate implementation can such an omission lead to a prima facie violation in itself.

One aspect is a clear shortcoming that could only be addressed by amending legislation: as mentioned in Chapter 1, neither Article 21A nor the Right to Education Act nor any other legislation effectively provide for *compulsory* education. Article 21A and Right to Education Act declare that elementary education shall be compulsory but they do not stipulate any sanctions to be imposed on parents if they do not follow their duty to enrol their children in school. Perhaps more importantly, there are especially no sanctions if they do not ensure that their children also attend regularly. There is also no other effective procedure that the State may follow to ensure that children do enrol in and regularly attend school, even, if need be, against the parents' wishes. Therefore, one may consider this a violation of international minimum standards.

As explained in Chapter 1, the most important reason why many parents in India do not regularly send their children to school is not that they are not interested in educating their children; most of the time, it is also not the highest priority to have the children work; rather, the lack of quality provided by the education system creates very little motivation for parents to ensure regular attendance, or for children themselves to regularly attend. Therefore, in the Indian context, fining parents who, for good reasons, see very little benefit in regularly sending their children to school, or who cannot send them because of economic necessities, may actually be counterproductive. Still, the international obligation to make primary education compulsory exists. More importantly, as shall be discussed below, the Indian legislature has also created a corresponding *constitutional* obligation.

As far as infrastructural shortcomings (for example, school facilities) are concerned (which are relevant as an aspect of the 'availability' of education), the problem appears to be the implementation of the legal framework rather than the framework itself. As mentioned in Chapter 1, the Act does contain several aspects that set infrastructural minimum standards. One may argue whether or not some additional aspects should be added, or if the benchmarks that are set are too low. Still, the Act does set them in the first place, and their implementation would be, at least on average, an improvement of the status quo.

Whether or not the fact that the implementation is lacking may constitute a violation of the right should be determined by process indicators. The time limit that the Act prescribes (that the infrastructural standards shall be fully adhered to within three years from the commencement of the Act, see Section 19(2, 3))[152]

[152] Section 19(2) states that schools that were already in existence before the commencement of the Act 'shall take steps to fulfil such norms and standards at [their] own expenses, within a period of three years from the date of such commencement', that is, by 2013. If private schools do not adhere to these standards, the state shall withdraw their recognition, Section 19(3). Furthermore, no new school shall be established or

may be seen as a temporal benchmark that the State has set for itself. This would have meant that by 2013, practically all schools should have managed to adhere to the minimum infrastructural requirements. Clearly, this goal was not reached (and has still not been reached today). This may be seen as a violation (or at least as a case of non-implementation) of the right, but not necessarily a violation of the ICESCR, as the Indian State did not commit to such specific benchmarks internationally. Also, there *has* been progress concerning infrastructural standards. It has just not been as quick as desired. Whether or not this slow pace of progress constitutes a violation is difficult to ascertain. For this, 'case law' will have to define the obligations more precisely. Kalantry, Getgen, and Koh had recognized a prima facie violation for cases in which indicators show that policies or plans *deliberately* halt or retard progressive realization (see above). Whether or not one could describe the Indian State's failure to reach its 2013 goals as 'deliberate' is difficult to ascertain.

The most pressing issue, however, appears to be the lack of quality of education, leading to low learning outcomes. This is relevant both for the availability and, especially, acceptability of education. The lack of improvement and even deterioration (in recent years) of learning achievements are process indicators that may suggest a prima facie violation as far as this parameter is concerned. Again, the question that arises is to what extent the lack of progress and deterioration are 'deliberate'. As mentioned in Chapter 1, the Right to Education Act is conspicuously silent about measures to improve quality, apart from a few aspects such as teacher–student ratio. While this, in itself, does not lead to a violation to be measured by a structural indicator, it may serve as evidence that the State did not prioritize this aspect as much as it should have. This is especially the case considering that there

---

recognized 'unless it fulfils the norms and standards specified in the Schedule' according to Section 19(1). 'Recognition' is only given to private schools, but it would be odd if the State did not intend to fulfil the minimum standards that it imposes on private parties itself. For the application of these standards to government schools, see Chapter 6.

has not been much of a focus on improving teacher training or even enforcement of regular teacher attendance and activity in the implementation process either.

One should also note that shortcomings in terms of quality, especially concerning teacher attendance, are so grave that one might consider them to be violations of minimum core obligations. If children, for a considerable amount of time that they are in school, do not receive any teaching whatsoever, one could barely state that they receive 'the most basic forms of education', even if one sets the threshold for that term very low.

Other shortcomings concern outcome indicators that may by themselves constitute violations. For instance, the fact that the percentage of girls enroled in school is still lower than the percentage of girls of elementary school age might constitute a violation as far as the immediate obligation to provide education without discrimination is concerned.

Thus, at least in some respects, the Indian State is not fulfilling its international obligations concerning the right to elementary education. However, as different courts in different jurisdictions around the world have employed very diverse approaches when adjudicating socio-economic rights, this observation alone does not allow a prediction of how the Indian courts might act because of these shortcomings. As mentioned above, it is ultimately the judiciary's task to define the contents of the right to education by identifying concrete violations. However, a prediction might be possible by assessing the approaches the Indian judiciary has followed when adjudicating socio-economic rights in the past.

## Socio-Economic Rights in India

As the Indian Supreme Court has often been hailed for its 'judicial activism', also internationally, one would assume that the remedies it has given when adjudication socio-economic rights are quite far-reaching. Notably, the Supreme Court is known to have asserted itself against the legislature and executive by essentially making policy decisions. However, the Court has, as far as the remedies given are concerned, often restricted itself to only ordering the implementation of schemes that are already in existence, rather than creating new schemes.

This self-restraint in terms of remedies is somewhat of a contrast to the Court's tendency to use strong language when declaring that violations of socio-economic rights have taken place. In the case of the right to education in particular, it would mean that Article 21A would essentially not call for more than the implementation of the Right to Education Act, meaning that the content of that article would be defined entirely by the legislature.

However, one may also argue to what extent the Court is actually consistent in restraining itself in this manner. One could also see this tendency as only one of the several strands of socio-economic rights adjudication by the Supreme Court.

After summarizing this debate, this part shall show that the existence of Article 21A actually creates an obligation for the judiciary to *not* restrain itself to merely test the implementation of the existing scheme defined by the Right to Education Act. This is the case even if one agrees that such a restriction may have been the dominating philosophy in socio-economic rights adjudication in the past. Furthermore, this part shall also show that Article 21A also applies (indirectly) in between private individuals, which will become more and more relevant as the privatization of primary education progresses.

## Scholarly Discussion of Socio-Economic Rights in India

The Supreme Court of India has often been hailed (and criticized) for a large amount of 'judicial activism'.[153] It has even been called 'the most powerful court in the world'.[154] The most prominent examples for these 'activist' tendencies are the court-made concept

[153] For an overview of its 'activism', see S.P. Sathe, *Judicial Activism in India*, 2nd edition (Delhi, Oxford: Oxford University Press, 2003).

[154] See, for instance, Lacanya Rajamani and Arghya Sengupta, 'The Supreme Court', in *The Oxford Companion to Politics in India*, ed. Niraja G. Jayal and Pratap B. Mehta (New Delhi: Oxford University Press, 2011), 86.

of PIL, which will be examined in more detail in Chapters 4 and 6, as well as the expansion of Article 21, as discussed in Chapter 2. On the face of it, the expansion of Article 21 suggests that the Court has played a great role in promoting socio-economic rights. However, this assumption may be put into perspective if one considers the actual remedies that were awarded (or not awarded) in some of the famous socio-economic rights cases.

Khosla has prominently analysed how Indian courts adjudicate socio-economic rights.[155] He argues that, considering the remedies awarded by the courts, they have actually displayed a high degree of judicial self-restraint, also when comparing them to courts in other jurisdictions. He categorizes both the 'minimum core doctrine' and the South African approach in the *Grootboom* case as forms of 'systemic' socio-economic rights adjudication, which lead to courts giving effect to 'a right to a certain minimum socio-economic standard, or to state action that undertakes reasonable measures to achieve that standard'.[156] In his view, the Indian judiciary has not employed such a systemic approach for socio-economic rights, but rather a 'conditional' approach to socio-economic rights, meaning that the judiciary restricts itself to merely ordering that schemes that the State has created be implemented. In other words, this means that remedies will only be rewarded under the 'condition' that the State has already created some sort of scheme that can be implemented.

In the *Grootboom* case, petitioners, who had been evicted from private land that they had occupied, invoked their right to housing against the State. Section 26(1) of the South African Constitution speaks of a 'right to *have access to* adequate housing', while Section 26(2) reads that the State 'must take *reasonable* legislative or other *measures*, within its available resources, to achieve the *progressive realisation* of this right' (emphasis added). The Constitutional Court, after highlighting the difference in wording to Article 11.1 of the ICESCR (which speaks of 'right to adequate housing' and 'appropriate steps'), restricted the

[155] Madhav Khosla, 'Making Social Rights Conditional: Lessons from India', *ICON* 8, no. 4 (2010).

[156] Khosla, 'Making Social Rights Conditional', 741–2.

scope of its judgment to the question whether or not the State had undertaken 'reasonable measures' that were 'capable of facilitating the realisation of the right' to housing.[157] The Court rejected the argument that the 'minimum core' of the right had to be provided, stating that the determination of a minimum core would be difficult, and that 'the real question in terms of our Constitution is whether the measures taken by the state to realise the right afforded by section 26 are reasonable'.[158] Thus, the Court decided to not answer the question of what the minimum core to the right may be. Consequently, it did not award an individualized remedy for the right-bearers. Thus, the *Grootboom* approach actually led to a relatively weak remedy.

Still, the approach commonly used by Indian courts (the 'conditional social rights approach') according to Khosla, leads to a remedy that is even weaker. Khosla observes a philosophy according to which the judiciary does not even ask whether or not measures undertaken by the State are 'reasonable', but only restricts itself to testing whether or not measures (whether they are reasonable or not) are properly implemented. 'No judicial review is conducted on the former question, making the right *conditional* upon state action.'[159]

Khosla names the case of *Francis Coralie Mullin*,[160] which is often cited as an illustration for the Supreme Court's judicial activism by expanding the scope of Article 21.[161] Khosla sees it

[157] *The Government of the Republic of South Africa and Others* v. *Irene Grootboom and Others* [2000] ZACC 19; 2001 (1) SA 46; 2000 (11) BCLR 1169, 42 (Constitutional Court of South Africa, 4 October 2000), http://www.saflii.org/za/cases/ZACC/2000/19.pdf, accessed on 16 November 2015.

[158] Note 157, 33.

[159] Khosla, 'Making Social Rights Conditional', 742.

[160] *Francis Coralie Mullin* v. *The Administrator, Union Territory of Delhi and Others* MANU/SC/0492/1981 (Supreme Court of India, 13 January 1981).

[161] It is therefore often named in the context of socio-economic rights, even though, as Khosla points out, the issue at hand was 'a classic civil liberties case' (see Khosla, 'Making Social Rights Conditional', 743). Singh and Sathe are two of the many scholars who quote it in the context of Article

as an example for many cases in which the court 'passionately expresses' the justiciability of socio-economic rights, but refrains from actually defining their nature and explaining to what extent the judiciary may order the delivery of the right's content to right-bearers.[162] Khosla therefore rejects the view (at least as far as tangible consequences of court decisions are concerned) that the Indian Supreme Court 'has developed the world's most comprehensive body of judgments dealing with social welfare rights'.[163] Khosla criticizes a lack of engagement with the actual *outcome* of socio-economic rights adjudication by other scholars. He believes that this might be explained by the fact that scholars have chosen to mainly focus on the procedural side of the Supreme Court's judicial activism, that is, PIL.[164] Contributions that do consider the substantive effects of socio-economic rights adjudication more specifically[165] do not really, Khosla notes, discuss the question of remedies, that is, whether the 'minimum core', 'reasonable measures', or other doctrines are applied with corresponding remedies.[166]

---

21 and—supposedly—extensive socio-economic rights adjudication. See Mahendra P. Singh, 'Constitutionalization and Realization of Human Rights in India', in C. Raj Kumar, K. Chockalingam, and V.R. Krishna Iyer, eds, *Human Rights, Justice, and Constitutional Empowerment*, 2nd edition (New Delhi: Oxford University Press, 2010), 34–5 and Sathe, *Judicial Activism in India*, 112.

162 Khosla, 'Making Social Rights Conditional', 743.

163 Ran Hirschl, *Towards Juristocracy: The Origins and Consequences of the New Constitutionalism* (Cambridge, Mass.: Harvard University Press, 2004), 246 fn. 81.

164 Khosla, 'Making Social Rights Conditional', 744.

165 For instance, Jayna Kothari, 'Social Rights Litigation in India: Developments of the Last Decade', in *Exploring Social Rights: Between Theory and Practice*, ed. Daphne Barak-Erez and Aeyal M. Gross (Oxford, Portland, Or: Hart Publishing, 2007), Arun Thiruvengadam, 'The Global Dialogue Among Courts: Social Rights Jurisprudence of the Supreme Court of India From a Comparative Perspective', in *Human Rights, Justice, and Constitutional Empowerment*.

166 Khosla, 'Making Social Rights Conditional', 743–4.

The author uses the famous case of Olga Tellis as an illustration that Indian courts apply socio-economic rights 'conditionally'.[167] In this case, which concerned eviction of 'pavement dwellers' in Bombay (now Mumbai), the Supreme Court declared that the right to life and personal liberty included the right to livelihood. Notably, it came to this conclusion by also considering directive principles.[168] However, as Khosla notes, the Supreme Court did not apply an individualized right to shelter or housing that would have given the pavement dwellers alternative accommodation or, at least, a right that would ensure that the State take 'reasonable measures' aimed at providing such accommodation.[169] Instead, Khosla observes, the Court merely ensured that a proper procedure for eviction is followed.[170]

For one group amongst the persons affected, however, the Court did decide that they should be provided with housing. This group consisted of those people who had been registered in a 1976 census that was conducted in preparation for providing land and shelter for pavement dwellers, and who had also been given identity cards as part of the census.[171] This serves as an illustration for what

[167] *Olga Tellis and Others* v. *Bombay Municipal Corporation and Others* MANU/SC/0039/1985 (Supreme Court of India, 10 July 1985).

[168] 'Therefore, directive principles, which are fundamental in the governance of the country, must serve as a beacon light to the interpretation of the Constitutional provisions. Viewed in this context, it is urged, the impugned action of the State Government and the Bombay Municipal Corporation is violative of the provisions contained in Articles 19(1)(e), 19(1)(g) and 21 of the Constitution' (see Note 167, 22).

[169] Khosla, 'Making Social Rights Conditional', 747. The Court, stating that there was no 'right to make use of a public property for a private purpose', decided that an eviction was not an infringement of the right as long as certain procedural standards (most importantly, giving notice to the persons affected—though exceptions to this rule, as prescribed by section 314 of the Bombay Municipal Corporation Act, were possible and also constitutionally permissible) were fulfilled (see *Olga Tellis and Others* v. *Bombay Municipal Corporation and Others* MANU/SC/0039/1985, 43 et seq.).

[170] Khosla, 'Making Social Rights Conditional', 747.

[171] *Olga Tellis and Others* v. *Bombay Municipal Corporation and Others* MANU/SC/0039/1985, 57.

Khosla calls the 'conditional social rights approach': only under the *condition* that a State scheme existed that promised shelter to a certain group of people did those people have an individual right to shelter. The author likens this approach to private contract law, meaning that the State provides certain goods or services to a certain group of people only if it has committed itself to do so for these individuals.[172] The courts may then only test whether the State fulfils this 'contractual' duty, that is, if it supplies what it has promised.[173]

In addition to naming another 'pavement dweller' case where the Court followed a similar approach,[174] Khosla also illustrates the 'conditional social rights approach' by referring to the right to education cases, *Mohini Jain*[175] and *Unni Krishnan.*[176] As mentioned in Chapter 2, 'capitation fees' charged by private higher education institutions were the immediate concern of these. However,

172 Khosla, 'Making Social Rights Conditional', 748.

173 For another group of cases, Khosla also draws another private law analogy, speaking of *torts*. In cases that are usually named as examples for the judiciary applying the right to health, Khosla recognizes what he calls 'constitutional tort actions', in which the courts recognize something that 'resemble[s] an instance of negligence' and therefore allow something similar to tort actions against the State—albeit under the common fundamental rights Article 32. He names the case of *Paschim Banga Khet Mazdoorsamity* as an example how this may lead to individual remedies that look as if the courts apply the minimum core doctrine 'systemically': the aggrieved person was awarded compensation for his medical expenses, but only after the Court had recognized administrative failures (as a form of 'negligence') in the government hospitals where he had previously tried to get treatment before turning to a private hospital: 'the Court focused on the state's inability to effectively run hospitals rather than on the creation of new hospitals'. See Khosla, 'Making Social Rights Conditional', 754–6.

174 *Ahmedabad Municipal Corporation* v. *Nawab Khan Gulab Khan and Others* MANU/SC/0051/1997 (Supreme Court of India, 11 October 1996), as quoted at Khosla, 'Making Social Rights Conditional', 748–9.

175 *Miss Mohini Jain* v. *State of Karnataka and Ors* MANU/SC/0357/1992 (Supreme Court of India, 30 July 1992).

176 *Unni Krishnan, J.P. and Ors* v. *State of Andhra Pradesh and Ors* MANU/SC/0333/1993.

the cases are better known for the fact that the Court recognized a right to education as part of Article 21. Khosla notes that in *Unni Krishnan*, the Court asked for an affidavit by the State concerning the measures that had been taken to provide elementary education, but that it did not call for specific programmes to ensure that education be provided to every child. Furthermore, in contrast to the South African Constitutional Court's approach, the Supreme Court did not test the reasonableness of State efforts. It also did not order that the State undertake measures to build schools.[177]

But at the same time, in the context of limited resources being available to the State, the Court stated that 'while allocating the available resources, due regard should be had to [...] Articles 45 and 46'.[178] This wording is indeed curious, considering the fact the same judgment also states that the right to *higher* education 'must necessarily be limited in any given country by its economic and social circumstances',[179] apparently drawing a contrast to the right to *elementary* education, which needs to be defined by Article 45 (in its original form). This implies that the right to elementary education (that is, education for children up to 14 years) is *not* limited by financial constraints. In this, the judgment seems to be contradictory.

Khosla believes that the decisions ultimately only mean that '*when* [elementary] education is imparted it must be free', but that they do 'not require that the state *must* in fact provide education to all children'.[180] The author believes that this is also the only interpretation that can explain why the Supreme Court elaborated on free elementary education in a case concerning tuition fees for higher education in the first place.[181]

The 'conditional social rights model', therefore, means that 'a violation can only occur when the state undertakes an obligation

[177] Khosla, 'Making Social Rights Conditional', 750–1.

[178] Khosla, 'Making Social Rights Conditional', 750–1; *Unni Krishnan, J.P. and Ors* v. *State of Andhra Pradesh and Ors* MANU/SC/0333/1993, 147.

[179] Note 178, 50.

[180] Khosla, 'Making Social Rights Conditional', 751.

[181] Khosla, 'Making Social Rights Conditional', 751.

but does not fulfil it'.[182] In contrast, a systemic, non-conditional minimum core approach would mean that the courts 'examine whether every child is being educated', while even a 'weak-form reasonableness approach' would mean that the courts would ask 'if a reasonable number of children are being educated'.[183] The Indian approach to socio-economic rights, according to Khosla, is therefore 'far weaker' than the one applied by the South African Constitutional Court: '[T]here is no systemic right, only a conditional one. This conditional approach does not guarantee any standard – minimum core or reasonableness – for any social right.'[184] Still, Khosla believes that the strong *rhetoric* the Supreme Court uses has a value in itself: it has transformed (non-justiciable) goals into rights, and 'the Court attempts to change the social meaning of socio-economic guarantees' and 'continually reminds the state of its obligations', as the State may otherwise not seriously consider the contents of the directive principles.[185]

Khosla's assessment of the Supreme Court's adjudication has not gone without criticism. Thiruvengadam is sceptical whether the Supreme Court's approach to socio-economic rights can be 'analytically characterised' at all, 'given its fluid and ever-changing character'.[186] He explains the 'fluid character', in part, by the fact that judges of the Supreme Court usually sit in small two- or three-judge benches, even though their decisions are at the same time considered to be representative of the entire Supreme Court.[187] This factor indeed becomes even more decisive if one considers

182 Khosla, 'Making Social Rights Conditional', 751.

183 Khosla, 'Making Social Rights Conditional', 751.

184 Khosla, 'Making Social Rights Conditional', 759.

185 Khosla, 'Making Social Rights Conditional', 762.

186 Arun Thiruvengadam, 'Characterising and Evaluating Indian Social Rights Jurisprudence into the 21st Century', in *Constitutional Rights to Welfare in India* (Forthcoming), ed. Sudhir Krishnaswamy and Malini Bhattacharjee (Oxford University Press, 2018), https://azimpremjiuniversity.edu.in/SitePages/pdf/Characterising-and-evaluating-Indian-social-rights-jurisprudence-into-the-21st-century.pdf, accessed on 16 August 2018.

187 Thiruvengadam, 'Characterising and Evaluating Indian Social Rights Jurisprudence into the 21st Century'.

the fact that the tenure of individual judges tends to be quite short.[188] Still, Thiruvengadam believes that in the last one and a half decades (that is, since 2000), the Supreme Court has become 'more confident about its authority' concerning socio-economic rights cases, and has begun focusing more on implementation and effective monitoring of its orders.[189] The author uses several cases as an illustration, including the ones that Khosla uses to illustrate his 'conditional approach' observation. For instance, according to Thiruvengadam, the reason that the Supreme Court was reluctant to give strong remedies in *Olga Tellis* (even after having used such strong language to evoke the existence of a right to livelihood) may be the fact that the idea of reading directive principles into the right to life was still quite new at the time. Therefore, one may hypothesize that the Court may have been of the opinion that reading a directive principle into a fundamental right would be sufficient for the time being, and that the government would act accordingly as a consequence.[190] Later on, as the government frequently did not react to such 'requests' by the Court, it ended up taking 'more expansive efforts'.[191]

Concerning other cases, Thiruvengadam notes that Khosla omits the fact that the Supreme Court did not only examine the working of a State scheme and asked it to improve it, but also obliged the State to take additional measures.[192] To illustrate that

[188] Supreme Court justices retire at age 65 (see Article 124(2) of the Indian Constitution). Andhyarujina notes that as a consequence, the judges generally only have a tenure at the Supreme Court of three to six years before retirement (see T.R. Andhyarujina, 'The Age of Judicial Reform', *The Hindu*, 1 September 2012, http://www.thehindu.com/opinion/lead/the-age-of-judicial-reform/article3845041.ece, accessed on 19 August 2018).

[189] Thiruvengadam, 'Characterising and Evaluating Indian Social Rights Jurisprudence into the 21st Century'.

[190] Thiruvengadam, 'Characterising and Evaluating Indian Social Rights Jurisprudence into the 21st Century'.

[191] Thiruvengadam, 'Characterising and Evaluating Indian Social Rights Jurisprudence into the 21st Century'.

[192] Thiruvengadam, 'Characterising and Evaluating Indian Social Rights Jurisprudence into the 21st Century'.

the Supreme Court has become a lot more willing to apply strong remedies, Thiruvengadam points to the *Right to Food* case.[193] In this case, PUCL, an NGO, had filed a PIL to compel the State to provide food (which was available in food stocks) to drought-stricken areas. Interestingly, the case did not result in a single judgment, but several separate orders that compelled the State to take on a range of measures. Thiruvengadam notes that the Court did take 'pains to emphasise that it was only requiring the implementation of pre-existing governmental schemes and policies'.[194] However, this was only the case in its initial orders. The author points to the fact that the Court extended the case to all Indian states and union territories, even though the initial respondents were only the Union of India and the Food Corporation of India.[195] Furthermore, the state governments were to reopen Public Distribution System (PDS) shops and to identify 'below poverty line families' within a certain period of time.[196] Also, the states and union territories were ordered to implement central government schemes and periodically send reports on implementation.[197] Thus, the Court 'gave new life and meaning to the schemes'.[198]

193 *People's Union for Civil Liberties* v. *Union of India and Others*. An overview of the orders given in that case can be found at http://www.righttofoodcampaign.in/legal-action/supreme-court-orders, accessed on 15 August 2018. For a more detailed assessment of the Right to Food adjudication in India, see Chapter 6.

194 Thiruvengadam, 'Characterising and Evaluating Indian Social Rights Jurisprudence into the 21st Century'.

195 Thiruvengadam, 'Characterising and Evaluating Indian Social Rights Jurisprudence into the 21st Century' (see Supreme Court orders of 23 July 2001 and 17 September 2001, available at http://www.righttofoodindia.org/orders/may203.html, accessed on 15 August 2018). For a more detailed assessment of the Right to Food adjudication in India, see Chapter 6.

196 Thiruvengadam, 'Characterising and Evaluating Indian Social Rights Jurisprudence into the 21st Century'.

197 Thiruvengadam, 'Characterising and Evaluating Indian Social Rights Jurisprudence into the 21st Century'.

198 Thiruvengadam, 'Characterising and Evaluating Indian Social Rights Jurisprudence into the 21st Century'.

However, one may note that it may sometimes be difficult to clearly distinguish between what is an improvement and what is an expansion of a scheme, so Khosla's argument may still apply insofar as the State did use the existing schemes as a starting point in the *Right to Food* case.[199] Consequently, Thiruvengadam concedes that Khosla would still call these measures a conditional approach, as the Court did not pass orders entirely independent of the existing schemes. Still, he believes that 'by reviving and expanding what had become moribund policies, the Court was adopting aspects of a systemic approach'.[200] The most important novelty was however the Court's 'strategic focus' for implementation of its orders, which included setting up monitoring structures.[201]

[199] For instance, Thiruvengadam cites the case of *Paschim Banga Khet Mazdoorsamity*, where the Court did issue

> fresh directions of its own, many of which required the creation of new systems and facilities, including a centralised communication system and an ambulance system for transporting patients between hospitals. [...] What is more striking is the fact that the Court directed that the ambit of the directions be expanded beyond the State of West Bengal where the case originated from, and required the Central government to ensure that the Court's directions were implemented across the nation.

See Thiruvengadam, 'Characterising and Evaluating Indian Social Rights Jurisprudence into the 21st Century'.

[200] Thiruvengadam, 'Characterising and Evaluating Indian Social Rights Jurisprudence into the 21st Century'.

[201] Thiruvengadam, 'Characterising and Evaluating Indian Social Rights Jurisprudence into the 21st Century'. Birchfield and Corsi note concrete achievements as results of the Supreme Court's orders (such as directions to implement specific schemes and funds (re-)allocations that followed), but also concede that '[t]hese achievements [...] substantially depend on a particularly ripe legal and political environment and on the contributions of the *PUCL* Commission for the Supreme Court, a federal oversight body appointed by the Court to monitor and enforce the interim orders, and the Right to Food Campaign, a network of civil society organizations' (see Lauren Birchfield and Jessica Corsi, 'Between Starvation and Globalization: Realizing the Right to Food in India', *Michigan Journal of International Law* 31, no. 4 (2010): 700–1).

Also, there is another interesting case in which an Indian court provided a strong remedy. Interestingly, in this case, it had also applied the minimum core doctrine, as mentioned above. In the 2014 case of *Mohd. Ahmed,*[202] the Delhi High Court decided that a child from a poor family, who suffered from a rare genetic disease and required very expensive recurring treatment, must be given treatment free of charge when required at a government hospital in Delhi, explicitly referring to the 'minimum core' guaranteed by the right to health as part of the right to life.[203] This case is therefore an example of 'non-conditional', 'systemic' socio-economic rights adjudication. Still, one should note that it is a singular case, decided by a single-judge bench in one high court, and Thiruvengadam admits that the remedy 'may be unusual in the Indian context'.[204] Nonetheless, it might be an indication that the Indian judiciary is more willing (or has become more willing) to apply strong remedies in socio-economic rights cases than Khosla believes.

## Non-Applicability of the 'Conditional Social Rights Approach' to the Right to Education

How, then, can one expect the Indian courts to adjudicate Article 21A? As mentioned above, Khosla described the effects of the 1990s decisions of *Mohini Jain* and *Unni Krishnan*. According to his reading, those Supreme Court decisions meant that education for children up to the age of 14 must be free, and that children have a corresponding right that they could enforce in courts, but nothing more. Most importantly, the effect of the right as read into Article 21 was not that the State would have to build more schools or employ more teachers, meaning that litigation could not be successful in calling for an expansion of existing schemes.

202 *Mohd. Ahmed (Minor)* v. *Union of India* MANU/DE/0915/2014. This case is also noteworthy for the fact that it is a social rights case that is not a PIL, but instead a case in which the petitioner is a seven-year old child represented by his father, a rickshaw puller.

203 Note 202, 66 et seq.

204 Thiruvengadam, 'Characterising and Evaluating Indian Social Rights Jurisprudence into the 21st Century'.

Since then, two decisive changes have occurred in the legal framework: the addition of Article 21A and the enactment of the Right to Education Act. If Indian courts indeed merely applied socio-economic rights 'conditionally', then they would now restrict their adjudication to the implementation of the Act (as well as state rules 'below' it).

As a consequence of the existence of the Right to Education Act, even when applying the 'conditional' approach, the judiciary would now be obliged to call for remedies that are more far-reaching than it did in the judgments of *Mohini Jain* and *Unni Krishnan*. The Act itself states that '[e]very child of the age of six to fourteen years [...] shall have the right to free and compulsory education in a neighbourhood school till the completion of his or her elementary education' (Section 3(1)), and also that children above six years of age that have not been admitted in any school 'shall be admitted in a class appropriate to his or her age' (Section 4). Furthermore, and most importantly, Section 6 prescribes that 'the appropriate Government and the local authority shall establish, within such area or limits of neighbourhood, as may be prescribed, a school, where it is not so established'. Implementing this scheme means that new schools must be established as long as children anywhere in India are out of school, meaning that a court could (even if the right to education is understood to be 'conditional') order the construction of schools. Existing schools would have to admit children, even if, for instance, they cannot provide documents to prove their age (see Section 14(2)).

Another provision for which the courts may call for implementation is the one concerning the pupil–teacher ratio (Section 25, read with the Schedule to the Act), meaning that the judiciary may order the recruitment of more teachers. Also, the infrastructural standards defined in Section 19 and the Schedule mean that the courts could direct the State to upgrade or renovate schools. The prohibition of private tuitions offered by teachers would allow the judiciary to order that the State ensure that the teachers refrain from providing these services (Section 28).

However, even if one agrees with Khosla's observation concerning socio-economic rights adjudication in India in the past, such limited adjudication cannot be employed for the right to education anymore. The existence of Article 21A mandates that the judiciary take a different approach. This may be demonstrated by considering the question of what the scope of adjudication could have been if the State had created Article 21A, but not passed the Right to Education Act, or if it had passed an Act with a more limited scope.

Hypothetically, one may consider a Right to Education Act that merely prescribed that children already admitted in government schools would not have to pay tuition fees, but not that all children must be admitted in a neighbourhood school. Or, similarly, an Act that prescribed that primary education would only be free to an extent that the State considers feasible in the current economic situation, or an Act prescribing that education would only be free for children aged 6 to 12 instead of 6 to 14 years.

In such a scenario, the courts could not have restricted themselves to the implementation of the Act. The fact that Article 21A speaks of compulsory education to be provided 'to *all* children of the age of six to fourteen years' makes it clear that it cannot be read as a 'right for education to be free wherever it is provided'. Instead, a fully justiciable obligation on the State is imposed directly by Article 21A to design an education system (which includes building more schools, employing more teachers, and so on) that provides all children with education. Therefore, an Act worded as described would clearly not fulfil the obligation created by Article 21A, meaning that the judiciary would have to order that its scope be extended.

In one respect, even the existing Right to Education Act does not live up to Article 21A. Currently, as mentioned above, neither the Act nor any other legislation contain provisions that effectively create a compulsion on parents to regularly send their children to school either through sanctions or other enforcement mechanisms. If the application of the right to education by the judiciary were restricted to implementing the scheme created by the Act, it would appear that they could not order the State to create such 'compulsion provisions' (or create them themselves, if the legislature refrains from creating them).

The Act does speak of 'compulsory' education, and Section 10 of the Act states that parents have a duty to admit their child in a neighbourhood school. Article 51A(k) of the Constitution declares that parents have a fundamental duty 'to provide opportunities for education' for their children. The Act also imposes a duty on the local authority to maintain records of children residing within its jurisdiction and to 'ensure and monitor admission, attendance and completion of elementary education' (Section 9(d)(e)).

However, no legislation provides for any sanctions to be imposed on parents who fail to send their children to school regularly, or for other procedures through which the State could enforce the parents' 'duty'. The Compulsory Education Bill, 2006, which was introduced in the Rajya Sabha (the upper house of Parliament), actually included a section (Section 7) that prescribed a punishment of imprisonment up to six years for parents 'preventing' any child from going to school.[205] However, the Bill was never passed.

Without any such sanctions, procedures, or mechanisms, one can hardly speak of having created a system of 'compulsory' education, as the 'compulsion' only exists on paper. As it is, parents who do not comply with it have no consequences to fear. Sanctions or compulsive measures by the State like fines against the parents and/or the authorization of State authorities to forcefully take children to school against the parents' will are only possible if they are prescribed by legislation. The necessity of legislation exists not only because of rule of law principles, but also because of Article 21 of the Constitution, even if the latter is understood in a very narrow sense, as the State may only restrict a person's personal liberty 'according to [a] procedure established by law'.[206] Merely stating that State authorities have the task to 'ensure attendance' in the Act does not allow such sanctions or forceful measures. As far as the creation of legal prerequisites for compulsion are concerned, the omission itself cannot be justified by any financial or other constraints. There is no conceivable reason to not prescribe sanctions, procedures, or mechanisms in the written law, even if their implementation may not be possible instantly.

[205] See the text of the Bill available at http://164.100.24.219/BillsTexts/RSBillTexts/AsIntroduced/lv_2006.pdf, accessed on 15 August 2018.

[206] For more on the broad interpretation of Article 21, see Chapter 2.

As mentioned above, one may question to what extent it is actually desirable to punish parents who refrain from sending their children to school regularly. Enlarging the appeal of education by improving its quality may therefore be a more sensible measure for increasing attendance. However, Article 21A is unambiguous in this regard, explicitly calling for legislation that provides for *compulsory* education, meaning that merely ordering the implementation of the existing Right to Education Act does not suffice in this regard.

Therefore, while the Supreme Court might have been reluctant to give strong remedies for those socio-economic rights that it 'created' by reading contents from the directive principles catalogue into Article 21, and while it may have previously focused on improving existing State schemes and on using a strong rights rhetoric to give more importance to those socio-economic rights, this cannot be sufficient for the one right that the Constitution now explicitly provides as a justiciable fundamental right. Article 21A obliges the State to create a scheme *and* to set minimum standards for the contents of such a scheme. It does not merely order the implementation of whatever scheme the State creates. If a scheme is not created or not sufficient, then the fact that Article 21A is fully justiciable means that the courts can, at the very least, direct the State to create such a scheme, or to improve it.

In other words, if Khosla's reading is accurate concerning the situation of socio-economic rights in India (as they have been read into Article 21), then this would provide a clear answer to the previously un-answered question of what the inclusion of Article 21A signifies: the right to education that, after *Mohini Jain* and *Unni Krishnan*, was a 'conditional socio-economic right', has been turned into a 'systemic socio-economic right' by adding Article 21A to the constitutional text. Importantly, this would also mean that it is the only socio-economic right that has achieved this position in Indian constitutional law so far.

## Horizontal Effect

As far as the obligation to *protect* is concerned, the question arises to what extent the State is under an obligation to protect the right-bearer against encroachments by third parties, or to what extent the right has (indirect) horizontal effect. For the right to education in India, this question is becoming increasingly relevant considering the ongoing privatization of elementary education.

Scholars differentiate between *direct* and *indirect* horizontal effect. Direct horizontal effect means that it is not only private law that may give claims between private individuals, but that fundamental rights may as well, that is, that these rights are directly applicable between private individuals. Indirect horizontal effect, on the other hand, means that when interpreting statutory law that is applicable between individuals, the courts take fundamental rights of the parties concerned into account, that is, that rights influence the application of other legal norms between private individuals.[207] While at first sight, the latter is a 'weaker' form of horizontal application, this is not necessarily the case. As the example of German constitutional law shows, an indirect application might lead to stronger results than a direct one.[208]

[207] On the difference between indirect and direct horizontal effect, see, for instance, Garvin Phillipson, 'The Human Rights Act, "Horizontal Effect" and the Common Law: a Bang or a Whimper?', *Modern Law Review* 62, no. 6 (1999): 826; Stephen Gardbaum, 'The "Horizontal Effect" of Constitutional Rights', *Michigan Law Review* 102, no. 3 (2003): 394 et seq; Eric Engle, 'Third Party Effect of Fundamental Rights (Drittwirkung)', *Hanse Law Review* 5, no. 2 (2009), https://papers.ssrn.com/sol3/papers.cfm?abstract_id=1481552, accessed on 19 August 2018. On horizontal effect in comparative constitutional law, see M. Tushnet, 'The Issue of State Action/Horizontal Effect in Comparative Constitutional Law', *International Journal of Constitutional Law* 1, no. 1 (2003). On direct and indirect horizontal effect of the ECtHR, see Evert A. Alkema, 'The Third-Party Applicability or "Drittwirkung" of the European Convention on Human Rights', in *Protecting Human Rights: The European Dimension: Studies in Honour of Gérard J. Wiarda = Protection des droits de l'homme: la dimension européenne*, ed. Franz Matscher and Herbert Petzold (Köln: Heymanns, 1988); Andrew Clapham, 'The "Drittwirkung" of the Convention', in *The European System for the Protection of Human Rights*, ed. Ronald J. St. Macdonald, Franz Matscher, and Herbert Petzold (Dordrecht, Boston: M. Nijhoff, 1993).

[208] Cherednychenko argues—convincingly—that the indirect horizontal application of fundamental rights in Germany is 'stronger' than the

There are different methods to construct an indirect horizontal application of fundamental rights doctrinally. In the 1950s, the German Constitutional Court recognized the Basic Law's fundamental rights as an 'objective order of values' (*objektive Wertordnung*) that will influence all statutory law. Therefore, when interpreting any law, the German courts need to take fundamental rights into account (otherwise the courts themselves may infringe fundamental rights).[209]

Another method is to construct (and then focus on) the State's positive duty to protect its citizens from infringements of their fundamental rights, rather than to just refrain from infringing them itself. The State is thus under an obligation to create and apply laws in a way that the interests of the citizens that are protected by fundamental rights are also protected against transgressions from other private parties. German scholarly opinion,[210] as

direct horizontal application of fundamental rights in the Netherlands (see Olha O. Cherednychenko, 'Fundamental Rights and Private Law: A Relationship of Subordination or Complementarity?', *Utrecht Law Review* 3, no. 2 [2007]: 21–2).

209 Lüth BVerfGE 7, 198 (Bundesverfassungsgericht, 15 January 1958).

210 Klaus Stern, *Allgemeine Lehren der Grundrechte* (München: Beck, 1988), III/1, 742 et seq; Claus-Wilhelm Canaris, 'Grundrechte und Privatrecht', *Archiv für die civilistische Praxis (AcP)* 184 (1984): 225 et seq; Claus-Wilhelm Canaris, 'Grundrechtswirkungen und Verhältnismäßigkeitsprinzip in der richterlichen Anwendung und Fortbildung des Privatrechts', *Juristische Schulung (JuS)* 29, no. 3 (1989): 163; Hans H. Klein, 'Grundrechte am Beginn des 21. Jahrhunderts', in Merten; Papier, *Handbuch der Grundrechte in Deutschland und Europa*, 305 / 67; Günter Krings, *Grund und Grenzen grundrechtlicher Schutzansprüche: Die subjektiv-rechtliche Rekonstruktion der grundrechtlichen Schutzpflichten und ihre Auswirkung auf die verfassungsrechtliche Fundierung des Verbrauchervertragsrechts* (Berlin: Duncker & Humblot, 2003), 74 et seq. Murswiek sees a necessity for the State to protect citizens against infringements of their fundamental rights in order to justify the existence of the state ('Diese Schutzpflicht [...] beruht auch auf [...] dem Prinzip der Staatlichkeit') (see Dietrich Murswiek, 'Zu den Grenzen der Abänderbarkeit von Grundrechten', in Merten; Papier, *Handbuch der Grundrechte in Deutschland und Europa* 2: 193).

well as the German Federal Constitutional Court,[211] now leans towards this doctrine. As shall be shown below, it is also more adequate to describe how the Indian Supreme Court has applied fundamental rights horizontally in the past.

Some provisions in Part III of the Indian Constitution are obviously meant to be applied (directly) horizontally, otherwise their existence simply would not make much sense. For instance, Article 17 abolishes the concept of 'untouchability'. As this is primarily a phenomenon of discrimination within the society between individuals, merely outlawing the exercise of the concept by the State would have only a very limited, if any, effect. Similarly, Article 15(2) prohibits discrimination on grounds of religion, race, caste, and so on, with regard to 'access to shops, public restaurants, hotels, and places of public entertainment', and so on, and Articles 23 and 24 prohibit human trafficking, forced labour, and employment of children in factories.[212]

For these articles to have a practical effect, implementing legislation would be desirable, or perhaps even necessary. If one considers it a necessity, this would mean that these fundamental rights offer a positive right against the State to pass legislation that would protect right-bearers against actions by other private individuals. Therefore, through the State's duty to *protect*, these rights would have *indirect* horizontal effect.[213]

[211] Handelsvertreter BVerfGE 81, 242 (Bundesverfassungsgericht, 7 February 1990); Bestandsübertragung BVerfGE 114, 1–72 (Bundesverfassungsgericht, 26 July 2005).

[212] For the horizontal effect of Articles 17, 15(2), 23, 24, and others, see Mahendra P. Singh, 'Fundamental Rights, State Action and Cricket in India', *Asia Pacific Law Review* (2005): 204. Krishnaswamy notes that in *People's Union for Democratic Rights* v. *Union of India* MANU/SC/0038/1982, 21 (Supreme Court of India, 18 September 1982), the Supreme Court has held Articles 17, 23, and 24 to be applicable to private persons, even though it does not specify whom they are addressed to (see Sudhir Krishnaswamy, 'Horizontal Application of Fundamental Rights and State Action in India', in *Human Rights, Justice, and Constitutional Empowerment*, 52).

[213] Shankar and Tyago argue in this direction (see Uday Shankar and Divya Tyagi, 'Socio-Economic Rights in India: Democracy Taking

However, the Indian judiciary has applied these rights horizontally even in the absence of implementing legislation. Concerning Article 24, it was initially understood to only become effective once such legislation was passed.[214] Then, in the case of *People's Union for Democratic Rights*,[215] the Supreme Court decided that construction work would be considered as a 'hazardous environment' under Article 24, and that even without this kind of work being included in the Employment of Children Act of 1938, employing children for construction work is made illegal by Article 24: 'This is a constitutional prohibition which, even if not followed up by appropriate legislation, must operate *propiro vigore* [...] it is clear that by reason of this Constitutional prohibition, no child below the age of 14 years can be allowed to be engaged in construction work.'[216] Without using the terminology, the Court sees an indirect horizontal effect based on the duty to protect: '[T]he Union of India as also every state Government must ensure that this constitutional mandate is not violated in any part of the country.'[217]

The arguments raised in the decision actually point in the direction of a *direct* horizontal effect.[218] But the Court has shied away from giving a direct horizontal remedy, which might be interpreted in a way that the Court believes that private parties can *violate* a fundamental right, but that the *remedy* that results from this is

---

Roots', *Law and Politics in Africa, Asia, Latin America [VRU]* 42, no. 4 [2009]: 535, https://www.nomos-elibrary.de/10.5771/0506-7286-2009-4-527/socio-economic-rights-in-india-democracy-taking-roots-jahrgang-42-2009-heft-4?page=0, accessed on 19 August 2018).

[214] Singh speaks of a 'general understanding' 'that the right secured by Article 24 will hardly be effective in the absence of legislation prohibiting and penalising its violation' that existed up until the 1980s (see Mahendra Pal Singh, *V.N. Shukla's Constitution of India*, 12th edition [Lucknow: Eastern Book Co., 2013], 256).

[215] *People's Union for Democratic Rights* v. *Union of India* MANU/SC/0038/1982, also known as the *Asiad Workers'* case.

[216] Note 215, 8.

[217] Note 215, 8.

[218] Krishnaswamy, 'Horizontal Application of Fundamental Rights and State Action in India', 60.

a claim against the State (which can be enforced through writ petitions), meaning that the State has to become active to protect the right-bearer by taking action against the violator.[219] This would mean that the Court gives both direct (as far as the determination of a violation is concerned) as well as indirect horizontal effect (as far as the remedy is concerned) to Article 24 (and Article 23).[220]

Articles 17, 15(2), 23, and 24 are somewhat of a peculiarity. Most of the fundamental rights in Part III of the Constitution do not *necessarily* apply horizontally, directly, or indirectly. In assessing whether or not they may nonetheless have horizontal effect, some scholars point to Article 12, the first provision in Part III. It defines the meaning of 'the State' for the entire Part, specifying that 'State' includes the governments and legislatures of the Centre, all Indian states, as well as 'all local or other authorities'. Some scholars, and also the Supreme Court in some of its judgments, read Article 12 in a way that it implies that all fundamental rights only apply in the relationship between the State and individuals (apart from the few rights mentioned above),[221] even though the term 'the State' is

[219] Krishnaswamy, 'Horizontal Application of Fundamental Rights and State Action in India', 60.

[220] Krishnaswamy, 'Horizontal Application of Fundamental Rights and State Action in India', 60.

[221] Seervai writes 'against whom were fundamental rights to be enforced? Broadly speaking, against "the State" [...] as widely defined by Art. 12', without differentiating in between such Articles whose wording includes 'the State' and those whose wording does not (see H.M. Seervai, *Constitutional Law of India: A Critical Commentary*, 4th edition, 3 vols [Bombay, Mumbai, Delhi: N.M. Tripathi; F.H. Seervai; Distributors, Universal Law Pub. Co, 1991–6], 349 et seq.). In the case of *P.D. Shamdasani* v. *Central Bank of India Ltd* MANU/SC/0017/1951, 3 (Supreme Court of India, 21 December 1951), the Supreme Court does not cite Article 12, but argues that the setting of Article 19 itself in Part III of the Constitution 'clearly show that the article was intended to protect those freedoms against State action [...] Violation of rights of property by individuals is not within the purview of the article'. Also see *The State of West Bengal* v. *Subodh Gopal Bose and Ors* MANU/SC/0018/1953, 11 (Supreme Court of India, 17 December 1953), which states that 'the whole object of Part III of the Constitution is to provide protection for the

not part of the wording of all fundamental rights.[222] Most notably, Article 21 (the right to life and personal liberty) makes no reference to 'the State', suggesting that its content cannot be defined by Article 12.[223]

Nonetheless, omission, according to several (older) Supreme Court decisions, does not mean that such articles should be interpreted in a way that there could potentially also be violations by non-state actors. Specifically for Article 21, the Supreme Court in *P.D. Shamdasani*[224] stated that the omission of 'the State' in that Article does not mean that it was intended to protect individuals from violations of their life and personal liberty by private individuals. The Court argued that the words 'except by procedure established by law' meant that such an interpretation was not permissible.[225] The Court's argument was that when drafting Article 21, the Constitutional Assembly had expressed that it could only be addressed to the State, as only the State could enact

---

freedoms and rights mentioned therein against arbitrary invasion by the State'. For an overview of adjudication concerning this question, see Surya Deva, 'Human Rights Realization in an Era of Globalization: The Indian Experience', *Buffalo Human Rights Law Review* 12 (2006): 121 et seq.

222 Krishnaswamy notes that this is a common argument against horizontal application (see Krishnaswamy, 'Horizontal Application of Fundamental Rights and State Action in India', 52–3).

223 Singh names Articles 19, 20, 22, 25, 26, 29(1), 30(1), and 32 as other examples for provisions that make no reference to 'the State' (see Singh, 'Fundamental Rights, State Action and Cricket in India', 204). He argues that the definition in Article 12 can therefore have no influence on their scope (see Singh, 'Fundamental rights, State Action and Cricket in India', 205).

224 *P.D. Shamdasani* v. *Central Bank of India Ltd.* MANU/SC/0017/1951. The core question in this case was whether Article 31, which had a similar meaning, could be applied horizontally. However, the Court pointed at Article 21 for illustration of its arguments concerning Article 31. The view was later specifically confirmed for Article 21 (see *Shrimati Vidya Verma* v. *Dr. Shiv Narain Verma* MANU/SC/0072/1955, 7 et seq. [Supreme Court of India, 11 November 1955]).

225 *P.D. Shamdasani* v. *Central Bank of India Ltd* MANU/SC/0017/1951, 5.

'law' in order to limit the scope of Article 21. However, this argument is not entirely convincing: the words 'except for procedure established by law' only states that whoever (the government or a private person) wants to limit the scope of a person's right must follow a legally established procedure. Therefore, it does not necessarily mean that the Article is addressed solely to the body that is capable of making law.[226] Thus, the question of whether or not such fundamental rights whose scope is not explicitly limited to violations by the State was not answered satisfactorily.

Based on the historical conditions of the Constitution's drafting process, one may find arguments for horizontal application of all fundamental rights, even those whose wording *does* contain 'the State'.[227] According to this argument, the historical background speaks against a narrow interpretation of fundamental rights that would restrict their scope to a vertical effect. While in the West, fundamental rights were created to protect citizens 'against an overbearing state', in India they must be seen 'against the background of a pre-colonial tradition'.[228] In pre-colonial India, violations of the interests or values that are today protected by fundamental rights were commonly performed by private parties and not by the State.[229]

The 'pre-colonial' background indeed explains the existence of those fundamental rights that must logically apply between individuals, especially those that protect against caste-based discrimination and forced labour. It does not, however, necessarily follow that other fundamental rights ought to apply horizontally, directly or indirectly. While one may find it more adequate when considering Indian conditions and traditions to apply

[226] Krishnaswamy, 'Horizontal Application of Fundamental Rights and State Action in India', 56–7.

[227] See Singh, 'Fundamental Rights, State Action and Cricket in India'.

[228] Singh, 'Fundamental Rights, State Action and Cricket in India', 205.

[229] 'Therefore', Singh claims, 'the Constitution makers sought to safeguard the rights of the individual not only against the state but also against those non-state actors' (see Singh, 'Fundamental Rights, State Action and Cricket in India', 205).

(all) fundamental rights horizontally, that does not necessarily mean that the Constitution must be read that way, or that the Constitutional Assembly had intended horizontal application.

However, the judiciary has in practice departed from the view that those fundamental rights whose wording is not restricted to State violations can nonetheless only be applied vertically. There are several cases in which the courts have essentially applied fundamental rights horizontally (without actually discussing the doctrinal question of horizontal effect), particularly in cases concerning environmental issues under the right to health as a part of Article 21.[230]

An instructive judgment in this group of cases is the one of *M.C. Mehta* of 1986.[231] This case concerned an incident where harmful oleum gas had escaped one factory owned by a fertilizer producer. The petitioners saw an infringement of the right to health as part of the right to life and personal liberty. As the fertilizer producer was a private company, the question arose whether or not it could be held responsible (and whether or not damages could be claimed) under fundamental rights. The question was ultimately not decided for this particular company (because of lack of time to investigate the details of the company, the petitioners, who had

[230] See, for instance, *Dr. Ashok* v. *Union of India* MANU/SC/0577/1997 (Supreme Court of India, 2 May 1997), where the Supreme Court examined and defined the extent of the State's duty to outlaw hazardous pesticides, without discussing the fact that the pesticides are used by private individuals; *Bandhua Mukti Morcha* v. *Union of India* MANU/SC/0051/1983, 14 (Supreme Court of India, 16 December 1983), a case of bonded labourers where the Supreme Court saw a violation of Article 21 (in addition to Article 23) and stated that '[t]he State is under a constitutional obligation to see that there is no violation of the fundamental right of any person, particularly when he belongs to the weaker sections of the community'; *M.C. Mehta* v. *Union of India* MANU/SC/0327/1999 (Supreme Court of India, 29 April 1999), where the Supreme Court ordered that after an expiry of certain deadlines, only such vehicles may be registered in the National Capital Region that fulfil certain emission standards (due to the threat they pose to the health of the citizens).

[231] *M.C. Mehta* v. *Union of India* MANU/SC/0092/1986 (Supreme Court of India, 20 December 1986).

filed the case as a PIL, were advised to support aggrieved persons in claiming damages under civil law). However, the Supreme Court did state that private companies may be bound by fundamental rights and discussed under which circumstances this might be the case, and, in doing so, compiled a number of judgments that may answer this question.[232] It noted that the scope of Article 12 had been extended by the Court 'not to destroy the raison d'être of creating corporations but to advance the human rights jurisprudence' and spoke of a 'creative interpretation and bold innovation' in the field of human rights jurisprudence which 'cannot be allowed to be halted by unfounded apprehensions expressed by status quoists'.[233]

The Court quoted the case of *Ramana D. Shetty*, in which it had identified the question of whether or not the private corporation is carrying 'a governmental function' as one decisive criterion.[234] It also quoted the case of *Sukhdev*, in which it had stated that '[a]ctivities which are too fundamental to the society are by definition too important not to be considered government functions.'[235] Basing its argument on this precedent, the Court stated that the activity of producing chemicals and fertilizers 'is deemed by the State to be an industry of vital public interest' and that 'the activity should be ultimately carried out by the State itself'.[236] The Court then stated that if the State acts as an 'economic agent, economic entrepreneur and allocator of economic benefits', then

[232] Among them were *Rajasthan State Electricity Board* v. *Mohan Lal* MANU/SC/0360/1967 (Supreme Court of India, 3 April 1967); *Sukhdev Singh, Oil & Natural Gas Commission* v. *Bhagat Ram* MANU/SC/0667/1975 (Supreme Court of India, 21 February 1975); *Ramana Dayaram Shetty* v. *The International Airport Authority* MANU/SC/0048/1979 (Supreme Court of India, 4 May 1979); *Ajay Hasia Etc* v. *Khalid Mujib Sehravardi* MANU/SC/0498/1980 (Supreme Court of India, 13 November 1980), as cited in *M.C. Mehta* v. *Union of India* MANU/SC/0092/1986, 11, 12, 17.

[233] Note 231, 30.

[234] *Ramana Dayaram Shetty* v. *The International Airport Authority* MANU/SC/0048/1979.

[235] *Sukhdev Singh, Oil & Natural Gas Commission* v. *Bhagat Ram* MANU/SC/0667/1975, 103.

[236] *M.C. Mehta* v. *Union of India* MANU/SC/0092/1986, 26.

this should also be the case for a private corporation that is under 'the functional control of the State' because of State regulation and licensing in the industry that it is active in.[237]

Of course, one should notice that these judgments were delivered prior to the liberalization of India's economy in the 1990s. Today, the argument that corporations are under the 'functional control of the State' because of licenses is weaker than it used to be in most industries.

Still, even in more recent years, there have been similar developments. Some of those point in the direction of those fundamental rights that *are* explicitly addressed at 'the State' having horizontal effect as well. In the case of *Vishaka*, the Supreme Court applied Articles 14 and 15, both guaranteeing the right to equality (in this case against gender discrimination and sexual violence against women), Article 19(1)(g) (guaranteeing, inter alia, the right to practise any profession), and Article 21 in order to create rules to protect women from sexual harassment at workplace.[238] The Court saw a constitutional duty to protect citizens against infringements by private parties flowing from the cited articles, which (apart from Article 21) are all explicitly addressed at 'the State'. As the petition was directed against the state (of Rajasthan), the result was a case of indirect horizontal effect. The Court saw a necessity for new law to be passed because of the constitutional duty flowing from fundamental rights. Unfortunately, the Court did not discuss the question of why it believed that Articles 14, 15, and 19(1)(g) could be applied horizontally; it just applied them without explaining itself in this regard.[239] The judgment does,

[237] Note 236, 28.

[238] The Court saw itself competent to essentially act as a legislative power because of continuous inactivity of Parliament in this field: 'The obligation of this Court under Article 32 [...] for the enforcement of these fundamental rights in the absence of legislation must be viewed along with the role of judiciary envisaged in the Beijing Statement of Principle of the Independence of the Judiciary in the LAWASIA region', *Vishaka & Ors* v. *State of Rajasthan & Ors* MANU/SC/0786/1997, 11.

[239] It merely stated that incidents like the one of a gang rape of a social worker that sparked the petition are 'a clear violation of the rights under Articles 14, 15 and 21 [...] [and] also the violation of the victim's

however, refer to one of the fundamental duties listed in Article 51A of the Indian Constitution: Article 51A(a) declares that it shall be the duty of every Indian citizen 'to abide by the Constitution'. But the Court did not elaborate on why this duty is relevant in the given case. Still, this reference could be a doctrinal explanation for a horizontal application of fundamental rights, though it would actually point to direct horizontal effect. If it is the duty of every citizen to abide by the Constitution and, therefore, to respect other citizens' fundamental rights, this could give those other citizens a direct claim against the infringer. In any case, so far, it does not appear that the judiciary has really adopted this argument as a doctrine.[240]

Also in other respects, *Vishaka* has remained an exceptional decision, but an important one with high authority, considering that the opinion of the three-judge bench was given by Chief Justice Verma. Some subsequent cases, like the case of *Zee Telefilms*, also point in a different direction.[241] In that case, the question arose whether or not the Board of Control for Cricket in India would have to be considered 'the State' in fundamental rights questions, even though it is a private society. Based on the reasons given in the pre-1990s judgments cited above, one could argue that this must be the case, as the Board held *exclusive* television rights to cricket matches. Nonetheless, the Supreme Court decided that 'unlike the rights under *Articles 17 and 21 which can be claimed against non-state actors* including individuals' (emphasis added), the right to practise any profession or carry on trade, occupation, or business under Article 19(1)(g) could only be asserted against the State and not a private institution.[242]

---

fundamental right under Article 19(1)(g) [...] Such violations, therefore, attract the remedy under Article 32 for the enforcement of these fundamental rights of women' (see Note 238, 3).

[240] Krishnaswamy, 'Horizontal Application of Fundamental Rights and State Action in India', 54.

[241] On this case, see Singh, 'Fundamental Rights, State Action and Cricket in India'.

[242] *Zee Telefilms Ltd* v. *Union of India* MANU/SC/0074/2005, 28 (Supreme Court of India, 2 February 2005).

At the very least, however, the judgment shows that the view that Article 21 can be applied both vertically and horizontally is, by now, relatively well established. The Supreme Court has just not discussed this issue or the theoretical foundation for the extension of the right's scope at length in any of the previous cases. Furthermore, the case of *Vishaka* shows that in addition to that, the limitation to vertical effect is not set in stone even for those articles addressed at 'the State'.[243] However, concerning those articles and fundamental rights, it remains to be seen in which direction adjudication will move in the future.

Considering this history of (non-)horizontal application of fundamental rights in adjudication, one may conclude that the question of whether or not the Indian Constitution's fundamental rights are applicable horizontally cannot be answered uniformly. Rather, the answer is different depending on the particular right. For some rights, the courts have argued towards direct horizontal effect (those rights that are logically aimed at private parties as well), some have been applied indirectly horizontally quite frequently (those that are, through their wording, not exclusively aimed at the State; primarily Article 21), and others have only been given indirect horizontal effect in exceptional cases (for example, the *Vishaka* judgment).[244]

The horizontal scope of Article 21 also has implications for the rights that have been found to be part of the right to life and personal liberty, including the right to education. This becomes especially relevant in an era of economic liberalization, which has, as described in Chapter 1, also shaped the field of elementary education.

[243] The Supreme Court had even entertained the idea of an indirect horizontal effect for Article 14 as early as in *People's Union for Democratic Rights* v. *Union of India* MANU/SC/0038/1982 (see Krishnaswamy, 'Horizontal Application of Fundamental Rights and State Action in India', 59).

[244] Krishnaswamy likens this to the rule given by Section 8(2) of the South African Constitution's Bill of Rights, which prescribes horizontal application 'taking account of the nature of the right and the nature of any duty imposed by the right' (see Krishnaswamy, 'Horizontal Application of Fundamental Rights and State Action in India', 63).

In those last couple of decades, the tendency or desire of the State to run 'industries of vital public interest' 'under its industrial policy' described in the Supreme Court decisions of earlier decades does not exist anymore. Rather, the opposite is the case. The State has shown more and more willingness to privatize such industries, and also to allow privatization of the 'public good' of education.

Privatization in itself evokes the question of horizontal application of fundamental rights. If the State decides that the private sector may henceforth supply public goods, at least in part, and if there is a right against the State to provide these goods, not giving a right against the private 'suppliers' would considerably weaken that right. At least there ought to be a right against the State to ensure that the contents of the right are provided by the private parties in a certain manner (that is, there ought to be indirect horizontal effect). Consequently, one may argue that the devolution of public power into the hands of private parties mandates an expansion of human rights that will accompany privatization.[245]

Under the Right to Education Act, the State has given itself a substantive amount of control over private schools by outlawing the running of schools without a license and naming minimum prerequisites for receiving (and keeping) a license (Sections 18 and 19). Perhaps even more importantly, the Act goes as far as compelling private schools (even such ones that are running entirely without state funds) to accept children from economically backwards families in 25 per cent of their total seats (Section 12). With these provisions, the State has decided to delegate part of its constitutional duty (that is, broadening the scope of free and compulsory elementary education) to private schools by making it *their* legal duty to provide their services to those children who are primarily targeted by the right, that is, the poor.

Even if one is sceptical concerning the general possibility of applying the Indian Constitution's fundamental rights horizontally, the right to education is a unique case in this respect as well. Even if one sees most of the rights in Part III as classical civil and political or 'first generation' rights without a positive scope (and

[245] Singh, 'Fundamental Rights, State Action and Cricket in India', 205–6.

without an obligation to *protect*) and followed the 'old view' that horizontal application is an exception applicable only for very few articles, one will still have to accept that Article 21A has a positive scope, imposing a duty on the State to provide a functioning primary education system, and to ensure that children attend school and receive adequate education. The children, represented by their parents, have a corresponding claim against the State. If the State decides to (in part) employ private parties in providing elementary education, then it needs to ensure that the education that they provide fulfils the standards that the fundamental right imposes on the State, as it would otherwise fail in providing for the right whenever it allows private initiative.[246] If the right did not have such an effect, the State would be able to dispose of its duties through privatization.

Because of this constitutional duty, the State needs to retain some control over the private education sector. For instance, it must define minimum standards that the private schools have to fulfil in terms of infrastructure, teacher qualifications, curricula, and so on, and also monitor the performance of private schools in order to be able to assess whether the private education sector is functioning and to be able to act if it is not. Concerning the rule of (minimum of) 25 per cent of children from economically backwards families in (non-minority) private schools, the State needs to undertake special efforts to ensure that they receive adequate education from their schools, as children from such backgrounds are the children at whom the fundamental right is primarily targeted.

This in turn means that the constitutionality (that is, whether or not the State lives up to its responsibility to *protect* as well as to *fulfil*, the latter with the help of private schools) of the education system created by the Right to Education Act can be tested in this respect as well. Courts may therefore assess whether or not the Act sets adequate minimum standards for private schools. They

[246] As the Supreme Court had stated in *Mohini Jain* (see Chapter 2), '[w]hen the State Government grants recognition to the private educational institutions it creates an agency to fulfil its obligation under the Constitution' (see *Miss Mohini Jain* v. *State of Karnataka and Ors.* MANU/SC/0357/1992, 17).

may also assess whether the Act and state rules under the Act provide an adequate system for children from economically backwards families to gain access to private schools, and to be educated in the schools without discrimination as compared to the children whose parents are paying the fees.

The Supreme Court has expressed such a view in a couple of its judgments that mention Article 21A, even though the cases themselves did not primarily deal with education. In the case of *Jatya Pal Singh*, the question arose whether or not the telecommunications company Videsh Sanchar Nigam Limited (VSNL) could be considered to be part of the State under Article 12.[247] Videsh Sanchar Nigam Limited had originally been founded by the Government of India, but was gradually privatized, with the state holding 26.97 per cent of the shares at the time of the judgment.[248] The Court noted that one would have to draw a line between a body performing a 'private function' or a 'public function', and that a public function would be exercised if a body intervenes or participates 'in social or economic affairs in the public interest'.[249] To illustrate what a 'public function' would be, the Court differentiated the activities of VSNL from imparting education to children, with the latter being, even if it is provided by private parties, 'a sovereign function which is required to be performed by the Union of India', as the right to education 'is a fundamental right [...] as provided in Article 21A'.[250] Interestingly, also in the case of *Zee Telefilms*, the Court suggested that Article 21A has horizontal effect. The Court stated that expansion of the concept of State may not only occur in business, but also in other activities that have 'a directive influence on the citizens'. Therefore, Article 21A required an expansion of the concept of State action. Once a school receives 'state patronage', 'its activities would be State activities and thus would be subject to judicial review'.[251]

[247] *Jatya Pal Singh and Ors* v. *Union of India and Ors* MANU/SC/0401/2013 (Supreme Court of India, 17 April 2013).

[248] Note 247, 21.

[249] Note 247, 50 et seq.

[250] Note 247, 52.

[251] *Zee Telefilms Ltd* v. *Union of India* MANU/SC/0074/2005, 96, 101.

As has been shown in Chapter 1, there is an enormous discrepancy in the quality standards between private schools. While they seem to perform better, on average, than government schools, it is clear that, at the very least, low-cost private schools do not provide an adequate level of education that Article 21A calls for. The State is, therefore, under an obligation to ensure quality improvement in these schools as well. How this scope of the right may be enforced shall also be discussed in the next chapters, particularly in Chapter 6.

## Adjudication of Article 21A by the Supreme Court

Since the creation of Article 21A, the Supreme Court has mentioned the provision in a total of 48 orders and judgments. The majority of those judgments (38) were passed after the Right to Education Act went into force in early 2010.[252]

Interestingly, most judgments do not concern the issues discussed above, such as discrimination of certain groups of children, the right of a child to be admitted, what the minimum quality standards should be, and so on. Many of the judgments mention Article 21A more or less 'in passing', and some do not even concern elementary education themselves. Others do make statements concerning its contents, but are not very specific.

Some judgments in which the Court mentions Article 21A are only indirectly related to its possible contents, such as cases concerning establishment of colleges for Bachelors of Education courses,[253] or whether there could be restrictions on 'Vedic' universities

[252] As of 18 August 2018, a search for 'Article 21A' in Supreme Court documents on the database Manupatra brings up 48 results. 10 judgments and orders were issued before, 38 after 1 April 2010. Seven of those 48 total documents concern three petitions (*Ashok Kumar Thakur*: two documents, *Environmental and Consumer Protection Foundation*: four documents, *J.K. Raju*: two documents), bringing the list of actual cases decided between 2002 and 18 August 2018 down to 43.

[253] *State of Maharashtra* v. *Sant Dnyaneshwar Shikshan Shastra Mahavidyalaya and Ors* MANU/SC/1756/2006 (Supreme Court of India, 31 March 2006).

that wish to teach science.[254] Several cases concern appointment, remuneration, and duties of teachers, for instance, concerning the question whether or not teachers in government-aided schools have to be paid at par with teachers in government schools,[255] appointment and remuneration of teachers as a general question,[256] as well as concerning special 'project schools' in a state[257] or concerning engineering colleges,[258] whether priority has to be given to trained teachers,[259] to what extent teachers may be obliged to work on election duty,[260] which teachers may be eligible for special trainings,[261] whether a state is required to provide salary to teachers of schools receiving state aid through grants,[262] and so on. Some of those merely mention Article 21A and state that it has 'made education a fundamental right', without discussing its contents.[263]

[254] *Maharshi Mahesh Yogi Vedic Vishwavidyalay* v. *State of M.P. and Ors* MANU/SC/0644/2013 (Supreme Court of India, 3 July 2013).

[255] *State of Rajasthan and Anr.* v. *S. R. Hr. Sec. School and Ors* MANU/SC/1264/2004 (Supreme Court of India, 15 September 2004).

[256] *State of U.P. and Ors* v. *Shiv Kumar Pathak and Ors* MANU/SC/0898/2017 (Supreme Court of India, 25 July 2017); *State of U.P. and Ors* v. *Anand Kumar Yadav and Ors* MANU/SC/0897/2017 (Supreme Court of India, 25 July 2017). In those cases, the question that was also raised was to what extent state governments are competent to define minimum qualifications for teachers' appointment.

[257] *State of Bihar and Ors* v. *Project Uchcha Vidy, Sikshak Sangh and Ors* MANU/SC/0054/2006 (Supreme Court of India, 3 January 2006).

[258] *Secretary Mahatama Gandhi Mission and Ors* v. *Bhartiya Kamgar Sena and Ors* MANU/SC/0024/2017 (Supreme Court of India, 5 January 2017).

[259] *Nand Kishoe Ojha* v. *Madan Mohan Jha* MANU/SC/7238/2007 (Supreme Court of India, 19 March 2007).

[260] *Election Commission of India* v. *St. Mary's School and Ors* MANU/SC/4627/2007 (Supreme Court of India, 6 December 2007).

[261] *State of U.P. and Ors* v. *Bhupendra Natz Tripathi and Ors* MANU/SC/0917/2010 (Supreme Court of India, 29 October 2010).

[262] *State of U.P.* v. *Pawan Kumar Divedi* MANU/SC/0753/2014 (Supreme Court of India, 2 September 2014).

[263] *State of Rajasthan and Anr.* v. *S. R. Hr. Sec. School and Ors* MANU/SC/1264/2004, 23; *State of Bihar and Ors* v. *Project Uchcha Vidy, Sikshak Sangh and Ors* MANU/SC/0054/2006, 2.

Interestingly, in some of those cases concerning teachers, the Court clarified that Article 21A calls for certain standards of *quality* in education, which may be achieved by ensuring that teachers have a certain level of competence.[264] In the case of *Nand Kishore Ojha*, the Court directed the state of Bihar to act upon an affidavit in which that state had declared that priority would be given to trained teachers in appointments 'to achieve the constitutional goal of free and compulsory education', and to enhance teachers' capability and quality of teaching.[265] Similarly, in the *Election Commission of India* case, which deals with the question of teachers' obligation to work on election duty, the Court ruled that teachers should ordinarily be obliged to perform duties of roll revisions and election works on holidays and non-teaching days, while non-teaching staff of schools may also be obliged to perform these duties on those days.[266] In the case of *Bhupendra Nath Tripathi*, the Court declared that the state must take adequate steps to ensure that there be an adequate number of efficient and qualified teachers in schools, and that teachers must receive appropriate and adequate training from recognized training institutes because otherwise Article 21A would 'remain illusory'.[267] In *Bhartiya Seva Samaj Trust*, the Court stated that in light of the existence of Article 21A, 'education *and particularly [...] elementary/basic education* has to be qualitative and for that the trained teachers are required' (emphasis added).[268]

264 See, for instance, *State of U.P. and Ors* v. *Anand Kumar Yadav and Ors* MANU/SC/0897/2017.

265 *Nand Kishoe Ojha* v. *Madan Mohan Jha* MANU/SC/7238/2007, 2, 4.

266 *Election Commission of India* v. *St. Mary's School and Ors* MANU/SC/4627/2007, 12. (b), 21., 29. In the reasons given for the judgment, the Court mentions Article 21A, but, more extensively, elaborates on the importance that the time limit in the original Article 45 had given to education.

267 *State of U.P. and Ors* v. *Bhupendra Nath Tripathi and Ors* MANU/SC/0917/2010, 11.

268 *Bhartiya Seva Samaj Trust Tr. Pres. and Anr.* v. *Yogeshbhai Ambalal Patel and Anr.* MANU/SC/0741/2012, 18 (Supreme Court of India, 14 September 2012).

Similarly, in the case of *Mamata Mohanty*, the Court highlighted the importance of high academic standards 'for the progress of a nation'.[269] However, that case actually concerned standards for teachers in *higher* education.[270] Still, in its arguments, the Court mentioned Article 21A in that context noting that quality of education depends on several factors, but that the 'most relevant of them' is 'excellence of teaching staff', without differentiating between elementary education, secondary education, or higher education as far as their constitutional positions are concerned.[271]

Recently, the Court has tested the validity the National Council for Teacher Education's system of Teacher Eligibility Test, a system that was created under Section 23 of the Right to Education Act to ensure a certain level of quality.[272] The system's concessions to aspiring teachers from certain categories (that is, general category versus 'reserved' categories such as Schedules Castes and Scheduled Tribes) were challenged, but upheld by the Court because of constitutional provisions allowing affirmative action, with the Court concluding that the system would still ensure a certain amount of quality due to the ultimate selection process still being based on merits.[273]

In *R.D. Upadhyay*, the Court ruled that the State is under an obligation to provide for children living in prisons with their mothers who are imprisoned while being under trial or as convicts.[274] The Court issued certain guidelines to be followed to ensure the safety and dignified living of such children, including that they must live in crèches and nurseries attached to prisons so that they

[269] *State of Orissa and Anr.* v. *Mamata Mohanty* MANU/SC/0110/2011, 17 (Supreme Court of India, 9 February 2011).

[270] Note 269. The Court even went as far as saying that '[d]emocracy depends for its own survival on a high standard of vocational and professional education'.

[271] Note 269.

[272] *Vikas Sankhala and Ors* v. *Vikas Kumar Agarwal and Ors* MANU/SC/1318/2016 (Supreme Court of India, 18 October 2016).

[273] Note 272.

[274] *R.D. Upadhyay* v. *State of A.P. and Ors* MANU/SC/2061/2006 (Supreme Court of India, 13 April 2006).

may receive education.[275] The decisions were based on Article 21A as well as other provisions.[276]

In some cases, the Court has also ruled that Article 21A imposes an obligation on the State to protect children from harm in educational institutions, also in private schools. In one case, the Court created guidelines to be followed by state governments as well as government schools and private schools for the safety of students after children had died in a fire in a private school. Such guidelines included ensuring that school buildings are constructed in accordance with safety norms as provided by the National Building Code of India, installing fire extinguishers in every school building, ensuring appropriate training of staff on how to use fire extinguishers, ensuring that school buildings are free from inflammable materials, and so on. The Court, again, cited Article 21A as one of the several provisions relating to education.[277] In another case, a child rights organization appealed against an acquittal by the Bombay High Court of three men accused of physical and sexual abuse of children in children's homes run by them. The Court also mentioned Article 21A, but only to illustrate the constitutional importance of protecting children, as this case was not related to an educational institution.[278] In the case of *Bachpan Bachao Andolan*, which dealt with a number of child rights issues such as child trafficking, the Court also discussed the issue of child labour, stating that Article 21A imposes a duty on the State to prevent it, specifically in circuses.[279]

Other cases concern the implementation of the provisions of the Right to Education Act concerning infrastructural standards. For the orders in the case of *Environmental and Consumer Protect. Found.*, the Court had called for affidavits to be filed by different state governments concerning improvements of schools'

[275] Note 274, 6.

[276] Note 274, 2.

[277] *Avinash Mehrotra* v. *Union of India and Ors* MANU/SC/0555/2009, 1, 24, 26, 27, 33, 34, 38, 40 (Supreme Court of India, 13 April 2009).

[278] *Childline India Foundation and Anr.* v. *Allan John Waters and Ors* MANU/SC/0254/2011, 24 (Supreme Court of India, 18 March 2011).

[279] *Bachpan Bachao Andolan* v. *Union of India and Ors* MANU/SC/0431/2011, 67, 68 (Supreme Court of India, 18 April 2011).

infrastructure, meaning that the Court sought to monitor (lack of) progress in implementation.[280] The Court also specifically ordered that drinking water must be provided in schools[281] and that there must be separate toilets for boys and girls.[282] In the cases of *J.K. Raju* and *Shiv Kumar Pathak*, the Court ordered that vacant teacher positions must be filled.[283]

Then there are cases in which the Right to Education Act and its implementation is challenged by private schools. As already mentioned in Chapter 1, in the cases of *Society for Unaided Private Schools of Rajasthan*, the Supreme Court first ruled that the provisions of the Right to Education Act does not apply for government-aided private minority schools,[284] and then in *Pramati Educational and Cultural Trust* went beyond that judgment by declaring that it applies neither to aided nor to un-aided private minority schools.[285] In those cases, the petitioners primarily opposed Section 12(b, c) of the Right to Education Act, which requires them to accept children from weaker sections of the society in 25 per cent of their seats.

[280] *Environmental and Consumer Protect. Found.* v. *Delhi Administration and Ors* MANU/SC/0822/2011 (Supreme Court of India, 29 March 2011).

[281] *Environmental and Consumer Protect. Found.* v. *Delhi Administration and Ors* MANU/SC/1366/2011 (Supreme Court of India, 29 April 2011).

[282] *Environmental and Consumer Protect. Found.* v. *Delhi Administration and Ors* MANU/SC/0393/2012 (Supreme Court of India, 12 March 2012); *Environment and Consumer Protection Foundation* v. *Delhi Administration and Ors* MANU/SC/0821/2012 (Supreme Court of India, 3 October 2012).

[283] *State of U.P.* v. *Shiv Kumar Pathak* MANU/SC/1241/2014 (Supreme Court of India, 17 December 2014); *J. K. Raju* v. *State Of Andhra Pradesh and Anr*. MANU/SCOR/30475/2015 (Supreme Court of India, 28 October 2015).

[284] *Society for Un-aided Private Schools of Rajasthan* v. *Union of India & Another* MANU/SC/0311/2012 (Supreme Court of India, 12 April 2012).

[285] *Pramati Educational & Cultural Trust* v. *Union of India & Ors* MANU/SC/0419/2014 (Supreme Court of India, 6 May 2014).

However, problematically, the Supreme Court went as far as ruling that private schools (aided or un-aided) are exempt from the *entire* Right to Education Act.[286] In these judgments, the Court ruled that the special protection given to minority education institutions by Article 30(1) of the Constitution weighed stronger than Article 21A concerning the question whether or not they can be obliged to accept a certain number of students from weaker sections. Considering this argument, it is unclear why it chose to exclude such schools from the effect of all other provisions of the Act as well, or why it did not rule that there may be an obligation to at least accept children from weaker sections within the respective minority. As mentioned in Chapter 1, there is little clarity on how one should actually define 'minority educational institution', leading to a situation in which many schools seek 'minority status' in order to avoid being bound by the Act.

However, with these judgments, the Supreme Court did follow its own precedent of giving special protection to minority schools. In the case of *Sindhi Education Society*, the Supreme Court had decided that rules for the Union Territory of Delhi with similar effect as Section 12(b, c) of the right to education were unconstitutional as they violated Article 30(1).[287]

[286] '[T]he said 2009 Act and in particular [not only!] Sections 12(1) and 18(3) infringes the fundamental freedom guaranteed to unaided minority schools under Article 30(1)' (see *Society for Un-aided Private Schools of Rajasthan* v. *Union of India & Another* MANU/SC/0311/2012, 20). The view was confirmed in *Pramati Educational & Cultural Trust* v. *Union of India & Ors* MANU/SC/0419/2014: 'In our view, if the 2009 Act is made applicable to minority schools, aided or unaided, the right of the minorities Under Article 30(1) of the Constitution will be abrogated. Therefore, the 2009 Act insofar it is made applicable to minority schools referred in Clause (1) of Article 30 of the Constitution is *ultra vires* the Constitution.'

[287] *Sindhi Education Society and Anr.* v. *The Chief Secretary, Govt. of NCT of Delhi and Ors* MANU/SC/0476/2010 (Supreme Court of India, 8 July 2010). Rule 64 of the Delhi School Education Rules, 1973 required schools to accept children from Scheduled Castes and Scheduled Tribes.

The most informative case concerning the scope of Article 21A is the one of *Ashok Kumar Thakur*.[288] The case was referred by a three-judge bench to a larger five-judge bench, including the chief justice, which gives the 2008 judgment particularly high authority as precedent.[289] The petitioner challenged the Constitution (Ninety-Third) Amendment Act, 2005, which added a new clause (5) to Article 15 of the Constitution that allowed special legal provisions for reservations in aided and un-aided private educational institutions, except for minority educational institutions referred to in Article 30(1). The petitioner argued that the amendment was unconstitutional because it violated the basic structure of the Constitution as it 'adversely affected' the doctrine of equality.[290] The Court, however, ruled that the Act did not violate the basic structure as it gave effect to Directive Principles of State Policy, particularly concerning education as expressed by Article 45 and now Article 21A.[291]

More importantly, though not directly related to the core questions of the case, Justice Bhandari, in his concurring opinion, also underlined the State's obligation to pass enabling legislation under Article 21A, and outlined standards that such legislation must fulfil, including concerning the question of compulsory education. He directed the central government to set a time limit for itself within which it aims to pass implementing legislation. He declared that the central government must set this time limit within six months, declaring that the Court may have to intervene if the central government fails to fulfil this duty in time.[292] Stressing the importance of regular attendance, Bhandari noted that parents should be given 'creative incentives' to send their children to school, which will be more effective

[288] *Ashoka Kumar Thakur* v. *Union of India and Ors* MANU/SC/1397/2008 (Supreme Court of India, 10 April 2008).

[289] *Ashoka Kumar Thakur* v. *Union of India and Ors* MANU/SC/3169/2007 (Supreme Court of India, 17 May 2007).

[290] *Ashoka Kumar Thakur* v. *Union of India and Ors* MANU/SC/1397/2008, 27, 30.

[291] Note 290, 40, 47.

[292] Note 290, 355.

than punishments.[293] However, he also argued that the fundamental duty of parents and guardians to send their children to school (Article 51A(k)) clarified that 'compulsory' in Article 21A must be understood as 'compulsion on parents/guardians',[294] meaning that the Article created an obligation on the State to define sanctions that may act as an effective deterrence.[295]

The judge also summarized experiences with compulsory education (with effective implementation) in other countries and the positive effects resulting from it.[296] Furthermore, he noted that the State had failed to give effect to this compulsion, as there were only some state laws levying very low fines on parents, and those laws were also not effectively enforced ('perhaps have never been implemented')[297]: 'If we analyze the legislation passed by different States, another conclusion becomes obvious: no State has provided for an adequate punishment whose effect would be to deter citizens from committing a violation'.[298] Therefore, because of the existence of Article 21A, fines would have to be increased.[299]

However, taking into account the fact that some parents may refrain from sending their children to school regularly because of economic necessities, he also called for a financial incentive programme to 'make education viable for the poor'.[300] Legislation should therefore only provide for penalization for those parents who accordingly receive financial benefits, but still refrain from sending their children to school regularly.[301] He explicitly reiterated that such penalties should even include imprisonment, as 'the State is obligated under Article 21A to implement free and compulsory education in toto'.[302]

293 Note 290, 424.
294 Note 290, 436.
295 Note 290, 464.
296 Note 290, 446 et seq.
297 Note 290, 461.
298 Note 290, 438, 457.
299 Note 290, 464.
300 Note 290, 465.
301 Note 290, 466.
302 Note 290, 472. The judge concluded by writing a list of standards that the State would have to fulfil with implementing legislation, with

As explained above, the Right to Education Act does not live up to those standards, as it neither gives parents financial incentives to send their children to school, nor does it provide for any sanctions against those who do not, and especially no sanctions going as far as imprisonment. The benchmarks set by Bhandari would first have to be confirmed by a majority opinion of a bench consisting of more than one judge, and not just one judge's concurring opinion. However, they do underline that there is a constitutional obligation to effectively compel parents to send their children to school, whether one agrees with the desirability of such a compulsion politically or not. The 'financial incentives' suggested by Bhandari are one idea to reconcile such political apprehensions with the constitutional duty.

Perhaps more importantly, his opinion shows that generally implementing legislation for Article 21A may be measured against the Article itself, that is, that the contents of the Article cannot be entirely defined by statutory legislation. The issue of compulsion is one of the most obvious aspects to demonstrate this, considering the clear wording of the Article.

Other than that, the conclusions that can be drawn from the Supreme Court decisions for the content of Article 21A are not very concrete. The decisions show that there is a constitutional obligation to implement the provisions of the Right to Education Act, but this may be considered a given. They also show that Article 21A calls for certain standards of quality in education, which justifies setting standards for teachers' qualifications, and that it obliges the State to create a safe environment for children's education.

For these standards to be defined more clearly, and for the Court to identify more aspects of the Article's content, more cases will have to be filed, especially concerning concrete on-the-ground violations. How effectively this will happen in the future also depends

---

financial incentives for parents to send their children to school being named first, followed by provisions for penalties for parents who receive such incentives but nonetheless send their children to work, as well as for those employing children.

on how frequently important on-the-ground issues can be raised in Court. Interestingly, all of the Supreme Court cases mentioned were raised in the Court by petitioners who ran private educational institutions, were teachers, or were acting in public interest.[303] None were children or parents affected by lack of implementation of the right themselves.

The lack of cases raised by right-bearers themselves may be seen as an indicator that the judiciary is not accessible for the persons that the right is primarily aimed at, that is, the poor parts of society that have previously been deprived of education. At least at the Supreme Court level, with a total lack of such cases, this conclusion is not far-fetched. A look at judgments and orders mentioning Article 21A in high courts shows that even there, cases raised by parents (themselves or on behalf of their children) are rare.

This is the case even in the Delhi High Court, which appears to be somewhat more accessible than other high courts. Even though the Delhi High Court has comparatively many such cases, the number is still quite low. Even in this Court, the majority of cases were raised by private parties, teachers, or persons acting in public interest. Exceptions include the case of *Birndavan Sharma*, in which the Court dealt with the situation of children whose father had murdered their mother, who, upon imprisonment of their father, were virtually living as orphans.[304] In that case, however, a 'compassionate citizen of this country' actually ended up taking care of the children. The Court stated that the State is under an obligation to provide benefits to such children, including education.[305] In the cases of *Abdullah (Minor) (Master Mohd)* and *Jatin Singh*, the petitioners, who belonged to weaker sections of the society, asked to be admitted (or have their children whom they represented be admitted), to a school.[306]

303 For the institution of PIL, see Chapters 4 and 6, p. 182 et seq., 272 et seq.

304 *Birndavan Sharma* v. *State* MANU/DE/2524/2007 (Delhi High Court, 24 August 2007).

305 Note 304, 9, 12.

306 *Abdullah (Minor) (Master Mohd.)* MANU/DE/2807/2011 (Delhi High Court, 23 May 2011); *Jatin Singh* v. *Kendriya Vidyalaya Sangathan* MANU/DE/5469/2012 (Delhi High Court, 9 November 2012).

In the case of *Siddharth International Public School*, the Delhi High Court was only approached indirectly. The aggrieved family of a child who had suffered an accident wished for the child to be admitted in the Siddharth International Public School under the Right to Education Act's 'Section 12 quota'. For this, they had approached the Motor Accident Claim Tribunal. That Tribunal ordered that the child be admitted to the school, which then itself challenged the Tribunal's order in the High Court.[307] The High Court clarified that the Tribunal did not have jurisdiction to give such an order. However, it ultimately passed a similar order itself.[308]

In the case of *Shishti Solkar*, the petitioners, a student and the father of that student, claimed that the respondent (a private school) was obliged to grant the student a fee concession, as the father belonged to an economically weaker section of the society as well as a scheduled caste.[309] However, it was questioned by the respondent whether this was really the case, as the father had admitted the child in the school more than 10 years earlier in the 'general category'. Therefore, it was questionable whether the family really qualified as one of a 'weaker section' or scheduled caste. In any case, the Court declared that the father had forfeited the benefits.[310]

Out of the cases mentioning Article 21A that the Delhi High Court has decided (in total, more than 50), these cases are rare exceptions. It therefore appears that at the high court level as well, instances of children or parents approaching the courts because of violations of the children's right to education are very few. This

[307] *Siddharth International Public School* v. *Motor Accident Claim Tribunal and Ors* MANU/DE/2218/2016 (Delhi High Court, 26 August 2016).

[308] Note 307, 44.

[309] *Shishti Solkar & Ors* v. *Mahavir Sr. Model School & Ors* MANU/DE/7010/2011 (Delhi High Court, 23 December 2011).

[310] Note 309, 10. A similar case (also concerning a parent possibly misleading authorities to benefit from rules concerning 'weaker sections') is *Master Singham* v. *Directorate of Education and Ors* MANU/DE/2625/2018 (Delhi High Court, 2 July 2018).

leads to the question of the reality of justiciability. As shall be shown in the next part, justiciability is in itself an important part of the content of the right.

## Justiciability as a Decisive Part of Article 21A's Content

One important effect of the creation of Article 21A does not follow from its wording, but from its position in the Constitution. Whatever stance one may have concerning the question of whether or not socio-economic rights should be justiciable, the Constitution now clearly states that the right to education must be. Articles 32 and 226 confer the right to every citizen to enforce fundamental rights against the State in the Supreme Court and the high courts. These provisions are themselves considered to be fundamental rights, meaning that the State is under an obligation to create effective enforcement mechanisms, as shall be discussed more in-depth in the next chapter.

As the potential beneficiaries of the right to education are primarily the poor (as mentioned in Chapter 1, more affluent families send their children to good private schools), the question of access to justice becomes especially relevant for this right for factual reasons as well. As described above, the question of whether or not the courts may restrict themselves to merely testing the implementation of schemes guaranteeing a right, and not the schemes itself, must be answered in light of the existence of Article 21A. Because of the existence of this Article, the courts are obliged to also test the schemes themselves. Similarly, the existence of Article 21A also widens the scope of the right concerning the question of access to justice, as compared to the previous situation, in which the right to education was 'merely' read into Article 21.

By reading 'new' rights into Article 21, the judiciary had gone beyond the constitutional text, therefore extending the scope of Article 21. Therefore, there may have been less of an urgency to ensure that the beneficiaries of those 'new' rights may claim their rights in court, as compared to those rights that were part of the constitutional text itself. With the placement of Article 21A in

Part III of the Constitution, the Constitution explicitly guarantees a justiciable right to education, with justiciability being the one decisive difference compared to the previous situation in which primary education was (according to the constitutional text itself) a non-justiciable directive principle, as prescribed by Article 45.

Many of the Supreme Court decisions described above could have also been decided similarly without the existence of Article 21A. The Right to Education Act could have been created without first creating Article 21A, and lack of its implementation could have been challenged in Court, especially with the right to education being understood as being a part of Article 21. Raising the minimum qualifications for teachers may have been justified with Article 45 as well. Furthermore, the provisions imposing an obligation on (non-minority) private educational institutions to accept children from weaker sections of the society could have also been created without Article 21A.

In the Constitution's doctrinal set-up, direct justiciability, without first having to take the 'detour' of extending the scope of an explicitly justiciable right, is the one decisive difference between fundamental rights and directive principles. This means that creating effective possibilities to enforce the right against the State in court may be the most important aspect of Article 21A as compared to the previous legal situation. In other words, while for Article 45 the Constitution did not include a promise that it will be enforceable against the State, it now does so for its 'successor': Article 21A.

Consequently, while aspects of the content of the right such as quality and infrastructural standards are subject to the judiciary defining its scope more or less broadly, providing practically effective and accessible justiciability is a necessity that directly follows from the constitutional text. Therefore, a court will have to order the State to take measures to improve access to justice if the question of access to justice concerning the right to education is raised and the court finds that the system currently provided by the State is lacking.

Thus, while somewhat symbolically declaring contents of directive principles to be 'rights', and thereby 'reminding' the states of its duties to implement its schemes alone may be sufficient for such rights that are not explicitly guaranteed to be justiciable by the constitutional text,[311] this limitation is constitutionally impermissible concerning Article 21A.

Consequently, the question arises whether or not the Indian State is currently fulfilling its duties in this respect. The fact that in spite of continuing widespread deprivation in the field of primary education very few parents of affected children approach the courts indicates that this is not the case. This question shall be studied more in-depth in the next chapter. It shall discuss several options of measures that the State may undertake to provide access to justice. This includes administrative grievance redress mechanisms, which the State has created under the Right to Education Act to provide for mechanisms of enforcement. Chapters 5 and 6 will then discuss whether these enforcement provisions live up to this constitutional obligation.

***

The aim of this chapter was to offer some waypoints concerning the contents of Article 21A, and for how the Indian courts may adjudicate on the right to education in the future. It was shown that the courts may draw on international human rights standards, but that those themselves often lack a clear definition of states' obligations concerning the right to education, meaning that the Indian courts will need to be innovative in defining those obligations for the Indian context. As demonstrated above, the Supreme Court has already defined the content of Article 21A concerning some issues, but many questions remain. Applying some international human rights standards shows that the Indian State is currently in violation of the right to education, particularly because it has not created measures to make elementary education compulsory in practice, but perhaps also because of other factors such as lack of and deterioration of quality.

Also, it was shown that even though the Indian Supreme Court has, in the past, been reluctant to go beyond ordering

311 As described by Khosla, 'Making Social Rights Conditional', 762, quoted above.

the implementation of schemes that the other branches of government had already created for the delivery of socio-economic rights, this reluctance cannot persist concerning the adjudication of Article 21A. Also, even though the courts were somewhat reluctant to recognize the indirect horizontal application of fundamental rights, this cannot be upheld in the case of the right to education, meaning that Article 21A has indirect horizontal effect between children admitted in private schools (or wanting to be admitted) and those schools.

However, as courts do not usually make abstract policy decisions, but rather decide cases that are 'given' to them by plaintiffs and petitioners, the question arises who the petitioners concerning the right to education may be, and what kinds of claims one might expect from them. For this, it is important to assess how realistic it is for different groups to approach the courts in practice. Past adjudication suggests that the State has thus far failed to provide mechanisms for right-bearers to effectively claim their right to education from the State in the higher judiciary, which may be a violation of the right in itself. The question of access to justice in India, and how the shortcomings might be overcome, shall be the topic of the following chapters.

# 4

# Enforcing Rights against the State in India

## The Problem of Access to Justice

As described in the last chapter, providing access to justice in order to facilitate enforcement of the right to education is part of the content of the right to education itself, as provided by Article 21A. The fact that none of the cases in the Supreme Court and hardly any cases at the high court level have been raised by right-bearers themselves suggests that access to justice is currently not provided in practice.

This chapter shall explain that this is indeed the case. It will then also offer an attempt to explain why India's higher judiciary is so inaccessible. Next, it will be explained that the Indian judiciary itself is also aware of this problem. After all, it has created the institution of PIL, which allows third persons acting in public interest to approach the courts to raise issues affecting others who might not be able to access the judiciary themselves. Even though many observers seem to believe that PIL is an adequate mechanism to compensate for lack of access to justice, the argument in this chapter will be that this is not the case, as the State's obligation to provide access to justice to the aggrieved persons themselves remains. The final portion of the chapter shall then begin to explore what alternative, potentially more accessible mechanisms for claiming one's right from the State may be. The institution of grievance redress mechanisms shall be discussed in detail in the next chapter.

## Enforcing Fundamental Rights in the Higher Judiciary

As mentioned in the previous chapter, the two decisive articles for fundamental rights enforcement in the Indian Constitution are Articles 32 and 226. With Article 32 being part of the fundamental rights catalogue itself, the constitutional framework has designated writ adjudication at the Supreme Court level as the primary one for enforcing one's fundamental rights against the State.

The powers conferred to the judiciary by these provisions are actually quite wide, meaning that effective enforcement of fundamental rights will not be hindered by a lack of competences given to the courts. From this point of view, approaching them in order to claim one's rights would appear to be an obvious solution, as the first portion of this section will discuss. It will then be explained that, because of a range of circumstances, the higher judiciary is very inaccessible, especially to the poor to whom the right to education is primarily addressed.

### Article 32 and Article 226

The most obvious option for enforcing one's fundamental rights against the State is given as part of the fundamental rights catalogue in the Indian Constitution itself. Article 32(1) guarantees '[t]he right to move the Supreme Court by appropriate proceedings for the enforcement of the rights conferred by this Part'. Article 32(2) confers the power on the Supreme Court to 'issue directions or order writs, including the writs in the nature of habeas corpus, mandamus, prohibition, *quo warranto*, and certiorari, whichever may be appropriate, for the enforcement of any of the rights conferred by this Part'. Additionally, Article 32(3) states that Parliament may empower 'any other court to exercise within the local limits of its jurisdiction all or any of the powers exercisable by the Supreme Court'.

Article 32 is in itself considered to be a fundamental right, as an 'aid' to other fundamental rights as well as a prerequisite for their effective enjoyment.[1] Ambedkar even went as far as stating that it might be 'the most important' Article of the entire Constitution.[2] The Supreme Court has also confirmed the provision's elevated position by stating that the concept of judicial review, guaranteed by Article 32 (as well as Article 226, which allows the enforcement of fundamental rights in the high courts), as being part of the 'basic structure' of the Constitution, meaning that this right must not be removed even by constitutional amendment.[3]

Article 32 confers very broad powers to the Supreme Court. Article 32(2) names specific writs that the Constitution adopted from English law, but the Court's powers are not restricted to them. The provision states that the Court may 'issue *directions or* order *writs, including* the writs *in the nature of* [...], *whichever may be appropriate*' (emphasis added). Consequently, the Court is empowered to order the writs named by the paragraph, order any other writs 'in their nature', or give any other 'directions'. In other words, the Court can give any kind of order that it considers to be appropriate 'for the enforcement of any [fundamental right]'.

The Supreme Court has been very creative as far as remedies are concerned,[4] going as far as effectively acting as an additional

[1] Mahabir Prashad Jain, Ruma Pal, and Samaraditya Pal, *Indian Constitutional Law*, 6th edition (Gurgaon: LexisNexis Butterworths Wadhwa Nagpur, 2010), 1430; H.M. Seervai, *Constitutional Law of India: A Critical Commentary*, 4th edition, 3 vols (Bombay, Mumbai, Delhi: N.M. Tripathi; F.H. Seervai; Distributors, Universal Law Pub. Co, 1991–6), 1449.

[2] Without it, he said in the Constitutional Assembly, the Constitution 'would be a nullity' (see *Constituent Assembly Debates*, Vol. VII, available at https://web.archive.org/web/20180205040135/http://parliamentofindia.nic.in/ls/debates/vol7p23.htm, accessed on 15 August 2018).

[3] *L. Chandra Kumar* v. *Union of India* MANU/SC/0261/1997 (Supreme Court of India, 18 March 1997). For more on the 'basic structure' doctrine, see Chapter 2 and Sudhir Krishnaswamy, *Democracy and Constitutionalism in India: A Study of the Basic Structure Doctrine* (New Delhi: Oxford University Press, 2009).

[4] Mahendra Pal Singh, *V.N. Shukla's Constitution of India*, 12th edition (Lucknow: Eastern Book Co., 2013), 344–5, lists a large number of cases with many very different kinds of orders.

executive or legislature in cases like the *Right to food* case[5] and *Vishaka*.[6] The Court has also clarified that it does not consider itself bound by concrete remedies that the petitioner asks for, but that it can rather choose any remedy that it considers appropriate.[7] The broad wording of Article 32(2) may also justify such far-reaching remedies which may be classified as 'structural injunctions', as will be discussed in Chapter 6.[8]

Article 32 also does not name specific procedural rules for submitting petitions to the Supreme Court. The Court has been similarly liberal, if not even more so, concerning this aspect. It has stated that there is 'no limitation in regard to the kind of proceeding', except for their appropriateness. Proceedings are, according to the Court, appropriate if they are suitable to further the enforcement of a fundamental right.[9] This wide interpretation has enabled the Court to invent the institution of PIL, which shall be looked at in more detail below. The judiciary has loosened the procedures to such an extent that it even accepts simple letters or postcards sent to individual judges as 'petitions' under Articles 226 and 32.[10]

[5] *People's Union for Civil Liberties* v. *Union of India and Others*, Supreme Court of India, Writ Petition (Civil) 196/2001. See Chapter 6 for a closer look at this case.

[6] *Vishaka & Ors* v. *State of Rajasthan & Ors* MANU/SC/0786/1997 (Supreme Court of India, 13 August 1997).

[7] Sathe notes that this wide interpretation started already with *T.C. Basappa* v. *T. Nagappa and Another* MANU/SC/0098/1954 (Supreme Court of India, 5 May 1954) (see S.P. Sathe, *Judicial Activism in India*, 2nd edition [Delhi: Oxford University Press, 2003], 199).

[8] See Chapter 6.

[9] *Bandhua Mukti Morcha* v. *Union of India* MANU/SC/0051/1983, 17 (Supreme Court of India, 16 December 1983).

[10] See, for instance, the cases of *Ram Kumar Misra* v. *State of Bihar and Others* MANU/SC/0251/1983 (Supreme Court of India, 21 September 1983); *Bandhua Mukti Morcha* v. *Union of India* MANU/SC/0051/1983; *Dr. Ashok* v. *Union of India* MANU/SC/0577/1997 (Supreme Court of India, 2 May 1997); *Avinash Mehrotra* v. *Union of India and Ors* MANU/SC/0555/2009 (Supreme Court of India, 13 April 2009), where the petitions were 'filed' by sending a letter. Cassels notes that petitions have also been filed by submitting postcards or newspaper clippings (see Jamie Cassels,

In sum, there are virtually no procedural restrictions in fundamental rights adjudication, neither concerning possibilities of approaching the Court nor concerning the kinds of remedies the Court might give once it has determined that a right has been violated.

Article 226, on the other hand, allows right-bearers to enforce their fundamental rights in the high courts. Similar to Article 32 (to which it refers), Article 226(1) states that every high court 'shall have power [...] to issue to any person or authority [...] orders or writs, including writs in the nature of *habeas corpus*, [etc.] [...] for the enforcement of any of the rights conferred by Part III and for any other purpose'. Therefore, the high courts are also empowered to issue writs other than those known in English law, and may also issue any other order (similar to 'direction' in Article 32(2)) that they see fit for the enforcement of fundamental rights. Within their jurisdictions, their powers are therefore as broad as the Supreme Court's are for the whole of the country.[11]

## The Problem of Access to Justice

When studying socio-economic rights cases, one notices that the subject that the courts adjudicate on were, most of the time, not raised by the bearers of those rights that the courts invoked. This is also the case concerning the right to education, as the examples cited in Chapter 3 demonstrate: cases brought to the court by poor parents or poor children themselves, who are the ones who ought to profit from the right, are a very rare exception.

Even the judgments of *Mohini Jain* and *Unni Krishnan* were initiated by a prospective university student who felt that college tuition fees were prohibitively high.[12] The student herself was

'Judicial Activism and Public Interest Litigation in India: Attempting the Impossible?', *The American Journal of Comparative Law* 37, no. 3 [1989]: 499–500).

[11] Singh, *V.N. Shukla's Constitution of India*, 658–9.

[12] See the facts in *Miss Mohini Jain* v. *State of Karnataka and Ors* MANU/SC/0357/1992 (Supreme Court of India, 30 July 1992). *Unni Krishnan* came as a reaction to the *Mohini Jain* judgment, with the

apparently not from a very wealthy background, as she stated that the medical college fees were too high for her or her family to afford. Still, students who even reach the point at which they can apply to universities in the first place are relatively affluent, while those whom the right to education is primarily aimed at often come from families without any educational background. They normally do not receive enough quality education at the elementary and secondary level to allow them to progress to higher education. Even though primary or secondary education was not the core question at hand, the Supreme Court saw the cases of *Mohini Jain* and *Unni Krishnan* as an opportunity to adjudicate on education as a whole, and elementary education in particular in the case of *Unni Krishnan*.

Therefore, while these cases are often cited as prime examples for socio-economic rights adjudication by the Indian Supreme Court, they too are examples that illustrate that the higher judiciary is not accessible to those who may benefit from socio-economic rights adjudication. Perhaps the Supreme Court did not expect that parents of children at the primary level would raise the question of universal elementary education in court, which may have motivated it to take up a case concerning higher education as an opportunity to adjudicate on the broader issue of universalization of education. Still, the question remains whether or not the judiciary is really so inaccessible, and if it is, why this is the case.

### *Empirical Studies on Access to the Lower Judiciary*

Interestingly, there appears to be no recent empirical study concerning (lack of) access to justice to India's higher judiciary, that is, the Supreme Court and the high courts. An explanation may

---

plaintiffs this time being private educational institutions; see in *Unni Krishnan, J.P. and Ors* v. *State of Andhra Pradesh and Ors* MANU/SC/0333/1993 (Supreme Court of India, 4 February 1993): 'In the writ petitions filed before this Court, the correctness of the decision of this Court in the case of Mohini Jain [...] was challenged by private educational institutions'. Thus, the cases are directly connected.

be that perhaps many observers believe that the problem has been solved with the invention of PIL, as shall be discussed below.

However, some recent work has been done on (lack of) access to justice in India's lower judiciary by Krishnan et al. in the three states of Maharashtra, Gujarat, and Himachal Pradesh.[13] Some of their findings may help in identifying factors that may play a role in making the *higher* judiciary inaccessible (and/or unattractive) for the poor as well.

Some aspects, like inferior infrastructure of the district courts[14] or incompetent and unhelpful staff[15] may not be as problematic as far as the higher judiciary is concerned. On the other hand, of course, physical distance to the courts will be more of a problem in the case of the higher judiciary.

Concerning the lower judiciary, the authors observe that poor litigants are often unfamiliar with legal processes and therefore require the help of lawyers. Those lawyers then have to invest a lot of time and energy into educating their clients on what is and what is not possible by means of litigation.[16] This will, of course, result in higher costs, which are especially problematic considering the fact that legal aid is in practice inaccessible to those potential litigants,[17] as shall be discussed in more detail below. Most likely, these factors will also hinder access to the higher judiciary, perhaps even more so than to the lower courts.

Generally, the litigants that Krishnan et al. interviewed named costs as a 'major barrier'. Costs include fees resulting from the

[13] Jayanth K. Krishnan et al., 'Grappling at the Grassroots: Access to Justice in India's Lower Tier', *Harvard Human Rights Journal* 27, no. 1 (2014).

[14] For example, non-digitalization, lack of internet access, 'cramped' storage spaces for physicals files, irregular electrical power or lacking sanitary facilities, water or food supplies that may be problematic especially for litigants who come from far away, and so on (see Krishnan et al., 'Grappling at the Grassroots', 515).

[15] Krishnan et al., 'Grappling at the Grassroots', 516–17.

[16] Krishnan et al., 'Grappling at the Grassroots', 518. This is the case even with those potential litigants who are not illiterate, though many of them are (see Krishnan et al., 'Grappling at the Grassroots', 520).

[17] Krishnan et al., 'Grappling at the Grassroots', 518.

litigation process itself, that is, court fees, photocopying fees, or 'file-retrieval fees, scheduling or calendar fees for court appearances', as well as fees charged by lawyers that 'seem quite arbitrary' to the litigants.[18] Also, the circumstance that litigants cannot work on the days that they would appear in court, and therefore lose wages for those days, is a major obstacle, with many litigants not even being able to afford to forego one day's wages.[19] The fact that the Indian judiciary is known to work quite slowly further intensifies this problem.[20]

Some of the additional problems that the authors identify, such as gender and caste discrimination,[21] or intimidation and corruption,[22] may be less relevant in the higher judiciary, though it cannot be ruled out that they play a role there as well.[23]

Several of these obstacles may be overcome with the help of proactive lawyers. Krishna et al., however, lament that most law schools do not focus on the values of helping the poor, professional ethics, and community responsibility as part of their legal education.[24] They also observe that whenever lawyers are willing to

[18] Krishnan et al., 'Grappling at the Grassroots', 521.

[19] Krishnan et al., 'Grappling at the Grassroots', 521.

[20] The problem may be especially grave in lower courts where 'delay tactics' by lawyers are quite common (see Krishnan et al., 'Grappling at the Grassroots', 521–2).

[21] Either directly by the courtroom staff by opposing, or also their own advocates, or indirectly such as by not providing available and clean washrooms or safe transportation to and from the courts (see Krishnan et al., 'Grappling at the Grassroots', 522–3).

[22] Krishnan et al., 'Grappling at the Grassroots', 525.

[23] Krishnan et al note that former chief justice S.H. Kapadia considerably reduced corruption in the high courts and the Supreme Court. They see his example as 'an inspiration [...] [that] can and should be replicated within the lower tier' and quote Kian Ganz, 'SH Kapadia, End of an Era: India's Greatest Ever CJI or Missed Opportunity? How will You Remember the Legacy?', *Legally India*, 28 September 2012, http://www.legallyindia.com/interviews/sh-kapadia-end-of-an-era-indias-greatest-ever-cji-or-missed-opportunity-how-will-you-remember-the-legacy, accessed on 19 August 2018. For an account of Kapadia's work, see Krishnan et al., 'Grappling at the Grassroots', 527.

[24] Krishnan et al., 'Grappling at the Grassroots', 519.

take up cases, the fact that their clients lack understanding of the legal processes and their rights often leads to frustration.[25]

Another, and also cost-related, aspect is the language barrier. Only more qualified lawyers will know good English, as English is 'not emphasized' in the majority of law colleges.[26] English, however, is the working language of the higher courts. Many judgments are only published in English, a large portion of legal literature is only available in English, and even statutes are often difficult to find in the respective local language.[27]

### *Judicial Backlog and the Importance of Qualified Advocates*

Even when considering those factors that (possibly) inhibit access to the higher judiciary, one still wonders why there are such few socio-economic right judgments in which the petitioners were the concerned persons themselves. It is especially surprising considering the fact that the higher judiciary has interpreted the rules for being approached so liberally. As mentioned above, even sending letters or postcards to judges can initiate procedures. Even if a poor person cannot afford a well-trained lawyer and afford to appear in court regularly, one would still assume that they would be able to write a simple letter to the high court or the Supreme Court, at least with the help of any literate person.

Gauri's empirical study of the Supreme Court's fundamental rights cases, which shall be discussed more extensively below, shows that a large majority of PILs that the Supreme Court actually accepts as writ petitions or 'cases' are submitted in the Court through formal channels. Letters or postcards are also categorized as PILs but the judiciary rarely accepts them in practice.

Even though the Supreme Court receives tens of thousands of informal petitions, such as letters or handwritten petitions every year, 'only a handful' of those are converted into formal

[25] Krishnan et al., 'Grappling at the Grassroots', 520.
[26] Krishnan et al., 'Grappling at the Grassroots', 519.
[27] Krishnan et al., 'Grappling at the Grassroots', 520.

cases pending in the Court.[28] For instance, in 2013, out of 45,588 such letters received by the Supreme Court, only 259 (that is, 0.6 per cent) were accepted as writ petitions.[29] The majority of petitions submitted as letters never appear before a judge, as they 'are combed through by Court staff'.[30]

Apparently, while in theory, the Supreme Court has completely abandoned all formal requirements for fundamental rights petitions, chances are a lot higher to actually be successfully heard by the Court if one does follow formal procedures. Thus, the loosening of procedural requirements may have made the Court appear very accessible, but this does not seem to translate into practice. One factor that may explain this is the problem of judicial backlog.

Judicial backlog is a well-known issue in India. Even India's former prime minister, Manmohan Singh, once claimed that it was 'the largest in the world'.[31] As of May 2018, 54,013 cases were pending in the Supreme Court alone.[32] The number has decreased slightly in recent years but is still much higher than in 1997, when the backlog was 19,032 cases.[33] In early 2015, in the 24 high

[28] Varun Gauri, 'Fundamental Rights and Public Interest Litigation in India: Overreaching or Underachieving?', *Indian Journal of Law & Economics* 1, no. 1 (2010): 83.

[29] Supreme Court of India, 'The Supreme Court of India. Annual Report 2014', https://web.archive.org/web/20161225150946/http://supremecourtofindia.nic.in/annualreport/annualreport2014-15.pdf, accessed on 19 August 2018, 64.

[30] Nick Robinson, 'A Quantitative Analysis of the Indian Supreme Court's Workload', 2012, http://papers.ssrn.com/sol3/papers.cfm?abstract_id=2189181, accessed on 19 August 2018, 36.

[31] BBC, 'Indian PM Plea on Justice Backlog', 17 September 2009, http://news.bbc.co.uk/2/hi/south_asia/8204607.stm, accessed on 19 August 2018.

[32] See https://www.sci.gov.in/statistics, accessed on 13 August 2018.

[33] See Supreme Court of India, 'The Supreme Court of India. Annual Report 2014', 78–79. Previously, in the 1990s, the number of backlogged cases had decreased considerably because the Court changed its method of accounting backlogged cases by not counting each hyphenated matter in a file, but rather counting only 'the entire file of clubbed matters', which were 'clubbed together' by district court judges and other judicial officers, of whom a large number was brought to the Supreme Court at the time

courts, the number of pending cases had reached 4,005,704 cases (that is, an average of 166,904 cases per high court), while in district and subordinate courts, the number was at 27,156,020 in the same year.[34] The total number was thus more than 31 million cases. Not surprisingly, the increasing backlog has also prolonged the delay for individual cases. While in 2004, in the Supreme Court, 7 per cent of the hearing matters had been pending for more than five years, that number had increased to 17 per cent in 2011.[35]

There are many possible reasons for the high number of pending cases. The most obvious is the fact that the number of judges in India is relatively low. Already in 1987, the Law Commission of India had recommended that the country increase its number of judges from 10.5 to 50 per million population.[36] To date, the number of judges per million population has only increased to 17.[37] This figure seems extremely low when compared to some Western countries like France (107) or, especially, Germany (247), but it is also almost half as high as in England and Wales (36).[38] The large

---

(see Robinson, 'A Quantitative Analysis of the Indian Supreme Court's Workload', 13). The number of cases pending decreased from 109,277 in 1990 (when it had reached its peak) to 19,032 in 1997. Since then, it has increased almost every year.

34 Supreme Court of India, 'Court News' X, no. 3, https://web.archive.org/web/20170428163330/http://supremecourtofindia.nic.in/courtnews/July,%202015-sept-2015.pdf, accessed on 19 August 2018, 6–7.

35 Robinson, 'A Quantitative Analysis of the Indian Supreme Court's Workload', 3, 26.

36 Law Commission of India, 'One Hundred Twentieth Report on Manpower Planning in Judiciary: A Blueprint' (1987), http://lawcommissionofindia.nic.in/101-169/report120.pdf, accessed on 2 March 2019, 3.

37 Pradeep Thakur, 'India Has 17 Judges for a Million People, 5,000 Posts Vacant', *Times of India*, 17 April 2016, http://timesofindia.indiatimes.com/india/India-has-17-judges-for-a-million-people-5000-posts-vacant/articleshow/51860142.cms, accessed on 19 August 2018.

38 2012 figures. See European Commission for the Efficiency of Justice, 'European Judicial Systems: Efficiency and Quality of Justice. An Overview' (2014), https://web.archive.org/web/20160625050701/http://www.coe.int/t/dghl/cooperation/cepej/evaluation/2014/synthese2014_en.pdf, accessed on 2 March 2019, 15.

difference between these countries shows that the context of the respective judicial system has to be taken into account, and that judicial systems can also function with a relatively low judge-per-population ratio.

Robinson has studied the workload of the Supreme Court and comes to some conclusions concerning the reasons behind it, with the caveat being that a lot of the available data is incomplete due to deficiencies in data collection and categorization.[39] He notes that the number of cases brought to the Supreme Court is increasing at a pace that is a lot faster than the country's increase in population. Both the number of admission matters as well as regular hearing matters had nearly doubled (from 24,747 to 48,677 and from 4,507 to 8,824) between 2000 and 2010.[40]

The majority of these cases are not such in which the Court is approached directly as a court of first instance. In recent years, the amount of writ petitions (under Article 32) have decreased, while Special Leave Petitions (SLPs) now constitute the vast majority of cases. Around 84.6 per cent of all admissions in 2011 were SLPs, while writ petitions only made up 1.8 per cent.[41] Public Interest Litigations only make up about 1 per cent.[42] Special Leave Petitions are effectively 'appeals' against such lower court judgments for which the respective lower court did not certify a (regular) appeal to the Supreme Court.[43] The Supreme Court may allow such 'irregular appeals' or SLPs at its discretion.

[39] Robinson, 'A Quantitative Analysis of the Indian Supreme Court's Workload', 2, 4 et seq.

[40] Robinson, 'A Quantitative Analysis of the Indian Supreme Court's Workload', 2–3.

[41] Robinson, 'A Quantitative Analysis of the Indian Supreme Court's Workload', 3, 17–18.

[42] Robinson, 'A Quantitative Analysis of the Indian Supreme Court's Workload', 3.

[43] See Article 136 of the Constitution. Regular appeals are only permissible if the high court certifies that the case 'involves a substantial question of law as to the interpretation of this Constitution' or 'a substantial question of law of general importance' (Articles 132(1), 133(1)(a), and 134A, which also include additional requirements).

Generally, one may argue that appeals to an apex court should be an exception and not the norm.[44] The Indian Constitution itself expresses this goal by creating SLPs (as their name already suggests) as an exception for extraordinary cases. However, the large number of SLPs to the Supreme Court demonstrates that the exception has now become the norm. Because of the high number of appeals, the modern Indian Supreme Court may be described as 'one mired in thousands of petitions and perpetual backlog with far less time for larger constitution benches and other important matters'.[45]

On the other hand, one reason why the share of writ petitions has declined is that the Supreme Court judges have, since the 1980s, encouraged petitioners to first file writ petitions in the high courts under Article 226, rather than directly approaching the Supreme Court.[46] Remarkably, the increase of the Supreme Court's workload is still disproportionately higher than that of the high courts and lower courts, which may potentially be explained by an 'increasing breakdown of the following of precedent'.[47] The increasing workload has led to an increase in the number of judges in the Supreme Court,[48] and also to the Court having cases be

[44] K.K. Venugopal believes that being a regular court of appeal 'is not the proper function of the apex court of a country', cited in Kian Ganz, 'Supreme Court's battle against backlog in cases', *Live Mint*, 7 June 2012, http://www.livemint.com/Politics/ziffwni3N64eFBcaWZobtL/Supreme-Court8217s-battle-against-backlog-in-cases.html, accessed on 19 August 2018.

[45] Robinson, 'A Quantitative Analysis of the Indian Supreme Court's Workload', 11.

[46] Robinson cites the order of *P.N. Kumar and Another* v. *Municipal Corporation of Delhi* MANU/SC/0127/1987 (Supreme Court of India, 2 November 1987), where the Supreme Court directed that the petitioner file a petition in the high court ('If the parties get relief in the High Court, they need not come to this Court, and, to that extent, the burden on this Court is reduced'), as an example (see Robinson, 'A Quantitative Analysis of the Indian Supreme Court's Workload', 19).

[47] Robinson, 'A Quantitative Analysis of the Indian Supreme Court's Workload', 3.

[48] The number has been progressively increased from 8 in 1950 to, currently, 31 (see https://www.sci.gov.in/history, accessed on 15 August 2018).

decided by smaller benches.[49] In addition to that, judges are only members of the Court for a relatively short period of time.[50] All these factors may lead to a situation in which the Court increasingly does not follow its own precedent,[51] in turn also making it more difficult for high courts to follow the Supreme Court's precedent.[52] This makes the content of the law less clear, which may, in turn, give more litigants an incentive to approach the judiciary with cases that involve questions of law that would have otherwise already been decided by precedent.[53] Therefore, this development

[49] The percentage of 'five+' judge benches, which rule on matters of 'constitutional importance', has decreased from 45.6 per cent in the years 1950–4 to just 6.4 per cent in the years 2005–9 (see Nick Robinson et al., 'Interpreting the Constitution: Supreme Court Constitution Benches since Independence', *Economic & Political Weekly* XLIV, no. 9 [2011]: 28).

[50] The list of former judges at Supreme Court of India, 'The Supreme Court of India. Annual Report 2014', 51 et seq. shows that being a Supreme Court justice for longer than five years is an exception. This is due to the fact that promotions from high courts to the Supreme Court occur following rules of seniority, and because of the mandatory retirement age of Supreme Court justices (65 years according to Article 124(2) of the Constitution) (see Marc Galanter and Nick Robinson, 'India's Grand Advocates: A Legal Elite Flourishing in the Era of Globalization', 2013, http://ssrn.com/abstract=2348699, accessed on 19 August 2018, 9). For the historical origins of the seniority principle, see Abhinav Chandrachud, 'Supreme Court's Seniority Norms. Historical Origins', *Economic & Political Weekly* XLVII, no. 8 (2012).

[51] Robinson hypothesizes that either 'high courts are no longer following precedent reliably [...] [or] [a]lternatively, the numerous benches of the Supreme Court might not be reliably following precedent themselves and/or giving conflicting precedent'—'[w]hatever the explanation [...] [it] is likely not a sign of a judicial system that is successfully implementing a system of precedent' (see Robinson, 'A Quantitative Analysis of the Indian Supreme Court's Workload', 16).

[52] Which they are obliged to do according to Article 141 of the Constitution.

[53] Robinson describes the disproportionate growth of the Court's hearing matters 'striking and the opposite of what one would intuitively expect'—as 'decisions should have precedential value', the Court 'generally should not have to hear a case involving the same issue again and

might only increase the Supreme Court's workload even more, as it has given litigants the impression that filing an 'appeal' (regular or irregular one) in the Supreme Court may always be worth a try.[54] There appears to be a 'rush of litigants towards the top of the system', with which 'the Supreme Court has seemed quite willing to oblige'.[55] To resolve this issue, it might be sensible for the Supreme Court to once again have more cases decided by larger benches. This would allow a more cohesive constitutional jurisprudence.[56]

Even though there appears to be a 'race to the top' of the judiciary by litigants, this does not mean that high courts have much less of a backlog problem. There are currently more than 3.3 million cases pending in India's 24 high courts, with more than 650,000 pending for more than 10 years.[57]

Judicial backlog might make the judicial process seem so unattractive that aggrieved persons do not even consider approaching the judiciary. Grievances concerning the right to education are usually relatively urgent, merely because of the facts that children age, and the fact that years lost in education are especially problematic when children are at an early age. Therefore, judicial backlog and the delays that come with it are particularly problematic when adjudicating the right to education.

---

may rely on the High Courts to implement its decisions in similar cases' (see Robinson, 'A Quantitative Analysis of the Indian Supreme Court's Workload', 15–16).

[54] Robinson, 'A Quantitative Analysis of the Indian Supreme Court's Workload', 16.

[55] Robinson, 'A Quantitative Analysis of the Indian Supreme Court's Workload', 16.

[56] On the other hand, Robinson notes, it would also make it more difficult for the Court to 'police' the lower courts in the larger mass of cases, as it could then accept a smaller number of appeals against judgments by those courts (see Robinson, 'A Quantitative Analysis of the Indian Supreme Court's Workload', 4). Therefore, it is important that the Supreme Court finds a certain balance.

[57] http://njdg.ecourts.gov.in/hcnjdg_public/main.php, accessed on 15 August 2018.

The question that arises is what litigants who believe that their grievances are particularly urgent can do in order to expedite their cases. If there are means for them to do so, then these means must be accessible for the poor as well in order to provide them with access to justice. Problematically, it appears that it requires skill and knowledge of the courts' workings in order to successfully 'jump' the 'queue' of pending cases, as there is no formalized and transparent 'expedition system'.

There are some written rules concerning urgency provided by the Supreme Court in its 'Practice & Procedure' handbook. However, they are, at least explicitly, only applied in the Court's holiday period.[58] Also, some of the parameters mentioned in the handbook are not very specific. The handbook lists requirements for urgency in the 'Allocation, Listing of Cases and Cause Lists' chapter under 'Listing – Urgent matters'. Matters are considered to be of urgent nature if, for instance, 'a death penalty has been awarded' or if matters relate 'to dispossession/eviction'. The latter is somewhat specific. However, matters are also considered to be urgent if they relate 'to violation of human rights' or are matters 'relating to and of public importance'.[59] In order to prove the urgency, litigants have to submit an affidavit 'indicating all the material facts necessary for formation of opinion about urgency'.[60]

The Supreme Court Rules of 1966 likewise only explicitly include orders concerning the treatment of urgent cases during vacations (Orders II 1, 6, Order VII 4 (1), (5–10)). Generally, it

[58] The sub-chapter on urgency describes the procedure for listing and hearing such cases 'during [the Court's] vacation/holidays', even though the headline is just 'urgent matters' (and not 'urgent matters in holiday period'). The list of prerequisites for urgency is introduced by the words '[t]he following matters are considered to be or urgent nature and may be listed and heard during vacation/holidays'. Therefore, it is not entirely clear whether these are requirements for urgency only during these times, or also generally (see Supreme Court of India, 'Practice & Procedure: A Handbook of Information', 3rd [Revised] Edition [2010], http://164.100.107.37/handbook3rdedition.pdf, accessed on 3 March 2019, 42).

[59] Supreme Court of India, 'Practice & Procedure', 42.

[60] Supreme Court of India, 'Practice & Procedure', 42.

appears that the Court has only created such a procedure for itself for times of the year when it is not in session.

However, advocates active in litigation report that they can submit proof establishing urgency to courts' registrars and/or judges (in both the high court and Supreme Court) in order to expedite cases.[61] Most high courts, however, appear to not have written rules that establish such procedures.[62] Notably, advocates active in litigation also report that informal knowledge about the inner workings of the courts and good relationships with the registrars may be of help to successfully expedite a case.[63] Thus, it appears that chances of success are higher for litigants who can afford qualified and experienced lawyers. However, it appears that there are no empirical studies on this issue.

However, a study of the work and role of advocates at the 'upper end' by Galanter and Robinson[64] does indicate that having a qualified and respected advocate creates a considerable advantage, specifically for expediting one's own case. Their study focuses on the country's 'Grand Advocates', that is, very prestigious and successful, but also very expensive advocates. They mostly litigate in the Supreme Court, but some of them also in the high courts.[65] Such advocates, who charged as much as 500,000 to 600,000 rupees per

[61] Several advocates described this procedure in interviews with the author. A form to claim urgency in matters pending at the Delhi High Court can be found at http://delhihighcourt.nic.in/writereaddata/upload/Downloads/DownloadFile_BF49033X.PDF, accessed on 15 August 2018.

[62] One notable exception is the Karnataka High Court, which does explicitly allow 'interlocutory applications for urgent orders' in pending cases (see the Karnataka High Court Rules, Chapter X, 4–6).

[63] Several advocates shared this assessment in interviews with the author.

[64] Galanter and Robinson, 'India's Grand Advocates'. The article's main observation is that even in the age of globalization, in which laws and proceedings are said to become increasingly similar in different legal systems and countries, the stronghold of the 'Grand Advocates', who are mostly not affiliated to any big law firm, still holds.

[65] They are mostly also designated as 'senior advocates' by the Supreme Court or a high court (see Galanter and Robinson, 'India's Grand Advocates', 4).

court appearance in 2012,[66] will usually only be hired by clients like large corporations and 'India's new uber-rich'.[67] While these advocates are therefore not accessible to middle-class or upper-middle-class citizens, the study sheds light on some interesting features of the workings of the judiciary. The study also allows some insight into the role and influence that qualified advocates (even those who are not part of the group of 'Grand Advocates') may have.

Specifically concerning the problem of judicial backlog, the authors report that Grand Advocates, in order to achieve interim orders in cases that may otherwise remain pending for years, use 'extensive human capital they have developed within the court system' as well as their knowledge of formal and informal judicial procedure.[68] According to the authors' findings, procedural aspects of law make up the bulk of these advocates' work.[69] One of the lawyers interviewed states that '[f]ace value matters in matters like SLPs [...] at the Supreme Court where a decision is made in a minute. A man that regularly appears will matter to that judge. That lawyer will know what that judge considers worth hearing'.[70] Once the importance of a case is thus established, the clients may then even pass the case on to another, less expensive, lawyer, but the influence of the Grand Advocate is required to first expedite the case.[71]

[66] Galanter and Robinson, 'India's Grand Advocates', 11.

[67] Galanter and Robinson, 'India's Grand Advocates', 2. Some take up pro bono matters as well, though they are only a 'tiny subset' among the lawyers focusing on public interest cases (see Galanter and Robinson, 'India's Grand Advocates', 18).

[68] Galanter and Robinson, 'India's Grand Advocates', 2.

[69] 'Pleading for stays and interim relief accounts for a substantial part of the advocates' work in court', Galanter and Robinson, 'India's Grand Advocates', 14.

[70] Galanter and Robinson, 'India's Grand Advocates', 14.

[71] Galanter and Robinson, 'India's Grand Advocates', 14–15. Therefore, the 'chief asset' of the 'Grand Advocate' in such cases is 'the time and sustained attention he can obtain for the client before a congested and otherwise impatient court' (see Galanter and Robinson, 'India's Grand Advocates', 15).

Generally, one may assume that familiarity with formal and informal procedures is especially important in a court system in which oral proceedings are much more important than written proceedings. The authors find that Grand Advocates focus much more on courtroom advocacy than advising, negotiating, or planning.[72] If they master the courtroom proceedings, their influence can apparently be enormous. One lawyer whom the authors interviewed even went as far as saying that 'judges are almost irrelevant. The counsel have [sic] learned to treat them with kid gloves. To guide them'. This may be attributed to an 'inferiority complex' of the judges, as the Grand Advocates often come from superior social and educational backgrounds.[73] Those advocates also frequently have more experience in the given court than the judges themselves. This is especially the case for the Supreme Court, considering that the judges' terms are quite limited due to the fact that they move up to the Supreme Court at a late stage in their careers and that their retirement age of 65 is mandatory.[74]

Another indicator for the importance of qualified advocates with good contacts within the judiciary is the fact that high courts that are closer to Delhi (and especially the Delhi High Court itself) are on average more likely to generate appeals to the Supreme Court.[75] This can also be seen as an indicator for the importance of physical proximity to the court one seeks to approach, and the advocate one intends to hire. Given the importance of oral proceedings, this

[72] Galanter and Robinson, 'India's Grand Advocates', 6. This factor also increases the problem of judicial backlog itself: senior advocates take on as many cases as possible, but then cannot make it themselves to many of their court appearances, meaning that their juniors have to ask for an adjournment (see Galanter and Robinson, 'India's Grand Advocates', 8). In practice, there are, apparently, also no negative consequences if (senior) advocates miss a hearing, at least not regularly (see Galanter and Robinson, 'India's Grand Advocates', 13).

[73] Galanter and Robinson, 'India's Grand Advocates', 8.

[74] Galanter and Robinson, 'India's Grand Advocates', 9–10.

[75] Robinson, 'A Quantitative Analysis of the Indian Supreme Court's Workload', 20–1.

is not surprising. The same correlation also exists for high courts from wealthier states,[76] which may be yet another indicator for the importance of wealth, in general, when wanting to approach the Supreme Court.

## *Inadequacy of Free Legal Aid*

Considering the lack of accessibility of the higher judiciary, especially for those who cannot afford qualified lawyers, the question arises as to what the State can do to facilitate access to justice. Perhaps the most obvious choice would be the provision of legal aid, as this could also provide right-bearers with access to at least somewhat qualified advocates.

Interestingly, the Constitution itself includes a call for the State to provide free legal aid. Article 39A, a directive principle, imposes a duty on the State to 'secure that the operation of the legal system promotes justice, on a basis of equal opportunity' and that the State 'shall, in particular, provide free legal aid, by suitable legislation or schemes or in any other way, to ensure that opportunities for securing justice are not denied to any citizen by reason of economic or other disabilities'.

The legislature did act on its obligation by passing the Legal Services Authorities Act of 1987. Section 12 of the Act states that any woman or any child (!) or any person in receipt of an annual income of less than 9,000 rupees (for any court other than the Supreme Court) or 12,000 rupees (for the Supreme Court) 'who has to file or defend a case' shall be entitled to free legal aid for cases before the Supreme Court or courts other than the Supreme Court. The provision also states that the figures concerning the annual income may be raised by the respective state government as well as the central government, which the governments have done several times in the past. The National Legal Services Authority (NALSA) most recently (in late 2016) named a figure of an annual

[76] Robinson, 'A Quantitative Analysis of the Indian Supreme Court's Workload', 20–1.

income that does not exceed 125,000 Rupees for cases before the Supreme Court.[77]

While an annual income of 125,000 Rupees, or 10,416.67 per month, may seem little, that definition of eligibility actually includes the vast majority of the population. The Socio-Economic and Caste Census 2011 found that for 91.7 per cent of the Indian population, the highest-earning household member earns less than 10,000 Rupees per month.[78] Furthermore, as mentioned above, the Legal Services Authorities Act prescribes that financial assistance shall be given to *all* children (and all women), apparently irrespective of their families' income, meaning that such assistance would be available for *all* potential litigants (who may then be represented by their parents or guardians) concerning the right to education.

Section 13(1) of the Legal Services Authorities Act declares that legal services shall be provided if 'the concerned Authority is satisfied that such person has a *prima-facie* case to prosecute or to defend'. Sections 14–16 prescribe that the central government must provide grants to the legal aid authority and order the creation of national, state, and district legal aid funds. The National Legal Service Authority states that persons eligible shall get 'free legal services' which include 'payment of court fee, process fee and all other charges payable or incurred in connection with any legal proceedings'. They shall also be provided with an advocate.

Thus, at least on paper, the State promises a far-reaching legal aid system to the vast majority of its citizens. The next question is, of course, how well this system works in practice. Surprisingly, it appears that there are few empirical studies on this question. Articles that deal with the legal aid system describe its conceptual

[77] See https://web.archive.org/web/20180117200623/https://nalsa.gov.in/content/rules, accessed on 15 August 2018). As of August of 2018, NALSA's website does not name an up-to-date figure anymore (see https://nalsa.gov.in/content/who-entitled-free-legal-service, accessed on 15 August 2018).

[78] http://secc.gov.in/categorywiseIncomeSlabReport?reportType=All%20Category, accessed on 15 August 2018.

set-up[79] or deal with the philosophical reasons why a State, specifically the Indian State, should provide legal aid for its weaker citizens.[80] More in-depth studies look at legal aid as an issue of access to *criminal* justice,[81] but do not do the same for access to justice in general, or for fundamental rights enforcement. Others deal with the work of non-state actors like law clinics.[82]

Many articles that mention the Legal Services Authorities Act focus on the institution of *Lok Adalats*, which shall be covered below. Scholars whose articles do not focus directly on the legal aid system, but mention it, state that it does not function well, but do not back this assertion up with empirical data.[83] One of those scholars told this author that '[m]ost of the legal aid at present is only at advisory level and at litigation it is very poorly organized even for prisoners'. He had done 'a preliminary study on how much of legal aid is provided to victims of domestic violence but

[79] See, for instance, Prativa Panda, 'Legal Aid in India—An Overview', *Indian Journal of Applied Research* 6, no. 2 (2016).

[80] Sushant Chandra and Nityash Solanki, 'Legal Aid in India: Returning Philosophical Chords', *BRICS LJ* 2, no. 2 (2015), https://web.archive.org/web/20160508190124/http://www.bricslawjournal.com/data/documents/Chandra-iz-BLG_2_2015.pdf, accessed on 19 August 2018.

[81] S. Muralidhar, *Law, Poverty and Legal Aid: Access to Criminal Justice* (New Delhi: LexisNexis Butterworth, 2004).

[82] Frank. S. Bloch and Iqbal S. Ishar, 'Legal Aid, Public Service and Clinical Legal Education: Future Directions firm India and the United States', *Michigan Journal of International Law* 12, no. 1 (1990): 92–120; Shuvro P. Sarker, 'Empowering the Underprivileged: The Social Justice Mission for Clinical Legal Education in India', in *Clinical Legal Education in Asia: Accessing Justice for the Underprivileged*, ed. Shuvro P. Sarker (New York: Palgrave Macmillan, 2015).

[83] Guruswamy and Aspatwar name 'a lack of efficient legal aid' as one of the 'major institutional barriers to accessing justice' (see Menaka Guruswamy and Bipin Aspatwar, 'Access to Justice in India: The Jurisprudence [and Self-Perception] of the Supreme Court', 2013, http://ssrn.com/abstract=2498459, accessed on 19 August 2018, 4–5). Karnam and Nanda look at the situation of undertrial prisoners and describe that 'dysfunctional legal aid' prevents them from exercising their rights (see Murali Karnam and Trijeeb Nanda, 'Conditions of Undertrials in India: Problems and Solutions', *Economic & Political Weekly* LI, no. 13 [2016]).

it was almost nothing [...] Only semblance of legal representation is provided in case of prisoners'. With the situation being this precarious, '[n]obody tried to study a system that does not exist in practice'.[84] The conclusion of the legal aid system being almost non-existent in practice is in line with a 1990s observation that even with the legal framework being in place, the legal aid programmes supports 'only a minuscule number of cases'.[85] It appears that not much has changed since then.

A survey of newspaper articles shows that the judiciary and politics aim to improve the system by various means,[86] also by providing more funds.[87] This may suggest that it is considered to be

[84] Murali Karnam of Tata Institute of Social Sciences in an e-mail exchange with the author (10 June 2016).

[85] Charles R. Epp, *The Rights Revolution: Lawyers, Activists, and Supreme Courts in Comparative Perspective* (Chicago: University of Chicago Press, 1998), 101.

[86] For instance, in one newspaper article, Justice Kabir, then executive chairman of the National Legal Services Authority, described the scheme of deploying 'para-legal volunteers' to 'bridge the gap between the common person and legal services institutions' (see Altamas Kabir, 'Bringing Legal Aid a Step Closer Home', *The Hindu*, 9 November 2011, http://www.thehindu.com/opinion/lead/bringing-legal-aid-a-step-closer-home/article2609718.ece, accessed on 19 August 2018). Apart from the institution of *Lok Adalats*, such legal awareness measures get the majority of media attention. See, for instance, *The Tribune*, 'Legal Awareness Camps for Teachers, Elderly in P'kula', 27 May 2016, http://www.tribuneindia.com/news/chandigarh/community/legal-awareness-camps-for-teachers-elderly-in-p-kula/242801.html, accessed on 19 August 2018; *Morung Express*, 'Awareness Programme Held in Zunheboto', 3 June 2016, http://morungexpress.com/awareness-programme-held-zunheboto/, accessed on 19 August 2018; *Morung Express*, 'NSLSA Holds State Level Training for PLVs', 22 May 2016, http://morungexpress.com/nslsa-holds-state-level-training-for-plvs/, accessed on 19 August 2018; *Assam Times*, 'Legal Awareness Campaign', 11 May 2016, http://www.assamtimes.org/node/16854, accessed on 19 August 2018; *Orissa Diary*, 'Odisha: Mobile Lok Adalat & Legal Awareness', 30 May 2016, http://orissadiary.com/CurrentNews.asp?id=67502, accessed on 19 August 2018.

[87] In early 2016, the central government decided to give 148 crore Rupees (1.48 billion Rupees) to the National Legal Services Authority

a known fact that the system is not working as it should. The fact that the State also wishes to nurture law clinics in law schools,[88] which is a different 'legal aid system' in itself, in addition to the existing one, may be another indicator.

Meanwhile, court decisions declare the importance of a legal aid system and order aid to be given to certain persons in specific cases, but do not make statements about the workings of the system itself, or what deficiencies it has in practice.[89]

Therefore, while there is no empirical data that assesses to what extent the legal aid system is working or not, and what its deficiencies are in practice, it does appear that the impact it has is quite limited. If it did work as desired, there would be many more fundamental rights cases, especially socio-economic right cases,

---

(see *The Economic Times*, 'Centre to Give Rs 148 Crore to National Legal Services Authority', 31 January 2016, https://economictimes.indiatimes.com/news/politics-and-nation/centre-to-give-rs-148-crore-to-national-legal-services-authority/articleshow/50795255.cms, accessed on 19 August 2018).

[88] For the development of clinical legal education in India, see Shuvro P. Sarker, 'Empowering the Underprivileged: The Social Justice Mission for Clinical Legal Education in India', *International Journal of Clinical Legal Education* 19 (2013).

[89] The Delhi High Court in 1999 wrote that 'the legal system should be able to deliver justice expeditiously on the basis of equal opportunity and provide free legal aid to ensure that opportunities for securing justice are not denied to any citizen by reasons of economic or other disabilities', and called for alternative forums to the courts like lok adalats to be strengthened (see *Abul Hassan* v. *Delhi Vidyut Board* MANU/DE/0011/1999, 3 [Delhi High Court, 15 January 1999]). Concerning giving free legal aid to an accused—and the judiciary's duty to make the accused aware of this possibility—the Supreme Court has stated that '[i]t would make a mockery of legal aid if it were to be left to a poor ignorant and illiterate accused to ask for free legal services', declaring that free legal aid is a fundamental right to be read into Article 21 (see *Suk Das* v. *Union Territory of Arunachal Pradesh* MANU/SC/0140/1986, 6 [Supreme Court of India, 10 March 1986]). However, that latter judgment was delivered before the current legal aid system was set up.

brought to the courts by poor litigants themselves. The fact that this is not the case illustrates the system's apparent deficiencies.

## Public Interest Litigation—the Solution?

The Indian judiciary is aware that accessing it is difficult for many groups of citizens, particularly the poor. This is demonstrated by the fact that the judiciary itself created a method to (seemingly) overcome this problem: PIL, sometimes also called 'Social Action Litigation' (SAL).[90]

### The Invention of PIL as a Compensation for Lack of Access to Justice

The Indian judiciary applied the traditional rules of *locus standi*, meaning that only 'an aggrieved person' could file a petition.[91] Starting in the 1980s, the Supreme Court, mostly driven by Justice Bhagwati, massively loosened the rules of standing by inventing the institution of PIL. The reasons given in famous PIL cases clearly shows that its primary goal was to compensate for lack of access to justice for the poor.

90 The term 'Social Action Litigation' was coined by Baxi (see Upendra Baxi, 'Taking Suffering Seriously', in *Law and Poverty: Critical Essays*, ed. Upendra Baxi [Bombay: N.M. Tripathi, 1988]). Sathe agrees that the term is more fitting, calling 'Public Interest Litigation' a 'misnomer', as '[a]ll public law litigation is inspired by public interest'. However, he himself uses the term 'Public Interest Litigation' 'because of its acceptance and familiarity at the popular level' (see Sathe, *Judicial Activism in India*, 202–3).

91 Singh cites the case of *Bokaro and Ramgur Ltd* v. *The State of Bihar and Another* MANU/SC/0404/1962 (Supreme Court of India, 14 March 1962), in which the Court stated that '[b]efore a party can complain of an infringement of his fundamental right to hold property he must establish that he has title to that property and if his title itself is in dispute and is the subject of adjudication in proceedings legally constituted, he cannot obviously put forward any claim based on his title'. See Singh, *V.N. Shukla's Constitution of India*, 354.

A predecessor to the long list of PIL cases may be seen in the case of *Sunil Batra*, in which a prisoner wrote an informal letter to the Supreme Court to draw its attention to mistreatment of fellow prisoners in Delhi.[92] The Court considered the 'scribbled [...] letter on a piece of paper' to Justice Krishna Iyer as an admissible petition.[93] In the case of *S. P. Gupta*,[94] Justice Bhagwati wrote that the rules of *locus standi* ought to be loosened

> where a legal wrong or a legal injury is caused to a person [...] by reason of violation of any constitutional or legal right [...] and such person [...] is by reason of poverty, helplessness or disability or socially or economically disadvantaged position, unable to approach the court for relief, any member of the public can maintain an application for an appropriate direction, order or writ.[95]

Similarly, in the case of *Bandhua Mukti Morcha*, Bhagwati described PIL's aim as 'so that the fundamental rights may become meaningful not only for the rich and the well to do'.[96] He justified this departure from *locus standi* by highlighting the fact that Article 32(1) does not specify who may move the Supreme Court in case of an infringement of a fundamental right.[97]

[92] *Sunil Batra (II)* v. *Delhi Administration* MANU/SC/0265/1979 (Supreme Court of India, 20 December 1979).

[93] Sathe, *Judicial Activism in India*, 203.

[94] Which actually did not concern fundamental rights, but was raised in the Supreme Court by advocates concerned about the independence of the judiciary because of several transfers of judges by the executive (see *S. P. Gupta* v. *Union of India and Ors* MANU/SC/0080/1981 [Supreme Court of India, 30 December 1981]). For a summary of the case, see Sathe, *Judicial Activism in India*, 215 et seq.

[95] *S. P. Gupta* v. *Union of India and Ors* MANU/SC/0080/1981, 17.

[96] *Bandhua Mukti Morcha* v. *Union of India* MANU/SC/0051/1983, 15.

[97] Bhagwati states that '[c]lause (1) of Article 32 confers the right to move the Supreme Court for enforcement of any of the fundamental rights, but it does not say as to who shall have this right to move the Supreme Court nor does it say by what proceedings the Supreme Court may be so moved' (see Note 96, 16).

In the *Asiad* case, contractors employed by the government had not complied with labour laws for their workers on construction sites for the Asian Games. The NGO People's Union for Democratic Rights brought the issue to the Supreme Court by writing a letter to Justice Bhagwati, whose bench considered the letter as a writ petition under Article 32. Bhagwati rejected the respondents' view that only the labourers themselves could raise the case in the court, stating that 'a new dimension' had been given to the concept of *locus standi*, and that this dimension had 'revolutionised the whole concept of access to justice in a way not known before to Western Systems of jurisprudence'.[98] Because of widespread 'poverty, illiteracy, and ignorance obstructing and impeding accessibility to the judicial process', it was necessary to 'evolve a new strategy' so that 'justice may become easily available to the lowly and the lost'.[99] Therefore, 'any member of the public acting *bona fide* and not out of any extraneous motivation' would henceforth be allowed to approach the Court for a wrong caused to another person, 'even by addressing a letter to the court'.[100] Bhagwati described PIL as 'a strategic arm of the legal aid movement' intended to 'bring justice within the reach of the poor masses'.[101] He therefore explicitly positioned it as a solution for the access to justice problem.

Bhagwati also envisioned that PIL would make a trial more of a collaborative than a contradictory procedure,[102] meaning that the Court would serve as a forum in which activist members of the society could discuss with the State how it could ensure that poor citizens without access to the Court enjoy their rights, rather than having two opposing parties argue about a specific case. The judges' role, on the other hand, is described as less neutral than in an adversarial procedure, as they are supposed to be 'proactive' if they recognize a violation of human rights or

98 *People's Union for Democratic Rights* v. *Union of India* MANU/SC/0038/1982, 10 (Supreme Court of India, 18 September 1982).

99 Note 98.

100 Note 98.

101 Note 98, 2.

102 Note 98, 3.

other public interests, such as rule of law or the environment.[103] Consequently, the Court can perform its own inquiries into the matter at hand, rather than requiring the petitioner 'to prove everything'.[104]

Subsequently, the Supreme Court and the high courts allowed PILs for a vast number of cases, not only those in the interest of 'the poor' who were unable to access the courts themselves,[105] but also for broader socio-economic and administrative issues, especially concerning environmental matters.[106] Judges have not only considered letters as 'petitions', but have even started becoming active entirely on their own, without any person or organization

[103] Sathe, *Judicial Activism in India*, 207.

[104] Sathe, *Judicial Activism in India*, 207–8.

[105] Jain names several of such cases (see Mahabir P. Jain, 'The Supreme Court and Fundamental Rights', in *Fifty Years of the Supreme Court of India: Its Grasp and Reach*, ed. S.K. Verma and K. Kusum [New Delhi, New York: Oxford University Press, 2000], 85).

[106] As examples for environmental cases, Jain names, among others, the judgments of *Rural Litigation and Environment Kendra Dehradun* v. *State of UP* MANU/SC/0043/1985 (Supreme Court of India, 12 March 1985) (several orders); *Consumer Education and Research Center and Others* v. *Union of India and Others* MANU/SC/0175/1995 (Supreme Court of India, 27 January 1995); *Indian Council for Enviro-Legal Action* v. *Union of India* MANU/SC/1112/1996 (Supreme Court of India, 13 February 1996) (see Mahabir P. Jain, 'The Supreme Court and Fundamental Rights', 85). Furthermore, as examples for cases in which issues like the misuse of power by politicians were raised in the courts, he names, among others, *N. Parthasarathy* v. *Controller of Capital issues and Anr.* MANU/SC/0592/1991 (Supreme Court of India, 16 April 1991); *Shiv Sagar Tiwari* v. *Union of India and Others* MANU/SC/0739/1997 (Supreme Court of India, 23 December 1996); *Chaitanya Kumar and Ors* v. *State of Karnataka and Ors* MANU/SC/0297/1986 (Supreme Court of India, 9 April 1986). Similarly, Singh cites the case of *Sub-Committee on Judicial Accountability* v. *Union of India* MANU/SC/0368/1991 (Supreme Court of India, 8 May 1991), in which the Supreme Court Bar Association and a sub-Committee Judicial Accountability filed a case to expedite impeachment proceedings against a Supreme Court judge (see Singh, *V.N. Shukla's Constitution of India*, 356).

approaching them, in so-called '*suo motu* petitions' or '*suo motu* public interest litigation'.[107]

Considering letters directly as petitions has, on the other hand, actually become rare. Instead, the Supreme Court usually resorts to appointing lawyers as *amicus curiae* who draft regular petitions 'on the lines of the letter'.[108]

## Criticism against PIL

The developments around PIL did not go without criticism. The most obvious point of criticism is an apparent breach of the rules of separation of powers. If courts detach their cases from individual complaints, and if virtually anyone can raise any political subject as a legal subject in court, then the judiciary ultimately takes up a political role that, according to some, should be reserved to the legislature. This problem is intensified if judges then also follow a non-contradictory but 'collaborative' approach concerning

107 In the case of the right to education, the Karnataka High Court acted *suo motu* after reading a newspaper article on out-of-school children in *The Hindu* (see *The Hindu*, 'High Court Initiates PIL on Out-of-School Children', 2 April 2013, http://www.thehindu.com/news/national/karnataka/high-court-initiates-pil-on-outofschool-children/article4570507.ece, accessed on 19 August 2018). The Supreme Court in *Joint Secretary, Political Department, Government of Meghalaya* v. *High Court of Meghalaya* MANU/SC/0317/2016 (Supreme Court of India, 18 March 2016) explained the aim of '*suo motu* public interest litigation' by summarizing the reasons for the creation of PIL itself, namely that '*[s]uo motu* public interest litigation can be initiated to ameliorate the conditions of a class of persons whose constitutional or otherwise lawful rights are affected [...] The Court has adopted the said tool so that persons in disadvantaged situation [...] are in a position to have access to the Court'; though one should add that it is not actually a case of the persons accessing (or 'having access to') the Court, but the Court considering their interests without them 'accessing' it. For an overview of the developments around *suo motu* petitions in India in general, see Marc Galanter, 'Snakes and Ladders: Suo Moto Intervention and the Indian Judiciary', *Florida International University College of Law (FIU) Law Review*, 2014.

108 Sathe, *Judicial Activism in India*, 206–7.

the question of how best to protect human rights and how to best deliver benefits to the citizens. These arguments shall be dealt with more depth in Chapter 6.

Concerning the question of whether or not PIL adequately compensates for the lack of access to justice, another point of criticism is more relevant. Many observers believe that the Supreme Court, after dealing with many human rights issues concerning the poor by allowing respective PILs in the late 1970s and 1980s, has since shifted the focus to other issues. It is argued that such issues are often topics that appear important to the judges themselves, based on their own everyday lives and their own experiences. Because of this, some observers describe an 'anti-poor bias'.[109]

[109] Balakrishnan Rajagopal, 'Pro-Human Rights But Anti-Poor? A Critical Evaluation of the Indian Supreme Court from a Social Movement Perspective', *Human Rights Review* 8, no. 3 (2007): 157–86. Similarly, Shukla observes that 'from the beginnings of PIL as pro-poor and trying to effectuate rights for the exploited, it is increasingly taking a diametrically opposite direction' (see Rakesh Shukla, 'Rights of the Poor: An Overview of Supreme Court', *Economic & Political Weekly* XLI, no. 35 [2006]: 3757). Thiruvengadam agrees insofar as that 'the Indian Supreme Court has, in a process that began in the 1990s and has continued across the 2000s, transformed the nature of PIL, turning away, in several cases, from concerns it embraced in its original phase' (see Arun Thiruvengadam, 'Revisiting the Role of the Judiciary in Plural Societies [1987]: A Quarter-Century Restrospective on Public Interest Litigation and the Global South', in *Comparative Constitutionalism in South Asia*, ed. Sunil Khilnani [New Delhi: Oxford University Press, 2013], 356). Even Baxi, who was originally very optimistic concerning the effectivity of PIL, appears to later have become very disenchanted by how the Supreme Court has used what he calls 'Social Action Litigation', and, generally, by the extent to which it has furthered social change. While in the 1980s, Baxi, when writing about 'Social Action Litigation', had stated that 'the Supreme Court of India is at long last becoming [...] the Supreme Court for Indians' (see Upendra Baxi, 'Taking Suffering Seriously: Social Action Litigation in the Supreme Court of India', *Third World Legal Studies*, 1985, 107), by the early 2000s, this euphoria faded. In 2000, once again writing about 'Social Action Litigation' and judicial activism, Baxi identifies 'disenchantment as well as constitutional chaos' (see Upendra Baxi, 'The Avatars of Indian Judicial Activism: Explorations in the Geographies of (In)Justice', in, *Fifty Years of the Supreme Court of India*, 157).

More fundamentally, PIL has been criticized for allowing the judiciary to depart from 'legalism' and to turn itself into a 'populist' institution.[110]

The topics that the Supreme Court deals with most frequently have indeed changed. In earlier decisions, the interests of disadvantaged groups were raised in Court through PIL, namely those of prisoners, labourers, disadvantaged children, and disadvantaged women.[111] Public Interest Litigation was therefore dominated by cases raised on behalf of oppressed people in the 1970s and 1980s.[112] This has been described as a stark contrast to the 'pre-Emergency era' in which most of the petitioners, even in fundamental rights cases, were affluent individuals like landowners or industrialists whom the government sought to expropriate or whose businesses were to be nationalized.[113] The focus of PIL then seems to have 'shifted towards prevention of government lawlessness and sustenance of the rule of law'[114] as well as, since the 1990s, environmental matters.[115]

[110] Anuj Bhuwania, *Courting the People: Public Interest Litigation in Post-Emergency India* (Cambridge: Cambridge University Press, 2017), 134 et seq.

[111] Sathe, *Judicial Activism in India*, 208.

[112] Sathe, *Judicial Activism in India*, 208–9.

[113] Sathe, *Judicial Activism in India*, 210.

[114] Sathe, *Judicial Activism in India*, 219. He cites Dhavan, who has compiled a long list of such cases (see Rajeev Dhavan, 'Law as Struggle: Public Interest Law in India', *Journal of the Indian Law Institute* 36, no. 3 [1994]: 309). Sathe names an extensive list of such cases at Sathe, *Judicial Activism in India*, 220 et seq. Many of the topics raised in these cases do appear mainly such that would be of interest mainly to more affluent parts of the society, for example, appointment of consumer courts, arbitrary allotment of houses, acts of corruption and breach of foreign exchange, non-implementation of a ban on imported drugs, improving the management and control of road traffic, the appointment of lecturers in college, or even the allotment of toll tax and fees paid by visitors to the Taj Mahal.

[115] See Sathe, *Judicial Activism in India*, 224 et seq. The fact that the State did not ensure environmental protection in the cases at hand was considered to be a violation of the citizens' right to (dignified) life guaranteed by Article 21 (Sathe names the case of *Indian Council for Enviro-Legal Action* v. *Union of India* MANU/SC/1112/1996 as an example of the Court applying Article 21 for environmental matters

Still, social movements in India often focus on the Supreme Court to achieve their goals.[116] However, the amount of on-the-ground success they have achieved in more recent decades is actually quite limited, which may be attributed, at least in part, to 'an ideological interpretation of human rights' by the Supreme Court's judges, who are said to be biased in favour of more affluent parts of the society.[117]

As examples of this 'shift', one may cite the 2003 case of *T. K. Rangarajan*, in which the Court denied government employees of Tamil Nadu the right to strike,[118] and the 2000 case of *Narmada Bachao Andolan*, in which the Court voted in favour of the government's plan of raising the height of a dam, leading to a large Court-sanctioned forced eviction of the people living in the area.[119] Similarly, in environmental PIL cases involving the

---

[see Sathe, *Judicial Activism in India*, 224]), which, as mentioned in Chapter 2, has been defined very broadly by the judiciary; it includes, among others, the right to health and, more generally, 'to a clean environment' (see *Virender Gaur* v. *State of Haryana* MANU/SC/0629/1995, 7 [Supreme Court of India, 24 November 1994]: 'hygienic environment is an integral facet of right to healthy life'), which also extends to less non-health-related aspects such as the conversation of wildlife and even the protection of the Taj Mahal against degradation because of pollution (*Pradeep Krishen* v. *Union of India* MANU/SC/0505/1996 (Supreme Court of India, 10 May 1996); *M.C. Mehta* v. *Union of India* MANU/SC/0175/1997 [Supreme Court of India, 30 December 1996]) (see Sathe, *Judicial Activism in India*, 224).

116 Rajagopal, 'Pro-Human Rights But Anti-Poor?', 157–8.

117 See Rajagopal, 'Pro-Human Rights But Anti-Poor?', 158, citing Epp, *The Rights Revolution*, 90 et seq. Rajagopal agrees, however, that the Court's judicial activism of the late 1970s—which he, as many others, sees as an attempt to compensate for the pro-government stance the Court had taken during the Emergency—gave 'the weak' 'a veritable weapon', and that the Court was 'riding a human rights wave' driven by social movements (see Rajagopal, 'Pro-Human Rights But Anti-Poor?', 160).

118 *TK Rangarajan* v. *Government of Tamil Nadu* MANU/SC/0541/2003, 15 et seq. (Supreme Court of India, 6 August 2003).

119 In this case, the Court effectively reasoned for judicial self-restraint:

closure of polluting industries in Delhi, the Court completely refrained from hearing the factories' workers.[120]

---

> In respect of public projects and policies which are initiated by the Government the Courts should not become an approval authority. Normally such decisions are taken by the Government after due care and consideration [...] The facts enumerated hereinabove clearly indicate that the Central Government had taken a decision to construct the Dam as that was the only solution available to it for providing water to water scare areas. It was known at that time that people will be displaced and will have to be rehabilitated. There is no material to enable this Court to come to the conclusion that the decision was mala fide. A hard decision need not necessarily be a bad decision.

See *Narmada Bachao Adolan* v. *Union of India* MANU/SC/0640/2000, 260 (Supreme Court of India, 18 October 2000). Sathe has also criticized the Court's final 2000 decision in the case, expressing a worry that 'the Supreme Court [...] seems unfortunately to be suggesting its withdrawal from the larger role which it had assumed in recent decades' (see S.P. Sathe, 'Supreme Court and NBA', *Economic & Political Weekly* XXXV, no. 46 [2000]: 399). On this case, also see Rajagopal, 'Pro-Human Rights But Anti-Poor?', 160, 162.

[120] Aggarwal refers to the case of *M.C. Mehta* v. *Union of India* MANU/SC/0570/1996 (Supreme Court of India, 8 July 1996), in which the Supreme Court ordered compensation only for permanent workers, who were only a minority group in the entire workforce of the factories involved (see Shobha Aggarwal, 'The Public Interest Litigation Hoax in India: Its Adverse Impact on the Poor and Working Class', *South Asia Citizens Web*, 23 April 2015, http://sacw.net/article11105.html, accessed on 19 August 2018, 5). Similarly, the Court did not hear affected persons in the case of *World Saviors* v. *Union of India* MANU/SC/1455/1998 (Supreme Court of India, 6 December 1996) (see Aggarwal, 'The Public Interest Litigation Hoax in India', 2). Also see the 'right to a clean environmental case', in which the Supreme Court, only gave non-enforceable recommendations (according to Aggarwal's interpretation) that affected mine workers 'shall, as far as practicable [...], be provided employment in [an] afforestation and soil conservation programme' (see *Rural Litigation and Environment Kendra Dehradun* v. *State of UP* MANU/SC/0043/1985, cited in Aggarwal, 'The Public Interest Litigation Hoax in India', 4). However, the wording 'shall' does have the meaning of a binding order, though it is limited considerably by the addition 'as far as practicable'. The

Even as far as the Court's environmental adjudication is concerned, an 'urban and elitist bias against the poor and the countryside' has been observed.[121] It is said that when the Court orders the closure of polluting industries, it ignores the interests of the workers, and mainly considers environmental issues that are of importance to urban parts of the society, rather than such that concern rural populations.[122] Furthermore, there are cases that illustrate that while giving orders on environmental matters, such as the implementation of environmental statutes, the Court tends to not see itself constrained by financial implications; however, when concerning socio-economic rights like the right to housing, it does.[123]

It is difficult to ascertain why this shift in PIL adjudication has taken place. It could be due to the fact that the Supreme Court,

---

author argues that this is especially problematic considering that there is no way to appeal against Supreme Court judgments, and suggests that PIL judgments should generally be open for review by a larger bench, and also that PILs should be treated like regular writ petitions or class actions suits in which third parties are affected, so that those persons would have to be able to file a representative suit on their behalf (see Aggarwal, 'The Public Interest Litigation Hoax in India', 6).

[121] Rajagopal, 'Pro-Human Rights But Anti-Poor?', 163. Similarly, Aggarwal agrees that the earlier cases had the aim of 'providing justice to the disadvantaged', but she now sees a shift to 'other interests' in later cases, which she believes is irreconcilable with the fact that PIL itself derives its legitimacy from being an instrument for 'justice to the underprivileged and downtrodden' (see Aggarwal, 'The Public Interest Litigation Hoax in India', 1).

[122] Rajagopal, 'Pro-Human Rights But Anti-Poor?', 163.

[123] Rajagopal, 'Pro-Human Rights But Anti-Poor?', 164, citing the cases of *Municipal Council, Ratlam* v. *Vardhichan* MANU/SC/0171/1980 (Supreme Court of India, 29 July 1980) and *M.C. Mehta* v. *Union of India* MANU/SC/0586/1988 (Supreme Court of India, 12 January 1988), in which the Court did indeed give specific orders for measures for the State to undertake for environmental protection, and *Olga Tellis And Others* v. *Bombay Municipal Corporation And Others* MANU/SC/0039/1985 (Supreme Court of India, 10 July 1985), where the Court saw a limitation on the scope of orders it could give to protect the right to housing, as examples.

since the invention of PIL, has seen itself as more of a political body and a legislator, and has therefore adopted the views concerning the definition of 'statism' and 'developmentalism' prevalent at the given time.[124] Indeed, the shift in the focus of PIL cases coincides with the era of economic liberalization which started in the early 1990s.[125] Using a terminology that Baxi has developed, one may say that the judges, therefore, have been merely 'active' rather than 'activist'.[126]

Another factor may be the establishment of the National Human Rights Commission, which was created by the Protection of Human Rights Act of 1991.[127] Possibly, the Supreme Court decided to 'yield' most of these cases to that body.[128] However, that Commission only has the power to make recommendations rather

[124] Rajagopal, 'Pro-Human Rights But Anti-Poor?', 166. He notes that the meaning of 'developmentalism' has changed 'from state-led industrial growth to sustainable development to rights-based development to neo-liberal development' over time. He also believes that the Court generally 'loathe[s] to find […] a petitioner who is asserting rights that openly contradict either the dominance of the state or vision of socioeconomic and cultural change that is implied in the grand vision of development'. In the case of *Narmada Bachao Adolan*, the Court 'found' an 'anti-dam organization', which presented the opportunity to declare that the displacement of the affected people, its negative effects notwithstanding, was justified as 'harvest[ing] a river [happens] for the larger good', quoting the judgment *Narmada Bachao Adolan* v. *Union of India* MANU/SC/0640/2000, 267.

[125] See, for instance, Rajagopal, 'Pro-Human Rights But Anti-Poor?', 160.

[126] Baxi believes that a differentiation between 'an active judge' and 'an activist judge' may also explain the discrepancies: 'An *active* judge regards herself […] as a trustee of state regime power and authority. Accordingly, she usually defers to the executive and legislature […] and overall promotes "stability" over "change"', while 'an *activist* judge regards herself as holding judicial power in fiduciary capacity for civil and democratic rights of all peoples, especially the disadvantaged' (see Baxi, 'The Avatars of Indian Judicial Activism', 165). In the 1980s, apparently, Baxi had hoped for a more activist Court that then, to his disappointment, often ended up not going beyond being active.

[127] Sathe, *Judicial Activism in India*, 218–19.

[128] Sathe, *Judicial Activism in India*, 218–19.

than passing binding orders, meaning that it is not an adequate alternative to 'traditional' fundamental rights adjudication.[129]

The Bar might also be indirectly responsible for the 'anti-poor bias'. It is said that in more recent years, Indian lawyers have pushed less aggressively for adjudication of socio-economic rights, and have especially refrained from drawing on trends in international and comparative law.[130] This reflects in judgments that are 'confusing and show a breezy familiarity with international law'.[131] Furthermore, one may note that many advocates at the appellate Bar initially did take up 'public interest' cases, but did not entirely focus on these issues. Instead, at the same time, they also defended individuals accused of corruption, arguing for environment causes and human rights one day 'and sculpt the next day unprecedented defences on behalf of a Union Carbide Corporation'.[132]

The criticism of the Supreme Court's more recent human rights record may be questioned itself, especially considering that there are numerous examples of cases in which the Court was 'pro-poor' in recent years as well. The *Right to food case*, which will be dealt with more in-depth in Chapter 6, is one prominent example. Furthermore, for a long time, there had been little empirical work

[129] Though it may in itself initiate litigation, see Section 18(b, e, f) of The Protection of Human Rights Act, 1993. Generally, the Commission appears to not have played a great role in effective rights enforcement, though the studies on its work are not up to date (Sripati studied the work of the National Human Rights Commission in 2000, speaking of an 'indifference' by the government to its recommendations, and calling for more political willingness to make the institution work, which ultimately depends on its personnel as well as it does on its powers, see Vijayashri Sripati, 'India's National Human Rights Commission: A Shackled Commission?', *Boston University International Law Journal* 18, no. 1 (2000): 44 et seq.), making it difficult to assess its role today. The working of a similar institution with similar powers, the National and State Commissions for Protection of Child Rights, shall be assessed more in-depth in the next chapters.

[130] Rajagopal, 'Pro-Human Rights But Anti-Poor?', 168.

[131] Rajagopal, 'Pro-Human Rights But Anti-Poor?', 168.

[132] Baxi, 'The Avatars of Indian Judicial Activism', 159.

to really confirm the validity of the narrative that PIL's focus shifted away from the poor.[133]

Gauri has performed such an empirical study to answer the question if PIL (still) benefits marginalized individuals and groups.[134] In trying to ascertain whether or not there is an anti-poor bias, the author analyses all cases involving fundamental rights, without being able to identify whether or not they were raised as PILs or 'normal' petitions. His analysis of these fundamental rights cases (which, because of the Supreme Court's broad understanding of Article 21, may also involve issues such as environmental concerns) shows that the number of claimants from 'advantaged classes'[135] has increased at almost the same rate as (but not at a higher rate than) the overall number of fundamental rights cases from the late 1960s up until 2007.[136] Gauri therefore comes to the conclusion 'that class bias concerns that stem from the organizational

[133] See Gauri, 'Fundamental Rights and Public Interest Litigation in India', 71–3. Indeed, while Rajagopal and Aggarwal name judgments that are convincing examples to support their arguments, they have not performed real empirical studies of judgments to verify whether or not the examples are really representative of a larger trend followed by the judiciary. Rather, they appear to describe their own experiences and (possibly subjective) general impressions of tendencies and possible reasons behind them. Even Baxi, when analysing the Supreme Court's activism and describing judges as 'active' and 'activist', does not base this on actual empirical work.

[134] Gauri, 'Fundamental Rights and Public Interest Litigation in India', 80 et seq. The author also notes that this study in itself is difficult. Whether or not PIL cases in particular have or have not increasingly involved 'middle class concerns' is difficult to ascertain because of lack of a record of identifiable PIL cases (see Gauri, 'Fundamental Rights and Public Interest Litigation in India', 83).

[135] Gauri identified a petitioner as belonging to 'advantaged classes' if he could identify them as 'a professional (doctors, teachers, members of the armed services, etc.), a landowner or business person, or someone otherwise in the global middle class (including formal sector workers and civil service employees not designated as workers or laborers)' (see Gauri, 'Fundamental Rights and Public Interest Litigation in India', 83).

[136] Gauri, 'Fundamental Rights and Public Interest Litigation in India', 84, 90.

advantages of the advantaged class are not as pronounced as some have feared'.[137]

The author reaches a similar conclusion by analysing the number of fundamental rights cases that have originated from India's poorest BIMARU states (Bihar, Madhya Pradesh, Rajasthan, and Uttar Pradesh). The share of cases from these states has actually been increasing since the late 1960s, albeit only slowly, even though their share still remains below the share of those states' population of the overall national population.[138] This suggests that inequalities exist, but that they have been declining.[139]

Gauri makes a third observation, which does allow some conclusions concerning PILs. The number of fundamental rights cases initiated by or involving an NGO or cooperative group has barely increased since the late 1960s, while the overall number of fundamental rights cases has steadily increased in the same period of time.[140] As NGOs are more likely to involve concerns of the poor than the middle or upper classes, and are also more likely to bring general benefits for a larger number of people than those raised on behalf of private individuals,[141] one may conclude that even though the numbers of fundamental rights cases has increased, this does not seem to be an effect of PILs, but rather 'increased mobilization by private individuals'.[142]

The results that Gauri has come to are, therefore, mixed. As he looks at the absolute number of cases, the increase of fundamental rights cases filed by individuals since the late 1960s is not really surprising, considering the fact that India's population has also greatly

[137] Gauri, 'Fundamental Rights and Public Interest Litigation in India', 84.

[138] Gauri, 'Fundamental Rights and Public Interest Litigation in India', 84, 90.

[139] Gauri, 'Fundamental Rights and Public Interest Litigation in India', 84.

[140] Gauri, 'Fundamental Rights and Public Interest Litigation in India', 84–5, 91.

[141] Gauri, 'Fundamental Rights and Public Interest Litigation in India', 84–5, 91.

[142] Gauri, 'Fundamental Rights and Public Interest Litigation in India', 85.

increased in the same period of time. The fact that at the same time the number of cases filed by cooperatives and NGOs has barely increased does suggest that PILs are not seen by them as a successful tool for 'helping the poor masses'. As mentioned above, PIL matters made up only 1–2 per cent of the Supreme Court's admission and regular hearing disposals between 2005 and 2011, which is in stark contrast to the media attention that they receive.[143]

The picture is also mixed concerning the outcome of cases, though Gauri's findings do suggest a tendency that is unfavourable for poorer claimants. The study finds that claimants in cases involving women's and children's rights are more likely to win than those in cases involving matters concerning Scheduled Castes, Scheduled Tribes, and Other Backward Classes (SC/ST/OBC). The claimants in the first group are actually, to a large extent, from affluent parts of the society; Gauri counts 72 per cent from advantaged classes.[144] On the other hand, the 'win rate' for the latter group of cases has actually decreased. This may suggest that judges are now less favourable towards claims from these disadvantaged classes than they used to be.[145] Furthermore, Gauri finds a clear tendency looking at the overall 'win rates' in fundamental right cases between those initiated by advantaged and those initiated by non-advantaged groups. Until the 1980s, the win rate for claimants from advantaged classes was below the one for members from non-advantaged classes. The situation has, since then, reversed. In the years 2000–8, the probability for an advantaged class claimant to win a fundamental rights case was at 73 per cent, while it was only at 47 per cent for those from non-advantaged classes.[146]

[143] Robinson, 'A Quantitative Analysis of the Indian Supreme Court's Workload', 27.

[144] Gauri, 'Fundamental Rights and Public Interest Litigation in India', 85.

[145] Gauri, 'Fundamental Rights and Public Interest Litigation in India', 85. However, he also notes that today, more claimants in cases involving SC/ST/OBC issues are themselves not members of these groups, which may have also played a role in this development (see Gauri, 'Fundamental Rights and Public Interest Litigation in India', 85).

[146] Gauri, 'Fundamental Rights and Public Interest Litigation in India', 85–6.

The author notes that while these findings might be a confirmation for the Supreme Court having become less receptive for fundamental rights claims made on behalf of the poor, there may be other explanations than a judicial bias as well. Perhaps the cases brought by poorer claimants are weaker in merits than they used to be, which may be explained by changes in statutes, an increase of more challenging cases brought by poorer claimants, or weaker legal representation.[147] While this explanation cannot be ruled out, it does not seem very likely.[148] Therefore, the author argues that there is a 'prima facie validation' that judicial attitudes are now less favourable towards claims of the poor than they used to be, likely 'in conjunction with changes in the political and legislative climate'.[149]

One may thus conclude that there are at least some indicators that in recent years there is a tendency of the judiciary deciding more favourably for advantaged classes. Perhaps also that it puts more emphasis on issues that are of larger concern to relatively affluent parts of the society. There may even be a preference of judges to such topics that they and their socio-economic peers consider important, meaning that 'pro-poor PILs' would remain pending for longer periods of time, or that they would not even be admitted as writ petitions. This alone may raise doubts whether PIL may be an adequate compensation for lack of access to justice for individuals with their specific grievances.

Furthermore, in practice, PIL does not actually make the courts as accessible even for relatively affluent groups as one might imagine. In theory, PIL promises that if one group merely points

[147] Gauri, 'Fundamental Rights and Public Interest Litigation in India', 86.

[148] Gauri notes that 'it is unlikely that the quality of legal representation has simultaneously increased for the advantaged and decreased for the marginalized, and sufficiently to explain the significant reversal in win rates', or that 'advantaged clients started to select a less challenging set of cases at the same time that marginalized claimants did the reverse' (see Gauri, 'Fundamental Rights and Public Interest Litigation in India', 86).

[149] Gauri, 'Fundamental Rights and Public Interest Litigation in India', 86.

a court's attention to violations of or lack of implementation of a right, then the court will take matters into its own hands, like it did in cases in which it became active merely because of becoming aware of a newspaper article identifying a social ill. In reality, however, a common complaint by PIL litigants is 'that they never realized how much time and money it would require'.[150]

## The Importance of Access to Justice for the Poor

But even if there were no such tendency, there are reasons to argue that fundamental rights, read with Article 32, still call for realistic possibilities of access to justice for the poor, in addition to PIL. As mentioned above, the question of access to justice does not feature much in discussions about socio-economic rights adjudication in India. It is difficult to assess why this is the case. Generally, the discussion focuses on the role and use of PIL and the Supreme Court's activism.[151] Activism, in this context, mostly has a positive connotation, as the judiciary's activism is considered to be almost a necessity in the Indian context.[152]

[150] Nick Robinson, 'Closing the Implementation Gap: Grievance Redress and India's Social Welfare Programs', *Columbia Journal of Transnational Law* 53, no. 2 (2015): 352.

[151] 'For the most part, the scholarship that takes note of social rights adjudication in India examines it only in passing. The primary focus is on "public interest litigation"' (see Madhav Khosla, 'Making Social Rights Conditional: Lessons from India', *ICON* 8, no. 4 [2010]: 743).

[152] For instance, the term is used positively by Jain, 'The Supreme Court and Fundamental Rights', 86. Sathe (when discussing the Supreme Court's loose application of the rule of 'prematurity', meaning that it frequently chose to resort to obiter dicta) notes that 'in a society where rights had been given to people who for generations had been powerless and exploited [...] [a] proactive judicial process was a condition precedent to the enforcement of fundamental rights' (see Sathe, *Judicial Activism in India*, 198). He also writes about 'a new paradigm of judicial process consistent with the rights discourse [the Court] has generated through judicial activism. The new paradigm envisions an affirmative, proactive role of the Court for facilitating access to justice for those who did not possess either the know-how or the resources for invoking the judicial process'

Specifically for the question of access to justice, it appears that most seem to believe that the problem has been 'solved' by creating PIL, at least if PIL is applied as it used to be before the 1990s. For instance, PIL has been described as offering a 'democratization' of access to constitutional remedies.[153] Also, the court's activism in loosening the rules of standing is said to have 'enabled the courts to reach victims of injustice who so far had remained invisible'.[154] It thus appears that PIL is considered to be an adequate solution for the access to justice problem.

But, as mentioned above, even Justice Bhagwati only described PIL as 'a strategic arm of the legal aid movement', meaning that there could be other 'arms' as well.[155] Perhaps it does not occur to some observers that the poor might want to claim their rights themselves rather than relying on NGOs or other groups that may help them, or perhaps those observers believe that enabling the poor to do so is not at all a realistic prospect.[156]

Whatever the reasons may be, both scholarly writings as well as NGOs working on the ground often seem to look only at PIL when

---

(see Sathe, *Judicial Activism in India*, 201). Also see Baxi's distinction between 'active and activist judge' described above.

[153] Upendra Baxi, 'Demosprudence Versus Jurisprudence: The Indian Judicial Experience in the Context of Comparative Constitutional Studies', *Macquarie Law Journal* 14 (2014): 3–23, at p. 8.

[154] Sathe, *Judicial Activism in India*, 209. The author also argues that PIL's goals are '(1) to enable the Court to reach the poor and the disadvantaged sections of society [...], (2) to enable individuals or groups of people to raise matters of common concern [...], and (3) to increase public participation in the process of constitutional adjudication' (see Sathe, *Judicial Activism in India*, 202).

[155] Jain also interprets Bhagwati's view in a way that PIL should be seen as one of several 'multi-dimensional strategies' (see Jain, 'The Supreme Court and Fundamental Rights', 82).

[156] Jain names the fact that the poor lack knowledge 'and the wherewithal' to approach the courts to enforce their rights themselves, and that this is one of the two main reasons for the invention of PIL, with the issue of certain 'diffused' rights inevitably concerning a multitude of persons rather than clearly identifiable individuals, being the other (see Jain, 'The Supreme Court and Fundamental Rights', 78).

considering raising 'the poor's' issues in court. While social movements that have become disenchanted with PIL have chosen to instead focus on grass-root/on-the-ground movements, those have been more political than legal, avoiding the judiciary altogether.[157] However, concerning elementary education, such a change in focus does not take advantage of the fact that a political claim has become an enforceable right.

As the Indian Constitution, like many other modern constitutions, includes the guarantee to judicially enforce one's rights (Article 32), the question arises whether lack of access to justice for the poor is merely an unfortunate circumstance or whether it in itself constitutes an infringement of an aggrieved person's fundamental rights that cannot be compensated for by an institution such as PIL.

## International Obligations

The special rapporteur on extreme poverty and human rights to the UN General Assembly notes that eradicating extreme poverty

[157] Thiruvengadam quotes, inter alia, Krishnan, who found that only policy groups with a large amount of resources employ litigation as a strategy—if at all (see Thiruvengadam, 'Revisiting the Role of the Judiciary in Plural Societies', 356). Krishnan, based on his interviews with civil society groups, reports that 'resource-poor policy groups commented that, even if they had a strong financial base, litigation would be the last course of action they would consider. [...] Movement leaders perceived that the government agency being sued would engage in endless delay and relentless appeals, even where the government's chance of winning was remote. Such an image seems to have documented support' (see Jayanth K. Krishnan, 'Social Policy Advocacy and the Role of the Courts in India', *American Asian Review* XXI, no. 2 [2003]: 112 et seq.). He also mentions the example of the PUDR, which, along with the PUCL, is one of the two successor groups to the PUCLDR. The PUDR believes that the PUCL relies too much on litigation, and instead itself employs a strategy (as it did in 1998 to oppose the expansion of capital punishment) of 'tactical pluralism', which also includes grass-roots measures such as 'holding vigils, public awareness meetings, and a series of protests and demonstrations' (see Krishnan, 'Social Policy Advocacy and the Role of the Courts in India', 115–16).

requires that the poor have 'the resources, capabilities, choices, security and power necessary to enjoy the whole spectrum of human rights'.[158] Furthermore, access to justice, in connection with a developed jurisprudence on social and economic rights, is 'crucial for tacking the root causes of poverty'.[159] Lack of access to justice, according to the special rapporteur, increases the poor's vulnerability both to poverty and rights violations because of which their abilities to use the justice system decreases even more—a 'vicious circle'.[160]

The rapporteur lists several sources in human rights declarations and treaties that impose a duty on states to provide access to justice, including the right to an effective remedy (Art. 8 UDHR, Art. 2.3 ICCPR), the right to a fair trial (Art. 10 UDHR, Arts. 14–15 ICCPR), the right to legal assistance (Art. 11.1 UDHR, Art. 14.3(b)-(d) ICCPR), the right to enjoy rights without discrimination (Art. 2 UDHR, Art. 2 ICCPR), and the right to recognition as a person before the law (Art. 6 UDHR, Art. 16 ICCPR).[161]

The rapporteur observes that therefore States have an obligation to design their judicial system in a way that it 'facilitates access to independent and effective judicial and adjudicatory mechanisms and ensures a fair outcome for those seeking redress, without discrimination of any kind'.[162] This system must also provide access to justice for the poor *in practice*, meaning that there is also an obligation to remove regulatory as well as social or economic obstacles in gaining access to justice.[163]

[158] United Nations General Assembly, 'Extreme Poverty and Human Rights: Note by the Secretary-General' A/67/278 (2012), 3.

[159] United Nations General Assembly, 'Extreme Poverty and Human Rights', 3.

[160] United Nations General Assembly, 'Extreme Poverty and Human Rights', 3–4.

[161] United Nations General Assembly, 'Extreme Poverty and Human Rights', 4.

[162] United Nations General Assembly, 'Extreme Poverty and Human Rights', 5.

[163] United Nations General Assembly, 'Extreme Poverty and Human Rights', 5.

## Bottom-Up vs. Top–Down or the Legal Empowerment of the Poor

Even with effective means of enforcement being seen a necessity for 'rights' (perhaps even a decisive part of what defines them as such), and even with the ICCPR and ICESCR having imposed respective international obligations for decades, reforms in poor people's access to justice and promoting their legal empowerment have become the focus of international development cooperation only relatively recently.[164] The United Nations Development Programme's (UNDP's) Commission for Legal Empowerment of the Poor, which brought this issue onto the international agenda, was only established in 2005[165] in spite of observations that laws benefitting the poor often only existed on paper 'unless the poor or their allies push for the laws' enforcement'.[166]

The idea of 'legal empowerment' seeks to go beyond focusing on 'law, lawyers and state institutions' by looking to provide the poor with 'legal and institutional tools'.[167] The idea of 'legal

[164] Van de Meene and van Rooij called access to justice and legal empowerment 'the latest trend in legal development cooperation' in 2008 (see Ineke van de Meene and Benjamin van Rooij, *Access to Justice and Legal Empowerment: Making the Poor Central in Legal Development Co-Operation* [Leiden: Leiden University Press, 2008], 5).

[165] See the website archived at https://web.archive.org/web/20080714163636/http://www.undp.org/legalempowerment/?, accessed on 15 August 2018. India was one of the countries supporting the Commission (see Dan Banik, 'Rights, Legal Empowerment and Poverty: An Overview of the Issues', in *Rights and Legal Empowerment in Eradicating Poverty*, ed. Dan Banik [Farnham, England, Burlington, VT: Ashgate Publishing, 2008], 11). Banik wrote as late as in 2008 that a 'strong claim that poverty persists partly because the poor do not enjoy legal rights' had been made 'in recent years', calling the 'legal empowerment of the poor' approach a 'relatively new and alternative development paradigm' (see Dan Banik, 'Introduction', in *Rights and Legal Empowerment in Eradicating Poverty*, 1).

[166] Stephen Golub, 'Beyond the Rule of Law Orthodoxy: The Legal Empowerment Alternative', 2003, http://carnegieendowment.org/files/wp41.pdf, accessed on 24 February 2019.

[167] Banik, 'Rights, Legal Empowerment and Poverty', 11.

empowerment' calls for measures that include reforming national and local judiciaries in order to facilitate access to justice.[168]

Considering the calls for access to justice and legal empowerment, there is a necessity to support the poor 'to seek and obtain justice and to use the legal system to improve their lives'.[169] 'Legal empowerment of the poor' may be described as a broader concept that includes the idea of 'access to justice', though the distinction is sometimes not completely clear.[170] One may say that access to justice reforms must focus on poor and marginalized people's lack of access to law and the legal system.[171] Legal empowerment, on the other hand, shall 'focus on the lack of power, opportunities and capacities that impede poor and marginalised people's use of law and (para) legal tools to take control of their lives and improve their livelihoods'.[172]

In international debates on law and development, the focus had previously been on promoting rule of law through legal reform and

[168] Banik identifies three major approaches that the legal empowerment concept follows: in addition to calling for reforms of national and local judiciaries, the other two measures are 'addressing the challenges posed by a rapidly growing informal sector' and 'formalising property rights' (see Banik, 'Rights, Legal Empowerment and Poverty', 11–12). The 'informal sector' and 'property rights' aspects relate to the poor's (in)ability to accumulate wealth and enjoy social security (because of labour and social laws not being applicable to them) and their (in)ability to enjoy legal protection of the wealth that they do have, for example, the ownership of land that they occupy. Both of these aspects are very relevant to India as well. However, in the present context, the aspect of access to justice and necessity of reforming judiciaries are most relevant.

[169] van de Meene and van Rooij, *Access to Justice and Legal Empowerment*, 6.

[170] '[L]egal empowerment may involve access to justice and access to justice may involve legal empowerment', Benjamin van Rooij, *Bringing Justice to the Poor: Bottom-up Legal Development Cooperation* (Amsterdam: Leiden University Press, 2008), 6.

[171] van de Meene and van Rooij, *Access to Justice and Legal Empowerment*, 6–7.

[172] van de Meene and van Rooij, *Access to Justice and Legal Empowerment*, 6–7.

institutional strengthening, also of the judiciary (so-called 'top-down' institutional reform measures).[173] It has been observed that the top–down approach was not able to overcome 'asymmetric power relations' that prevented benefits for the poor, even when such benefits were intended to be the result of these measures.[174] Therefore, more recently, legal reform programmes have shifted their focus 'to the justice seeker' (and therefore, to bottom-up intervention).[175] Legal empowerment, therefore, calls for a stronger focus on the 'demand side of governance' rather than 'empowerment from above'.[176]

There are different measures that are discussed at the international level to further legal empowerment. Interestingly, one of them is 'collective litigation and public interest law'.[177] A tool like the Indian institution of PIL is therefore also considered as a method to strengthen access to justice and legal empowerment. In fact, India's experience with PIL, particularly in the *Right to Food* case, is actually cited as a positive example for legal empowerment of the poor.[178] However, it is also conceded that 'it does not

[173] van de Meene and van Rooij, *Access to Justice and Legal Empowerment*, 6.

[174] van de Meene and van Rooij, *Access to Justice and Legal Empowerment*, 10.

[175] van de Meene and van Rooij, *Access to Justice and Legal Empowerment*, 6. The authors see this development as a part of a 'shift in emphasis from macro-economic growth to micro-level relief'.

[176] Kenneth Nielsen, '"Not on Our Land!" Peasants' Struggle against Forced Land Acquisition in India's West Bengal', in Banik, *Rights and Legal Empowerment in Eradicating Poverty*, 219, with reference to Ana Palacio, 'Legal Empowerment of the Poor: An Action Agenda for the World Bank: To the attention of the World Bank', December 2005, http://siteresources.worldbank.org/INTLAWJUSTINST/Resources/LegalEmpowermentofthePoor.pdf, accessed on 19 August 2018, 8.

[177] van de Meene and van Rooij, *Access to Justice and Legal Empowerment*, 13. The authors name this measure in addition to measures such as improving legal aid, introducing 'hybrid courts and procedures' that 'combine litigation and reconciliation', and strengthening civil society and community organizations.

[178] Banik, 'Rights, Legal Empowerment and Poverty', 26.

directly enhance [poor people's] ability to use the legal system for solving individual issues'.[179]

The legal empowerment debate identifies two problems: the fact that the judicial system does not provide effective means for disadvantaged persons to claim their rights, and also that certain characteristic inhibitions are also found in the sphere of the poor.[180] In addition to lack of financial capacity and experience, there is also a lack of legal awareness and knowledge and a negative perception of and distrust towards the legal system.[181] Legal empowerment and access to justice, therefore, have two dimensions. The 'supply side' calls for reforms of the judiciary to make it work more effectively and efficiently, and the 'demand side' calls for a wide range of measures to ensure that the judiciary is more accessible, and that the people also access it in practice.[182]

Generally, for the Indian context, one may raise the question of why legal 'bottom-up' mechanisms are actually necessary in a democracy, where the larger political system itself offers measures to exert pressure 'from below'. Groups of people who believe that they are entitled to certain benefits can 'lobby' for those benefits to be provided to them. They can exert political pressure on the State, particularly through elections, if provision is lacking. Indeed, as far as directive principles are concerned, Ambedkar had pointed out that the State may not be answerable to the judiciary, but that it would be answerable to the electorate.[183] Apparently, he hoped that this 'accountability' mechanism would eventually suffice for achieving the goals set out by the principles. Concerning education as well as many other socio-economic goals set by the

[179] van de Meene and van Rooij, *Access to Justice and Legal Empowerment*, 14.

[180] van Rooij, 'Bringing Justice to the Poor', 9–11.

[181] van Rooij, 'Bringing Justice to the Poor', 9–11.

[182] Yash Ghai and Jill Cottrell, 'The Rule of Law and Access to Justice', in *Marginalized Communities and Access to Justice*, ed. Yash P. Ghai and Jill Cottrell (Abingdon [England], New York: Routledge, 2010), 4–5.

[183] As quoted in Granville Austin, *The Indian Constitution: Cornerstone of a Nation* (Oxford, New York: Oxford University Press, 1999), 78.

principles, this did not happen in reality. Merely relying on the State being answerable to the electorate did not suffice.

Concerning the right to education, Article 21A itself mandates that there must be effective means to claim education from the State *in addition* to the option of exerting pressure through elections and other means of political agitation. Ideally, having both of these tools should put the right-bearers in a stronger position to exert pressure on the State *themselves* to receive what they are entitled to. Consequently, the use of legal services to increase the control that disadvantaged persons have over their own lives is seen as one decisive feature of the legal empowerment approach.[184] The approach seeks to give the poor 'new power to use law and legal tools' to escape poverty, in addition to the powers that they already had.[185]

In India, one factor inhibiting people from lobbying for the 'benefits they are *entitled* to', either through democratic or through the legal system, seems to be that the sense of entitlement itself appears to be missing, particularly concerning education. Even though the Indian State has, for a long time, rhetorically positioned itself as a welfare State, with the Constitution including welfare promises in both its Preamble and the directive principles catalogue, the public often does not actually expect the State to fulfil its promises, as has been described in Chapter 1. The fact that there is such a lack of public and media attention for low quality of primary education, particularly government education, is one of the several indicators for this phenomenon.

Particularly concerning education, many citizens do not think of it as a 'public good' at all, meaning that many may not realize that the government is supposed to offer decent quality education for free, in spite of it being a fundamental right (or previously a directive principle, which had put the same obligation on the State). When questioned about private and government schools, parents tend to express the view that government schools are

[184] Golub, 'Beyond Rule of Law Orthodoxy', 25.

[185] John W. Bruce et al., 'Legal Empowerment of the Poor: From Concepts to Assessment', ARD, Inc. for the USAID, March 2007, http://pdf.usaid.gov/pdf_docs/Pnadm500.pdf, accessed on 19 August 2018, 29.

'meant for the poor',[186] possibly indicating a view that quality education can only be expected if one has to pay for it. In other words, most parents seem to consider it their own responsibility that their children receive good quality education, and not the State's. The fact that the media pays little attention to government elementary education might be a result of such a mindset.

In any case, when 'the poor' in India do believe that the government infringes their rights, the amount of pressure that they exert on the State can actually be considerable. An interesting example is the peasants' struggle against forced land acquisition in West Bengal for a car factory in Singur in the 2000s, where peasants truly exerted pressure 'from below'.[187] In Singur, the state government of West Bengal had expropriated peasants in the interest of 'economic development' of that region.[188] Critics rejected this notion of 'development' and noted that the inhabitants at Singur, on average, did not have the skills to work in a car factory, and that taking their land would harm a relatively prosperous agricultural economy.[189]

The peasants felt that they were entitled to their land and that the State was committing an injustice. In such cases, where citizens are aware of their rights, more focus should be put on strengthening the demand-side and helping the poor to organize themselves and to mobilize in order to facilitate legal empowerment.[190] Legal empowerment calls for a 'transformation of the poor into citizens who are aware of their rights, are able to assert

[186] 'The discourse commonly heard during the village studies was that government schools are "bad" and meant for low-caste and poor children only' (see Anuradha De, *Probe Revisited: A Report on Elementary Education in India* [New Delhi: Oxford University Press, 2011], 51).

[187] Nielsen, 'Not on Our Land!', 217.

[188] For the developments in Singur, see Walter Fernandes, 'Singur and the Displacement Scenario', *Economic & Political Weekly* XLII, no. 3 (2007); D. Bandyopadhyay, 'Singur: What Happened, What Next and Time to Pay the Cost', *Economic & Political Weekly* XLIII, no. 48 (2008).

[189] Nielsen, 'Not on Our Land!', 230.

[190] Nielsen, 'Not on Our Land!', 219, with reference to Palacio, 'Legal Empowerment of the Poor', 24.

them and also to hold the state accountable for their adequate enforcement'.[191]

Another interesting example is Chatterjee's study of urban slums in Kolkata, which shows that the poor exert pressure and claim benefits in other ways than the educated urban middle/upper class (who are those whom the State may consider to be 'full citizens') do. This happens, for instance, by measures such as occupying land, electrical power theft, or, more generally, not paying for public utilities that they use.[192] Such illegal measures of claiming benefits are made possible over longer periods of times through 'clandestine arrangements [...] with influential politicians', but the fact that they remain illegal is one factor preventing the poor from achieving full 'citizenship', which they would only gain if they could use legal and organized means to claim their rights.[193]

To an extent, the events at Singur are a case of the people 'claiming citizenship'. The affected peasants formed a coordination committee and started agitations on and off the streets. This included petitions and deputations to officials and politicians, as well as protest meetings, rallies, and fasts.[194] Sometimes they also used illegal means like violence against the police.[195] The committee gained support of a multitude of organizations, and also of the biggest opposition party in the state at the time, the Trinamool Congress, with local representatives of that party becoming influential members of the committee.[196]

[191] Palacio, 'Legal Empowerment of the Poor', 21. This description has been criticized by Nielsen, who notes that it sounds as if the poor 'appear as "not-yet" or "not-quite" citizens waiting to be rather passively granted the status of "full citizens"', which he finds to be an apt description of how they are generally viewed in India (see Nielsen, 'Not on Our Land!', 220).

[192] Nielsen, 'Not on Our Land!', 220, referring to Partha Chatterjee, *The Politics of the Governed: Reflections on Popular Politics in Most of the World* (New York: Columbia University Press, 2004), 52 et seq.

[193] Nielsen, 'Not on Our Land!', 220.

[194] Nielsen, 'Not on Our Land!', 230–1.

[195] Nielsen, 'Not on Our Land!', 230–1.

[196] Nielsen, 'Not on Our Land!', 231. The Trinamool Congress also supported the movement by providing services like food supplies and

NGOs, on the other hand, helped the peasants prepare for fighting their case in the High Court, and ultimately acted as petitioners themselves. The NGOs compiled data like 'fact finding mission reports, survey results, and reports from people's hearings', which helped the peasants 'speak the language of governance' so that they could 'challenge government policies on its own turf and in its own specialist language'.[197] Effectively, the NGOs 'translated' emotive expressions and subjective feelings into 'the powerful language of rights, citizenship and democracy'.[198] This process helped peasants become more familiar with 'the language of citizenship' as well as with laws and institutions.[199] This became especially relevant once the state government banned public gatherings, which led to the peasants taking 'their struggle from the streets to the court room'.[200]

Interestingly, also in this case, even though the peasants were already quite actively trying to vindicate their rights, the 'struggle in the courtroom' ended up being an 'indirect' one. Rather than filing their own petitions (which NGOs that were supporting them could have helped them with), the peasants mostly relied on the NGOs filing petitions in their interest (that is, PILs) in the High Court.[201] Some peasants also filed their own petitions, but those were eventually dismissed by the Court, which demonstrates how difficult it is to access the higher judiciary even in a case that is already receiving a court's attention.[202]

In this particular case, there were several factors inhibiting access to the High Court: when challenging acquisitions, one of the major problems for the peasants was to prove their own existence in formal documents.[203] Also, using the alternative to

---

paying for medical costs for those injured in agitations, as well as paying bail for imprisoned peasants (see Nielsen, 'Not on Our Land!', 232).

[197] Nielsen, 'Not on Our Land!', 233.

[198] Nielsen, 'Not on Our Land!', 233.

[199] Nielsen, 'Not on Our Land!', 234.

[200] Nielsen, 'Not on Our Land!', 234.

[201] Nielsen, 'Not on Our Land!', 234.

[202] Nielsen, 'Not on Our Land!', 234.

[203] Nielsen, 'Not on Our Land!', 237.

documental proof, that is, giving sworn testimonies or affidavits, proved difficult, as the peasants were unable to obtain official stamp papers. The Court refused to recognize the statements given on plain paper as legally valid.[204] Those stamp papers were then sometimes given to the peasants by 'middlemen' who charged additional 'fees'. Ultimately the papers could also be obtained by the leadership of the peasants' committee.[205] Nielsen concludes that 'the entire process demonstrates how the poor are disadvantaged when confronting a hostile government'.[206]

The High Court eventually ruled in favour of the government. Still, the case shows how on-the-ground mobilization for a cause that concerns many poor people can exert pressure on the State.[207] Also, even without being successful in the High Court, the peasants did achieve what they had aimed for 'on the ground'. Because of the agitations and the support they received from the main opposition party, the car company ultimately decided not to build the car factory in Singur.[208] Furthermore, the central government reacted by drafting a new law for land acquisition, which was passed in 2013.[209]

In addition to this extensive organizational and political support, the peasants' struggle also received extensive regional and national media attention,[210] and is even said to have been essential

[204] Nielsen, 'Not on Our Land!', 237.

[205] Nielsen, 'Not on Our Land!', 237–8.

[206] Nielsen, 'Not on Our Land!', 238.

[207] Nielsen believes that 'the peasants of Singur have done most things right' and that they 'achieved remarkable results in terms of both policy and collective capacity' (see Nielsen, 'Not on Our Land!', 241).

[208] *Financial Express*, 'Tata Pulls Out of Singur, Blames Trinamool Stir', 4 October 2008, http://www.financialexpress.com/archive/Tata-pulls-out-of-Singur-blames-Trinamool-stir/369241/, accessed on 19 August 2018.

[209] The Right to Fair Compensation and Transparency in Land Acquisition, Rehabilitation and Resettlement Act, 2013 (see http://www.legislative.gov.in/sites/default/files/A2013-30.pdf, accessed on 15 August 2018). This Act replaces the Land Acquisition Act of 1894 (see http://pib.nic.in/newsite/PrintRelease.aspx?relid=122150, accessed on 15 August 2018).

[210] Nielsen, 'Not on Our Land!', 232.

for the outcome for the next state election in 2011, which the Trinamool Congress won.[211] Ultimately, the movement successfully appealed to the Supreme Court, which in 2016 ruled that the land acquisition was illegal as it was not for a 'public purpose'.[212]

The example of Singur shows that the poor are able to exert a tremendous amount of pressure from 'below' when they believe their rights are being infringed by the government. It also shows that such agitation can also lead to tangible results, at least when the poor form alliances with NGOs and opposition parties.

One wonders why similar agitations do not happen when the State fails to deliver benefits that the Constitution promises to every citizen, particularly primary education. When comparing the issue of land acquisition with the non-delivery of quality education, one decisive difference may be that the State takes something of utmost important from the people that they already have (land), rather than 'just' refraining from delivering something to them. The injustice may be more obvious in the former case.

Also, the example shows that even when the poor do become active, both on and off the streets, fighting their own case in the courts is so difficult that they had to rely on NGOs doing it for them. This means that even in this case, they were only 'indirectly' empowered as far as adjudication was concerned.

This demonstrates the problem of seeing PIL as a means of legal empowerment. Public Interest Litigation does not provide access to justice to the right-bearers *themselves*. Rather, as in the Singur case, beneficiaries of public interest petitions are still reliant on help from third parties to take up their case for them. Public Interest Litigation cases do come from within the 'civil society', but they do not actually come 'from below'. Rather, in the Singur case, as well as in the *Right to food* case, a group that was already

[211] *Economic Times*, 'Assembly election 2011 West Bengal: Trinamool Congress Rises Like a Phoenix', 13 May 2011, https://economictimes.indiatimes.com/news/politics-and-nation/assembly-election-2011-west-bengal-trinamool-congress-rises-like-phoenix/articleshow/8293363.cms, accessed on 19 August 2018.

[212] *Kedar Nath Yadav* v. *State of West Bengal & Ors* MANU/SC/0964/2016 (Supreme Court of India, 31 August 2016).

somewhat 'empowered' (an NGO) lobbied for the interests of those who are not. An NGO may then be successful in making an institution that is at the 'top' (the Supreme Court) order another institution at the top to change its policies. This way, the interests of those at the 'bottom' are served, but not as a result of their own actions; in the Singur case, at least not directly.

Non-Governmental Organizations (NGOs) and public interest lawyers might also be more likely to lobby for the poor's interests if they concern more general, politically 'important' matters, which they consider detached from the large number of individual cases that may, in isolation, not be considered to be of high importance. This means that right-bearers with everyday grievances that do not carry the potential for ground-breaking judgments may still remain without help from such groups, and ultimately without even 'indirect' access to justice.

To use an example in the field of education, if in one village a school's teachers are frequently absent, then the affected children's interests would best be served if those particular teachers were ordered to perform their duties by the local authority. This should also happen quickly. However, NGOs preparing public interest petitions might be more interested in considering teacher absence as a structural problem that may be solved by the judiciary ordering the legislature and executive to change their policies. The organizations might then (also with good reasons) find it more useful to draw a court's attention to these policy shortcomings rather than using their energies to help one group of parents, or even just one parent, trying to ensure that their children's teachers perform their duties. Consequently, very few PIL cases concern the violation of just one person's or one family's rights. Rather, they tend to concern a large group of people whose rights are infringed because of larger shortcomings that may be described as 'systemic'.

Successful PILs may therefore end up benefitting a larger number of children in the entire state or country. However, this will only happen if the policy changes are implemented properly and lead to the desired results. Imposing sanctions on one particular teacher at the local level directly would only have an effect for that particular school, but this effect would potentially follow a lot more quickly, and it would be more tangible for the aggrieved right-bearer.

Therefore, PIL only provides *empowerment* in a limited, very indirect sense, even if it may lead to the delivery of benefits. But even if it does, the beneficiaries will still not feel that they claimed the benefits from the State themselves because they had a right to do so. Rather, that 'someone else' lobbied for their interests at a higher level. That is not full 'empowerment', and also not what the Constitution envisions in the case of elementary education by virtue of it being a justiciable fundamental right. Rather, being able to effectively claim one's rights, and therefore enjoying the right conferred by Articles 32 and 226 itself, remains an unfulfilled constitutional promise.

Without the fulfilment of this promise, most of the right-bearers cannot yet fully feel as 'citizens', as they cannot make themselves be heard as much (not even remotely) as the privileged can in the legal sphere.

As far as the 'sense of entitlement' is concerned, the current situation might be described as a vicious circle. If a group of persons feels that they are entitled to certain benefits, they may become more active in claiming them from the State. However, even if the State is under an obligation to deliver certain benefits, the non-delivery of such benefits is not felt as strongly as in a situation in which the State takes property or other assets from its citizens. A sense of entitlement, on the other hand, may grow if there are effective avenues through which the citizens may claim these benefits. But only if these prove to be successful will it be more obvious to the right-bearers that they truly are entitled to the benefits.

## Mobilizing Citizens for Rights Implementation

Even when viewed from the State's perspective, enabling citizens to effectively access the judiciary may have important advantages. Ineffective administration and corruption inhibit effective implementation of the Right to Education Act and the education system as a whole. In order to act on shortcomings in the implementation process, these shortcomings have to first be precisely identified. This in itself requires effective monitoring of the implementation process, which may also be difficult to achieve when the administration process is ineffective.

If the aggrieved persons themselves (and/or their parents, in this case) approach courts with grievances resulting from shortcomings in the implementation process, such cases may help the State to more effectively identify these shortcomings, and then to remedy them. If there is indeed a rights violation, the judiciary would award remedies in the individual case. However, in addition to that, the cases may help the executive and legislature in identifying why such a violation occurred in the first place, and if similar violations may be prevented by policy decisions in the future. Thus, citizens going to court or using other complaint mechanisms provides an avenue for the State to gather information about the implementation of its policies.[213] One may even describe rights as a 'tool' for Indian officials at the higher level 'to monitor and control the bureaucracy by encouraging complains from citizens and then penalizing erring behavior'.[214] Courts may thus act 'like an alarm bell' informing the government about implementation and therefore administration failures.[215] For such an 'alarm system' to work, however, the 'bell' has to be accessible, it has to be rung in the first place.

This effect has been described by Masing, writing about the idea of 'mobilising citizens for the implementation of laws',[216] though in a very different environment to the one in India. He points out that in the European Union (EU),[217] the vast amount of highly specialized laws in many different areas of life have led to a situation in which authorities and administrative agencies find it increasingly difficult to ensure implementation of these laws.

213 Robinson, 'Closing the Implementation Gap', 345.

214 Robinson, 'Closing the Implementation Gap', 350.

215 Robinson, 'Closing the Implementation Gap', 360. For the process of 'fire alarm monitoring' through grievance redress, also see Varun Gauri, 'Redressing Grievances and Complaints Regarding Basic Service Delivery', 2011, http://elibrary.worldbank.org/doi/pdf/10.1596/1813-9450-5699, accessed on 19 August 2018, 5.

216 Johannes Masing, *Die Mobilisierung des Bürgers für die Durchsetzung des Rechts: Europäische Impulse für eine Revision der Lehre vom subjektiv-öffentlichen Recht* (Berlin: Duncker & Humblot, 1997).

217 At that time, the 'European Communities'.

This effect is increased by the fact that the EU is reliant on the member states' administrations' implementation of its laws.[218] A 'decentralized' demand for the implementation of laws by citizens may therefore be more effective in the EU and in a modern state with highly specialized laws. The citizens may then compensate for the lack of capacity of the authorities.[219]

The situation in the EU (being a supranational body with only very limited administrative powers of its own, having to rely mostly on member States for implementation of its laws) and India (being a 'regular' nation State in which the lack of effective implementation of laws is a result of an often ineffective and corrupt administration) is, at first sight, very different. However, in both jurisdictions the legislatures may find that 'their' laws are not implemented as desired because of barriers in the administration system, even though the nature of these barriers is very different in both contexts. In both of them, monitoring and ensuring implementation 'from above' may be difficult, so added pressure 'from below' may make a decisive difference.[220] The European Court of Justice has recognized the importance of this effect in numerous cases, for instance, concerning the direct application of

[218] Masing, *Die Mobilisierung des Bürgers für die Durchsetzung des Rechts*, 231.

[219] Masing, *Die Mobilisierung des Bürgers für die Durchsetzung des Rechts*, 232. He also cautions that thus empowering citizens may also have negative effects if this empowerment motivates them to become denunciators against fellow citizens, which would become extremely problematic in the fields of welfare of aliens' laws (see Masing, *Die Mobilisierung des Bürgers für die Durchsetzung des Rechts*, 233).

[220] Generally, considering India's diversity, it has been argued that comparing India and the EU is actually more apt than comparing India with one EU member state (see Philipp Dann, 'Federal Democracy in India and the European Union: Towards Transcontinental Comparison of Constitutional Law', *Law and Politics in Africa, Asia, Latin America (VRU)* 44, no. 2 [2011], https://www.nomos-elibrary.de/10.5771/0506-7286-2011-2-160/federal-democracy-in-india-and-the-european-union-towards-transcontinental-comparison-of-constitutional-law-jahrgang-44-2011-heft-2?page=0, accessed on 19 August 2018).

provisions in directives.[221] One might even state that the citizens themselves become 'part of the administration' by ensuring that laws are implemented.[222]

Public Interest Litigation may play a role in this respect as well. In fact, Masing argues that in Germany, one might broaden the rules of standing by re-defining the German administrative law concept of 'subjective public rights'.[223] This way, one could mobilize society to help in identifying a lack of implementation of laws for a wider range of issues. One could argue that the Indian institution of PIL also has a 'mobilizing effect', enabling the civil society to ensure the implementation of laws. But, as mentioned above, because of lack of access to justice for a large part of the population (which is by far less of an issue in Germany), this only happens in parts 'from below'. It is also somewhat selective, as only those

221 *Andrea Francovich and Danila Bonifaci and others* v. *Italian Republic* (European Court of Justice, 19 November 1991). However, in that case, it is the legislature and not the administration in a member State that fails to act.

222 Masing, *Die Mobilisierung des Bürgers für die Durchsetzung des Rechts*, 51.

223 The German administrative law concept of 'subjective public rights' states that legal norms of a certain category give an individual the authority to have a direct claim against the State to pursue their own interests (see Hartmut Maurer, *Allgemeines Verwaltungsrecht*, 18th edition [München: Beck, C H, 2011], Chapter 8, No. 2). Masing gives a detailed overview of how this concept has developed since the nineteenth century (see Masing, *Die Mobilisierung des Bürgers für die Durchsetzung des Rechts*, 56 et seq.). 'Objective law', on the other hand, is made up of all legal norms that may or may not give such claims to individuals; the State (or the administration) has to follow these laws, but individuals might not have individual claims that the State will actually follow them in practice (see Maurer, *Allgemeines Verwaltungsrecht*, Chapter 8, No. 3, 4). In judicial practice, the consequence of this categorization is that as a general rule, individuals can only approach administrative courts if they can assert that one of their 'subjective rights' might have been infringed by the State (Section 42(2) Verwaltungsgerichtsordnung). Re-defining the 'subjective public rights' concept would therefore have a similar effect as the loosening of the common law rules of *locus standi*.

matters taken up by human rights advocates, NGOs, and other 'empowered' parts of the society will make it to the courts (and will actually be given attention by the courts).

In order to fill gaps in the system of monitoring through adjudication, the State's attention has to be drawn to on-the-ground shortcomings in implementation even at the 'lowest level', which is most difficult to monitor, and not just those shortcomings that are addressed by more vocal parts of the society such as NGOs. Therefore, the vast majority of citizens must be mobilized at least potentially. Every citizen who becomes a witness of laws not being implemented, or is directly affected by the non-implementation, has to be able to also act on that shortcoming and demand implementation. Only then, comprehensive monitoring with the help of courts as 'alarm bells' will be possible.

## Alternatives to the Higher Judiciary

Thus, PIL is not an adequate alternative to right-bearers themselves claiming their fundamental right to education in the Supreme Court or the high courts. Still, these courts remain inaccessible to them in practice. Therefore, the question arises whether or not there are other forums in which right-bearers can claim their fundamental rights. In order to provide adequate compensation, these forums would have to be more accessible than the higher judiciary, while at the same time promising effective remedies.

Providing such mechanisms might be an alternative solution by which the State could fulfil its obligation to provide justiciability, even if it is not the 'justiciability' in the higher judiciary that the Constitution actually guarantees. Pragmatically, one could argue that the State may provide 'justiciability' (or, rather, enforceability, as it might happen outside of the judiciary) also by offering alternative systems that lead to the same results.

The State is obviously aware of a need to facilitate access to justice for the majority of the people. Both constitutional as well as statutory law does provide some alternative means that could also be used for fundamental rights adjudication, including socio-economic rights adjudication. Still, as shall be shown below, most of these forums have not been empowered to adjudicate on fundamental rights.

The only institutions whose functions currently include enforcement of fundamental rights outside of the 'regular' judiciary are statutorily created grievance mechanisms and human rights commissions, which shall be the focus of the final two chapters.

## District Courts

As mentioned above, Article 32(3) allows Parliament to empower 'any other court' to exercise the powers given to the Supreme Court within that court's jurisdiction. As those powers are already given to the high courts by Article 226, that is, by the Constitution itself, the provision means that Parliament may choose to empower India's lower judiciary, that is, the district courts to adjudicate fundamental rights. As of now, it has not done so.[224]

However, even in the current legal set-up, the Specific Relief Act of 1963 may allow right-bearers to move the district courts against the State concerning such parts of the content of fundamental rights that have been further defined by statutory law, such as the Right to Education Act. The Specific Relief Act empowers courts to issue injunctive relief to compel performance concerning obligations under statutory law.[225] The Specific Relief Act is usually applied in civil (particularly contractual) matters. However,

224 The Delhi Advocate Dhamija calls for legislation to empower the district courts with fundamental rights adjudication in order to make justice more accessible for those right-bearers who do not live in a city with a high court (see Ashok Dhamija, 'Empowering District Courts to enforce Fundamental Rights', 3 May 2012, http://tilakmarg.com/opinion/empowering-district-courts-to-enforce-fundamental-rights/, accessed on 19 August 2018). In addition to the issue of physical distance, the reasons he gives include lower costs for lawyers for district courts, a relief for the backlogged higher courts who may then be able to focus on the more important cases that may be brought to them through appeals, and so on.

225 Malini Bhattacharjee, Dolashree Mysoor, and Arun Sivaramakrishnan, 'RTE Grievance Redress in Karnataka', *Economic & Political Weekly* XLIX, no. 23 (2014): 40.

the 'obligations' that the Act speaks of (for instance, in Section 38)[226] are defined as 'every duty enforceable by law' by Section 2(a), meaning that the wording of the Act itself is not restricted to these matters. It might therefore also be used to enforce obligations addressed at the State.[227]

However, this is only a theoretical possibility. So far, district courts have not adjudicated cases that involve infringements or enforcement of fundamental rights.[228] It remains to be seen whether or not their idea may be taken up in practice by the courts. Also, so far, this possibility has not found widespread scholarly attention. Furthermore, the Specific Relief Act allows injunctive relief only if there is no 'equally efficacious relief' (Section 41(h)). Such relief could be provided for by the grievance mechanisms given by the Right to Education Act,[229] which shall be described below and in the next chapters.

There have been calls for lower court judges to become 'activist'. They should go beyond conventional constraints and adjudicating fundamental rights, specifically socio-economic rights, thus taking part in furthering 'social change'.[230] Although scholarly opinion has thus far only considered the higher judiciary for adjudication of these matters,[231] there already are some isolated cases in which the lower judiciary may encounter questions of fundamental rights as well, even without specifically being approached for fundamental rights enforcement. In one district court case, a defendant had threatened a witness, causing the witness to file a petition for a court order to provide police protection to him.[232]

[226] Section 38 states that 'a perpetual injunction may be granted to the plaintiff to prevent the breach of an obligation existing in his favour'.

[227] Bhattacharjee, Mysoor, and Sivaramakrishnan, 'RTE Grievance Redress in Karnataka', 40.

[228] Bhattacharjee, Mysoor, and Sivaramakrishnan, 'RTE Grievance Redress in Karnataka', 40.

[229] Bhattacharjee, Mysoor, and Sivaramakrishnan, 'RTE Grievance Redress in Karnataka', 40. The authors are of the opinion that the grievance mechanisms, as they are currently designed, do not offer 'equally efficacious relief'—a view that shall be discussed in Chapter 5.

[230] Krishnan et al., 'Grappling at the Grassroots', 531.

[231] Krishnan et al., 'Grappling at the Grassroots', 531.

[232] Krishnan et al., 'Grappling at the Grassroots', 533.

The Court of the Judicial Magistrate First Class dismissed the petition stating that 'issues concerning the right to life can only be raised before the High Court'.[233] The matter then came to a district court judge, who allowed the petition and ordered police protection. However, his order was reversed on the ground that a district court did not have jurisdiction for such a petition.[234] The judge, in an interview with Krishnan et al., argued that '[t]he applicant was a poor man who would never be able to afford the expenses of filing an application before the High Court. What use is right to life being a justiciable right if it cannot be accessed in any court by any common person?'[235]

Another judge whom Krishnan et al. interviewed had not had specific fundamental rights petitions brought before him. He explained that nonetheless, he generally considered such rights (essentially, the right to housing as part of the right to life)[236] in his judgments. He describes how in cases concerning the eviction of 'squatters' or illegal occupants of private property, he would allow the occupants to stay on the property until alternative arrangements could be made.[237] An immediate eviction, he notes, would leave the people with 'no shelter, no privacy, and no protection'.[238] As the State 'at some level' would be responsible for that situation, 'at such times, I take into consideration the emergency that must have compelled the persons to take recourse to an illegal act and I give precedence to the principles of natural justice over all other procedures'.[239]

By quoting these cases, the authors essentially argue that lower-judiciary judges may bring social change by stretching the rules that have traditionally limited their powers, and by thus becoming activist as the higher-judiciary judges have been in the past decades.[240] They do note, however, that such an expansion could

233 Krishnan et al., 'Grappling at the Grassroots', 533.

234 Krishnan et al., 'Grappling at the Grassroots', 533.

235 Krishnan et al., 'Grappling at the Grassroots', 533.

236 Declared to be part of Article 21 in *Olga Tellis and Others* v. *Bombay Municipal Corporation and Others* MANU/SC/0039/1985.

237 Krishnan et al., 'Grappling at the Grassroots', 537.

238 Krishnan et al., 'Grappling at the Grassroots', 537.

239 Krishnan et al., 'Grappling at the Grassroots', 537.

240 Krishnan et al., 'Grappling at the Grassroots', 533.

also be seen critically, considering the fact that lower courts suffer from systemic deficiencies that impede predictability and equitable justice delivery.[241]

While one may raise doctrinal, ethical, or political arguments for why the lower judiciary could, or should, adjudicate fundamental rights, such adjudication does not occur in practice—at least not yet. It is also not envisaged (at least not explicitly) by the constitutional and legal set-up as it is in place today, as long as Parliament does not explicitly empower the district courts with fundamental rights adjudication. Therefore, the lower courts currently do not offer an opportunity for effective enforcement of these rights against the State.

## Tribunals

The Indian State has attempted to create several kinds of alternative forums in addition to the regular judiciary with the aim of offering faster and more accessible justice. 'Tribunals' are institutions that are, today, independent of the regular judiciary and are each specialized on certain subjects.

The provisions in Part XIV-A of the Constitution allow Parliament (Article 323A) and the state legislatures (Article 323B) to 'provide for the adjudication or trial by (administrative) tribunals'. Tribunals had already existed prior to 1976, when Articles 323A and B were added to the Constitution by the Forty-Second Amendment Act. They were under the appellate jurisdiction of the respective high court according to Article 227.[242] Part XIV-A gave them additional constitutional sanction and even made it possible for the legislature to exclude the possibility to appeal against tribunals' decisions to the higher judiciary, except for the possibility to approach the Supreme Court with a Special Leave Petition under Article 136 (see articles 323A(2)(d) and 323B(3)(d)).[243]

241 Krishnan et al., 'Grappling at the Grassroots', 533.

242 Singh, *V.N. Shukla's Constitution of India*, 711 et seq.

243 However, as far as judicial review under Articles 32 and 226 is concerned, this restriction for appeals was held to be unconstitutional by the Supreme Court in *L. Chandra Kumar* v. *Union of India* MANU/SC/0261/1997.

Administrative tribunals, according to Article 323-A, are to be concerned with 'recruitment and conditions of service of persons appointed to public services and posts'. Article 323-B(2) includes an extensive list of subjects for which the central and state legislatures may create tribunals (for instance, tax and foreign exchange issues as well as industrial and labour disputes). Even though the constitutional text makes it appear that tribunals may only be created for the matters listed, the Supreme Court has decided that tribunals may be set up by the central and state legislatures for any matter that they are competent to legislate on.[244] A large number of tribunals have been set up for very different kinds of subjects.[245] However, so far, no tribunals have been set up for fundamental rights adjudication.

In theory, tribunals could also be a faster, less costly and more accessible option for adjudication than the regular judiciary, as they too could be empowered with fundamental rights adjudication (at least to a certain extent) through simple statutory legislation. However, the legislature has not done so until today.

The case of *Siddharth International Public School* mentioned in Chapter 3, in which the Motor Accident Claim Tribunal decided to enforce Section 12 of the Right to Education Act by declaring that the child injured in an accident must be admitted to a private school, appears to be an odd exception.[246] Considering that the Delhi High Court then ruled that the tribunal had acted outside of its jurisdiction, this case does not demonstrate how tribunals may viably adjudicate fundamental rights.

As far as the subject of education is concerned, different states have created 'school tribunals'.[247] However, those only deal with

[244] *Union of India* v. *Delhi High Court* MANU/SC/0194/2002 (Supreme Court of India, 14 March 2002).

[245] Several of the current 37 tribunals at the national level actually perform 'identical functions', which leads to calls for their number to be reduced (see *Times of India*, 'Fresh Move to Decrease Number of Tribunals', 25 November 2015, http://timesofindia.indiatimes.com/india/Fresh-move-to-decrease-number-of-tribunals/articleshow/49918099.cms, accessed on 19 August 2018).

[246] See Chapter 3.

[247] See, for instance, the Delhi School Tribunal set up by Section 11 of the Delhi School Education Act, 1973, or the Maharashtra School Tribunal

disputes between teachers and private schools that employ them and therefore do not offer means for children to evoke their right to education.

## Lok Adalat

The problems of access to justice and an overburdened judiciary have also led to calls for alternatives to the regular courts at the lowest-possible level, particularly in villages. The calls for such alternative forums were often joined by an evocation of the pre-British Indian self-government institution of panchayats, whose re-introduction was called for by a directive principle (Article 40) when the Constitution came into force. The seventy-third and seventy-fourth constitutional amendments did (re-)introduce a *panchayati raj* system in India. However, as far as village-level 'courts' are concerned, a system using the traditional name already existed shortly after Independence, the *nyaya panchayat*s. Nyaya panchayats were introduced in the late 1950s and dealt mainly with relatively petty cases.[248] But the 'new' nyaya panchayat system ultimately did not work. The reasons were, among others, lack of independence of the 'judges' from the parties, lack of enforcement possibilities, and, ultimately, lack of support from the villagers.[249]

---

set up by Section 8 of the Maharashtra Employees of Private Schools (Conditions of Service) Regulation Act, 1977.

248 Upendra Baxi and Marc Galanter, 'Panchayat Justice: An Indian Experiment in Legal Accesss', in *Access to Justice*, ed. Bryant Garth and Mauro Cappelletti (Alphen aan den Rijn: Sijthoff and Noordhoff, 1978), http://upendrabaxi.in/documents/Panchayat%20justice_%20an%20indian%20experiment%20in%20legal%20access.pdf, accessed on 9 December 2016, 364–5. As Galanter and Krishnan point out, they had very little to do with the traditional system: the traditional system, unlike the post-Independence system, had applied indigenous norms rather than statutory law, and only 'leading men of a caste' could be members (see Marc Galanter and Jayanth K. Krishnan, '"Bread for the Poor": Access to Justice and the Rights of the Needy in India', *Hastings Law Journal* 55, no. 4 [2004]: 792).

249 Galanter and Krishnan, 'Bread for the Poor', 792. As a consequence, '[i]n little more than a decade, *nyaya panchayats* were moribund' (see Galanter and Krishnan, 'Bread for the Poor', 793).

Still, the idea of alternative forums of adjudication at a lower level did survive and led to the creation of so-called lok adalats or 'people's courts'.[250] Such institutions were first created (without official legal sanction) in the 1970s, and later became more formalized.[251] One might describe them, in legal terms, as private arbitration or mediation forums.[252] They developed into an alternative to the lower judiciary for, mostly, relatively small civil and even criminal matters.[253] In the case of the 'High Court Lok Adalat' in the state that Galanter and Krishnan studied,[254] the panel (or 'bench') is compromised by a retired high court judge and two advocates.[255]

Lok adalats ultimately received legislative sanction. For instance, Section 22D of the Legal Services Authorities Act, 1987, explicitly refers to a 'Permanent Lok Adalat'.[256] Still, whether or

[250] At the village level, there are now also village courts called *gram nyalaya*s that have mandatory jurisdiction for certain petty civil and criminal matters (see Krishnan et al., 'Grappling at the Grassroots', 511).

[251] Galanter and Krishnan, 'Bread for the Poor', 794.

[252] Galanter and Krishnan refer to the 1976 report by Baxi on the lok adalat in a tribal area of Gujarat run by the social worker Harivallabh Parikh, who acted as a mediator for the community (see Upendra Baxi, 'From Takrar to Karar: The Lok Adalat at Ragpur—A Preliminary Study', *Journal of Constitutional and Parliamentary Studies* 10, no. 52 (1976): 56 et seq., http://upendrabaxi.in/documents/From%20takrar%20to%20karar_%20the%20lok%20adalat%20at%20rangpur%20a%20preliminary%20st.pdf, accessed on 19 August 2018 cited in Galanter and Krishnan, 'Bread for the Poor', 794).

[253] As far as criminal law is concerned, they were responsible for 'petty criminal cases', for which they are supposed to find resolutions described as 'plea bargains between the state's public prosecutor and the petty criminal defendant' (see Galanter and Krishnan, 'Bread for the Poor'). In civil matters, the lok adalats deal with, for instance, claims by accident victims under the Motor Vehicle Act (see Galanter and Krishnan, 'Bread for the Poor', 801).

[254] They do not disclose which state this was to ensure the anonymity of persons that they interviewed, but say that it is 'one of India's most politically and economically important states' (see Galanter and Krishnan, 'Bread for the Poor', 809).

[255] Galanter and Krishnan, 'Bread for the Poor', 822.

[256] Section 22D reads: 'The Permanent Lok Adalat shall, while conducting conciliation proceedings or deciding a dispute on merit under this

not lok adalats have been a success is debatable. They do tend to settle cases more quickly than regular courts do. Their main achievement is that they provide a system through which claimants can secure at least a partition of what they are entitled to 'without the aggravation, extortionate expense, inordinate delay and tormenting uncertainty of the court process'.[257] To illustrate, Galanter and Krishnan cite the example of a motor accident claimant who might end up receiving compensation of 50,000 rupees 'after an expensive ten-year struggle in the courts', or half of that amount in a lok adalat 'in just a few months'.[258] However, one should keep in mind that the claimant is actually entitled to the full amount. The only reason why receiving half of what one is entitled to can be considered a success is because the only alternative for receiving the full amount is 'a disastrously flawed judicial system'.[259] Therefore, one may ask if the resources invested in the lok adalat system would not better be invested in improving that 'disastrously flawed' judicial system itself.[260]

Still, the 'people's courts' (which also have other flaws in addition to offering 'discounted' remedies)[261] are yet another indicator that the State is aware of accessibility problems in the judiciary, and is trying to compensate for it by creating (or, in this case, endorsing) alternative mechanisms. The lok adalats do offer an alternative that may be adequate and beneficial for plaintiffs in certain situations.[262]

---

Act, be guided by the principles of natural justice, objectivity fair play, equity and other principles of justice, and shall not be bound by the Code of Civil Procedure, 1908 and the Indian Evidence Act, 1872'.

257 Galanter and Krishnan, 'Bread for the Poor', 808.

258 Galanter and Krishnan, 'Bread for the Poor', 808.

259 Galanter and Krishnan, 'Bread for the Poor', 808.

260 Galanter and Krishnan, 'Bread for the Poor', 829.

261 Galanter and Krishnan give a detailed account about oftentimes paternalistic judges, struggles of lawyers who ultimately prefer the regular judiciary, and so on (see Galanter and Krishnan, 'Bread for the Poor', 809 et seq.).

262 However, creating several kinds of alternative forums has also led to a situation in which cases are transferred from one forum to another, which may create additional delays (see Krishnan et al., 'Grappling at the Grassroots', 528).

However, the lok adalats too have not (yet) been endowed with powers to adjudicate on fundamental rights.

***

Even though the Indian State is aware of the problem of access to justice, and has, through legislative and judicial means, created several forums and mechanisms to compensate for the deficiencies, the problem has not been solved by the measures described in this chapter, especially not in the field of fundamental rights.

Considering the fact that the defining feature of fundamental rights in Indian constitutional law is their enforceability against the State, especially when compared to the directive principles, this deficiency is especially grave. Ultimately, one has to conclude that the State is not fulfilling its constitutional duties in this respect, neither with the regular judicial system nor with the alternatives mentioned above. Even if some systems show promising features, those systems have not yet been employed for fundamental rights 'adjudication'.

There are, however, additional grievance redress mechanisms created by the Right to Education Act itself, as well as the Commissions for the Protection of Child Rights Act of 2005, which may provide compensation for this deficiency at least to a certain extent. These measures shall be dealt with in the two final chapters.

# 5

# The Grievance Redress System under the Right to Education Act

The Right to Education Act itself provides for a grievance redress system that may compensate for the inaccessibility of the 'regular' enforcement mechanism for the right to education provided by the constitutional framework. The system provided by the Act builds upon the system created by the Commissions for Protection of Child Rights Act of 2005, with local grievance redress authorities assigned by the Right to Education Act acting at the first instance and Child Rights Commissions acting at the 'appellate' level.

A functioning grievance redress mechanism could possibly fulfil the State's obligation to provide access to justice. One may argue that Articles 32 and 226 guarantee access to the higher judiciary and therefore to all the powers of the judicial branch. Therefore, a system within the executive branch of power might never fully compensate for lack of access to justice. However, as mentioned in the previous chapter, a system that provides citizens with remedies that are somewhat comparable to judicial remedies in a considerable amount of cases would provide a certain degree of compensation.

Whether the State decides to provide access to justice by making the judiciary more accessible or by creating other powerful forums is a political decision that the government must take. Also, the government will have to decide if it chooses grievance redress mechanism, tribunals, or other forums that may compensate for lack of access to justice. Articles 32 and 226 of the Constitution, if understood broadly in a sense that compensation through other forums than the judiciary is possible, merely mandate that the State undertake measures in order to provide access to justice to its citizens. Concerning the right to education, there is an additional amount of urgency because of the existence of Article 21A, and the fact that the right is primarily aimed at those for whom the judiciary is particularly inaccessible.

For this fundamental right, the State has decided to provide access to justice through administrative grievance redress mechanisms, and thus, this chapter shall examine to what extent they fulfil the constitutional mandate. If the system is found to be lacking, then this means that the State does not provide citizens with the means of enforcement that they are entitled to. This does not mean that the Constitution obliges the State to change this particular system in a certain manner. The State could always choose other means such as empowering the district courts (as described in the previous chapter) to provide access to justice. However, for the right to education, the only alternative to the higher judiciary that is currently available is the grievance redress mechanism. It shall thus be examined further.

This chapter shall proceed as follows. First, it will explain the design of the grievance redress system created by these statutory provisions. In order to assess whether or not that system may adequately compensate for the lack of access to the regular judiciary, one first has to assess what minimum standards for a judicial system for rights enforcement may be, and how an extra-judicial grievance redress system may be designed in order to fulfil these standards. This will be discussed in the second portion of this chapter. It will then come to the conclusion that, measured by these standards, the current grievance redress system for the right to education is deficient. The final portion of this chapter shall provide an overview of similar systems for enforcement of other rights in India. It will be shown that those systems tend to have similar deficiencies. But they also include aspects that make them more powerful, particularly the system provided by the Right to Information Act.

## Legal Empowerment Measures Provided by the Right to Education Act

The Right to Education Act itself provides some measures that may compensate for the lack of access to the higher judiciary for enforcement of the right to education. These measures may therefore act as tools for legal empowerment of the right-bearers. One is the institution of School Management Committees, which shall be examined in the first part of this section. School Management Committees could, if the conceptual set-up as well as its implementation are optimized, act as a tool for legal empowerment. However, they cannot be a real alternative to providing access to the high courts and the Supreme Court in case of grievances, as they do not 'emulate' a judicial system. Consequently, they also do not provide similar remedies. The grievance redress system provided for by the Act, however, could provide such remedies, as the second part of this section shall explain.

### School Management Committees

Section 21 of the Right to Education Act requires all government and government-aided schools to create School Management Committees (SMCs).[1] According to Section 21, the SMCs' functions include monitoring the working of the school, preparing and recommending a school development plan, and 'monitoring the utilization of grants received from the government'. Three-fourths of the members of SMCs shall be parents or guardians. Parents and guardians of children belonging to disadvantaged and weaker parts of the society shall be represented proportionally. Women shall make up at least half of all SMC members. One-fourth of the membership shall

[1] For the role that SMCs may play in legal empowerment, see Florian Matthey-Prakash, 'School Management Committees as a Means for Bottom-Up Implementation of the Right to Education in India', *Law and Politics in Africa, Asia, Latin America (VRU)* 49, no. 2 (2016), https://www.nomos-elibrary.de/10.5771/0506-7286-2016-2-193/school-management-committees-as-a-means-for-bottom-up-implementation-of-the-right-to-education-in-india-jahrgang-49-2016-heft-2?page=1, accessed on 19 August 2018.

be representatives of the local authority and teachers. All members (parents as well as other members) shall be elected.[2]

Further rules concerning SMCs are found in the 'state rules' that every state government in India ought to enact to adapt the provisions of the Act to the conditions in the state (Section 38). The central government created 'model rules' that may serve as an orientation for the states. Many states have, at least concerning the majority of the provisions, merely copied these model rules.

The model rules include provisions concerning the time in which the SMCs must be created (six months after the state rules come into force, Section 13(1)). They also prescribe who the non-parent/guardian members shall be. Furthermore, they also prescribe that every SMC shall have a chairperson and vice chairperson (Section 13(2-4)), that SMCs shall meet once a month, that minutes shall be taken for all meetings, and that the meetings shall be public (Section 13(5)).

Furthermore, according to the model rules, SMCs shall have functions that are not prescribed by the Right to Education Act itself. Such functions include, for instance, communicating the rights of children to the community, ensuring the fulfilment of teachers' duties, ensuring enrolment and attendance of children, monitoring the compliance with infrastructural norms as defined by the Right to Education Act's Schedule, monitoring the implementation of the Mid-Day Meal Scheme, and so on. Section 14 gives additional details for the School Development Plans, which shall contain, inter alia, estimates for future enrolment figures and the number of teachers required at the school, assessments of the need for infrastructural measures, as well as assessments of the need for additional funding.

Giving parents the possibility to take part in managing their children's schools may be an important step for their empowerment, especially considering that they are prescribed to be the dominating group in the managing body. Thus, SMCs may be a means for 'bottom-up implementation' of the right to education. Parents may voice their concerns 'upwards' and exert pressure

2 The election process is defined by rules created by state governments for their jurisdiction (see http://mhrd.gov.in/rte_smc, accessed on 13 August 2018).

on the State to deliver the right to their children.[3] However, the SMCs' powers are currently very limited. Even more importantly, lack of implementation of the existing provisions means that SMCs have not (yet) truly given parents decisive powers in the running of their children's schools.[4]

## Grievance Redress Mechanisms

The Right to Education Act's grievance redress system has some features that are similar to a judicial system. Therefore, unlike SMCs, it could compensate for the deficiencies in access to the judiciary.

### *Grievances Submitted to the 'Local Authority'*

Section 32(1) of the Act states that 'any person having any grievance relating to the right of a child under this Act may make a written complaint to the local authority having jurisdiction'. The 'local authority' shall then decide within three months 'after affording a reasonable opportunity of being heard to the parties concerned' (Section 32(2)). Any person aggrieved by the decision of the local authority may then appeal to the State Commission for Protection of Child Rights (Section 32(3)).

### *The Appellate Authority: The States' Child Rights Commissions*

The State Commissions for Protection of Child Rights as well as the National Commission are also entrusted with several monitoring functions for the education system by Section 31 of the Right to Education Act. That section states that they shall 'examine and review the safeguards for rights provided by or under this Act' and 'recommend measures for their effective implementation'. In addition to the appellate function as part of the grievance redress system, they shall also directly 'inquire into complaints relating to child's right to free and compulsory education'. Section 31(1)(c)

[3] See Matthey-Prakash, 'School Management Committees', 206 et seq.

[4] See Matthey-Prakash, 'School Management Committees', 206 et seq., 210 et seq.

and Section 31(2) refers to Sections 14 to 24 of the Commissions for Protection of Child Rights Act of 2005. The latter declare that the Commissions shall take 'necessary steps' in order to address grievances. They also define the powers that it shall have when inquiring into matters concerning a child's right to education.

The Commissions for Protection of Child Rights Act mandates the creation of a National Commission as well as commissions in every state (Sections 3, 17). Sections 3 to 12 describe the constitution of the National Commission and also prescribe procedures such as appointment of its chairperson and members. It also declares what salary the chairperson and members shall receive, how often the Commission shall have meetings, and so on. Sections 13 to 15 define the actual powers of the Commission, while Section 16 prescribes that it shall create an annual report as well as special reports. Section 24 entrusts the state commissions with the same powers that the National Commission receives through Sections 13 to 15.

Those powers include inquiring into violations of child rights and recommending initiation of proceedings in such cases, looking into the matters relating to children in need of special care and protection, and recommending appropriate remedial measures. The commissions shall also promote research in the field of child rights and spreading child rights awareness (Section 13(1)).

More importantly, the state and National Commissions have original jurisdiction to inquire into complaints and take *suo motu* notice of any deprivation or violation of child rights or non-implementation of laws 'providing for protection and development of children' (Section 13(1)(j)). This original jurisdiction for violations of any child right is an additional task to the appellate and original 'jurisdiction' that the state commissions are given through Right to Education Act.

When exercising these inquiry powers, the commissions have 'all the power of a civil court trying a suit under the Code of Civil Procedure', including summoning and enforcing the attendance of any person and examining him on oath, discovery and production of any document, receiving evidence on affidavits, requisitioning any public record or copy thereof from any court or office, and issuing commissions for the examination of witnesses or documents (Section 14(1)). The Commissions may also forward cases to a magistrate. The magistrate may then 'proceed to hear the complaint against the accused as if the case had been forwarded to him under [...] the Code of Criminal Procedure' (Section 14(2)).

### *A 'Judicial' System?*

The system created by the Right to Education Act and the Commissions for Protection of Child Rights Act clearly 'emulates' a judicial system to a certain extent. Persons can bring 'cases' against a 'defendant' (that is, the state bodies that might have violated or not fulfilled a child's right to education) and also appeal to a higher authority, which has powers that are explicitly in line with those of a civil court.

These similarities are clearly not accidental. However, this emulation needs to fulfil some minimum standards in order to really compensate for the lack of access to justice to the 'regular judiciary'. An 'alternative' system to the judiciary would have to guarantee a level of relief to the aggrieved persons that is at least somewhat comparable to the 'original' system in order to fulfil the constitutional mandate of providing citizens with effective judicial enforcement mechanisms for their rights.

## Minimum Standards for a Functioning Judicial System

How may one define the 'minimum standards' for a functioning and effective judicial system, specifically in the Indian context, and particularly for the enforcement of fundamental rights? One may, again, first look towards international treaties that India has ratified, as well as customary international law.

Article 14(1) of the ICCPR guarantees that 'everyone shall be entitled to a fair and public hearing *by a competent, independent and impartial tribunal established by law*' (emphasis added), both when facing criminal charges as well as concerning a person's 'rights and obligations in a suit at law'. Similarly, Article 10 of the UDHR[5] states that '[e]veryone is entitled in full equality to

[5] Which, of course, is not legally binding in international law, but has still been cited by the Indian judiciary in numerous fundamental rights cases.

a fair and public hearing *by an independent and impartial tribunal*' (emphasis added). The Human Rights Committee has held in a 1992 decision that 'the right to be tried by an independent and impartial tribunal is an absolute right that may suffer no exception'.[6] As the Office of the High Commissioner for Human Rights notes in a manual on human rights for judges, prosecutors, and lawyers, the principle of an independent and impartial judiciary is also considered to be part of customary international law and general principles of law.[7] In 1985, the General Assembly unanimously adopted the Basic Principles on the Independence of the Judiciary by the Seventh United Nations Congress on the Prevention of Crime and the Treatment of Offenders, which may thus be considered to be 'declaratory of universally accepted views [...] by the State Members' of the United Nations.[8]

The Basic Principles state that the judiciary must be both *independent* as well as *impartial*.[9] Concerning independence, they state that it is necessary for the Constitution, the law, and all government and other institutions to guarantee and respect the independence of the judiciary.[10] Independence means that the other branches of power (the executive and other authorities as well as the legislature) 'must respect and abide by the judgments

[6] *Gonzalez del Rio* v. *Peru U.N. Doc.* CCPR/C/46/D/263/1987 (1992), 5.1 (Human Rights Committee, 2 November 1992).

[7] Office of the High Commissioner for Human Rights, *Human Rights in the Administration of Justice: A Manual on Human Rights for Judges, Prosecutors and Lawyers* (New York, Geneva: United Nations, 2003), 118.

[8] Office of the High Commissioner for Human Rights, *Human Rights in the Administration of Justice*, 119.

[9] In addition to listing other important features like freedom of expression and association for members of the judiciary, professional secrecy, immunity to protect their work, and also a system of discipline, suspension, and removal of judges.

[10] Seventh United Nations Congress on the Prevention of Crime and the Treatment of Offenders, Basic Principles on the Independence of the Judiciary: Endorsed by General Assembly resolutions 40/32 of 29 November 1985 and 40/146 of 13 December 1985 (1985), http://www.ohchr.org/EN/ProfessionalInterest/Pages/IndependenceJudiciary.aspx, accessed on 2 March 2019, 1.

and decisions of the Judiciary, even when they do not agree with them'.[11] Such respect for the judiciary is 'indispensable for the maintenance of rule of law'.[12]

Impartiality, on the other hand, focuses more on the motivations of the individual judge. Judges, according to the Basic Principles, shall decide matters 'on the basis of facts and in accordance with the law, without any restrictions, improper influences, inducements, pressures, threats or interferences, direct or indirect, from any quarter or for any reason'.[13] The Human Rights Committee has stated that impartiality 'implies that judges must not harbour preconceptions about the matter put before them, and that they must not act in ways that promote the interests of one of the parties'.[14]

Scholars argue that a judge is *independent* if there is no 'pressure or interference from other sources, especially government'.[15] An *impartial* judge must not 'decide for reasons other than the merits of the issue for resolution'.[16] Impartiality and independence may also mandate that judges' job security and salaries, as well as the process of decision-making, are protected against political manipulation.[17] The government, on the other hand, must accept

[11] Office of the High Commissioner for Human Rights, *Human Rights in the Administration of Justice*, 121.

[12] Office of the High Commissioner for Human Rights, *Human Rights in the Administration of Justice*, 121.

[13] Seventh United Nations Congress on the Prevention of Crime and the Treatment of Offenders, 'Basic Principles on the Independence of the Judiciary', 2.

[14] *Karttunen* v. *Finland*, Communication No. 387/1989, 7.2 (Human Rights Committee, 5 November 1992).

[15] Daniel C. Prefontaine and Joanne Lee, 'The Rule of Law and the Independence of the Judiciary', *Revue québécoise de droit international*, 1998, 164.

[16] B.N. Srikrishna, 'Judicial Independence', in *The Oxford Handbook of the Indian Constitution*, ed. Sujit Choudhry, Madhav Khosla, and Pratap B. Mehta (Oxford, New York: Oxford University Press, 2016), 350.

[17] Charles R. Epp, *The Rights Revolution: Lawyers, Activists, and Supreme Courts in Comparative Perspective* (Chicago: University of Chicago Press, 1998), 11. Referring to Dicey, Epp also observes that

the primacy of law and must itself seek to be law-abiding, meaning that the government must create (and then maintain) 'competing centers of authority beyond [its] control'[18] and 'subordinate' itself to the law.[19] One may note that in addition to the freedom of the judge, for the effective protection of human rights, it is also crucial that a judge is *perceived* to be free to make impartial decisions,[20] as otherwise the trust in the judiciary as an institution would be undermined.

Of course, one could argue that this understanding of separation of powers and the prerequisites for a functioning judiciary and rule of law is 'Western' and should not be transferred into the Indian context. It has been observed that Asian politicians tend to 'focus on the regular, efficient application of law' rather than submitting themselves to it. They often do not see law as a limitation for the State's powers, but rather as a tool used to exert power; their idea is a 'rule *by* law rather than rule of law'.[21] However, as far as Indian constitutional law and the role of the higher judiciary is concerned (and especially how it has developed since Independence), separation of power and especially the independence of the judiciary is seen as essential.[22] The higher judiciary has even strengthened its

---

'constitutional right guarantees [are] meaningless in the absence of ordinary legal remedies to invoke them', for which an effective, independent judiciary is a necessity (see Epp, *The Rights Revolution*, 14 and A.V. Dicey, *Introduction to the Study of the Law of the Constitution* [Indianapolis: Liberty/Classics, 1982], 118).

[18] Thomas Carothers, 'The Rule of Law Revival', *Foreign Affairs* 77, no. 2 (1998): 96.

[19] Prefontaine and Lee, 'The Rule of Law and the Independence of the Judiciary', 164.

[20] Prefontaine and Lee, 'The Rule of Law and the Independence of the Judiciary', 164.

[21] Carothers, 'The Rule of Law Revival', 96.

[22] As described in Chapter 2, the Supreme Court has given the judiciary extensive powers to review acts by the executive and legislature: in the 1970s case of *Kesavananda Bharati*, the Court had asserted its power by declaring that it could even review constitutional amendments, *Kesavananda Bharati* v. *State of Kerala* MANU/SC/0445/1973 (Supreme Court of India, 24 April 1973). Also see Chapter 2. Furthermore, in the

own structural independence to an extent that goes far beyond the provisions that are commonly found in 'Western' constitutions.[23]

---

*Maneka Gandhi* decision, the Supreme Court declared that 'law' defining the procedure by which the life or personal liberty of an individual (Article 21) may be compromised must be '*just* law', essentially introducing 'substantive due process' into constitutional adjudication and putting itself in a position in which it acquired 'vast power to supervise and invalidate any union or state action [...] perceived [...] to be "arbitrary" and "unreasonable"', see T.R. Andhyarujina, 'The Evolution of Due Process of Law by the Supreme Court', in *Supreme but not Infallible: Essays in Honour of the Supreme Court of India*, ed. B.N. Kirpal (New Delhi, New York: Oxford University Press, 2000), 193, referring to *Maneka Gandhi* v. *Union of India* MANU/SC/0133/1978 (Supreme Court of India, 25 January 1978), see Chapter 2.

[23] After the 'power struggle' between the government of Indira Gandhi and the judiciary in the 1970s, the judiciary has gone to great lengths to secure its independence in the post-Emergency era. In the 1970s, the government had transferred high court judges and superseded Supreme Court judges who were in line for becoming Chief Justice of India as 'punishments' for disagreeable decisions (see S.P. Sathe, *Judicial Activism in India*, 2nd edition [Delhi, Oxford: Oxford University Press, 2003], 249). The original constitutional set-up, which already included several safeguards to protect the judiciary's Independence, prescribed that Supreme Court and high court judges be appointed 'after consultation' with the Chief Justice of India (Articles 124, 217, 222 of the Constitution). In the 1970s and also 1980s, the Supreme Court had stated that 'consultation' meant that the president (as advised by his government) could also appoint judges against the Supreme Court's wishes (see *Union of India* v. *Sankal Chand Himatlal Sheth* MANU/SC/0065/1977, 41 [Supreme Court of India, 19 September 1977]; *S.P. Gupta* v. *Union of India and Ors* MANU/SC/0080/1981, 28, 29 [Supreme Court of India, 30 December 1981]). In the 1990s, the Supreme Court reversed this stance in the 'Second Judges' case' (see *Supreme Court Advocates-on-Record Association and another* v. *Union of India* MANU/SC/0073/1994 [Supreme Court of India, 6 October 1993]). The Supreme Court then, in the 'Third Judges' case', created a 'collegium system' for judicial appointments. In this, the judiciary would always have a majority, meaning that the executive cannot appoint judges against the judiciary's will, see In the Supreme Court of India, In *Re: Appointment & Transfer of Judges* v. *Civil Advisory Jurisdiction* MANU/SC/1146/1998 (Supreme

Thus, separation of powers and the independence of the higher judiciary is taken very seriously in Indian constitutional law. This is the case in a material sense, as the higher judiciary has asserted itself in decisive cases against the legislature and executive, gaining and maintaining extensive powers of judicial review. It is also true in an institutional sense, as the judiciary has created a position of almost absolute power concerning judicial appointments, transfers of judges, and also criminal inquiries against judges.[24] Such strong measures against external influences should also provide for a considerable amount of impartiality of the judges, as defined above.

Whoever accesses the higher judiciary for rights enforcement against the State through Articles 32 and 226 can therefore expect

---

Court of India, 28 October 1998). Then, in 2015, the Supreme Court ruled that a 2014 constitutional amendment and an Act creating a National Judicial Appointments Commission violated the basic structure of the Constitution (see *Supreme Court Advocates-on-Record Association and another* v. *Union of India* MANU/SC/1183/2015 [Supreme Court of India, 16 October 2015]). The Commission was to consist of the Chief Justice of India (as Chairperson), two other senior Judges of the Supreme Court, the Union Minister in charge of Law and Justice, and two 'eminent persons to be nominated by the committee consisting of the Prime Minister, the Chief Justice of India and the Leader of Opposition'. This set-up would have actually given the executive and legislature *less* power in appointing judges than it is the case in many Western countries. For instance, in USA, Supreme Court judges are nominated by the president and confirmed by the Senate (see Article 2(2) of the US Constitution). The German Basic Law in Article 94 prescribes that the judges of the Federal Constitutional Court are elected by the two houses of Parliament. Still, the Supreme Court considered even this Commission to be impermissible.

24 In the case of criminal proceedings against a judge, the Supreme Court decided that a criminal case must only be registered under Section 154 of the Code of Criminal Procedure against a judge if the Chief Justice of India was consulted (see *K. Veeraswami* v. *Union of India and Others* MANU/SC/0610/1991, 62 [Supreme Court of India, 25 July 1991]). If the case is against the Chief Justice themselves, then the president would have to consult other judges of the Supreme Court and 'shall act in accordance with the advice given to him' by them (see Note 23, 12).

to have one's case decided by judges that are not influenced by institutional pressure from the executive and legislature, or that do not see themselves in a position to review the executive's and legislature's actions. Nonetheless, of course, the issue of a possible 'anti-poor bias', as described in the last chapter, remains.

More recently, the independence of the judiciary has been questioned by several Supreme Court judges in an open letter to Chief Justice Dipak Misra.[25] However, the '2018 Supreme Court of India crisis' demonstrates that the power of a chief justice, who might act based on their own political inclinations, can be misused. It does not show that there are *institutional* weaknesses that allow a government to improperly influence the judiciary, unless one considers the powers of the chief justice as an institutional weakness.

## Standards to be Fulfilled by a Grievance Redress System

Therefore, Articles 32 and 226 still guarantee access to a judiciary that is exceptionally strong and independent. Of course, the same degree of independence and impartiality cannot be expected from an alternative system within the administration.[26] Nonetheless, the importance that the constitutional framework places on judicial independence, especially as interpreted by the judiciary itself, does call for a relatively high degree of impartiality and independence of decision-makers (acting similar to judges) in a grievance redress system that is supposed to compensate for the lack of access to the 'regular' judiciary. At the same time, the system needs to be at least somewhat as effective as the judiciary, meaning that the decision-makers need to have some sort of means of

[25] *Times of India*, 'Full Text of Letter: Four Senior Judges Say Situation in SC "not in order"', 12 January 2018, https://timesofindia.indiatimes.com/india/full-text-of-letter-four-senior-judges-say-situation-in-sc-not-in-order/articleshow/62472957.cms, accessed on 12 August 2018.

[26] Robinson notes that 'judicial officials [...] are created to be more impartial than other redress options' (see Nick Robinson, 'Closing the Implementation Gap: Grievance Redress and India's Social Welfare Programs', *Columbia Journal of Transnational Law* 53, no. 2 (2015): 341).

enforcement against the persons and institutions that are obliged to act or obliged to refrain from certain actions.

Based on such considerations, Gauri has carved out some standards that a functioning and effective grievance redress mechanism has to live up to. The author argues that grievance redress systems may provide additional benefit to other accountability enhancing systems, such as social audits, as they provide persons who have been harmed with some sort of direct remedy.[27] Systems such as social audits may provide information to enhance service delivery in the future, without rectifying what has gone wrong in the past.[28] The latter must be a task that grievance redress mechanisms can fulfil.

The author names some features of a judicial process, specifically independent review, as being of core importance.[29] He calls for 'legal attributes' concerning standards for evidence to be presented, public availability of documented petitions and reasons given for decisions, and, generally, the incorporation of 'trial-like characteristics'.[30] Grievance redress procedures outside of the judiciary will need additional safeguards to ensure quality of the adjudication process, 'even if those safeguards are not identical to the legal ideal'.[31]

[27] Varun Gauri, 'Redressing Grievances and Complaints Regarding Basic Service Delivery', http://elibrary.worldbank.org/doi/pdf/10.1596/1813-9450-5699, accessed on 19 August 2018, 3–4.

[28] Gauri names the example of social audits finding that slum dwellers have not been provided with citizen scorecards that they are actually entitled to (see Gauri, 'Redressing Grievances and Complaints Regarding Basic Service Delivery', 3–4).

[29] Gauri, 'Redressing Grievances and Complaints Regarding Basic Service Delivery'.

[30] Gauri, 'Redressing Grievances and Complaints Regarding Basic Service Delivery', 10.

[31] Gauri, 'Redressing Grievances and Complaints Regarding Basic Service Delivery', 10. Such safeguards are especially necessary 'to handle significant harms, such as sexual assault on the part of a medical provider or a teacher, or a significant loss of earnings from the denial of benefits', Gauri, 'Redressing Grievances and Complaints Regarding Basic Service Delivery', 10.

A functioning grievance redress will also support rule of law in their 'jurisdiction', for instance, by treating like cases alike.[32] This may be ensured by application of 'routinized and nearly identical practices' to all individuals. Also, there must be a certain amount of transparency ensured by giving reasons for administrative decisions.[33] Only then will grievance redress bodies be able to consider their own precedent.

While transparency may be achieved by publishing regular reports with information such as the number and nature of appeals, effectiveness may be achieved by delegating as much authority to the redress bodies as possible.[34] Gauri notes that experience has shown that some of the most effective redress procedures grant significant competences to grievance redress officials, which includes imposing penalties or sometimes even changing certain policies.[35]

As far as accessibility is concerned, redress procedures may be naturally more approachable if they are part of local government agencies. However, the system will only work efficiently if independent review is possible, meaning that the State may have to make such bodies that are more independent than such agencies more accessible.[36] Thus, the institutional set-up must find a balance between accessibility and independence.

Independent review, which may increase confidence in objectivity and neutrality of grievance redress mechanisms, may be realized by creating and using sources for funding that are 'somewhat autonomous of political powers', and by creating bodies

[32] Gauri, 'Redressing Grievances and Complaints Regarding Basic Service Delivery', 4.

[33] Gauri, 'Redressing Grievances and Complaints Regarding Basic Service Delivery', 4.

[34] That is, as may be allowed by legal, political, and economic constraints (see Gauri, 'Redressing Grievances and Complaints Regarding Basic Service Delivery', 13).

[35] Gauri, 'Redressing Grievances and Complaints Regarding Basic Service Delivery', 13.

[36] Gauri, 'Redressing Grievances and Complaints Regarding Basic Service Delivery', 8–9

that are designed in a way that they are institutionally isolated from 'politically, economically and socially powerful individuals and groups'.[37] Importantly, redress mechanisms also need to be credible in order to ensure that there will be sufficient demand. Promoting rights awareness could help in this respect as many citizens will not know of their entitlement, not to mention their right to complain if they do not receive the services they are entitled to.[38]

## Deficiencies in the Education Grievance Redress System

Based on these standards, one may now examine the design and the functioning of the grievance redress system for the right to education in India. Thus, in this part, the provisions creating the grievance redress mechanisms in the Right to Education Act and the Commission for the Protection of Child Rights Act shall be examined and measured against this yardstick. It will be shown that the current legal and institutional set-up does not offer the amount of institutional independence and effective means of enforcement that would be required to compensate for lack of access to the judiciary.

This shall be explained in three steps. First, the grievance redress mechanism provisions in the Right to Education Act and state rules, as well as orders passed under the Act that concern complaints at the 'first instance', that is, to the 'local authority', shall be examined. Then, moving on to the 'appellate' authority, the workings of the Commissions for the Protection of Child Rights and similar commissions, particularly the National Human Rights Commission, shall be assessed. Finally, it shall be explained how evidence shows that even this deficient system is not implemented properly in practice.

[37] Gauri, 'Redressing Grievances and Complaints Regarding Basic Service Delivery', 9.

[38] Gauri, 'Redressing Grievances and Complaints Regarding Basic Service Delivery', 8.

## Conceptual Deficiencies in Right to Education Act Concerning the 'First Instance'

As mentioned above, Section 32(1) of the Right to Education Act states that 'any person having any grievance relating to the right of a child under this Act may make a written complaint to the local authority having jurisdiction'. The 'local authority', according to Section 2(h) of the Act, is a body of lower level of administration in a city, town, or village that has administrative control over the schools within its jurisdiction.[39] The 'local authority' may also be the district-level administration (*zila parishad*) as well 'other authorities and bodies' in the education administration system. Therefore, according to the definition given by the Act, the functions assigned to the local authority by the Act are actually given to a multitude of bodies at the same time.

Consequently, how the administrative functions are distributed among different lower-level administrative bodies is far from clear. As shall be discussed below, this makes the practical application of the provisions difficult. Even more problematically, the Act assigns both implementation as well as grievance redress functions to the local authority.[40] This means that the Act allows a system in which a body has to decide about complaints against itself, which would mean that the system guarantees neither independence nor impartiality of the 'judges'.

[39] This authority may have different names in different states with different administrative systems.

[40] The Act assigns several implementation functions to the 'local authority'. For instance, a duty to establish a school in every neighbourhood (Sections 6, 9(b)), to 'provide free and compulsory education', ensure that children from weaker sections or disadvantages groups are not discriminated against, maintain records of children within its jurisdiction, ensure and monitor admission, attendance, and completion of elementary education, provide infrastructure, provide training facilities, ensure good quality elementary education, and so on (Section 9), ensuring the maintenance of the pupil–teacher ratio prescribed by the Act (Section 25(1)) as well as following other directions given by the state or central government (Section 35).

Aware of this problem, the Ministry of Human Resource Development of the central government in 2012 sent a (non-binding) 'Advisory on implementation of Sections 31 and 32' of the Right to Education Act to all state governments.[41] The advisory suggested that local authority in Section 9 should be a different body than the local authority in Section 32, although it does not explicitly instruct states to ensure that this should be the case.[42] The problem could have been avoided easily by not assigning both grievance redress as well as implementation functions to a local authority and/or not giving a single definition for the term 'local authority' applicable for the entire Act.

The states have come up with different solutions for assigning implementation and grievance redress duties to local authorities, and the extent to which the 'grievance redress local authorities' are independent of the 'implementing local authorities differs.[43] Some states (or union territories) have not passed rules explicitly identifying local authorities for the purpose of grievance redress under Section 32 in their jurisdiction at all.[44] Some do identify a local authority for grievance redress, but actually name the same authority as the one to whom they assign responsibilities for the

[41] Advisory F.No. 1-18/2010-EE-4 (pt. I) dated 14 February 2012, available at http://mhrd.gov.in/sites/upload_files/mhrd/files/upload_document/30.pdf, accessed on 15 August 2018.

[42] The advisory also explains that the states should 'identify' the 'local authority(ies) [...] for performing the functions envisaged in section 32 (1) and (2) of the Act' and '[n]otify the local authority at the village, block/mandal and district level having jurisdiction in respect of the responsibilities specified for local authorities under section 9, who would perform the functions envisaged in section 32 (1) and (2)'.

[43] An overview with links to the rules and notifications published by the states can be found on the Ministry of Human Resource Development website at http://mhrd.gov.in/rte_rules, accessed on 12 August 2018. It lists 'State RTE Rules' concerning the local authority as well as concerning the respective Local Grievance Redressal Mechanism.

[44] For instance, Arunachal Pradesh, Daman and Diu, Goa, Jharkand, Kerala, Lakshadweep, Manipur, Puducherry (Pondicherry), and Tamil Nadu.

other provisions of the Right to Education Act.[45] Others assign grievance redress functions to higher administrative bodies rather than the implementing local authorities.[46] Some of them have created matrixes assigning certain responsibilities to certain authorities and assigning grievance redress authorities that are higher in the administrative structure for each of these functions.[47] Yet, another group of states have created, by notification, committees (one or several ones in the same state) responsible for grievance redress,[48] sometimes in addition to grievance redress functions given to local authorities, and sometimes as the only grievance redress body or bodies. Members of the committees are usually persons from within the (education) administration.[49]

Bhattacharjee and Mysoor have studied the grievance redress provisions in Karnataka and their implementation in-depth—something that had previously not been done and has not been done since, in Karnataka or any other state.[50] They find that the

[45] For instance, Himachal Pradesh names the Block Elementary Education Officers and Deputy Directors of Elementary Education as local authorities both for implementation as well as for grievance redress.

[46] For instance, Karnataka, Odisha, and West Bengal.

[47] For instance, Assam, Gujarat, Meghalaya, and Rajasthan.

[48] For instance, Andhra Pradesh, Delhi, Haryana, Maharashtra, Nagaland, and Sikkim. Andhra Pradesh names the same local authorities as for other provisions of the Right to Education Act for grievance redress at the first level, but different authorities (a committee for grievance redress) at higher administration levels. Chandigarh assigns the District Education Officer both as a local authority concerning other Right to Education Act rules as well as a grievance redress authority, though the actual decisions are to be made by the District Education Officer, the Deputy District Education Officer, and two heads/principals of government schools.

[49] In Sikkim, however, at the block and district levels, one of the seven members of each committee is a local NGO member (see the notification at http://mhrd.gov.in/sites/upload_files/mhrd/files/upload_document/GR-sikkim.pdf, accessed on 12 August 2018).

[50] The authors themselves note that even the institutions and mechanisms of grievance redress as a whole have received only limited attention, citing Robinson, 'Closing the Implementation Gap', and Gauri, 'Redressing Grievances and Complaints Regarding Basic Service Delivery' as two scholars who have studied them. However, even those do not offer

redress procedures under the Right to Education Act in the state are 'perplexing and poorly designed and have not led to enforcement of the right', and that in order to effectively enforce the right, significant changes in the law and a redesign of the institutions involved are required.[51] The example of Karnataka is interesting because at first glance it appears to guarantee a certain degree of independence for the decision-makers, but in reality, it actually does not.

The 'perplexity' that Bhattacharjee and Mysoor speak of partly lies in the fact that in Karnataka there seems to be an 'official' as well as an additional 'unofficial' grievance redress mechanism under the Right to Education Act. The government of Karnataka has notified municipal corporations, municipal councils, zila parishads, nagar panchayats, or panchayats as 'local authorities' for implementing the Right to Education Act, especially concerning the duties under Section 9.[52] Another notification has identified the District Level Education Regulating Authority (DLERA) in each district as the 'local authority' for grievance redress.[53] That notification also states that Block Education Officers (BEOs),

---

'an in-depth examination of these procedures with respect to any particularly statutory right'. Their article(s) 'responds to the surprising lack of scholarly attention to this important area of law and policy by providing a few insights into how the design of institution responsible for grievance redress under the RTE Act impacts the common man' (see Malini Bhattacharjee and Dolashree Mysoor, '"Unredressed" Grievances under RTE: Navigating the State Labyrinth', *Governance: An International Journal of Policy, Administration, and Institutions* 29, no. 1 [2016]: 33).

51 Bhattacharjee and Mysoor, '"Unredressed" Grievances under RTE', 31.

52 See government Notification dated 16 September 2013, available at http://mhrd.gov.in/sites/upload_files/mhrd/files/upload_document/LA-karnataka.pdf, accessed on 15 August 2018. Local authorities are also 'such other authority or body having administrative control over the school or empowered or under any law [...] to function as a local authority'. This echoes the wording of Section 2(h) of the Right to Education Act.

53 See government Notification dated 12 July 2012, available at http://mhrd.gov.in/sites/upload_files/mhrd/files/upload_document/Karnataka.pdf, accessed on 15 August 2018.

the Deputy Director of Public Instruction (DDPI) of the educational district, and the Chief Executive Officer (CEO) of the Zila Panchayat (CEO-ZP) are to execute the orders of the DLERA in their district. While these are separate administrative bodies at different hierarchical levels, the DDPI and CEO-ZP are also members of the DLERA. However, it seems that the state government did not consider this conflict of interest when drafting the Notification.[54] Generally, one may conclude that the system in Karnataka does not appear to provide independence or guarantee impartiality concerning the decision-makers.

One other aspect increases the 'perplexity' in the Karnataka set-up even further. The state rules give the BEO the power to receive complaints and, upon receipt, issue notices to schools and seek explanations. If they are not satisfied with the response, they shall bring the violation to the notice of the DDPI and the CEO-ZP (Clause 23(2)).[55] Consequently, in addition to the formal grievance redress mechanism created by Section 32 of the Right to Education Act, there is an additional 'grievance redress mechanism' that is just not explicitly called by that name. These authorities are thus 'implicitly' responsible for grievance redress without ever having been notified as 'grievance redress authorities'.[56] As shall be described below, this creation of two parallel systems leads to additional problems in practice.

But even within the 'official' grievance redress mechanism, there are additional perplexities that make the system in Karnataka an even less adequate alternative to an independent and impartial judiciary. While the government rules mentioned above seem to make a clear distinction between 'implementing local authorities' and 'grievance redress local authorities', this distinction is undone by the annexures to these orders. The annexures of 16 September 2013 assign *both* grievance redress and certain implementation

54 Bhattacharjee and Mysoor, '"Unredressed" Grievances under RTE', 37.

55 See government Notification dated 28 April 2012, available at http://mhrd.gov.in/sites/upload_files/mhrd/files/upload_document/Karnataka_RTE_1.pdf, accessed on 15 August 2018.

56 Bhattacharjee and Mysoor, '"Unredressed" Grievances under RTE', 37.

functions to the exact same authorities.[57] The charts in the annexures even list the duties under Section 9 of the Act read with the state rules separately, only to then assign all of them *and* the responsibility for redressing grievances concerning all of them to all of the authorities at the same time. In other words, the system created by the Act and the state government orders fails to provide for any institutional independence of the decision-makers.[58] As shall be described below, these perplexities also translate into further problems in implementation.

One may conclude that, while in some states such as Karnataka, independence and impartiality of the officials deciding at 'first instance' is not at all guaranteed (as those officials are, at least in some constellations, the ones against whom the complaints are raised), there is a certain extent of institutional and personal distance in those states that do identify separate grievance redress bodies. Partiality of the decision-makers seen as a whole may also be reduced when setting up committees rather than having one single person as the decision-maker in a given case. Still, the majority of members in the committees are usually also involved in the implementation as bureaucrats.

Furthermore, even if upper-level education administrative bodies or committees comprised of representatives of such bodies control lower ones, conflicts of interest may arise. In many cases, there might be a sufficient amount of distance between the officials that have caused a grievance and the one 'judging'. For instance, if a teacher has physically abused a child and the complaint is

[57] That is, the Zila Panchayat Standing Committee of Education & Health at the district level, the Taluk Panchayat Social Justice Committee at the taluk level, and the Public Health, Education, and Social Justice Committee of Urban Local Body in municipal corporations, Bhattacharjee and Mysoor, '"Unredressed" Grievances under RTE', 37. See the annexures with charts at http://mhrd.gov.in/sites/upload_files/mhrd/files/upload_document/LA-karnataka.pdf, accessed on 15 August 2018.

[58] Bhattacharjee and Mysoor note that 'a situation where the authority is mandated to decide upon complaints brought against itself [...] goes against the very principle of a fair and independent redress procedure and raises serious conflicts of interest' (see Bhattacharjee and Mysoor, '"Unredressed" Grievances under RTE', 37).

submitted to the block or district administration body, it is not a case of one official judging a colleague's actions. Other cases, however, may be related to structural deficiencies in the education system that involve decisions like allocation of funds. Such cases may, for instance, concern the questions whether an additional teacher needs to be employed to fulfil the student–teacher ratio prescribed by the Act or whether the school's premise's infrastructure has to be improved.[59]

Therefore, as long as officials involved in the implementation of the education system are also the ones making decisions about complaints against its deficiencies, independence and impartiality cannot be guaranteed. However, this shortcoming could be compensated for to some extent by the appellate authority, that is, the State Commissions for Protection of Child Rights.

## Human Rights and Child Rights Commissions: An Independent Appellate Authority?

The obligation to create the State (and National) Commissions for Protection of Child Rights arises from The Commissions for Protection of Child Rights Act, 2005 (hereafter Child Rights Commissions Act), which came into force in 2006. Its preamble refers to UN declarations and conventions, particularly the Convention on the Rights of the Child of 1990, to which India acceded in December 1992.

As mentioned above, the state commissions are given both appellate and original jurisdictions to decide grievances and complaints submitted to them under the Right to Education Act as

[59] For instance, Bhattacharjee, Mysoor, and Sivaramakrishnan note that in Karnataka, the head of one grievance redress authority—the District Level Education Regulatory Authority—is the deputy district commissioner, 'an official who performs several key administrative, revenue and magisterial functions'. Them already being entrusted with such important functions may also mean that they may not have the additional capacities required to perform grievance redress functions effectively (see Malini Bhattacharjee, Dolashree Mysoor, and Arun Sivaramakrishnan, 'RTE Grievance Redress in Karnataka', *Economic & Political Weekly* XLIX, no. 23 [2014]: 39).

part of the grievance redress regime under Section 32 and as part of their monitoring duties under Section 31. The state commissions and the National Commission are also given original grievance redress competences under the Child Rights Commission Act itself. Therefore, the state commissions can be approached through appeals as well as directly; the National Commission may also be approached directly, but only if the case is not already pending in a state commission (see Section 13(2) of the Child Rights Commissions Act).

The personal set-up of the Commissions is defined by Sections 3 and 17 of the Child Rights Commissions Act. Section 3(2) states that the National Commission shall have a chairperson and six members. The chairperson shall be a 'person of eminence' who 'has done outstanding work for promoting the welfare of children'. The members, of whom at least two shall be women, shall be chosen 'from amongst persons of eminence, ability, integrity, standing', and experience in fields such as education, child health, and juvenile justice. While the members shall be appointed by the central government on its own discretion (Sections 3(2)(b), 4), the chairperson shall be appointed by central government 'on the recommendation of a three member Selection Committee constituted by the Central Government under the Chairmanship of the Minister in-charge of the Ministry of Human Resource Development' (Section 4). This is the ministry that is in charge of the implementation of the Right to Education Act and education as a whole at the national level.[60]

The standards for qualification of the chairperson and members (also six) in the states prescribed by Section 17 are the same as for the National Commission. Meanwhile, Section 18 states that the chairperson shall be 'appointed on the recommendation of a three [m]ember Selection Committee constituted by the State Government under the Chairmanship of the Minister in-charge of the Department dealing with children. The department dealing with children' in the states is usually the Department of Women and Child Development or the Social Justice Department, while

60 See http://mhrd.gov.in/school-education, accessed on 15 August 2018.

a separate department is responsible for education, usually called the Department of Education. Therefore, at least the decision for the appointment of the state commissions' chairpersons are somewhat independent from the education administration, especially considering that the other two members of the selection committee are usually also not part of the education administration.[61] Therefore, the grievance redress system at this level is sufficiently independent of the education bureaucracy.[62]

After their appointment, the chairperson and the members shall hold office for a term of three years, with the maximum tenure being two terms (Sections 5, 19). Chairpersons and members shall be given a salary which, like the terms and conditions of service, must not be lowered after their appointment (Sections 6, 20). However, the central and state governments do have the power to remove the chairperson 'on the ground of proved misbehaviour or incapacity', and also to remove members for similar reasons.[63]

Still, generally, these provisions guarantee independence of the commissions from political influence at least to a certain degree. They may also create a system in which the decision-makers are somewhat impartial, considering that they are not involved in

[61] See the State Commission for the Protection of Child Right (SCPCR) notifications and rules available at http://mhrd.gov.in/constitution_scpcr, accessed on 15 August 2018.

[62] Bhattacharjee, Mysoor, and Sivaramakrishnan, 'RTE Grievance Redress in Karnataka', 39.

[63] For instance, if the member 'engages during his term of office in any paid employment outside the duties of his office', 'refuses to act or becomes incapable of acting', 'has so abused his office as to render his continuance in office detrimental to the public interest', and so on (Sections 7(1, 2), 24). As far as the powers of the government over the commissions is concerned, one may also note that the central and state governments appoint a member-secretary (in the case of the National Commission) or a secretary (in the case of the state commissions) for each commission 'responsible for the proper administration of the affairs of the [...] Commission and its day-to-day management' (Sections 11(1, 2), 21(1, 2)). Furthermore, the governments 'shall make available to the [...] Commission such other officers and employees as may be necessary for the efficient performance of its functions' (Sections 11(1), 21(1)).

the implementation process and should be relatively free from conflicts of interests, especially in comparison to the lower local authority level of grievance redress.

However, there is one other decisive shortcoming in the commissions' institutional set-up. While the commissions, to a degree, act like courts, having 'all the powers of a civil court trying a suit under the Code of Civil Procedure' (Section 14(1), 24), these powers only concern the fact-finding case of their 'trials' (for instance, summoning persons and summoning them under oath and discovery and production of documents). However, the 'judgments' or 'decisions' made by the commissions are mere recommendations (Sections 13(1), 24). While the commissions may 'recommend measures' for the 'effective implementation' of child rights (Section 13(1)(a)), they cannot force the administration to follow these recommendations, or give any sort of binding orders, like a court could.

Therefore, if one considers the entire set-up of the grievance redress mechanism, one may conclude that it only provides independent decision-making at a level where decision-makers have no power to effectively enforce their decisions. The committees were therefore described as 'toothless tigers' that are 'the weakest link in the entire grievance redress chain'.[64] This is, of course, especially problematic considering that they are the only link in the chain that offers some degree of independence and impartiality.

However, in addition to their own (very limited) decision-making powers, the commissions are empowered to approach the Supreme Court or high courts (Sections 15(ii), 24), which may then judge independently and enforce their judgments. This could potentially offer a channel through which right-bearers could eventually access the judiciary. However, as shall be shown below, this does not happen in practice.

## Lack of Implementation

Several of the conceptual shortcomings described above translate into problems in the workings of the grievance redress system in

[64] Bhattacharjee and Mysoor, '"Unredressed" Grievances under RTE', 44.

practice. Furthermore, the system becomes even more flawed by additional shortcomings that do not directly result from the flaws in the institutional set-up.

As far as the state commissions are concerned, several states have not even properly created these bodies. An overview of the state commissions at the website of the National Commission for Protection of Child Rights shows that the key positions of several commissions are currently vacant (even though this situation has improved, particularly in the last couple of years).[65] States in which (almost) all membership positions are vacant include India's largest state of Uttar Pradesh.[66] A curious (but, apparently, isolated case) is the one of the union territory of Dadra and Nagar Haveli in which the members of the commission are not selected by a committee. Instead, according to a notification by the administrator, several members of the bureaucracy automatically become chairperson and members of the commission in spite of the clear rules provided for by the Child Rights Commission Act,[67] raising concerns regarding its independence and impartiality. The notification is especially surprising considering the fact that the territory is administered by the central government.

Generally, the states were late in creating the commissions in the first place. Many of them were only created or started functioning several years after the Right to Education Act came into force, even though at that time, the obligation to create the commissions had already existed for four years since the Child Rights Commissions Act had gone into force. As late as in 2014, several states (including India's largest state of Uttar Pradesh) had not yet

[65] http://ncpcr.gov.in/statecom.php; http://ncpcr.gov.in/index1.php?lang=1&level=0&lid=1309&linkid=100, accessed on 12 August 2018.

[66] See http://ncpcr.gov.in/index1.php?lang=1&level=2&&sublinkid=1168&lid=1341, accessed on 12 August 2018. The Uttar Pradesh Commission does not have a website.

[67] See Notification dated 12 May 2011, No DNH/Police/COP/2010/240, available at http://mhrd.gov.in/sites/upload_files/mhrd/files/upload_document/Dadra%20&%20Nagar%20Haveli-SCPCR.pdf; also see http://ncpcr.gov.in/index1.php?lang=1&level=1&&sublinkid=1026&lid=1316, accessed on 12 August 2018.

set up a working commission.[68] Therefore, the amount of time in which it was possible to study the working of the entire grievance redress was quite limited in many jurisdictions.

The empirical work done by Bhattacharjee and Mysoor in Karnataka shows how the system may work, what problems may arise, and how the shortcomings in the legal set-up translate into practice.

For instance, they find that perplexity of the rules that makes a multitude of administrative bodies responsible for grievance redress makes citizens apprehensive about approaching the system in the first place. This is worsened by the fact that there are no guidelines advising citizens whom to approach for what kind of grievances.[69] Citizens who do attempt to use the grievance redress system often approach several authorities at the same time or are sent from one authority to the other to even get a case registered.[70]

[68] Ananya Sengupta, 'Child Rights Panels Exist but on Paper', *The Telegraph*, 6 January 2014, http://www.telegraphindia.com/1140106/jsp/nation/story_17756333.jsp#.V55QnGVwPws, accessed on 19 August 2018. The Supreme Court had ordered the states to create the commissions in 2013 (see *Re. Exploitation of Children in Orphanages in the State of Tamil Nadu* v. *Union of India* MANU/SC/1304/2013 [Supreme Court of India, 16 December 2013]). Through the Model Rules for the Right to Education Act, the central government also recommended that such states that had not constituted a state commission at the time constitute an interim authority known as the Right to Education Protection Authority (REPA) (Rule 24(2)), though those governments also 'may take immediate steps to set up the Commission' (Rule 24(1)). A REPA shall consist of a chairperson 'who is a person of high academic repute or has been a High Court Judge or has done outstanding work for promoting the rights of children' and two members 'from the following areas, from amongst persons of eminence, ability, integrity, standing and experience in' education, child health care, juvenile justice, and so on, that is, the same fields as the members of the state commissions (Rule 24(3)). In several states, particularly in West Bengal, the REPA and state commission had existed parallel to each other, creating confusion as far as the jurisdiction for grievance redress are concerned; however, this does not seem to be the case anymore.

[69] Bhattacharjee and Mysoor, '"Unredressed" Grievances under RTE', 37.

[70] Bhattacharjee and Mysoor, '"Unredressed" Grievances under RTE', 44.

This also complicates the situation insofar as there are also no rules concerning how 'judgments' by the 'official and unofficial' grievance redress mechanisms relate to each other, particularly whether a decision by the DLERA shall prevail over a decision by the Social Justice Committee (SJC) or vice versa.[71]

Also, the large number of 'entry points' for complaints make it difficult to study the workings of the system, as they make it practically impossible to check pendency of complaints.[72] The fact that local authorities at several levels may have received all kinds of grievances, ranging from relatively minor issues such as availability of school uniforms to very serious ones such as physical abuse, not only leads to confusion, but also to inordinate delays.[73]

According to the authors, 'anecdotal evidence' shows that the BEO is the most sought-after authority to look into complaints.[74] Interestingly, as mentioned above, BEOs are not a formal grievance redress authority, but rather an informal authority that may receive complaints according to Rule 23(1) of the Karnataka State Rules. As mentioned above, according to the rules, the BEO must send a notice to the concerned school, its management, and/or the School Development and Monitoring Committee and must then forward the case to the DDPI and the CEO of the zila panchayat if the reply is not satisfactory or the school fails to respond to the notice. The zila panchayat, on the other hand, is actually a body that is also explicitly entrusted with grievance redress under Section 32 of the Right to Education Act. Bhattacharjee, Mysoor, and Sivaramakrishnan note that the cases should actually be forwarded to the DLERA or SJC (also formal grievance redress authorities), but that this is 'yet to happen'.[75]

[71] Bhattacharjee, Mysoor, and Sivaramakrishnan, 'RTE Grievance Redress in Karnataka', 38.

[72] Bhattacharjee, Mysoor, and Sivaramakrishnan, 'RTE Grievance Redress in Karnataka', 39.

[73] Bhattacharjee, Mysoor, and Sivaramakrishnan, 'RTE Grievance Redress in Karnataka', 39.

[74] Bhattacharjee, Mysoor, and Sivaramakrishnan, 'RTE Grievance Redress in Karnataka', 38.

[75] Bhattacharjee, Mysoor, and Sivaramakrishnan, 'RTE Grievance Redress in Karnataka', 38.

In any case, it seems that the complaints do not proceed through the grievance redress system as they should. The Karnataka SCPCR, at the time of the authors' research in September 2013, had not received a single formal appeal against the order of any local authority.[76] Instead, the Karnataka State Commission for Protection of Child Rights (KSCPCR) is usually approached directly, without aggrieved persons first filing cases at the local authority level of the formal grievance redress system. It seems that the KSCPCR appears to the citizens as a viable option for grievance redress, even though it has no powers to enforce its decisions.[77] The authors find that the KSCPCR seems to be 'by far the most approachable institution in the entire grievance redress structure'. They also find it to be 'the only institution that seems to be responding to the complaints of citizens'.[78]

Considering the fact that the local authorities do have the power to enforce their decision against lower-level administrative bodies and the schools, and also considering the fact that they are geographically more accessible as they are found in every block and every district, it is somewhat surprising that citizens still choose not to approach these authorities at all, but rather directly approach the KSCPCR. It therefore appears that the lower-level grievance redress system is so ineffective, or perceived to be so ineffective, or perhaps so confusing to citizens that they choose to instead approach the KSCPCR directly.[79] Problematically, though, as the KSCPCR only has an office in Bengaluru, a 'dominant percentage of cases' submitted to it in the two-year period that Bhattacharjee, Mysoor, and Sivaramakrishnan have studied are from Bengaluru city itself, 'indicating a clear urban bias'.[80]

[76] Bhattacharjee, Mysoor, and Sivaramakrishnan, 'RTE Grievance Redress in Karnataka', 39; Bhattacharjee and Mysoor, '"Unredressed" Grievances under RTE', 39.

[77] The authors note that the Commission is 'hardly in a position to effectively resolve any grievances' (see Bhattacharjee and Mysoor, '"Unredressed" Grievances under RTE', 44).

[78] Bhattacharjee and Mysoor, '"Unredressed" Grievances under RTE', 44.

[79] Bhattacharjee and Mysoor, '"Unredressed" Grievances under RTE', 44.

[80] Bhattacharjee, Mysoor, and Sivaramakrishnan, 'RTE Grievance Redress in Karnataka', 39; Bhattacharjee and Mysoor, '"Unredressed" Grievances under RTE', 39.

The KSCPCR, because of its lack of legal authority, has chosen to use 'popular mechanisms'. This includes public hearings, which are intended to heighten awareness in addition to redressing grievances.[81] In particular, the authors have studied a 'right to Education public hearing' in September 2013 in Bengaluru, where 32 cases were heard and disposed of,[82] conducting interviews with members and employees of the state commission as well as complainants in 15 of the 32 cases that were sampled to respect a wide array of violations.[83] Disappointingly, the authors conclude that 'none of the complaints that were taken up at the public hearing [...] were effectively resolved',[84] and that 'the exercise resulted merely in public reprimand of schools without any penalties and misapplication of the law in a few instances'.[85] The interviews with the parents 'revealed a narrative of frustration and despair about the manner in which the public hearing was conducted'.[86] Furthermore, many parents did not feel that the remedy that was provided for their cases was adequate for their complaints.[87]

The parents interviewed reported that they had approached multiple institutions without any remedies before finally turning to the KSCPCR.[88] Those 'multiple institutions' were apparently

[81] Describing this development, the authors also critically speak of 'populist processes [...] which [have] no legal sanction whatsoever' (see Bhattacharjee, Mysoor, and Sivaramakrishnan, 'RTE Grievance Redress in Karnataka', 39, 40).

[82] Bhattacharjee, Mysoor, and Sivaramakrishnan, 'RTE Grievance Redress in Karnataka', 39.

[83] Bhattacharjee and Mysoor, '"Unredressed" Grievances under RTE', 32 et seq.

[84] Bhattacharjee and Mysoor, '"Unredressed" Grievances under RTE', 40.

[85] Bhattacharjee, Mysoor, and Sivaramakrishnan, 'RTE Grievance Redress in Karnataka', 39; Bhattacharjee and Mysoor, '"Unredressed" Grievances under RTE', 39.

[86] Bhattacharjee and Mysoor, '"Unredressed" Grievances under RTE', 40.

[87] Bhattacharjee and Mysoor, '"Unredressed" Grievances under RTE', 40.

[88] Bhattacharjee and Mysoor, '"Unredressed" Grievances under RTE', 39.

not part of the formal grievance redress system. Many of the parents interviewed were unaware of the regular grievance redress bodies (the DLERA and SJC) and instead approached the BEO (as the informal grievance redress authority) and sometimes even the Karnataka chief minister.[89] Ultimately, they were referred to the KSCPCR by the other bodies and authorities,[90] in spite of the Commission's lack of legal authority. Consequently, the authors find that in the cases that they have studied, the KSCPCR failed to provide adequate remedies.[91]

[89] Bhattacharjee and Mysoor, '"Unredressed" Grievances under RTE', 39.

[90] Bhattacharjee and Mysoor, '"Unredressed" Grievances under RTE', 39.

[91] The authors summarize four of the cases that they have studied in more detail. For instance, in one case, a child was victim of severe corporal punishment in a private school. The parents complained to the school, resulting in the expulsion of the child. The child's mother filed a complaint with the KSCPCR in July 2013, with the Commission scheduling the case for public hearing in September 2013. The Commission summoned the school's authorities, the BEO, and the child's family and recommended that the school pay compensation of 20,000 Rupees and that the child be admitted to another school. The BEO was 'advised to ensure that the family is compensated'. The parents apparently first tried to get their child readmitted in the same school, but were refused. Later, that same school did agree to admit the child (also stating that it would do so before the BEO), but then created further barriers, possibly motivated by the fact that the child had previously complained against it. For instance, the school stated that it would only readmit the child for a readmission fee. Then, the parents considered admitting the child in a different school, but were not able to do so, as the previous school refused to issue a transfer certificate to them. This certificate is a requirement to move to another school. The BEO simply informed the parents that they must obtain a transfer certificate or wait for the 'upcoming round of admission', that is, the next school year. Consequently, the child ended up being (for a considerable amount of time) out of school, creating the additional problem of the mother having to quit her job to take care of the child during the day. The case not only demonstrates the problems resulting from the fact that the KSCPCR has no means to enforce its 'judgments', but also that it does not adequately use the powers that it does have. In cases of

physical assault, the Commission generally does not recommend criminal proceedings against teachers, even though it is empowered to do so (see Section 15(i) of the Child Rights Commission Act). The authors note that 'instead, the solutions provided were extremely broad and generic and did not sufficiently enforce the right of a child not to be physically harassed'. In another case, a child was expelled from a private school because of suffering from a non-contagious genetic condition causing dry skin. Other parents had started 'pulling out' their children, thinking that the disease was communicable. The father had approached several administrative institutions to no avail, and eventually even contacted Karnataka's chief minister. The issue was still not resolved after approaching the KSCPCR (one of its members had wrongfully concluded that the parents had wilfully withdrawn the child). This led to the father approaching the chief minister again, who instructed the BEO to have the child readmitted, which was then prevented by the school's parents' community that had been mobilized by the school. The case was then included in the September 2013 public hearing, where the KSCPCR recommended that the school readmit the child. Even then, the school initially refused to do so, stating that it had not yet received the recommendation from the Commission (which was, of course, not binding anyway). The father then approached the chief minister a third time, following which the school did re-admit the child, but only conditionally. The school got the parents to agree to not seek admission for their child again in the next year. The authors note how this case 'demonstrates the prevalence of practice of schools forcing parents to enter into such illegal agreements that lead to denial of admission'. In the 15 public hearing cases the authors have studied, there were two or three such schools 'indulging in such extra-legal practices' as a reaction to parents successfully approaching the grievance redress system. They see this as an indicator that the schools, being aware of the limitations of the system (especially, the Commission's lack of power), resort to 'arm-twisting tactics'. The current system is, the authors conclude, 'not capable of dealing with the subtle power relations that exist between schools and parents'. On the other hand, resolutions of cases outside the grievance redress system, which are not uncommon, are usually also not beneficial to the child. One reason for parents choosing 'settlements' outside of the system may be that schools and teachers subtly threaten parents and children with repercussions if they file a formal complaint. In one of the public hearing cases they studied, such threats led to the parent withdrawing a complaint altogether. A monitoring and grievance redress body that can pass binding orders and ensure that they be enforced by effective follow-ups might be able to prevent such occurrences. See Bhattacharjee and Mysoor, '"Unredressed" Grievances under RTE', 40 et seq.

As there are no studies similar to the one undertaken by Bhattacharjee and Mysoor for other states' grievance redress systems concerning the right to education, it is difficult to assess to what extent their findings for Karnataka are representative. However, of course, some of the on-the-ground problems seem to be a direct reflection of systemic deficiencies that are universal, particularly concerning the lack of legal authority of the state commissions.

It appears that in Delhi, the State Commission, in addition to being approached directly, has received appeals against orders of local authorities, suggesting that the relationship between the Commission and the authorities as redress bodies of first and second instance is working there at least to some extent.[92] However, this, of course, does not change the fact that the appellate body does not have powers of enforcement.

Still, even within their limited powers, the commissions could perform more effectively. Currently, their work is hampered by factors such as lack of personnel, apparently sometimes also lack of commitment, and inadequate funding. It appears that the personnel are often not aware of the powers that the commissions do have, and, in particular, also not aware about how to effectively handle complaints. Reportedly, they frequently do not follow up on cases once they have passed recommendations as they have not created a system to monitor individual cases until they are actually resolved. The cases are often considered 'closed' once a reply from a school expressing the will to act on the matter has

[92] Former Delhi Commission for the Protection of Child Rights (DCPCR) member Mamta Sahai reported that the Commission received both original as well as appellate submissions in an interview with the author (which took place in March 2015 when she was with the DCPCR). She also noted that overall, less grievances have been coming to the Commission ever since the local authorities for grievance redress have been notified in Delhi. Also see Urmi Ramchandani, 'Evaluation of Monitoring Mechanisms of DCPCR to Ensure the Implementation of RTE Act in Delhi', Working paper no. 337, Centre for Civil Society, http://ccs.in/internship_papers/2015/337_evaluation-of-monitoring-mechanisms-of-dcpcr_urmi-ramchandani.pdf, accessed on 19 August 2018, 14. However, the DCPCR's official reports do not differentiate between appellate and direct submissions.

been received.[93] Lack of funding and staff is said to be one cause of this deficiency.[94] Generally, it appears that the commissions are not adequately equipped to perform their two core duties, that is, monitoring and grievance redress.[95]

Even though the personnel should be somewhat independent, the government is said to treat the commissions (also the National Commission) as 'subordinate departments', which has the effect that the personnel often see themselves as part of 'the government'.[96] The fact that many state governments leave the commissions' key positions vacant for months at a time might be an expression of lack of respect for their work as an independent body.[97]

Bhatty, former national coordinator for the right to education of the National Commission for the Protection of Child Right

[93] Archana Mehendale of Tata Institute of Social Sciences and Swagata Raha, an Independent Human Rights Consultant and Consultant at Centre for Child and the Law, National Law School of India University, in an interview with the author (March 2015).

[94] Mehendale and Raha in an interview with the author (see note 93). Kiran Bhatty of Centre for Policy Research and former national coordinator for the Right to Education of the NCPCR, in an interview with the author (March 2015), reports that on average, only 50 Rupees are given to the Commissions per school per year. Oxfam India notes that 'most SCPCRs are staffed by part time people' who, in the example of Maharasthra, receive only 5000 (chairperson) and 3000 (members) Rupees 'honorariums' per month (see Oxfam India, 'Oxfam India Newsletter. May 2014', https://www.oxfamindia.org/sites/default/files/Oxfam%20India%20Newsletter%20May%202014.pdf, accessed on 19 August 2018, 2).

[95] Robinson notes that rights commissions are empowered to investigate complaints, 'but they spend significant time examining large-scale failures in governance or systemic rights abuses', making the fact that their resources are very limited is even more problematic, especially considering that '[i]nvestigations that are aimed at addressing individualized instances of maladministration or illegality [...] tend to be more legalistic and expensive' than such 'large-scale failures', even though they may ensure that a remedy is given to a particular aggrieved person (see Robinson, 'Closing the Implementation Gap', 358).

[96] Mehendale and Raha in an interview with the author (see note 93).

[97] Mehendale and Raha believe that the governments simply do not want these bodies to be strong—in an interview with the author (see note 93).

(NCPCR), reports that a lack of clear rules made it difficult to process complaints in the National Commission. Consequently, once a complaint was received, it was difficult to assess whom to address a recommendation to.[98] As far as the option of referring a case to the higher judiciary is concerned, the lack of funding meant that even the National Commission did not have the capacity for litigation.[99] Generally, it is reported that the commissions hardly ever initiate litigation,[100] with the lack of funding and personnel being a possible reason for this. As the pendency of, for instance, a case on corporal punishment in the Supreme Court would stay litigation in similar cases (potentially for several years), litigating might also have a detrimental effect.[101] Therefore, Bhatty believes that litigating would be a more sensible option if a case concerned larger, more general questions concerning the interpretation of the Right to Education Act itself, and not for routine complaints or grievances,[102] an idea that will be entertained in more detail in the next chapter.

Of course, the views quoted on the general functioning of the commissions are subjective. It becomes clear that more empirical work as undertaken by Bhattacharjee, Mysoor, and Sivaramakrishnan (who also only worked with a small sample) is required to really assess how the system is working in practice. However, even with the limited amount of data, one may conclude that it does not appear that the deficiencies in the legal set-up are being compensated for. This would only have been the case if the system was working better than expected.

## Other Examples of (In)effective Grievance Redress Regimes in India

Education is, of course, only one of the many services to be provided by the government. Also, the education system is not

[98] Bhatty in an interview with the author (see note 94).
[99] Bhatty in an interview with the author (see note 94).
[100] See Robinson, 'Closing the Implementation Gap', 355.
[101] Bhatty in an interview with the author (see note 94).
[102] Bhatty in an interview with the author (see note 94).

the only system that includes a grievance redress mechanism. Therefore, the question arises whether grievance redress works better in different fields, or whether the shortcomings described above are universal.

At least some conceptual shortcomings are not exclusive to the right to education grievance redress regime. For instance, as already mentioned in the last chapter, the Human Rights Commission (which clearly acted as a role model for the Child Rights Commissions, as the acts establishing them are in many parts almost identical) is only able to pass recommendations rather than binding decisions. Therefore, lack of legal authority is indeed universal at the commissions level.

Generally, the question arises which prerequisites a grievance redress regime must fulfil in order to work effectively. Also, one may ask which design features it needs to have to be accessible in order to allow citizens to effectively claim benefits from the State. As State officials are obliged to provide services to those who are entitled to them, a grievance redress system will have to ensure that they be held accountable if they do not fulfil their obligation, and/or that a higher instance can ensure the provision if they do not fulfil their duties. A functioning grievance redress system would be an important factor in increasing accountability in India.[103] Generally, accountability of governance institutions in India is weak in various fields, including the judiciary.[104]

In administrative law literature, several kinds of accountability have been defined. One may differentiate between administrative, political, and legal accountability. Administrative or 'bureaucratic' accountability means that superiors control subordinates through hierarchical control mechanisms. Legal accountability is achieved through authoritatively applying law to facts, as courts

[103] Bhattacharjee and Mysoor, '"Unredressed" Grievances under RTE', 32.

[104] See, for instance, Yamini Aiyar and Bala Posani, 'State of Accountability: Evolution, Practice and Emerging Questions in Public Accountability in India', Accountability Initiative, http://accountabilityindia.in/sites/default/files/working-paper/34_1244199435.pdf, accessed on 19 August 2018, 15.

do. Political accountability, on the other hand, means that grievances are submitted to political leaders, who may then use their powers to redress these grievances.[105]

A grievance redress regime within the administration is somewhat of an 'in-between' of a system guaranteeing administrative accountability and one guaranteeing legal accountability. In the case of grievance redress within the education administration, teachers, schools, or lower-level officials would be held accountable by higher-level officials, which is a feature of administrative accountability. Legal accountability would usually require that they be held accountable by the judiciary. However, as described above, the legal provisions creating the grievance redress system 'emulate', to a certain extent, a judicial system, at least at the appellate level (that is, the Child Rights Commissions). Therefore, in the grievance redress system, the members of the commissions are supposed to act as 'judges' (or rather, a quasi-judiciary) that are at least somewhat independent and impartial, applying the law to a given case that was brought to them as a specific complaint, rather than generally monitoring the performance of the lower-level bodies (which, of course, is a function that they also fulfil in addition to their grievance redress competences).

While Bhattacharjee, Mysoor, and Sivaramakrishnan have studied the performance of India's grievance redress regime concerning the right to education in particular in one state, Robinson has, more generally, studied how grievance redress regimes work in India for

[105] Bhattacharjee and Mysoor, '"Unredressed" Grievances under RTE', 32, citing Mashaw. Mashaw writes that 'in a *legal* public accountability regime, *public officials* are responsible to *individuals and firms*, about their respect or lack of respect for legal requirements or legal rights *through* processes of administrative and judicial review, *judged* in accordance with law, *resulting in* either validation or nullification of official acts'. In a public administrative regime, 'lower-ranking officials are responsible to superiors for their compliance with official instructions' (see Jerry L. Mashaw, 'Accountability and Institutional Design: Some Thoughts on the Grammar of Governance', Public Law Working Paper No. 116, Yale Law School, Yale University, Connecticut, USA, http://papers.ssrn.com/sol3/papers.cfm?abstract_id=924879, accessed on 19 August 2018, 120).

different kinds of services to be provided by the State.[106] Stressing the importance of a responsive grievance redress systems in India, he believes, that they have become a key tool for policymakers for addressing implementation failures.[107] Noting that, in spite of this importance, there has been 'surprisingly little theorization, or even description, of grievance redress mechanisms', he examines the grievance redress mechanisms for different social welfare programs in the states of Madhya Pradesh and Bihar, which he visited for on-the-ground studies, and categorizes his observations by different kinds of 'grievance redress regimes' with similar categories as the 'accountability regimes' mentioned above.[108]

The author develops a 'grievance redress matrix' in which he compares different kinds of grievance redress systems categorized as 'political redress', 'legal redress', and 'administrative redress' and measures them according to 'access', 'impartiality towards complainant', 'impartiality towards local administration', 'power to remedy', and 'cost to government to create'.[109] The parameters are often inter-related. For instance, in order for a system to be *impartial*, the grievance redress actor would have to be independent of both the political and administrative process. This means that the state will have to create the post of a judge or some other independent arbitrator, which generates higher *costs* for personnel than a system in which citizens may merely complain to politicians or existing administrators does.[110] Such trade-offs may indicate that the state should employ a mixture of different regimes in order to maximize efficacy.[111]

The goal of the categorization is to help policymakers identify strengths and weaknesses of specific grievance redress

[106] Robinson, 'Closing the Implementation Gap'; Nick Robinson, 'Right to Public Service Acts in India: The Experience from Bihar and Madhya Pradesh', Accountability Initiative, http://accountabilityindia.in/sites/default/files/policy-brief/right_to_public_services_act_nick_robinson.pdf, accessed on 19 August 2018.

[107] Robinson, 'Closing the Implementation Gap', 326.

[108] Robinson, 'Closing the Implementation Gap', 321, 326, 328–9.

[109] Robinson, 'Closing the Implementation Gap', 329.

[110] Robinson, 'Closing the Implementation Gap', 330.

[111] Robinson, 'Closing the Implementation Gap', 330.

mechanisms, and also to allow them to design different systems in a way that they work in a parallel manner that allows them to support each other rather than one system undermining the other.[112]

## Political Redress Mechanisms

'Political redress' means that complaints are raised directly with a (local) politician (commonly to a panchayat leader, a ward member, a member of the respective Legislative Assembly, or even a Member of Parliament or the chief minister), as observed by Bhattacharjee, Mysoor, and Sivaramakrishnan in Karnataka as well.[113] In fact, in Bihar, the chief minister receives a larger number of complaints than all the district collectors in the state combined, indicating that citizens there prefer approaching politicians rather than using administrative grievance redress mechanisms.[114] While politicians do not have direct authority over members of the administration, they do have subtle powers over the bureaucracy, even when their own political parties are not in power.[115] For instance, local politicians, especially members of the opposition, may organize public protests,[116] as described concerning the case of Singur in the last chapter.

These avenues are generally informal, but may be formalized as well. For instance, legislation like the Panchayat Raj Acts gives relatively wide powers to the *Gram Sabha*, which is 'essentially a town hall meeting of a village'.[117] Still, such bodies' powers are limited even when they are formalized, as they are not empowered to penalize local officials.[118]

112 Robinson, 'Closing the Implementation Gap', 321.

113 Robinson, 'Closing the Implementation Gap', 335–6.

114 Robinson, 'Closing the Implementation Gap', 337.

115 Robinson, 'Closing the Implementation Gap', 337–8.

116 Robinson, 'Closing the Implementation Gap', 338.

117 Robinson, 'Closing the Implementation Gap', 340. See, for instance, Sections 3–10 of the Bihar Panchayat Raj Act of 2006, available at http://www.panchayat.gov.in/documents/10198/350801/BiharPRAct_2006_English.pdf, accessed on 17 December 2016.

118 Robinson, 'Closing the Implementation Gap', 340.

The reason why scholarly literature is 'so quiet' concerning this form of grievance redress might be that politicians are seen as a '"politicizing" and corrupting influence on policy' and 'antithetical to both a technocratic or legalistic view of grievance redress'.[119] However, to citizens, politicians often appear to be more accessible than bureaucrats, as the process is less formalized, and also because the (local) politicians are known to the community.[120] They also tend to be more responsive.[121] At the same time, politicians tend to not be impartial towards their constituents. There have been accusations of both complicity in and outright corruption.[122] Furthermore, their power to effectively 'enforce' their decisions (even through the 'subtle means' described above) largely depends on their own political standing and their relationship to the local administration.[123]

## Administrative Redress Mechanisms

Robinson finds that administrative redress systems are at least somewhat effective. However, this has been the case only in more recent years. While grievance redress cells were already introduced in the late 1960s, they were both lacking in terms of political support and motivated staff.[124] He quotes a former 'high ranking bureaucrat' who was a district collector in the 1970s.[125] He remembers that 'no one would complain because inspectors wouldn't listen to them'.[126] A deputy district collector from Madhya Pradesh reports that also in the 1980s, grievances could only be redressed if the aggrieved party had personal connections with local officials or politicians.[127] A government consultant in Bihar is of the view

[119] Robinson, 'Closing the Implementation Gap', 338–9.

[120] Robinson, 'Closing the Implementation Gap', 340.

[121] Robinson, 'Closing the Implementation Gap', 340.

[122] Robinson, 'Closing the Implementation Gap', 340

[123] Robinson, 'Closing the Implementation Gap', 340

[124] Robinson, 'Closing the Implementation Gap', 332.

[125] The district collector is the 'most powerful administrator at the local level' (see Robinson, 'Closing the Implementation Gap', 331).

[126] Robinson, 'Closing the Implementation Gap', 332.

[127] Robinson, 'Closing the Implementation Gap', 332.

that even today bureaucrats see the delivery of services as 'providing a personal gift to the citizen', and not as a service that the citizens are entitled to.[128]

Still, formalized grievance redress mechanisms in several states are at least somewhat more effective than their predecessors. For instance, the so-called *janta darbar*s are a common practice in both Bihar and Madhya Pradesh. These are public hearings held by district collectors and other high-ranking officials.[129] In Bihar, retired state civil servants have been appointed as grievance redress officers (who also have the power to penalize other officials) to follow up on such public hearings.[130]

### *State Public Services Acts*

In several states, there are also formalized systems for a range of state services regulated by 'public services acts', with the first such act having been passed in Madhya Pradesh in 2010.[131] The Madhya Pradesh Act also acted as a role model for many of the acts that were later passed in other states.[132] The systems created by these acts allow citizens to get more clarity on what services they may expect from the state in the first place.[133] They also set time

[128] Robinson, 'Closing the Implementation Gap', 332.

[129] Robinson, 'Closing the Implementation Gap', 333.

[130] Robinson, 'Closing the Implementation Gap', 333.

[131] Robinson, 'Closing the Implementation Gap', 333. Such state services include the provision of documents and certificates such as 'Below Poverty Line' cards or income or residency certificates. See The Madhya Pradesh Lok Sewaon Ke Pradan Ki Guarantee Adhiniyam Act, 2010, available at http://aiggpa.mp.gov.in/images/files/pdf/regulation/1-Right%20to%20services%20Act.pdf, accessed on 15 August 2018.

[132] Robinson, 'Right to Public Service Acts in India', 5.

[133] Robinson, 'Closing the Implementation Gap', 335. Some groundwork was done in this respect already by the 'Citizen's Charter movement' in the late 1990s and early 2000s, though these may have 'lacked the precision necessary to be effective' (see Robinson, 'Right to Public Service Acts in India', 4). The Madhya Pradesh Act, in Section 3, requires that the state government notify services, designated officers, first appeal officers, second appellate authority, and stipulated time limits.

limits within which officials shall decide whether or not a service will be provided.[134]

The acts also provide possibilities of appeal. An appeal is usually filed with senior administrative officials, meaning that the complaint remains within the bureaucracy.[135] The appeal officers may, however, also impose penalties on lower officials, meaning that they do have effective means of enforcement as part of their grievance redress powers.[136] Nonetheless, in practice, appeals and especially penalties are rare.[137] Generally, awareness about the complaints procedure (and about the acts in general) appears to be low.[138]

Robinson quotes one civil society advocate in Madhya Pradesh who believes that 'the act is more about administrative relationships' and 'systematizing things at the government level', rather than having the goal of actually mobilizing the people.[139] The author also notes that the acts were largely promoted by politicians and top bureaucrats rather than civil society groups. This may indicate that these acts were seen as a tool for top level officials

[134] See Section 5 of the Madhya Pradesh Act.

[135] Robinson, 'Closing the Implementation Gap', 334. The Madhya Pradesh Act provides for a two-level appellate procedure in Section 6.

[136] Section 7(1) of the Madhya Pradesh Act allows lump sum penalties between 500 and 5,000 Rupees.

[137] Robinson, 'Closing the Implementation Gap', 334; Robinson, 'Right to Public Service Acts in India', 7–8. Generally, one may also question whether or not penalties are actually the right choice. It is not clear how effective penalization is, as other countries as well as Indian states with better public service implementation like Kerala or Gujarat do not use such a strategy. This means that while it might improve implementation, it is not a necessity (see Robinson, 'Right to Public Service Acts in India', 11). Also, the strategy may demoralize officials, especially considering the fact that officials may sometimes not be fully responsible for a delay in responding (see Robinson, 'Right to Public Service Acts in India', 11; Robinson, 'Closing the Implementation Gap', 351).

[138] Robinson, 'Right to Public Service Acts in India', 8, notes that in 2011, only 2 per cent of applicants for services covered under the system knew about the Act in Madhya Pradesh.

[139] Robinson, 'Right to Public Service Acts in India Pradesh', 8.

and politicians to control the lower ties of bureaucracy rather than as a tool for empowerment of citizens.[140] Still, the acts seem to have had a positive effect. Generally, the persons whom Robinson has interviewed believe that the acts have 'helped improve services by creating simpler and more legible processes for applying'.[141] Furthermore, 'there is a potential for these acts to have a lasting institutional culture affect'.[142]

However, it appears that these benefits are the result of the acts' effect of making the bureaucracy more efficient rather than of successful grievance redress. Grievance redress in itself does not seem to function as desired under these acts, at least not in Madhya Pradesh and Bihar. The improvements in service delivery are rather the result of the fact that while creating these acts, the states also made service delivery systems simpler, more legible, and more robust. For instance, it is now far easier to receive certificates because of the simplification of the rules according to which they have to be provided.[143]

The fact that the appeal system hardly leads to punishments may also be explained by design deficiencies. Civil society representatives believe that the lack of penalties are a sign for bureaucrats 'looking out for each other'.[144] On the other hand, lower officials themselves state that the mere possibility of being penalized made them prioritize processing applications for the respective services, but sometimes at the expense of their other work.[145] The officials believe that because of the time limit within which they have to respond, the system would only be fair if there were also a limit for the number of applications they have to process.[146] Top officials, on the other hand, are generally sceptical of the system concerning some of the services. They believe that the acts should only be applied to such services that are 'easy to quantify or track', and

140 Robinson, 'Right to Public Service Acts in India', 5.
141 Robinson, 'Right to Public Service Acts in India', 8.
142 Robinson, 'Right to Public Service Acts in India', 9
143 Robinson, 'Right to Public Service Acts in India', 10
144 Robinson, 'Right to Public Service Acts in India', 9.
145 Robinson, 'Right to Public Service Acts in India', 9.
146 Robinson, 'Right to Public Service Acts in India', 9.

that the system should not be 'a one-size-fits-all approach to service delivery'. Specifically, they believe that it would not work for more complicated issues such as health or education.[147]

### *The Right to Information Act*

Another piece of legislation that offers a grievance redress system is the Right to Information Act, which was passed in 2005. Unlike the states' services acts, it had received 'vigorous backing from civil society'.[148]

The Act requires public authorities to maintain all their records duly catalogued and indexed (Section 1(a)) and to publish information concerning their organization (such as the powers and duties of their officers and employees, the procedure they follow in decision-making processes, and so on [see Section 1(b)]). Every public authority shall also designate Public Information Officers in all administrative units or offices under it (Section 5(1, 2)). Any person may send requests to receive information to these Public Information Officers (Section 6(1)). They shall then be responsible for providing the requested piece of information and shall work with other officers in their department if they are required to obtain it from them (Section 5 (3, 4)). They must provide it 'as expeditiously as possible, and in any case within thirty days of the receipt of the request' (Section 7(1)). If they do not provide the piece of information within that period of time, they 'shall be deemed to have refused the request' (Section 7(2)).

Right to Information Act allows appeals to the State and Centre Information Commissions (Section 18). This part of the system is comparable to the education grievance redress system, where an appeal is possible to the (somewhat independent) Child Rights Commissions. The Information Commissions shall consist of one (state) chief information commissioner as well as several (up to 10) central/state information commissioners, who shall be appointed on recommendation of the prime minister/chief minister, the leader of the opposition, and a cabinet minister (Sections 12(1-3), 15

[147] Robinson, 'Right to Public Service Acts in India', 10.

[148] Robinson, 'Closing the Implementation Gap', 344.

(1-3)). In practice, the commissioners are usually retired civil servants.[149] These Commissions, like the Child Rights Commissions, have the powers of a civil court concerning fact-finding (Section 18(3)). Importantly, the Commissions are also able to 'impose a penalty of two hundred and fifty rupees each day till [...] information is furnished' on the Public Information Officer (Section 20). Therefore, unlike the Child Rights Commissions, the Information Commissions have the power to enforce their decisions.

Interestingly, even though the Right to Information Act does not provide citizens with means to enforce the provision of government services (except, of course, receiving information), it has still become an important tool to further the implementation of such services. Citizens have been able to acquire services through the right to information system simply by inquiring about why certain services have not been provided.[150] For instance, one right to information commissioner in Bihar reports that requests inquiring about a person's application to be included in the 'Below Poverty Line' list often result in the bureaucrats then processing the request faster.[151] A study of service delivery in Delhi has found that filing an information request under the Act in Delhi

[149] Robinson quotes Daruwala, Nayak, and Parwar, who have found that 90 per cent of central and state chief information commissioners and 53 per cent of information commissioners were retired civil servants (see Maja Daruwala, Venkatesh Nayak, and Amikar Parwar, 'A Rapid Study of Information Commissions Established Under the Right to Information Laws in India', Commonwealth Human Rights Initiative, May 2012, http://humanrightsinitiative.org/old/publications/rti/ICs-compstudy-final-Delhi-May12-VenkatN&AmikarP.pdf, accessed on 19 August 2018, 11–12, cited in Robinson, 'Closing the Implementation Gap', 344).

[150] Robinson cites Shrinivasan, who reports that 'for common people, especially slum dwellers, RTI applications have become a means to access basic government services' (see Rumini Shrinivasan, 'Paper Power', *Times of India* (The Crest Edition), 13 April 2013, https://web.archive.org/web/20160417132947/http://www.timescrest.com/society/paper-power-10113, accessed on 19 August 2018, cited in Robinson, 'Closing the Implementation Gap', 344).

[151] Robinson, 'Closing the Implementation Gap', 344.

was almost as successful as paying a bribe and more successful than having an NGO write a letter of support.[152]

However, on average, the persons filing right to information requests tend to have a relatively high educational background,[153] meaning that (like it is the case with PIL in the courts) the poor often rely on more affluent persons or groups like NGOs taking up the cases for them. Generally, 'much like the judiciary', the Commissions are inaccessible to 'those who lack the knowledge or resources to vigorously contest their rights'.[154] Additional complaints about the system include officers' failure to provide information even after being fined, as well as a slow appeals process.[155]

Still, the right to information regime seems to be working comparatively well. It also enhances legibility, as it 'provides citizens, journalists, and civil society with access to much of the same information that officials have, meaning new sets of eyes can watch official action'.[156]

152 'While bribery still appears to be the fastest way to obtain the desired public good, the RTIA is nevertheless impressively effective. [...] [R]ecourse to the RTIA is considerably more effective than standard application procedures and is almost as effective as bribery' (see Leonid Peisakhin and Paul Pinto, 'Is Transparency an Effective Anti-Corruption Strategy? Evidence from a Field Experiment in India', *Regulation & Governance* 4, no. 3 [2010]).

153 Robinson cites the RTI Assessment & Analysis Group & National Campaign for People's Right to Information, who have found that only 30 per cent of rural and only 15 per cent of the urban applicants belonged to the economically weaker class of society (see 'Safeguarding the Right to Information. Report of the People's RTI Assessment 2008. Executive Summary', RTI Assessment & Analysis Group & National Campaign for People's Right to Information, 2018, http://freedominfo.org/documents/india-safeguarding-executivesummary.pdf, accessed on 19 August 2018, 8–9, cited in Robinson, 'Closing the Implementation Gap', 344).

154 Robinson, 'Closing the Implementation Gap', 345.

155 Waiting time for disposal of appeals is several months in most states and more than a year in some states (see 'Safeguarding the Right to Information', RTI Assessment & Analysis Group & National Campaign for People's Right to Information, 17).

156 Robinson, 'Closing the Implementation Gap', 346.

## The Benefits and Dangers of 'Level Jumping'

Even though none of the grievance redress regimes work perfectly, and even though some of them have inherent problems such as lack of independence and impartiality or lack of remedial powers, there are some positive aspects: for instance, each avenue provides the government with opportunities to gather information on implementation of its policies.[157] In Bihar and Madhya Pradesh, the public hearings by administrators seem to fulfil that purpose particularly well, as one district collector reported to Robinson that 'it's the biggest feedback I use to assess performance'.[158]

Such effects of public hearings are an example of 'level jumping'. Complainants 'bypass the morass of local bureaucracy, politicians, or judicial system and bring their concern to a higher level'.[159] While citizens are 'jumping up' in this manner, higher-level officials and politicians (especially the chief minister) might also 'jump down' by reacting to complaints that are addressed at them directly without referring citizens to the grievance redress mechanisms.[160]

However, at the same time, it is a time-consuming and costly exercise for top-level officials and politicians. The whole system might also benefit particularly those citizens who already have access to these officials and politicians to begin with.[161] It does not particularly empower those citizens whose voices are currently unheard.

Therefore, level jumping is an effective tool that may help in instances where the regular grievance redress mechanisms fail. But it cannot be as effective and especially cannot have the same outreach as a functioning lower-level grievance redress mechanism with a well-functioning and organized appellate system. Only a system that also functions at the lower level can provide a 'fishing net' that is fine-meshed enough to 'catch' cases of lacking

157 Robinson, 'Closing the Implementation Gap', 345.

158 Robinson, 'Closing the Implementation Gap', 347.

159 Robinson, 'Closing the Implementation Gap', 347–8. He also sees PIL as an example for such a 'level jump'.

160 Robinson, 'Closing the Implementation Gap', 348.

161 Robinson, 'Closing the Implementation Gap', 348.

implementation. Level jumping may therefore be an effective 'transitional strategy' while other systems are malfunctioning, but the goal must be to improve those systems.[162] If level jumping became a permanent solution, then it would result in centralizing power around few top-level officials, meaning that service delivery would be entirely up to their discretion,[163] which is a situation that a grievance redress system must seek to avoid.

The system created by the Right to Education Act and Child Rights Commissions Act does have potential in this respect, as it relies both on lower-level grievance redress as well as a higher-level appellate body that are somewhat independent. Until a state is reached in which the lower-level system functions as desired, governments may also employ strategies of 'level jumping', as the Karnataka SCPCR has done by holding its public meetings. In fact, with the Right to Education Act and Child Rights Commissions Act allowing a direct complaint to the commissions, avenues for 'level jumping' are even formally provided for.

However, the problem of lack of legal enforcement mechanisms for the commissions' decisions remains. The system created by the Right to Information Act shows how this may be improved.

* * *

In this chapter, it has become clear that the grievance redress mechanism under the Right to Education Act is deficient in many respects, with some deficiencies being common to other grievance redress regimes as well. Some deficiencies, on the other hand, have been avoided in other systems. In particular, the Right to Information Act demonstrates how such a system can work more effectively, albeit also not perfectly.

One may conclude that the system created by the Right to Education Act features both lack of independence for some of the decision-makers and lack of competences for those decision-makers who are somewhat independent. The system therefore does not compensate for the lack of access to a judiciary. The judiciary is

[162] Robinson, 'Closing the Implementation Gap', 349.
[163] Robinson, 'Closing the Implementation Gap', 349.

both independent and powerful; it just remains inaccessible. The grievance redress system, on the other hand, lacks independent decision makers that are also powerful. In conclusion, this means that the State has not fulfilled its duty under the Constitution to make the right to education an effectively enforceable right.

As shown in the previous chapter, the grievance redress regime is just one of several potential solutions that the State could choose to fulfil its constitutional duty of making the right enforceable. If a court were to test whether or not the State has acted on its obligation in this respect, it might restrain itself to stating that one of these paths has to be taken. It could thus leave it entirely up to the discretion of the State to choose which path it will take and how it will design the alternative mechanism, or how it will provide for access to the courts such as by improving the legal aid regime.

However, in the Right to Education Act itself, the state has already chosen the grievance redress system as a solution (in addition to the inaccessible higher judiciary). It just has not designed this solution in a constitutionally acceptable manner. If the judiciary were to assess State measures for making the right to education effectively and practically enforceable, it would not stretch its competences by focusing on this one system and accordingly ordering that it must be improved.

Considering the experience with this system, as well as other grievance redress regimes, the question arises how the system may be improved, and how it could work in practice to provide for effective enforceability of the right. The next question would then be how the courts could play a role in identifying the shortcomings and defining to what extent the State is under a constitutional obligation to improve the system. The courts could perhaps even define the concrete measures that the State must take. The judiciary should act alongside grievance redress systems with different actors that support each other, ensuring that the burden is not placed on few persons and institutions alone. How this may work in practice, particularly for the right to education, shall be explored in the final chapter.

# 6

# Grievance Redress and the Judiciary

## Enforcing the Right to Education through 'Macromanagement and Micromanagement'

This chapter shall give some answers to the question of what concrete measures the State has to take to fulfil its constitutional obligation under Article 21A. Such measures concern the question of access to justice and effective enforcement of the right, but not exclusively. The chapter shall show which measures may be taken in order to make the Right to Education Act's grievance redress system functional. However, while assessing this issue, it will also differentiate between such measures that may be a necessity prescribed by the Constitution and such where discretion may be left to policymakers.

Obviously, the body that will ultimately, at last instance, decide whether or not the State has fulfilled its constitutional obligations is the higher judiciary, that is, the high courts and the Supreme Court. How much of that discretion policymakers will actually be left with in practice is therefore a question that the higher judiciary will have to decide. As mentioned in Chapters 2 and 3, the question of delineating the concrete constitutional obligations is inherently linked to the question of division of power and to what extent the judiciary is allowed to 'interfere' in policy decisions that should ordinarily be made by the legislature and the executive.

Considering the fact that Article 21A was added to the Constitution at a time when the judiciary, especially the Supreme Court, had already 'interfered' to a large extent in policy-making concerning socio-economic rights, and that the amendment adding it to the constitutional text was nonetheless passed unanimously, the case against such 'interference' has become much weaker for the right to education. However, it is still difficult to predict what lengths the judiciary would go to if, for instance, the question of lack of quality of (government) schools were raised in court: the fact that quality standards are extremely low and have even been decreasing, combined with the fact that the State is not employing all possible measures in order to reverse or at least halt this development, may be seen as a prima facie violation, as described in Chapter 3. However, as also mentioned in that chapter, there are different kinds of measures that the State could take, which may or may not include amending the Right to Education Act or state rules under the Act. The judiciary might merely identify a violation of the right and leave it up to the other branches of power to decide which measures ought to be taken. Alternatively, it may decide to order specific policy alterations itself. It is also up to the courts to decide how far-reaching measures ought to be and in what period of time they must be taken.

Concerning the question of access to justice, it might be easier and more justified for the judiciary to order specific measures than it is for questions such as lack of quality. As explained in Chapter 3, the principal question of whether or not the court must measure statutory legislation against Article 21A has to be answered affirmatively. This then raises the question whether or not the grievance redress mechanisms created by the Right to Education Act as well as the Child Rights Commissions Act, which the Right to Education Act refers to, fulfil the obligation of the State to provide access to justice and mechanisms through which the right can be effectively enforced.

As mentioned in Chapter 5, it is also important to note that the State is not constitutionally obliged to necessarily create an administrative grievance redress mechanism. Shortcomings in that system are therefore not in themselves a 'violation' or non-fulfilment of the right to education. Because of Article 21A, however, the State *is* obliged to provide access to justice. Articles 32 and 226 mean that primarily it must make the high courts and the Supreme Court more accessible. Grievance redress mechanisms may just become an adequate compensation for lack of access to the judiciary. A properly functioning grievance redress system may thus be a decisive step forward in order to fulfil this duty imposed on the State by Articles 21, 32, and 226. As such, its adequacy may be assessed by the judiciary.

Amongst the various measures that the State may take to provide compensation for lack of access to the higher judiciary described in Chapter 4, the legislature has decided to provide an alternative through grievance redress mechanisms within the administration, with the state child rights commissions acting as appellate bodies, as described in Chapter 5. Therefore, concerning the question to what extent the State has fulfilled its obligation and what measures it must take, there is more tangible 'material' (the acts, the state rules, and notifications, as well as reports about their implementation) that can be evaluated from a constitutional law perspective than concerning other questions such as (lack of) measures concerning quality issues.

If the grievance redress system worked as it should, there would ultimately be two levels of 'adjudication': one outside of and one within the judiciary. The Supreme Court and the high courts would be at the 'upper end', the local authorities and the Child Rights Commissions would be at the 'lower end'. This chapter shall not only show what measures the Constitution obliges the State to take to make this 'division of labour' functional, but also provides a small outlook at how the system might work once such steps are taken. Even though the necessity for a system such as the administrative grievance redress regime arises from the fact that the system that the Constitution had originally created is malfunctioning (because it is not accessible), it shall also be argued that the division of labour system may actually be superior to that original idea.

The first part of this chapter shall assess the question of what measures must be taken to 'fix' the grievance redress system, so that it may live up to the constitutional requirements. This includes not only improving shortcomings in its formal set-up, but also clear definitions of some of the matters that the grievance redress authorities shall adjudicate on. Importantly, the higher judiciary is the only body empowered to perform judicial review, and therefore the only body that is competent to declare what measures need to be taken to improve the implementation of the Right to Education Act (including the grievance redress mechanisms). Therefore, the next question will be how, in spite of its inaccessibility, it might be able to do so in practice. Public Interest Litigation, in spite of all its shortcomings, can be a decisive tool in this respect (as shown in the second part of the chapter). The last section of this chapter shall then show that a division of responsibilities concerning 'macromanagement' and 'micromanagement' between the 'upper and lower levels' of 'adjudication' might actually be more effective than the system that the Constitution had originally created.

## Grievance Redress System: Constitutional Obligations for Its Improvement

Chapter 5 highlighted severe deficiencies in the grievance redress system. If certain measures are taken to optimize its formal set-up, however, it could become a system that might indeed serve as an adequate and more accessible alternative to adjudication of the right to education in the higher judiciary, as the first part of this section shall explain. It shall then be argued that it might be necessary to not only change the design of the system, but to also re-draft some provisions in the Right to Education Act (as well as the rules made under it) for the grievance redress bodies to adjudicate them effectively.

### Improvements Required in the System's Design

As described in the last chapter, one shortcoming in the grievance redress system that hinders its effectiveness is the fact that 'jurisdiction' is not clearly defined at the local authority level. The extent of lack of clarity differs between different states, with some states not having made any specific rules identifying grievance redress local authorities at all, and others having created relatively detailed matrixes with responsibilities assigned to different authorities for different issues. The case of Karnataka appears to be especially problematic in this regard, with somewhat clearly defined jurisdictions on one hand clashing with an 'informal' grievance redress mechanisms on the other.

Consequently, state governments must define jurisdictions of different authorities clearly, meaning that they should clearly design 'channels' through which complaints should be processed. They should also clearly define which authorities are competent to process what kind of grievances.[1] For this, each state should develop a matrix identifying authorities and creating clearly defined appellate structures and powers.[2] States may also consider creating 'one-stop windows' at which citizens could fill all kinds of complaints that could then be processed by different authorities.[3] This would remedy the current situation in which parents, who are often themselves uneducated, do not know whom to turn to or are sent from one authority to the other.

In order to ensure at least a minimum amount of independence and impartiality by officials responsible for grievance redress at the lower level, the decision-makers in a given case must not be the same persons who are responsible for the grievance. Such authorities that themselves have either actively violated the aggrieved person's right or have failed to provide a service should not be those that decide grievances. Ideally, it should be an authority that is hierarchically above the 'implementation local authority' so that it may enforce its decisions effectively. The central government's non-binding 'Advisory' on this issue does call for such a design at the state level,[4] however, as the formal set-up of

[1] Malini Bhattacharjee, Dolashree Mysoor, and Arun Sivaramakrishnan, 'RTE Grievance Redress in Karnataka', *Economic & Political Weekly* XLIX, no. 23 (2014): 39.

[2] Bhattacharjee, Mysoor, and Sivaramakrishnan, 'RTE Grievance Redress in Karnataka', 40.

[3] Bhattacharjee, Mysoor, and Sivaramakrishnan, 'RTE Grievance Redress in Karnataka', 40.

[4] Advisory F. No. 1-18/2010-EE-4 (pt. I) dated 14 February 2012, available at http://mhrd.gov.in/sites/upload_files/mhrd/files/upload_document/30.pdf, accessed on 15 August 2018.

the systems in many states show, this has not been implemented accordingly. It may therefore be required to oblige the states to design their grievance redress systems in a way that may guarantee such basic levels of independence and impartiality. This could be achieved by adding more specific minimum standards to the Right to Education Act.

In any case, being part of the bureaucracy themselves, the extent to which local authorities will be independent and impartial, especially when compared to the judiciary, is limited. Therefore, by assigning an institutionally independent body (the Child Rights Commissions) as the appellate authority (in addition to it being an authority of original jurisdiction under Sections 13(1)(c), 24), the State has taken an important step towards fulfilling its constitutional obligation. However, the fact that the Commissions' 'judgments' are not binding is a shortcoming that cannot be reconciled with the constitutional obligation to provide *effective* accessible enforcement mechanisms. The Commissions must have means to enforce their decisions so that they can play an important part in compensating for the lack of access to the judiciary.

If the Supreme Court were to test the design of the system against this constitutional obligation, it would be reasonable for it to order that the rules be changed in a way that the appellate authorities' decisions are binding.[5] It might then be up to policymakers, and not the court, to decide on the remedies. For instance, they would have to decide whether non-performance by bureaucrats should allow the appellate authorities to impose fines.

If the Supreme Court ordered the legislature to change the Right to Education Act and Child Rights Commissions Act to make the Commissions' decisions binding, it would venture into the legislature's authority to a lesser extent than it has in many of its past

[5] Bhattacharjee, Mysoor, and Sivaramakrishnan also argue that the SCPCR would be a 'credible original or appellate authority' if the CPCR Act were amended to 'substantially increase its powers and authority in ways that can enforce bureaucratic action and enforce sanctions against schools'. They do not, however, go as far as identifying this as a constitutional necessity (see Bhattacharjee, Mysoor, and Sivaramakrishnan, 'RTE Grievance Redress in Karnataka', 40).

judgments. Importantly, the grievance redress system has already been designed by the legislature, and passing such an order would only change one detail. That detail is, of course, a decisive one. However, such an order would be less intrusive than ordering that the system has to be redesigned in its entirety, or that another system has to be created or redesigned to fulfil the constitutional obligation. Ideally, the Court would clarify that the State may choose to take any other measures, but that they be as effective as empowering the Commissions in this sense would be.

The Court might also restrain itself to identifying the lack of powers of the appellate authority as a shortcoming without ordering the change itself. Even then, changing the statutory provisions to make the Commissions' judgments binding would be the most obvious and easiest way to fulfil the constitutional obligation. If policymakers remained inactive, however, then ordering a change of the provisions (or another, equally effective measure to provide access to justice) would become a necessity.

## Lack of Clarity in Definition of Obligations

In addition to the structural shortcomings, there is also one aspect of material law that inhibits the effective working of the grievance redress regime. The statutory provisions on education, especially the Right to Education Act, lack clarity. Some provisions are so opaque that 'adjudication' would be almost impossible for grievance redress authorities. One may therefore argue that the legislature must clarify the content of existing provisions so that the grievance redress system may become functional.

Of course, the issue could also be solved by 'case law' to a certain extent. However, with the courts being as inaccessible as they are, and with alternative forums being dysfunctional, one cannot expect a development of precedent.

### *'The Right of a Child Under This Act'*

When trying to assess how grievance redress authorities might adjudicate on violations of provisions in the Right to Education Act, one quickly realizes that it is difficult to identify which provisions shall be adjudicated upon in the first place. Section 32(1) states that 'any person having any grievance relating to the right of a child under this Act may make a written complaint' to the grievance redress authorities. Clearly, the jurisdiction of the grievance redress authorities is limited to complaints concerning the non-implementation of provisions of the Act and those provisions created 'under' it (that is, especially the state rules). It is not clear, however, whether this includes *all* of the Act's provisions and the rules made by the states, that is, whether the non-implementation of *any* of the provisions also constitutes a violation of 'the right of a child under this Act'.[6]

Some (but very few) provisions of the Act are unambiguous. Section 3(1) reiterates a 'right to free and compulsory education' for every child aged six to fourteen years and, read with Section 15, specifies that this right includes admission in a 'neighbourhood school' until elementary education is completed. Section 4 prescribes that a child above six years of age who had previously not been admitted to any school shall be admitted in a class appropriate to their age. Such a child then has 'a right to receive special training, in such manner [...] as may be prescribed'. Section 5(1) gives a 'right to seek transfer to any other school' to children who are enrolled in a school that does not provide for completion of elementary education.

Most provisions, however, are worded less clearly and do not speak of a 'right'. This leaves some uncertainty as to whether or not implementation can be enforced under Section 32. Still, for

[6] Bhattacharjee and Mysoor believe that the 'right of a child' should be defined very broadly: they believe that the right of a child should include 'effective regulation of schools and the implementation of the [25 per cent] reservation policy' by state officials, local authorities 'implementing the RTE Act', teachers imparting education in a meaningful and stress-free manner, monitoring by the parents community, and provision of access to education and compliance with regulatory standards by schools themselves (see Malini Bhattacharjee and Dolashree Mysoor, '"Unredressed" Grievances under RTE: Navigating the State Labyrinth', *Governance: An International Journal of Policy, Administration, and Institutions* 29, no. 1 [2016]: 4). However, when analysing the wording of the Act, it is not clear whether or not the 'right' can really be defined so broadly.

some of those provisions, it is obvious that the legislature intended for them to be 'justiciable' in the grievance redress system. For instance, Section 13(1) states that no school or person shall collect any capitation fee while admitting a child. With Section 13(2) even imposing a fine for persons or schools that act in contravention to this provision, the Act also prescribes a specific remedy for violations. Considering this remedy, and also the fact that the issue of 'capitation fees' was the 'trigger' for the Supreme Court declaring that education is a fundamental right in the first place,[7] it is almost inconceivable that the legislature did not intend for this provision to offer a claim under Section 32. Section 13 therefore illustrates that Section 32 does not only refer to those provisions that explicitly declare that they constitute a 'right of a child'.

The central government's advisory on implementation of Section 32 seemingly suggests that grievance redress bodies should adjudicate *all* of the Act's provisions.[8] However, such an 'advisory' is not binding on state governments. Also, concerning some provisions, one might actually question whether or not they *can* be enforced through the grievance redress system. Instead, they might only give instructions to the executive for organizing the education system. For instance, one may consider a private school that has to admit children from economically weaker families under the '25 per cent rule' according to Section 12(1)(c). If such a school is not adequately reimbursed for admitting those children, this will hardly constitute a violation of 'a right of a child'.[9]

To name another example, Section 7 includes some provisions concerning how the central and state governments shall share financial and other responsibilities. Section 7(2–5) state that the

[7] See Chapter 2.

[8] It states that '[g]rievances may relate to violation of any of the provisions under the RTE Act and may be against any public office, public servant, private institution, private person or any other agency responsible [...] for the effective implementation of the provisions of the RTE Act' (see Number 4 of the Advisory available at http://mhrd.gov.in/sites/upload_files/mhrd/files/upload_document/30.pdf, accessed on 15 August 2018).

[9] Or at least only very indirectly, as that school might then face difficulties in providing quality education because of budgetary constraints.

central government shall estimate required capital and recurring expenditure for the implementation of the Act, that the central government shall then accordingly provide grants-in-aid to the state governments, and that the central government may request the president to make a reference to the Finance Commission to examine the need for additional resources. The state government shall then use the funds received from the central government, as well as additional funds that it may have, for implementation of the Act.

The question is: does a right-bearer have a claim for the central and state governments to follow these provisions? One could imagine a situation in which the state governments cannot build enough schools because of the central government not giving grants-in-aid according to Section 7(3). In such a case, a grievance redress body or a court could act upon a complaint or petition and identify a violation (indirectly) giving a claim for implementation of Section 7(2, 3) to the individual right-bearer.[10]

If, however, the central and state governments did not follow the procedure prescribed in Section 7, but were able to sufficiently implement other provisions nonetheless (because of some informal alternative financing arrangement), it is, at the very least, debatable whether or not an individual right-bearer should then have a claim to have a grievance redress body or court order that the executive follow the prescribed procedure.

Similarly, it is not clear whether or not it constitutes an infringement of an individual's right if the central government does not develop a national curriculum, does not develop and enforce standards for teachers' trainings, or does not provide technical support and resources to the state governments (Section 7(6)(a–c)) as long as the 'end results' are acceptable. Also, one may debate whether or not the right of a child is violated if a teacher is deployed for non-educational purposes or engages in private tuition or teacher activity in addition to their regular school services (which is prohibited by Sections 27 and 28), but nonetheless performs their regular teaching duties adequately.

[10] However, as shall be discussed below, one may question to what extent a grievance redress body is competent to give such orders.

## *Lack of Clarity Concerning Remedies and Sanctions*

Even when a provision of the Right to Education gives a direct claim to a right-bearer, the grievance redress mechanism will then face the challenge of choosing certain remedies or sanctions to rectify the violation. Many of the Act's provisions do not define clear consequences for violations. At least for several of them, a wide range of consequences is perceivable. Not defining them further gives a problematically wide discretion to the grievance redress system.[11] The intensity to which right-bearers would benefit, and to which the body or official accused of violation of a right would be affected, varies greatly between such remedies. In practice, as of now, the recommendations or orders the system may come to is entirely unpredictable concerning many of the Right to Education Act's provisions.[12] This may seriously impede the workings of the system, as decision-makers will often not know what remedy is adequate.

However, as far as some provisions are concerned, the legal consequences of their non-implementation are quite clear. For instance, Sections 3(1), 4, and 15 state that all children aged between six and fourteen years have a right to be admitted in a neighbourhood school. If such schools refuse admission to a child in this age group, this constitutes a violation of that right. A grievance redress authority would then have to pass an order against the school stating that it must admit the child immediately. If a child is expelled in contravention of Section 16, the child will have to be readmitted without delay. Similarly, if schools do not allow the transfer of a child between them in contravention of Section 5, the authority would order the child's new school to accept the

[11] Bhattacharjee and Mysoor, '"Unredressed" Grievances under RTE', 39.

[12] Bhattacharjee and Mysoor report about the experience in Karnataka (see Bhattacharjee and Mysoor, '"Unredressed" Grievances under RTE', 44). The authors criticize that '[n]either the law nor the KSCPCR has formulated a standardized rubric for resolving complaints in a manner that is appropriate for the claim', and argue that the RTE Act itself must 'stipulate specific remedies for specific grievances' (see Bhattacharjee and Mysoor, '"Unredressed" Grievances under RTE', 43).

child immediately and the old school to issue a transfer certificate according to Section 5(3).

Some provisions even explicitly prescribe a concrete remedy. As mentioned above, Section 13(2) states that schools that charge capitation fees shall be fined. Section 5(3) explicitly states that if the head teacher of the child's former school refuses to issue a transfer certificate, they will be liable to disciplinary action according to the service rules. Such disciplinary actions can also be taken against a teacher who subjects a child to physical punishment or mental harassment in contravention of Section 17(2).

Other provisions, however, only seem to offer clear remedies, but raise more complicated questions at second glance. Sections 8 and 9 define some specific duties of the state governments and the local authorities.[13] For instance, Sections 8(b) and 9(b), read with Section 6, oblige these authorities to establish a school in every neighbourhood.[14] If a complainant rightly points out that a school has not been established in a given neighbourhood, a grievance redress body may order that the state and/or government establish a school in that neighbourhood, perhaps also ordering that this be done within a certain period of time. However, can a grievance redress body at the local authority level give such an order to the state government, even though the latter is higher in bureaucratic hierarchy? What if new schools cannot be established because of budgetary constraints that only the state legislature, or perhaps even the central government or Parliament, could remedy?[15] Similarly, if a school does not offer special training to a child above the age of six who is entitled to such training according to Section 4, the grievance redress authority could simply order that such training must be provided to that child immediately. However, what consequences should a grievance redress authority call for

[13] Many of those duties are assigned to both the government as well as the local authority, which also makes responsibilities somewhat less clear.

[14] 'Neighbourhood' is defined further by state rules under the Act.

[15] Section 7, as mentioned above, states that the central and state governments have concurrent responsibility for providing the funds for carrying out the provisions of the Act.

if the training prescribed by the rules made under the Act is not adequate to effectively achieve the goal of bringing the child to a level that is at par with other pupils?[16]

Also, as already mentioned in Chapter 3, it is unclear what the consequences will be if the government or local authority does not ensure compulsory admission and attendance of a child (as they are obliged to do by Section 8(a)(ii), Section 9(a)). The Right to Education Act (and no other law made under its regime) does not provide for any fine or other sanctions to be imposed on a parent who does not regularly send their child to school.[17] Without such negative consequences being prescribed by law,[18] a grievance redress body cannot go much further than identifying children who do not attend regularly and then asking their parents to send their children to school.

[16] In fact, the central government's Model Rules (in Rule 3) do not prescribe more than an obligation on the School Management Committee or local authority to identify children who require special training, and that the special training shall be organized with 'specifically designed, age appropriate learning material', that it shall be held on the premises of the school or 'in safe residential facilities', that is shall be provided by teachers working for the school or teachers specifically appointed, and that it shall be offered for a minimum period of three months and a maximum period of two years. Children shall also receive 'special attention' even after the conclusion of the special training. This still leaves many open questions, for example, how the child's advances towards the goal of parity with other children of the same age shall be assessed, how big the 'special training groups' may be, how many hours of special training should be offered in a day, and so on. Many states have adopted the Model Rules as state rules with few alterations. See http://mhrd.gov.in/rte_state_rules, accessed on 15 August 2018, for an overview.

[17] As mentioned in Chapters 1 and 3, curiously, Section 10 declares a duty of every parent or guardian to admit their child in a school, but not to ensure attendance. This clearly falls short of the obligation imposed on the State by Article 21A (see Chapter 3).

[18] According to Article 21 of the Constitution, the parents' personal liberty must be limited only by a 'procedure established by law'. Therefore, such a provision is a prerequisite to imposing such consequences because of the parents' fundamental rights.

## *Application of the Schedule's Standards to Government Schools*

In addition to unclarity concerning remedies and sanctions, it is not even clear to whom decisions based on Right to Education Act provisions could be addressed. In particular, this is the case concerning provisions concerning infrastructure, even though the Schedule to the Act sets relatively clear standards. For instance, it states that a school building must have one classroom for every teacher, must have barrier-free access, must have separate toilets for boys and girls, and so on. If a school lacks these facilities, a grievance redress authority might order the local authority and/or the state government that such facilities must be provided for within a certain period of time.

Clearly, the Schedule's provisions concerning infrastructure are binding for private schools. The Act threatens that they may lose recognition and will therefore not be allowed to operate if they do not adhere to the Schedule's standards. However, it is unclear whether or not these provisions apply to government schools as well, as already mentioned in Chapter 1.[19]

Sections 8(d) and 9(f) state that local authorities and state governments shall 'provide infrastructure including school building, teaching staff and learning equipment/material', without referring to the Schedule. Sections 8(g) and 9(h) refer to the 'standards and norms specified in the Schedule', but do not refer to infrastructure. Instead, they state that the authorities shall conform to the Schedule's standards concerning 'good quality education'. One may argue that adequate infrastructure is, to an extent, a prerequisite for good quality education. However, this does not explain why the sections refer to infrastructure separately in Sections 8(d) and 9(f), without those sub-sections themselves referring to the Schedule. Section 25, which is explicitly applicable to 'each school', also refers to the Schedule, but only concerning pupil–teacher ratios and not concerning infrastructure.

[19] Chapter 1, 'Problems Concerning Elementary Education in India Today/Infrastructure'.

Section 19(1) states that '[n]o school shall be established, or recognised, under section 18, unless it fulfils the norms and standards specified in the Schedule'. Section 19(3) states that schools that do not fulfil these standards shall lose recognition. This means that they must not continue operations (Section 18(1)). While Section 18(1) explicitly only refers to private schools operating without recognition,[20] 'established' in Section 19(1) may also refer to government schools. The wording 'shall be established, or recognised, under section 18' would actually make little sense if the provision were only applicable to private schools, as for them, the recognition is a prerequisite to be legally established.[21]

This would mean that the government must not establish new schools that do not fulfil the Schedule's infrastructure standards, but that it is not under an obligation to upgrade schools that already existed at the time of the commencement of the Act (that is, beginning of 2010). Still, it has been said that 'there is an implicit understanding' that government schools are not bound by the infrastructural norms and standards set by the Schedule at all, without any differentiation concerning schools that were established before or after 2010.[22] Because of the wording of Sections 18 and 19, such an understanding would not be very convincing, however. Ideally, adjudication and/or the legislature will have to clarify the provisions' ambiguity.

### *General Application to Private Schools*

Concerning private schools, of course, it is clear that the infrastructural provisions in the Act's Schedule are addressed at them. Still, there are other provisions for which it is unclear whether or not they can apply to private schools at all. Also, concerning those

[20] The provision states that this is applicable to schools 'other than a school established, owned or controlled by the appropriate Government or the local authority'.

[21] Section 18 states that 'no school [...] shall [...] be established [...] without obtaining a certificate of recognition'.

[22] Bhattacharjee and Mysoor, '"Unredressed" Grievances under RTE', 42.

provisions that do, it is unclear what the consequences will be if they do not adhere to them.

As explained in Chapter 3, Article 21A has (at least indirect) horizontal effect, meaning that the State is under a constitutional obligation to ensure that the contents of the right be fulfilled through private schools. However, several of the Right to Education Act's provisions that are clearly (also) addressed at private schools are effectively un-enforceable. The Right to Education Act either lacks clear provisions that oblige private schools to perform certain duties or refrain from certain actions, or it lacks effective enforcement mechanisms for such provisions. Therefore, neither the education administration nor the grievance redress authorities would be able to enforce them, meaning that the State is not fulfilling its constitutional duty.

In addition to that, as mentioned in Chapter 1, after the Supreme Court's decisions of *Society for Un-aided Private Schools of Rajasthan* and *Pramati Educational & Cultural Trust*, none of the provisions of the Act are applicable to private un-aided minority schools (with repercussions further amplified by the fact that there is lack of clarity concerning what a 'minority school' is).[23] Therefore, currently, these minority schools are entirely unregulated under the Right to Education Act regime.

As mentioned above, 'non-minority' private schools must fulfil 'the norms and standards specified in the Schedule'.[24] Otherwise, the authority empowered by Section 18(1) 'shall withdraw recognition granted to such school' (Section 19(3)), meaning that, according to Section 18(1), the school must cease operations.

The three-year period within which the schools may take steps towards fulfilling the standards prescribed by the Schedule (see

[23] *Society for Un-aided Private Schools of Rajasthan* v. *Union of India & Another* MANU/SC/0311/2012, 20 (Supreme Court of India, 12 April 2012), confirmed in *Pramati Educational & Cultural Trust* v. *Union of India & Ors* MANU/SC/0419/2014 (Supreme Court of India, 6 May 2014). Also see Chapters 1 and 3.

[24] This concerns all of the Schedule's provisions, for example, pupil–teacher ratios, infrastructure, working days and instructional hours, teaching learning equipment, library, play material, games and sports equipment, and so on.

Section 19(2)) has expired in 2013, meaning that schools not fulfilling the norms would have to now lose recognition and, consequently, be closed. If a parent of a child raised a complaint to the grievance redress authority that their child's school does not fulfil some of the standards set by the Schedule, then that authority would have to order that the school lose recognition and be closed. Usually, this would not be in the interest of the children enrolled in that school or of their parents. Rather, it might be more appropriate to first set another time limit within which the school must fulfil the standards. The authority could then also decide that the school will indeed lose recognition if it does not fulfil the standards upon expiry of that deadline. This threat, if taken seriously, might ensure that schools actually take action.

As mentioned in Chapter 1, the authorities have indeed often refrained from actually revoking recognition and closing schools even after the passing of the deadline in 2013 (though they were not acting as grievance redress authorities in those cases). Such a decision might be pragmatic and sensible. However, the provisions given by Sections 18 and 19 actually unambiguously call for the de-recognition of such schools, and do not give any discretion to authorities to first set additional individual time limits. Thus, concerning these provisions, the issue is actually not that they suffer from a lack of clarity concerning remedies, but that they give *too little* discretion to the authorities.

Some other provisions are explicitly or implicitly aimed at private schools. Some of them apply exclusively to private schools, some to private schools as well as to government schools. Some of those provisions also prescribe explicit sanctions specifically aimed at private parties as a consequence in case of violations. For instance, Section 13, which prohibits collecting 'capitation fees' from children upon admission, is exclusively aimed at private schools. Section 13(2)(a) names a fine of up to 10 times the capitation fee charged. Also, Section 18(5) states that establishing or running a school without having a certificate of recognition (or after the recognition has been revoked) is punishable with a fine up to 100,000 Rupees or 10,000 Rupees for each day during which the violation continues.

The most important provision in the Act exclusively addressing private schools might be Section 12(1)(c), which prescribes that private un-aided schools must admit children from weaker sections and disadvantaged groups in class I to the extent of at least 25 per cent of the strength of that class. These children shall be given 'free and compulsory education' until the completion of that class. The schools receive money for each child thus admitted according to Section 12(2). However, even though this provision is of crucial importance for the 'privatizing' part of the implementation of the right to education, the Act does not prescribe any fines or any other sanctions if private schools refuse to accept children from weaker sections and disadvantaged groups. If a school refuses to accept children under the '25 per cent rule' and a parent of an eligible child complains to a grievance redress authority, that authority might then order that the child must be admitted. However, if the school refuses to follow that order, that authority cannot enforce its decision by threatening fines or other sanctions like fines or revocation of recognition as the law does not prescribe any such consequences, unlike for other provisions. The rights of the private schools, including fundamental rights like Article 21, require that such sanctions be explicitly prescribed by law for any authority to impose them on a private party. If private schools are found to violate these provision, the only authority that could impose such sanctions on them is the higher judiciary by means of applying the rules of contempt of court, as shall be explained below.

Interestingly, the Central Board of Secondary Education (CBSE) has recently (in September 2016) disaffiliated a prominent group of schools in Karnataka for forging documents to prove its minority status in order to 'escape' the provisions of the Right to Education Act, especially the '25 per cent rule' of Section 12(2).[25] Section 17(2a) of the CBSE Affiliation Bye-Laws states that proceedings for withdrawal of affiliation may be initiated in a wide range of cases, including any 'misconduct in connection with the admissions/examinations/any other area which in the opinion of the Board

[25] *New Indian Express*, 'CBSE Disaffiliates Six National Public Schools in Karnataka', 7 September 2016, http://www.newindianexpress.com/states/karnataka/CBSE-disaffiliates-six-National-Public-Schools-in-Karnataka/2016/09/07/article3614785.ece, accessed on 19 August 2018.

warrants immediate disaffiliation of the school'.[26] Not surprisingly, the group of schools challenged the disaffiliation. The High Court eventually quashed the CBSE's disaffiliation, stating that even if a forgery had taken place, it would not be a criminal act, as no one benefitted from such a fraud, and also noting that the question of linguistic minority status was a 'grey area' that still needed to be addressed.[27]

Still, the case does show that disaffiliation by the CBSE may be a possible consequence whenever it can be undoubtedly established that a school refrains from fulfilling its obligations under Section 12 of the Right to Education Act. In any case, while losing affiliation with the CBSE (or other boards providing class X and XII examinations) is a harsh sanction, it is weaker than de-recognition. Unlike schools that have not received or have lost recognition according to Sections 18, 19 of the Right to Education Act, non-affiliated schools are still allowed to operate up to the level of class VIII, that is, all classes covered by the Right to Education Act.[28] Disaffiliated schools are also still allowed to seek affiliation with another board. Still, the threat of disaffiliation may have a strong detrimental effect on schools that offer education up to class X or XII. This is especially the case for such schools that otherwise have a high reputation, which may be hurt severely by such actions by the respective boards. These repercussions are, however, outside the scope of the regime created by the Right to Education Act.

[26] See the CBSE Affiliation Bye-Laws at http://cbseaff.nic.in/cbse_aff/Attachment/OnlineServices/AffiliationByeLaws_14112012.pdf, accessed on 15 August 2018. Section 17 itself applies only to provisionally affiliated schools; however, regularly/permanently affiliated schools may be 'downgraded' to the provisional affiliation status according to Section 18 and may then eventually lose affiliation as prescribed by Section 17.

[27] *K.P. Gopalakrishna and Ors* v. *The State of Karnataka and Ors* MANU/KA/0778/2017 (Supreme Court of India, 5 April 2017).

[28] See the CBSE notice to schools conducting classes without affiliation quoted at Preetu Nair, 'Get Affiliation or Face Action, CBSE Schools Told', *Times of India*, 8 April 2015, http://timesofindia.indiatimes.com/city/kochi/Get-affiliation-or-face-action-CBSE-schools-told/articleshow/46843140.cms, accessed on 19 August 2018.

Another provision for which the Act does not provide for effective enforcement is found in Sections 8(c) and 9(c). Those provisions state that state governments and local authorities shall ensure that children belonging to weaker sections and disadvantaged groups are not discriminated against. More specifically, the central government's 'Model Rules'[29] state that such children 'shall not be segregated from other children in the classrooms nor shall their classes be held at places and timings different from the classes held for the other children' and that those children 'shall not be discriminated from the rest of the children in any manner pertaining to entitlements and facilities' (Rule 7(1, 2)). Here, as well, a local authority may recognize a violation and may order that the provisions be followed. But it cannot enforce its decision by imposing sanctions such as fines or revoking the school's recognition, as such sanctions are not prescribed by the Act or other legislation.

Another aspect is the issue of physical punishment. Section 17(1) states that '[n]o child shall be subjected to physical punishment or mental harassment', making no distinction between private or government schools. However, Section 17(2) states that '[w]hoever contravenes the provisions of sub-section (1) shall be liable to disciplinary action under the *service rules applicable to such person*' (emphasis added). This effectively restricts the scope of the provision to teachers and other persons in service of government schools, as 'service rules' are not applicable to private schools' teachers, whose relationship to their school is that of a private employment contract.[30] Therefore, it appears that Section 17(1) is only aimed at government schools in the first place. This would be highly problematic, as it would be in violation of the State's constitutional obligations interpreted in according to

[29] Which have been adopted by most states without little alterations as state rules under the Right to Education Act, as prescribed by Section 38 of the Act.

[30] See the overview of 'service rules' at the central level in India, which are all applicable only to government servants, at https://dopt.gov.in/vol1; https://dopt.gov.in/revised-all-india-services-rules-vol-ii; https://dopt.gov.in/revised-all-india-services-rules-vol-iii, accessed on 15 August 2018.

international law standards setting the 'minimum core' of the right to education, as mentioned in Chapter 3.

Even if Section 17 is to be understood broadly (in a way that it refers to private schools' rules of conduct for their teachers as well), then, under the Act, there would still be no means for authorities to ensure that such rules prescribe disciplinary actions in case of physical punishment. This is the case because, again, there are no statutorily prescribed sanctions such as fines. Therefore, the provision would be effectively unenforceable against private schools that tolerate corporal punishment and private school teachers who abuse children, at least within the Right to Education Act regime, which the grievance redress authorities' jurisdiction is limited to under Section 32 (right of a child under this Act).

The state child rights commissions, on the other hand, might refer such cases to a magistrate in order to initiate criminal proceedings (Sections 14(2), 24 of the Child Rights Commissions Act) against teachers and/or the school's management. Members of the education bureaucracy might also do so, but not when acting as grievance redress authorities under Section 32 of the Right to Education Act.

However, even if cases are referred to a magistrate, this might not help in effectively preventing corporal punishment, as it is actually not necessarily a crime. Section 82 of the recently passed Juvenile Justice (Care and Protection of Children) Act of 2015 prescribes a punishment of imprisonment of up to three months and a fine for corporal punishment, but only by persons in charge of or employed in 'child care institutions', which, according to the Act's definitions, does not include schools.

Instances of corporal punishment are complicated further by the fact that in many cases, parents do not have a problem with corporal punishment and are allowed to physically punish their children themselves. They may also consent to others (like teachers) doing so. Section 89 of the Indian Penal Code of 1860 allows corporal punishment by parents, guardians, and other persons having lawful charge of children under the age of 12 years.[31] Section 75 prescribes

[31] For the (il)legality and realities of corporal punishment at home, in schools, and elsewhere, see Global Initiative to End All Corporal Punishment of Children, 'Corporal Punishment of Children in India' (2015), https://web.archive.org/web/20160122194628/http://www.endcor

a punishment of imprisonment of up to three years and/or a fine for parents and 'rigorous imprisonment' up to five years and a fine for persons in charge of or employed in child care institutions for several acts of cruelty against children. However, such acts go beyond 'normal corporal punishment' as far as severity is concerned.

Therefore, the only provision that effectively prohibits all kinds of corporal punishment in schools is Section 17 of the Right to Education Act. But, as stated above, it cannot be effectively enforced against private schools. As explained, this is also the case with many other important provisions of the Act. At least as far as corporal punishment is concerned, the State is in violation of its international obligations and also of its constitutional obligation if they are interpreted according to international law.[32]

As far as other provisions of the Act applicable to private schools are concerned, one may argue that if the State decides to fulfil its constitutional duties by also including private parties in the implementation process, then it will also have to ensure that it can effectively enforce the standards that it sets for those parties. Therefore, the constitutional duty to make obligations of private parties enforceable in practice extends to other provisions as well. The fact that the law does not provide right-bearers with means to effectively enforce their rights against private schools may therefore be considered a violation of the right.

## *Case Law*

Generally, statutory provisions that are worded ambiguously have to be further defined through adjudication or 'case law'. Some

---

poralpunishment.org/assets/pdfs/states-reports/India.pdf, 2 March 2019. The report finds that corporal punishment is still very widespread in both government and private schools.

[32] If Article 21A is to be interpreted in light of international human rights standards, then the State is also under a constitutional obligation to protect children against physical punishment in private schools. As shown in Chapter 3, there is little reason to believe that the judiciary, especially the Supreme Court, would not refer to international human rights standards when interpreting Article 21A.

'precedent' could be set by Child Rights Commissions for their jurisdiction, though, of course, it would only be *binding* precedent if they could actually enforce their orders. Concerning other provisions, however, the legislature and/or the judiciary will have to become active.

Some of the shortcomings named above (for instance, the lack of powers of the Child Rights Commissions or the lack of effective enforcement possibilities against private schools) can only be remedied by the legislature or by the judiciary ordering legislative measures. The legislature would either have to amend the Right to Education Act and/or the Child Rights Commissions Act or pass entirely new legislation.

Furthermore, only courts, and not grievance redress authorities, can effectively order high-level authorities (especially the legislature) to take certain actions, for example, making budgetary decisions facilitating the establishment of new schools or employing more teachers. As mentioned above, courts may also sanction private parties that act in contravention of their decisions based on the rules of contempt of court.[33] Section 2(b) of the Contempt of Courts Act of 1971 defines 'civil contempt' as 'wilful disobedience to any judgment, decree, direction, order, writ or other process of a court'. Ignoring a Supreme Court or high court order against oneself is 'wilful disobedience of a judgment'. Section 12(1) of the Contempt of Courts Act stipulates imprisonment and/or a monetary fine for contempt of court. This way, the higher judiciary could actually impose sanctions on private schools that, for instance, discriminate against children accepted under Section 12(1)(c), or who refuse to admit those children in the first place. Of course, those schools would first have to be ordered by the courts to fulfil their duties. Only if they then still refrain from doing so can the contempt of court rules be applied. Grievance redress authorities and even lower courts, on the other hand, do not have such powers in the first place.

As far as the lack of clarity concerning the questions of which provisions confer a right of a child and of specific remedies for

[33] See Articles 129 and 215 of the Constitution for the Supreme Court and the high courts.

specific violations is concerned, precedents and 'case law' may rectify the situation to an extent. Grievance redress authorities could first attempt to find adequate legal consequences whenever they identify a violation of a right of a child. They would thus set precedent for themselves, and higher-level grievance redress authorities (if a State has created appellate levels for grievance redress at the local authority level) may set precedent for lower ones in their respective jurisdiction.

State child rights commissions could then set precedents and create 'case law' applicable in the entire state and publish their decisions with reasons for why they chose a specific remedy in order to also give guidelines for other commissions in other states. However, a system of binding precedent that lower forums have to follow can only work if the 'judgments' of a higher 'court' are actually legally binding, which the decisions of the Child Rights Commissions are not. With their decision being mere recommendations, the Commissions cannot effectively 'overrule' local authorities' decisions in the first place.

Furthermore, a prerequisite of development of 'case law' is that a noteworthy number of cases enters the system.[34] As described in Chapter 5, the institutional set-up of the grievance redress system is severely lacking in several states, which leads to many aggrieved persons using informal grievance redress mechanisms and/or directly approaching the Child Rights Commissions rather than following the regular procedure. Therefore, the ability of the grievance redress system is quite limited, also inhibiting the potential for development of precedent and 'case law'.

Of course, actual case law can be developed by the higher judiciary. Such judgments could also overcome institutional shortcomings by ordering legislative measures. However, with the judiciary being as inaccessible as it is, the problem that many cases never actually become judgments is even more severe. Nonetheless, the judiciary can still play an important role, as shall be explained below.

[34] As Bhattacherjee and Mysoor note, 'in the absence of specific remedies, the task of decision making while redressing any complaint of RTE purely rests on the ability of the grievance redress system' (see Bhattacharjee and Mysoor, '"Unredressed" Grievances under RTE', 34).

## Conclusion

Clearly, the performance of the grievance redress system is impaired by institutional shortcomings (some of them severe) that can only be rectified by legislative amendments, either passed by the legislature itself or to be ordered by the judiciary. Concerning many of the shortcomings, the constitutional obligation on the legislature is relatively clear. For instance, the Child Rights Commissions need to be empowered to pass binding judgments if the legislature chooses to assign them as the one independent adjudication authority within a system that may compensate for lack of access to courts. Also, the consequences of violations of specific provisions of the Right to Education Act need to be defined, and fines and other sanctions for violations committed by private schools need to be stipulated. Of course, only the higher judiciary is able to clearly demarcate the content of the right to education in this respect, and able to order that (and how) the legislature has to become active.

## Courts' 'Macromanagement' at the 'Upper End'—PIL Revisited

In order for the judiciary to test the Right to Education Act and the grievance mechanisms created for its enforcement against the constitutional obligation, the question would have to be raised in the high courts and the Supreme Court in the first place. In theory, right-bearers themselves could raise larger questions concerning the adequacy of the legal framework in court. However, this is unlikely to happen because of their lack of access to justice, which the grievance mechanisms are supposed to compensate for.

As long as the shortcomings remain, other parties will have to raise these issues in court, which is what the institution of PIL was invented for. As described in Chapter 4, PIL in itself cannot compensate for the lack of access to justice for right-bearers, but it could play an important role in overcoming these deficiencies.

Once these questions are raised in court, possible outcomes depend on the judiciary's willingness to effectively take policy decisions. The degree to which courts order specific legislative acts differs greatly between different jurisdictions. Ultimately, courts have to decide to which extent they themselves want to give 'strength' to constitutional obligations, or exercise judicial self-restraint because of balance of power considerations (which, of course, also have constitutional value in themselves). As the first part of this section shall explain, adjudication by the Indian Supreme Court in the past has shown that the Court often leans towards judicial activism as far as socio-economic rights are concerned, even if it does also sometimes shy away from awarding strong remedies. However, self-restraint in defining the scope of rights and awarding remedies is less justified concerning the right to education after the inclusion of Article 21A in the Constitution.

At the present time, the judiciary remains inaccessible for aggrieved right-bearers. Therefore, as the second part of this section shall argue, PIL initiated by persons and groups such as human rights advocates, NGOs, and so on (in short, the 'civil society') may play an important role for raising questions concerning the (in)adequacy of the grievance redress system as well as other doctrinal and implementation questions in court. Such groups should, therefore, focus more specifically on the question of access to justice. The existence of Article 21A gives a stronger case for the judiciary's willingness to accept petitions calling for such measures as PIL, in spite of balance of power considerations still being raised as an argument against the institution of PIL itself.

Once the cases are brought to the judiciary (realistically, most likely through PILs) it may thus adjudicate not only on the implementation of the Right to Education Act, but also decide to what extent the Act fulfils the constitutional obligation. This includes the question to what extent the obligation to provide accessible enforcement mechanisms is concerned. The courts could then also award remedies accordingly. How far-reaching these remedies will be is ultimately up to the courts to decide. However, the existence of Article 21A creates a strong case for what has been described as 'structural injunctions', which have also been shown to be most beneficial to the poor, as the final part of this section shall explain.

## Possible Degrees of Judicial Activism

As far as measuring the design of the grievance redress regime against the constitutional obligation arising out of Articles 21A and 32 is concerned, a high court or the Supreme Court may restrict itself to stating that the system created by the Right to Education Act, the Child Rights Commissions Act, and the respective state rules is not sufficient. It may then rule that the State must either improve the grievance redress regime, make the judiciary more accessible, or offer other, more accessible alternative enforcement mechanisms, ultimately leaving the choice for or against certain paths of rights enforcement up to policymakers.

A court may also suggest, or even order, that specific measures ought to be taken to bring the existing system in line with the constitutional obligation. As mentioned above, considering the fact that the legislature has already chosen one of the several options for compensating lack of access to justice described in Chapter 4 for the right to education, suggesting specific measures to make that system fulfil the constitutional obligation would still be a relatively modest intrusion into the competences of the legislature. Such measures could include enabling the Child Rights Commission to make binding 'judgments'.

The most intrusive option, on the other hand, is a court making policy decisions itself rather than ordering the legislature and/or executive to become active. Past adjudication shows that the Indian Supreme Court is not averse to taking even this 'extreme' route.[35]

Therefore, while the constitutional obligations described above and in the previous chapters have focused on what may be considered clear or indisputable obligations for the State to fulfil under Article 21A,[36] the judiciary's definition of obligations and the remedies that it might ask for in given cases might go far beyond that.

[35] See, for instance, the case of *Vishaka*, in which the Court effectively created legislation to protect women from sexual harassment at work (see *Vishaka & Ors* v. *State of Rajasthan & Ors* MANU/SC/0786/1997 [Supreme Court of India, 13 August 1997]).

[36] Including providing for accessible and effective enforcement mechanisms for the right, at least concerning such entitlements as have been delineated in the Act (when Article 21A is read with Article 32).

## Role of Civil Society: PIL for Implementation of Right to Education Act and Challenging Right to Education Act

As explained in Chapter 3, the higher judiciary is not just obliged to test the implementation of the Right to Education Act, but also its constitutionality. Importantly, whether or not the Act lives up to the constitutional obligations also includes the question whether the grievance redress mechanisms may compensate for the lack of access to justice that inhibits right-bearers from claiming their benefits (as guaranteed by the Act) themselves.

Obviously, because of the lack of access to the higher judiciary, the right-bearers themselves will not be able to raise these questions in court. Therefore, for the enforcement of Article 21A, the institution of PIL must play an important role.

While PIL does not in itself compensate for lack of access to justice by the right-bearers, as has been noted in Chapter 4, it may still be an important tool in strengthening mechanisms for access to justice. Members of the civil society (for example, NGOs, human rights advocates, or advocacy groups) could, in addition to pointing out shortcomings in the general implementation of the Right to Education Act, raise the question of effective enforcement and lack of access to justice in the Supreme Court and the high courts through PIL. The courts could then adjudicate on the entire scope of Article 21A.[37]

Judges could then decide whether the State has fulfilled its constitutional obligations by creating the Right to Education Act and the state rules under the Act. This would include the substantive contents of the right, for example, infrastructural and quality standards. They could also decide whether or not the Act lives up to the State's constitutional obligation to provide the procedural scope of the right, that is, assess whether the Act provides effective and accessible enforceability by designing a functioning grievance redress system. Of course, the courts could also assess the implementation of these provisions in practice.

[37] In addition to the option of them acting entirely on their own in '*suo motu* petitions', which is, however, a rare occurrence.

In doing so, the courts would end up measuring both legislative as well as executive measures (or lack thereof) against the 'public interest', detached from individual cases. This raises the question to what extent such intrusions into the legislative and executive powers are justified—generally, but also specifically in the context of adjudication under Article 21A.

As has already been mentioned, the Indian higher judiciary, especially the Supreme Court, is known for such 'intrusions'.[38] Still, judges of the Supreme Court have criticized instances of 'law-making' by the Court.[39] Recent scholarly opinion, as

[38] Consequently, Mehta describes that the Supreme Court is 'a *politically* significant institution' and 'a powerful actor in Indian politics': 'There is a not a single important issue of political life in India that has not been, by accident or design, profoundly shaped by its interventions'. The courts, he states, 'participate and collaborate in governing India' (see Pratap B. Mehta, 'India's Judiciary: The Promise of Uncertainty', in *The Supreme Court Versus the Constitution: A Challenge to Federalism*, ed. Pran Chopra [New Delhi, Thousand Oaks: SAGE, 2006], 162).

[39] Justice Hidayatullah, speaking in 1984, agreed that within limits, 'a little incursion into law making' may be permissible. He also stated that drawing the attention of the legislature or executive to a 'flaw' may be permissible in other cases. However, developments such as the court basing its judgments entirely on the investigation of its own registrar or accepting letters by anyone as petitions for the sake of a 'pro-active goal-oriented approach' may be described as 'annihilation of all procedure'. He criticized an expectation by some for the courts to 'run the government' (see M. Hidayatullah, 'Highways and Bylanes of Justice', *Supreme Court Cases [Journal]*, no. 2 [1984]: 5). In the case of *Divisional Manager, Aravali Golf Club*, the Court itself stated that judges must not try to 'run the government'. 'They must have modesty and humility, and not behave like Emperors' (see *Divisional Manager, Aravali Golf Club & Anr.* v. *Chander Hass & Anr.* MANU/SC/4463/2007, 20 [Supreme Court of India, 6 December 2007]). Similarly, in *Suresh Kumar Koushal*, the judgment on the appeal against the Delhi High Court's *Naz Foundation* judgment (*Naz Foundation* v. *Government of NCT of Delhi* MANU/DE/0869/2009 (Delhi High Court, 2 July 2009)), the Supreme Court ruled that when testing the constitutionality of a law, judges must work with a certain amount of self-restraint and with the 'presumption of constitutionality'. It also stated that '[i]t is [...] apposite to say that unless a clear constitutional violation is

mentioned in Chapter 3, voices more criticisms against an ideological shift in the Court's judgments rather than judicial activism in itself. Still, there are voices that criticize a violation of the principle of separation of power in several of the Supreme Court's judgments, noting that some of them 'amount to legislating like a legislature'.[40]

However, one may observe that such 'judicial excessivism'[41] is mostly criticized whenever the scholar does not agree with the result of the judgment. Sometimes, the same scholars hail the judiciary acting like the legislature in some cases and criticize them for such violations of the separation of powers principle in others.[42] While the Court's activism, including intrusions in the executive's and legislature's spheres, were generally praised in the late 1970s and 1980s, when the Court had followed a 'pro-poor' strand, it is exactly this positive stance that may have allowed it to become 'activist' in a direction that is now seen negatively

---

proved, this Court is not empowered to strike down a law merely by virtue of its falling into disuse or the perception of the society having changed as regards the legitimacy of its purpose and its need' (see *Suresh Kumar Koushal & Anr.* v. *Naz Foundation & Ors* MANU/SC/1278/2013, 32, 33 [Supreme Court of India, 11 December 2013]).

40 Sathe argues that this constitutes 'judicial excessivism that fl[ies] in the face of the doctrine of separation of powers', that 'the making of an entirely new law' by the judiciary 'is not a legitimate judicial function', and that it is 'a well-established policy that a court of law cannot and should not ask the legislature to pass a law or not to pass a law in a particular manner' (see S.P. Sathe, *Judicial Activism in India*, 2nd edition [Delhi, Oxford: Oxford University Press, 2003], 250, 282).

41 Sathe, *Judicial Activism in India*, 282.

42 Sathe uses one case in which the Court decided in favour of landlords rather than tenants (see, *Malpe Vishwanath Acharya & Ors* v. *State of Maharashtra & Anr.* MANU/SC/0905/1998 (Supreme Court of India, 19 December 1997)) as an illustration for his argument arguing that by judging in favour of the landlords, 'the Court had clearly exceeded its limits', as '[i]t should never have taken up the cause of an economically powerful group', as, in doing so, it 'acted against the philosophy of judicial activism' (see Sathe, *Judicial Activism in India*, 282).

by the same observers.[43] The previous 'pro-activism' climate may have led to judges believing that they were 'all powerful and fully justified in incorporating their own understanding of the values of the Constitution into their decisions'.[44] Therefore, in hindsight, from the point of view of progressive scholars who are critical of the judiciary's 'neo-liberal turn', 'the deification of activist judges' may have been a mistake.[45]

Thus, whether or not judicial activism and judicial encroachment into the spheres of the legislature and executive are justified should be assessed from a politically neutral, legal point of view, rather than an ideological point of view. Also, concerning Article 21A, there is an even stronger constitutional case for extensive adjudication through PIL, even though the judiciary may act as a 'secondary government' in these cases to a considerable degree.

In right to education cases, possible judgments by the higher judiciary could be quite far-reaching, especially if they are brought to the court as PIL. An 'isolated' case initiated by an aggrieved individual might raise the question whether a child should be admitted in school, whether a child had been discriminated against by a teacher, or whether a new school should be built in a village. A PIL would usually raise much broader questions, for example, whether the central government should provide more funds for implementation of the Right to Education Act in the states (see Section 7 of the Right to Education Act), or whether the State should create

[43] Thiruvengadam observes that 'an astonishingly instrumental vision advanced for the judiciary' in 1980s scholarly literature, which may have allowed the Supreme Court judges to 'flex their muscles, particularly in the 1990s, when the weakened political executive had no choice but to tolerate such judicial adventurism' (see Arun Thiruvengadam, 'Revisiting the Role of the Judiciary in Plural Societies [1987]: A Quarter-Century Restrospective on Public Interest Litigation and the Global South', in *Comparative Constitutionalism in South Asia*, ed. Sunil Khilnani, 1st edition [New Delhi: Oxford University Press, 2013], 358 et seq.).

[44] Thiruvengadam, 'Revisiting the Role of the Judiciary in Plural Societies', 358.

[45] Thiruvengadam, 'Revisiting the Role of the Judiciary in Plural Societies', 359. He therefore also cautions progressive scholars against calling for a return of more progressive activist judges.

schemes to prevent discrimination against children in schools, or whether it should take certain steps to implement such schemes. Cases raised by individuals might lead to the courts assessing such questions as well (if, for instance, a school could not be built because of lack of funds in a state), but with a PIL, a petitioner may directly focus on these larger implementation questions independently of such individual cases.

Still, the judiciary entertaining such extensive questions raised through PIL is justified. This justification is based on the existence of Article 21A. As described in Chapter 2, the insertion of Article 21A into the constitutional text is somewhat of a climax of the developments around Article 21/the right to life, directive principles, and socio-economic rights adjudication in India. These developments are also intrinsically linked to the 'invention' of PIL.[46] While the first PIL cases focused on civil and political rights,[47] it quickly became a common tool for socio-economic rights adjudication. This is not surprising, given the fact that people for whom socio-economic rights are most relevant are usually the ones who

[46] Robinson sees a direct causality between the two, stating that '[t]he growth of article 21 jurisprudence also led to the development of a new form of legal practice, called public interest litigation' (see Nick Robinson, 'Expanding Judiciaries: India and the Rise of the Good Governance Court', *Washington University Global Studies Law Review* 8, no. 1 [2009]: 43). Similarly, Thiruvengadam notes that socio-economic rights jurisprudence in India started with the foundation laid out in the case of *Maneka Gandhi* v. *Union of India* MANU/SC/0133/1978 (Supreme Court of India, 25 January 1978), as discussed in Chapter 2, and led to a stronger emphasis of socio-economic rights cases—rather than the civil and political rights that the Supreme Court had focused on before—and in this context, 'judges in India adapted and modified American public interest law strategies in innovative ways to fashion [India's] own PIL jurisprudence' (see Thiruvengadam, 'Revisiting the Role of the Judiciary in Plural Societies', 348–9). Khosla notes that the procedural developments around PIL 'took place almost alongside an important substantive one: the 'right to life' [...] was interpreted to include several socio-economic guarantees' (see Madhav Khosla, 'Making Social Rights Conditional: Lessons from India', *International Journal of Constitutional Law* 8, no. 4 [2010]: 743).

[47] For instance, those of prisoners, as discussed in Chapter 4.

lack financial and other means to access the courts, as well as the fact that lack of implementation of these rights often involves larger policy issues. Consequently, many of the famous socio-economic rights decisions are PILs.[48] Article 21 has therefore been described as the substantive link and PIL as the procedural link between Parts III and IV of the Constitution (that is, fundamental rights and directive principles).[49]

Furthermore, in the case of the right to education, the legislature did not only passively accept the judgments stating that education is a fundamental right (as a part of the right to life), but it also actively confirmed this qualification by adding a new justiciable right to the fundamental rights catalogue. The constitutional amendment adding Article 21A was passed at a time when extensive adjudication on the right to life and PIL had already become well-established practices. By adding Article 21A, the legislature confirmed both of these practices. It was aware of the fact that socio-economic rights adjudication commonly occurs through PIL, and therefore (with a *unanimous* vote in the Lok Sabha) gave constitutional sanction to this form of adjudication, at least as far as the right to education is concerned.

Therefore, the existence of Article 21A not only empowers the judiciary to adjudicate on the right to education (and also to test implementing legislation), but also to do this by accepting PILs that raise larger policy and implementation questions. While one may see the institution of PIL, the far-reaching judgments resulting from such petitions, and 'judicial law-making' in general critically, one must at the same time accept that Article 21A permits it and even calls for it.

## The Benefits of 'Structural Injunctions'

As described in Chapter 3, one may see a tendency in the Indian higher judiciary, specifically the Supreme Court, to 'compensate'

[48] Though some like the 'Right to Education decisions' of *Mohini Jain* and *Unni Krishnan* are not. On those cases, see Chapters 2 and 3.

[49] P.P. Craig and S.L. Deshpande, 'Rights, Autonomy and Process: Public Interest Litigation in India', *Oxford Journal of Legal Studies* 9, no. 3 (1989): 365.

for its activism in the field of socio-economic rights by first 'creating' them, but then giving a relatively narrow definition of their scope. The judiciary appears to be particularly activist by first solemnly declaring that the given right must be read into the right to (dignified) life, but then actually awards somewhat weak remedies. However, Article 21A not only permits departing from such judicial self-restraint. Instead, whenever the government remains passive it even *calls* for far-reaching judgments, including those which have been described as 'structural injunctions', also because those may benefit the poor the most.

As argued in Chapter 3, the 'conditional social rights approach' described by Khosla[50] is not permissible in the case of the right to education. This also extends to the procedural aspects of its enforcement. Interpreted 'conditionally', the judiciary would restrain itself to testing whether or not the grievance redress provisions of the Right to Education Act and Child Rights Commissions Act are implemented properly, not whether they are themselves sufficient to fulfil the State's constitutional obligations. It would therefore not entertain the question whether or not they have to be amended or additional provisions have to be created. However, because of the existence of Article 21A read with Article 32, there is an *explicit* constitutional obligation to provide effective means of enforcement for the right to education through independent judges.

Therefore, the State must provide justiciability in reality by creating an effective and accessible judiciary. If the State chooses to compensate for access to the judiciary by providing alternative mechanisms, then it has to create a functioning and effective enforcement system. In order to achieve this goal, it must delineate its workings in statutory laws *and* implement these laws effectively.

If the judiciary 'creates' new fundamental rights itself, then it may also define their scope, as it goes beyond the constitutional

[50] Which, as explained in Chapter 3, may also not fully describe how the Supreme Court has in the past applied socio-economic rights, as the example of the *Right to food* case shows. This case shall be described more extensively below.

text. However, as described in Chapter 3, for a right that the Constitution guarantees itself, this is not permissible to the same extent. For such constitutionally guaranteed rights, the judiciary cannot limit adjudication to existing schemes rather than ordering the alteration or extension of existing schemes, or even creation of new schemes if the current schemes are not sufficient. Otherwise, the legislature could freely limit the scope of the positive effect (that is, obligations to *fulfil* and *protect*, as described in Chapter 3) of any constitutionally guaranteed right. Therefore, the Court must go beyond a 'conditional' application of the right to education. This includes the right to be able to effectively enforce that right against the State.

Because of this, the Court may even go as far as employing a strategy of 'structural injunctions'. Structural injunctions are court orders which may be described as 'aggressive, unconventional enforcement strategies'[51] that bring 'broad orders aimed at reforming institutional practice over a long period of time'.[52] Other forms of injunctions are an 'individualized model' in which 'courts give a single remedy to a single plaintiff',[53] or a 'negative injunction model' in which 'courts strike down benefit cuts or other laws that change the social benefits being given in the status quo'.[54] Landau argues that only 'structural injunctions' will effectively benefit the poor and thus further the implementation of socio-economic rights.[55] To illustrate, he cites several examples of cases and their effect in different developing countries.

The author recognizes that courts are more likely to choose 'individualized' or 'negative' injunctions, as such do not require that courts interfere in public policy, meaning that they are also less likely 'to get into trouble'.[56] At the same time, these two

[51] David Landau, 'The Reality of Social Rights Enforcement', *Harvard International Law Journal* 53, no. 1 (2012): 192.

[52] Landau, 'The Reality of Social Rights Enforcement', 201.

[53] Landau, 'The Reality of Social Rights Enforcement', 192.

[54] Landau, 'The Reality of Social Rights Enforcement', 192.

[55] Landau, 'The Reality of Social Rights Enforcement'.

[56] Landau, 'The Reality of Social Rights Enforcement', 196. This is particularly the case for the 'negative injunction model', as the 'individualized model' may still have large aggregate effects on the public budget,

models of injunctions are more likely to benefit middle class and even upper income groups, rather than furthering actual socio-economic change for the benefit of the poor.[57] As far as individual enforcement is concerned, relatively wealthy petitioners have the advantage of awareness about their rights and of being able to 'navigate' the legal system.[58] Negative injunctions might often not benefit the poor, or at least not the very poor, as such injunctions are only advantageous for such persons who already own some assets or are already recipients of some sort of benefits.[59] Structural enforcement, on the other hand, may be primarily targeted at and may also be beneficial for lower income groups. However, this method is actually used quite rarely.[60]

Landau illustrates the (non-)effectiveness of the different approaches by using the example of the Colombian Constitutional Court.[61] Since the late 1990s, the number of individualized socio-economic rights cases in Columbia has grown considerably, with the Court becoming increasingly often concerned with health

---

which may cause resistance by the other branches of power. However, judges might still be particularly open to employing this method, as the individual decisions are to them 'familiar court-like work' and as they do not involve 'complex management issues' (see Landau, 'The Reality of Social Rights Enforcement', 199).

57 Landau, 'The Reality of Social Rights Enforcement', 199.

58 Landau, 'The Reality of Social Rights Enforcement', 200.

59 Landau, 'The Reality of Social Rights Enforcement', 200.

60 Landau, 'The Reality of Social Rights Enforcement', 201.

61 He believes this example to be particularly insightful because that Court has been very active in enforcing socio-economic rights, because it has used all three types of remedies, because it is committed to socio-economic change, because it has been vested with a large amount of power, and because its magistrates 'have generally stated that they may legitimately substitute for the roles of other branches of government if necessary in order to further constitutional values'. Therefore, 'one would expect that were *any* court going to be successful in targeting lower income groups with its social rights jurisprudence, it would be the Colombian Constitutional Court' (see Landau, 'The Reality of Social Rights Enforcement', 202).

care and pension cases.[62] The Court's system of constitutional complaints (called *tutelas*) allows comparatively easy and inexpensive access to the Court.[63] Also, tutelas were designed to only be invoked by marginalized groups.[64] Nonetheless, as time progressed, the percentage of tutelas coming from relatively wealthy petitioners increased steadily.[65]

Landau confirms that these observations may, at least to an extent, be generalized with a comparative outlook: he highlights the findings of the empirical study by Hoffmann and Bentes on right to health litigation in Brazil,[66] according to which the Brazilian judiciary almost exclusively uses individualized remedies, and

[62] By 2003, half of the constitutional complaints dealt with these issues (see Landau, 'The Reality of Social Rights Enforcement', 202, 209 et seq.).

[63] Landau believes a tutela to be 'among the cheapest and easiest devices of its kind in the world [...] Thus, these results are likely to hold even more strongly in other systems' (see Landau, 'The Reality of Social Rights Enforcement', 205, 210).

[64] Landau, 'The Reality of Social Rights Enforcement', 208.

[65] By 2003, the petitioners in 73 per cent of all right to health tutelas 'were filed by members of the contributory regime, or those who generally have formal employment and a reasonable income'. One reason for this development may be that 'virtually any household in the country' could show that it is overwhelmed by certain expensive medical costs. Still, relatively affluent petitioners have the 'competitive advantage' of rights awareness and at least a certain amount of financial means. As far as pension cases were concerned, the petitioners were persons who were entitled to state pensions in the first place, and thus already comparatively privileged (see Landau, 'The Reality of Social Rights Enforcement', 209, 213, 214). Also, some of the tutelas were even filed by former congressmen and judges—Landau cites the case of a former Supreme Court judge as an extreme, but 'illustrative' example (see Landau, 'The Reality of Social Rights Enforcement', 213).

[66] The authors note that '[m]ost of the demands are individual demands, for specific health-care-related goods and services and are concentrated in the more developed states' (see Florian F. Hoffmann and Fernando R.N.M. Bentes, 'Accountability for Social and Economic Rights in Brazil', in *Courting Social Justice: Judicial Enforcement of Social and Economic Rights in the Developing World*, ed. Varun Gauri and Daniel M. Brinks [Cambridge, New York: Cambridge University Press, 2008], 101).

according to which the poor in the country often refrain from approaching the judiciary because of a general lack of rights consciousness and trust in the judiciary.[67]

It appears that this almost exclusive focus on individualized remedies by courts adjudicating socio-economic rights leads to a situation in which there is neither much of a positive effect on the performance of the bureaucracy in implementing benefits nor on the actual living conditions of the poor.[68]

There are, however, two cases in which the Colombian Constitutional Court issued structural orders. These are the only instances in which it did so 'in a full-fledged way'.[69] In a 2004 case, the Court created an entirely new scheme concerning aid for displaced persons.[70] In 2008,[71] it used structural injunctions ordering alterations to the entire state health care system, which had already existed previously, but was malfunctioning.[72] In both cases, the Court was able to get the other branches of power to become (more) active in the respective field.[73] However, the progress in the health care case has been a lot more limited, which

67 Hoffmann and Bentes, 'Accountability for Social and Economic Rights in Brazil', 113. He also cites the work by Ferraz, according to which 'the richest states [in Brazil] file the bulk of the claims' (see Octavio L. Motta Ferraz, 'Brazil: Health Inequalities, Rights, and Courts: The Social Impact of the Judicialization of Health', in *Litigating Health Rights: Can Courts Bring More Justice to Health?*, ed. Alicia E. Yamin and Siri Gloppen [Cambridge, MA: Human Rights Program, Harvard Law School, Harvard University Press, 2011], 87–8).

68 Landau, 'The Reality of Social Rights Enforcement', 232.

69 Landau, 'The Reality of Social Rights Enforcement', 223.

70 See Sentencia T-025/04 (Constitutional Court of Colombia, 22 January 2004), http://www.corteconstitucional.gov.co/relatoria/2004/t%2D025%2D04.htm, accessed on 17 November 2015, summarized in Landau, 'The Reality of Social Rights Enforcement', 223 et seq. Importantly, there had previously been no public policy at all.

71 See Sentencia T-760/08 (Constitutional Court of Colombia, 31 July 2008), http://www.corteconstitucional.gov.co/relatoria/2008/t%2D760%2D08.htm, accessed on 17 November 2015, summarized at Landau, 'The Reality of Social Rights Enforcement', 223 et seq.

72 Landau, 'The Reality of Social Rights Enforcement', 223–4.

73 Landau, 'The Reality of Social Rights Enforcement', 225–6.

indicates that structural injunction cases require certain contexts to work.[74] In the displaced persons case, it had been advantageous that the Court was able to write 'on a virtually clean slate', while in the health care case, the Court had to attempt improving a well-developed, but flawed system, fighting policymakers who believed the modifications were too costly.[75] Still, one may conclude unlike the other two kinds of remedies, the structural injunction approach may successfully target lower-income groups and may also effectively lead to positive changes in the bureaucracy.[76] However, managing only these two cases already takes up a large amount of the Court's resources.[77]

Internationally, structural enforcement cases are so rare that this 'remedy [...] exists in journal articles but is almost never seen in reality'.[78] One of the few examples is the Indian Supreme Court's *Right to food* case,[79] which has 'striking' similarities to the Colombian displaced persons case.[80] The case shall be dealt with in more detail below.

## Conclusion

The existence of Article 21A gives a mandate to the higher judiciary to adjudicate legislation in the field of education, the State's policy decisions, as well as the (in)adequacy of implementation measures. While the discretion given to the courts is especially wide when combining these substantive powers with the procedural aspect of PIL, the historical background of the constitutional amendment shows that such wide discretion was intended by the legislature when amending the Constitution.

The higher judiciary therefore has a mandate for strong 'structural injunctions' concerning the right to education as well. But

[74] Landau, 'The Reality of Social Rights Enforcement', 225.

[75] Landau, 'The Reality of Social Rights Enforcement', 227–8.

[76] Landau, 'The Reality of Social Rights Enforcement', 230.

[77] Landau, 'The Reality of Social Rights Enforcement', 225.

[78] Landau, 'The Reality of Social Rights Enforcement', 235.

[79] *People's Union for Civil Liberties* v. *Union of India and Others* (Supreme Court of India).

[80] Landau, 'The Reality of Social Rights Enforcement', 237.

this makes the courts face the challenge of being an effective 'secondary government'. This raises the question to what extent the higher judiciary, specifically the Supreme Court, is capable of living up to this practical challenge. If it is not, then again, little tangible benefit will be gained from its theoretical powers.

## Distribution of Micromanagement and Macromanagement: A Superior System to 'Conventional' Socio-Economic Rights Adjudication?

An individual aggrieved person will only be motivated to claim their right in court or through a court-like system if they can expect concrete and tangible remedies for their grievances. Swift remedies are especially important concerning a child's education, where every year lost can only be compensated for with much difficulty, if at all. Grievance redress systems at the lower level should be able to provide swift and effective resolution at least to a certain kind of grievances. This would be possible for those grievances that do not necessarily require that larger policy decisions be made first.

Larger policy decisions such as an increase in budgetary allocations can often not be taken instantly, and will also often have on-the-ground effects only with a certain amount of delay. It may not be adequate to expect parents who have very limited time and resources to approach the judiciary seeking orders for such policy decisions that may only benefit the next generation of children.

The Constitution had designed a system that gave powers for fundamental rights enforcement exclusively to the higher judiciary. Meanwhile, the question of alternative enforcement mechanisms only arose because of the inaccessibility of the judiciary. But the grievance redress system cannot, and should not, fully replace the judiciary as far as fundamental rights enforcement is concerned. Instead, both systems may be most powerful if they complement each other. In fact, a system that combines lower-level grievance redress outside of the judiciary and fundamental rights adjudication through writs at the higher level may actually be superior to the system that was originally designed by the Constituent Assembly. This may be achieved by combining the grievance redress system with PIL.

Aggrieved persons themselves may submit their 'simpler' grievances to the grievance redress systems at the 'bottom', with some hope that their issues will be resolved quickly. More complicated and broader policy issues, on the other hand, may be raised at the 'top' by third parties acting in public interest. This set-up may, if designed properly, be more adequate than raising all questions with the higher judiciary, that is, at the 'top'.

This section shall offer some suggestions and an outlook on how such a system may work in practice. Concerning 'structural injunctions' for cases raised as PIL to be taken by the higher judiciary, the experience with adjudication of the right to food may offer some guidelines. Against that backdrop, one may make some careful predictions about how a 'division of labour' between the lower-level grievance redress system and the higher judiciary may work.

## The Right to Food Adjudication: Possible Blueprint?

The *Right to food* case is an example of the Supreme Court both defining the scope of a right broadly *and* awarding strong and creative remedies that may be qualified as 'structural injunctions'.[81] Importantly, in addition to this substantive significance, the case also shows how a civil society campaign may influence and even drive forward socio-economic rights litigation in the Indian judiciary.

Interestingly, the case of *People's Union for Civil Liberties*,[82] also known as the *Right to food* case, remained pending for more than 15 years.[83] For that period of time, the Supreme Court did

[81] Landau explicitly names it as an example for this mode of injunctions (see Landau, 'The Reality of Social Rights Enforcement', 237).

[82] *People's Union for Civil Liberties* v. *Union of India and Others*.

[83] The case was only disposed of in February of 2017 (see the documents at https://www.sci.gov.in/case-status for Writ Petition [Civil] 196/2001). On 10 February 2017, it was dismissed as the right to food is

not pass any judgment. Instead, it chose to pass a series of interim orders.[84] At the same time, it continuously monitored the implementation of these orders, the policy decisions taken by the central and state governments, and on-the-ground developments concerning the provision of food to citizens. It also monitored related issues, such as (lack of) shelter for homeless persons in cities in winters.[85] The *Right to food* case is not the only one of its kind. In fact, the Court had employed the strategy of keeping cases pending in order to continuously pass orders several times.[86] But this case is perhaps the most extensive one as far as the strategies used are concerned.[87]

The case was initiated by the PUCL as a PIL against the Union of India, the Food Corporation of India,[88] and six state governments in 2001.[89] The petitioner called for government action because

---

not governed by the National Food Security Act, 2013 (see https://www.sci.gov.in/jonew/ropor/rop/all/901064.pdf, accessed on 18 August 2018).

[84] Summaries of and links to individual orders are available at http://www.righttofoodindia.org/orders/interimorders.html and at https://www.sci.gov.in/case-status for Writ Petition (Civil) 196/2001, accessed on 13 August 2018.

[85] See the orders of 20 January 2010; 27 January 2010; 10 February 2010; 16 March 2010; 5 May 2010; 21 July 2010; 15 November 2010; 24 November 2010; 26 November 2011; 16 December 2010; 3 January 2011; 7 January 2011; 27 February 2012.

[86] See Thiruvengadam, 'Revisiting the Role of the Judiciary in Plural Societies', 350 et seq. Baxi originally described this strategy of one of '"creeping" jurisdiction', which 'typically consists in taking over the direction of administration in a particular arena from the executive' (see Upendra Baxi, 'Taking Suffering Seriously: Social Action Litigation in the Supreme Court of India', *Third World Legal Studies*, 1985, 122).

[87] Nick Robinson in his article, 'Closing the Implementation Gap: Grievance Redress and India's Social Welfare Programs', *Columbia Journal of Transnational Law* 53, no. 2 (2015): 342, calls the case the 'largest and best-known instance' of PIL cases.

[88] A corporation established by the central government to fulfil its food policies under the Food Corporations Act, 1964.

[89] The original petition is available at http://www.righttofoodindia.org/case/petition.html, accessed on 15 August 2018.

of starvation deaths in the state of Rajasthan after a drought.[90] The situation was aggrieved by the fact that the central and state governments failed to properly implement food distribution and employment relief schemes.[91] In Rajasthan itself, a surplus amount of food that was available was not adequately provided through the PDS.[92] The Supreme Court relied on its precedent declaring a right to food to be part of the right to life under Article 21.[93] It initially ordered that the respondents (the Union of India, the states, and the Food Corporation of India) provide affidavits concerning the (lack of) implementation of food provision schemes. It also ordered that all PDS in the six states must reopen and 'start functioning' within a week.[94] The Court later extended the list of respondents to the Union of India, the Food Corporation of India, and 16 states and union territories,[95] and, eventually, passed orders binding all states and union territories in the country.[96]

Subsequent orders obliged the states to inform the central government about the number of 'below poverty line families'

[90] For the background history of the case, see Lauren Birchfield and Jessica Corsi, 'Between Starvation and Globalization: Realizing the Right to Food in India', *Michigan Journal of International Law* 31, no. 4 (2010): 697 et seq.

[91] See Birchfield and Corsi, 'Between Starvation and Globalization', 697–8.

[92] See Birchfield and Corsi, 'Between Starvation and Globalization', 698.

[93] The Court had declared that the right to life 'includes the right to live with human dignity and all that goes along with it, namely, the bare necessaries of life such as adequate nutrition' in *Francis Coralie Mullin* v. *The Administrator, Union Territory of Delhi and Others* MANU/SC/0492/1981 (Supreme Court of India, 13 January 1981)—a case which the petitioners in the *Right to food* case had referred to in their initial 2001 petition (see the petition available at http://www.righttofoodindia.org/case/petition.html at 26, accessed on 15 August 2018). The Court explicitly referred to the 'right to life' in orders of 2 May 2003 and 20 April 2004. However, it did not indulge in doctrinal questions in its orders, instead, it immediately proceeded to define state obligations.

[94] See the order of 23 July 2001.

[95] See the order of 17 September 2001.

[96] See, for instance, the order of 7 October 2004.

eligible under one food provision scheme.[97] The states were also to inform the central government's cabinet secretary about the status of implementation of relevant schemes 'and if all or any of the Schemes have not been implemented, then the reasons for the same', with the central government being ordered to subsequently 'take necessary action in order to ensure implementation' and to submit a status report.[98] Upon identification of eligible families, the states were also ordered to commence provision of a specific amount of food (25 kg of grains per family per month under the 'Targeted Public Distribution Scheme') by a specific date.[99] In order to create awareness about entitlements, the Court also directed state media to 'adequately publicise various Schemes and this order'.[100] The Court also called for a computerization of the food provision programmes.[101]

In addition to the provision of food, the Court also gave orders aimed at bringing citizens into a position that they could 'feed themselves'. Gram panchayats (that is, village level administration bodies) were ordered to frame 'employment generation proposals' under the *Sampoorna Gramin Rozgar Yojana* scheme in order to bring village population into a position in which they may sustain themselves.[102] The Gram Sabhas (institutionalized town hall meetings of a village)[103] were given the function of conducting social audits into food and employment schemes, and of reporting all instances of misuse of funds.[104] The employment programme focused on agricultural wage earners, non-agricultural unskilled wage earners, marginal farmers, and SCs and STs, for whom the

97 See the order of 17 September 2001.

98 See the order of 17 September 2001.

99 See the order of 28 November 2001. The provision was ordered to commence latest by 1 January 2002.

100 See the order of 28 November 2001.

101 See the order of 12 August 2010.

102 See the order of 8 May 2002.

103 Robinson, 'Closing the Implementation Gap', 340.

104 See the order of 8 May 2002: the CEO of the Zila Panchayat were ordered to record such complaints and 'scrutinize the action taken by all the implementing agencies', and the 'responsibility for implementation of the order of this Court shall be that of the CEO'.

states were to ensure wage payment on a weekly basis.[105] For this, the central government was ordered to provide funds under different employment generation schemes.[106]

Importantly, the Court also ordered the provision of free mid-day meals to children in all government and government-assisted elementary schools in all states, giving specific instructions concerning the minimum calories and protein content to be provided to each child each day of school.[107] It, therefore, ordered the implementation of a scheme that had previously been a voluntary national programme.[108] It also extended its scope by, for instance, ordering that mid-day meals must be provided in drought-affected areas even during summer vacations.[109]

To support the strategy of continuous orders over several years in the same case, rather than coming to one singular judgment at one point in time, the Supreme Court also created a commission with the task of monitoring implementation of its orders.[110] The commissioners were given the task to recommend 'a course of action to ensure compliance with this Court's orders'. The state governments were, in turn, ordered to follow the recommendations and to report compliance with them.[111] The commissioners, who were former bureaucrats,[112] were empowered to seek assistance of individuals and 'reliable organizations' in the states. Those individuals and organizations were, in turn, 'directed to fully cooperate'.[113] To ensure that the commissioners can work effectively, the state governments were ordered to appoint government

[105] See the order of 8 May 2002.

[106] See the order of 8 May 2002.

[107] See the order of 28 November 2001.

[108] See Robinson, 'Expanding Judiciaries', 50.

[109] See the order of 20 April 2004. It also referred to a mere suggestion by the prime minister, who stated that the scheme could be extended up to 10th standard, and called for the Government of India to provide an affidavit informing the Court by what time such an extension could be possible.

[110] See the order of 29 October 2002.

[111] See the order of 8 May 2002.

[112] See the order of 8 May 2002.

[113] See the order of 8 May 2002.

officials as 'Assistants to the Commissioners'.[114] Each state and the central government were to each appoint one nodal officer, whose task would be to provide full access to relevant records, and to provide information to the commissioners.[115] The commissioners and nodal officers thus essentially became ombudsmen for the Court-ordered social welfare programmes.[116]

The Court also aimed to continuously ensure compliance with its orders by directing that schemes 'shall not be discontinued or restricted in any way without the prior approval of this Court'.[117] Consequently, when the Union of India planned to modify an existing scheme and to create a new scheme (*Janani Suraksha Yojana* [JSY]) under which some of the benefits of the old scheme (National Maternity Benefit Scheme [NMBS]) were to be supplied, it sought prior permission from the Court.[118] The Court pointed out that the coverage under the new scheme was below the coverage of the previous one and reported that the central government, after discussions with the commissioner appointed by the Court, decided to modify the new scheme to continue the benefits of the NMBS.[119]

At a later stage (in 2006), reacting to a lack of monitoring over the sums allotted for the PDS by the central government, the Court created an additional 'Central Vigilance Committee' to be headed by a retired Supreme Court judge who would be assisted by one of the commissioners.[120] The Central Vigilance Committee's task is to take measures against 'large scale corruption' in the service delivery process.[121] Based on the findings of the Committee, the Court gave concrete policy suggestions to the government. For instance, it recommended that before aiming for universal food

114 See the order of 29 October 2002.

115 See the order of 29 October 2002.

116 Robinson, 'Closing the Implementation Gap', 342.

117 See the order of 27 April 2004.

118 See the order of 11 November 2007.

119 See the order of 11 November 2007.

120 See the order of 12 July 2006. The Committee was also called 'Wadhwa Committee', named after the retired judge leading it.

121 See the order of 12 July 2006.

security, the government should ensure that at least the vulnerable sections of the society be provided with food, and that in order to ensure that this is done, the central government 'may consider distributing food on an individual basis rather than on a family basis', as it had been done previously.[122] The Court also requested that the Committee identify the poorest districts and poorest segments of the society, and ordered that available food stocks be allocated to the 150 poorest districts 'or other poorer segments of the society on the recommendation of the Committee' in consultation with the representatives of the Government of India and the case's petitioners.[123] Furthermore, the Court empowered the Committee to co-opt 'any individual or organization to assist them'.[124]

The Court, in addition to merely expressing a certain degree of frustration with officials not following its orders as desired[125] and reminding the state governments that it is their 'constitutional duty' to implement its orders,[126] also explicitly threatened that in case of 'persistent default in compliance' with its orders, the concerned members of the higher bureaucracy of the states and union territories 'shall be held responsible'.[127]

[122] See the order of 14 May 2011. The Court pointed at Tamil Nadu as a positive example where the state government distributed food in such a manner.

[123] See the order of 14 May 2011.

[124] See the order of 14 May 2011.

[125] See, for instance, the orders of 2 May 2003: 'Ten months have passed. We do not know what consideration the report has received if at all it has been considered by the Government. [...] The affidavit could not be more vague than it is'; of 20 April 2004: 'Some of the States/Union Territories have not made even a beginning despite lapse of so many years'; of 7 October 2004: 'It is most unfortunate that instead of three months, nearly six months have expired, the Government of India has still not filed the affidavit [...] We are shocked at the attitude of the Central Government'; or of 29 October 2010: 'Mere schemes without any implementation are of no use'.

[126] See the order of 20 April 2004.

[127] Namely, the chief secretaries and administrators of the states and union territories; see the order of 29 October 2002. The Court stated that in case the commissioners' reports identified instances of starvation deaths, it would deem itself 'justified in presuming that its orders have not been

Looking at these orders, it becomes clear that the Court used existing state schemes at a starting point in order to define the content of the right to food. At first glance, this may indeed be seen as a 'conditional' or 'non-systemic' social rights approach that Khosla had described.[128] However, the Court did not limit itself to merely testing the implementation of existing schemes. Instead, the Court extended the scope of such schemes, most notably by turning the Mid-Day Meal Scheme into a binding obligation on the states. Also, the fact that the Court directed the government(s) to not reduce the scope of certain schemes, and even intervened when the central government wanted to partly replace the NMBS with the JSY, goes beyond a 'conditional socio-economic rights' approach. Instead of applying the right to food 'conditionally', the Court limited the legislature's discretion to define (and limit) the 'conditions' for socio-economic rights provision.[129] Therefore, the *Right to food* case allows a serious challenge to the 'conditional socio-economic rights' hypothesis.[130]

---

implemented', triggering a case in which the administrators would be held responsible; see the order of 29 October 2002. In another order (dated 7 October 2004), the Court warned that, as the central government had not filed an affidavit, '[i]n absence of the affidavit, we could have straightaway issued directions for the sanction of the remaining AWCs [Aanganwadi Centers, which supply food to children, pregnant and lactating women, etc.] and for increase' of the money to be supplied to each AWC—'but having regard to the totality of the circumstances, we grant one final opportunity to the Central Government'. If the affidavits were not filed in time, however, 'this Court will be left with no option but to issue directions for implementation of the two aspects'.

[128] See Khosla, 'Making Social Rights Conditional', as described in Chapter 3. Birchfield and Corsi, 'Between Starvation and Globalization', 701, also concede that the 'concrete ramifications' of the case 'are perhaps somewhat narrow in that the case directs the government to implement schemes it had already enacted for itself'.

[129] An example for the principle of 'non-retrogression' guiding socio-economic rights adjudication, Chapter 3.

[130] Arun Thiruvengadam, 'Characterising and Evaluating Indian Social Rights Jurisprudence into the 21st Century', in *Constitutional Rights to Welfare in India* (Forthcoming), ed. Sudhir Krishnaswamy and

The orders in the *Right to food* case also display what has been described as a shift from 'an adversarial to a more inquisitorial judicial model'.[131] The process of the central and state governments providing affidavits to the Court, the Court's commissioners' monitoring and reporting on implementation, and the petitioners, the civil society, the commissioners, and the Court itself making policy suggestions also present a case of a 'dialogue' between the executive, the legislature, the judiciary, and the civil society about adequate socio-economic rights adjudication and implementation.[132]

Perhaps the most interesting aspects about the *Right to food* case is the creation of the Commission. It was not the first time

---

Malini Bhattacharjee, https://azimpremjiuniversity.edu.in/SitePages/pdf/Characterising-and-evaluating-Indian-social-rights-jurisprudence-into-the-21st-century.pdf, accessed on 16 August 2018, see Chapter 3. As described above and in Chapter 3, for the right to education under Article 21A, the judiciary must not limit the effect of the right to a 'conditional' one in any case, see 'Non-Applicability of the "Conditional Social Rights Approach" to the Right to Education' in Chapter 3.

[131] Robinson, 'Expanding Judiciaries: India and the Rise of the Good Governance Court', 44.

[132] The benefits of such a 'dialogue' has been described by Tushnet, who, however, generally sees benefits in judicial restraint: if courts refrain from taking policy decisions, they may avoid conflicts with the legislative and executive branches, which may make their judgments more acceptable and thus actually strengthen the rights in practice. The legislature and executive might then be more willing to act on the court's decisions, rather than trying to resist them. This way, a 'dialogue' between the different branches of power may further the implementation of the right (see Mark V. Tushnet, *Weak Courts, Strong Rights: Judicial Review and Social Welfare Rights in Comparative Constitutional Law* [Princeton, N.J., Woodstock: Princeton University Press, 2009], 43 et seq., 242 et seq.). Tushnet's prediction may not be adequate for the Indian context, however, as the Court's 'strong' judgments have, in the post-Emergency era, led to much less resistance than they had before, in spite of the judiciary being more activist, judicial self-restraint is probably required to a lesser extent than elsewhere to nurture an atmosphere of productive 'dialogue' in court.

that the Court created such a commission.[133] But in this case, the Commission's work was especially important, as the Court based many of its orders on data provided by the Commission over the course of many years.

The Commission fulfils several roles. It monitors the implementation of the orders and provides the Court with reports, and also recommends specific orders to the Court based on its findings.[134] In addition to providing the Court with information, the Commission also directly communicates with the governments and even 'mediates and negotiates' policy and changes in legal provisions with them, using its 'diplomatic relations with state governments' in doing so.[135] After all, as mentioned above, the commissioners themselves are former bureaucrats.

The commissioners have to employ 'diplomatic' methods as the Commission does not have any authority to enforce its decisions, which is similar to the Human Rights Commission or the Child Rights Commissions. Therefore, to further the implementation of the right to food, they must rely on either good relationships with the governments and, or, as an alternative, on the Supreme Court acting on their recommendations by issuing orders.[136] This, of course, requires finding a right balance. Birchfeld and Corsi, who have interviewed commissioners' personnel, note that generally, 'Commissioners have found that autonomous resolution of

133 Baxi names several examples of Court-appointed 'socio-legal commissions of public citizens, social scientists and others' who, in PIL cases (or Social Action Litigation (SAL) cases, as the author calls them), helped the Court in 'the collection of social data and legal evidence concerning the plight of these impoverished groups' (see Upendra Baxi, 'Judicial Discourse: Dialectics of the Face and the Mask', *Journal of the Indian Law Institute [JILI]* 35, no. 1 and 2 [1993]: 7).

134 Birchfield and Corsi, 'Between Starvation and Globalization', 728.

135 See Birchfield and Corsi, 'Between Starvation and Globalization', 728–9. The authors highlight the Commission's success in 'building relationships with state officials and using those successfully forged partnerships to resolve grievances and foster political will for implementation of court orders'.

136 See Robinson, 'Closing the Implementation Gap', 343.

problematic implementation policies without court involvement best serves implementation objectives'.[137]

As far as the actual enforcement of the Court's orders (either based on recommendations by the Commission or on other grounds) is concerned, it is interesting to see that the Court has, in several orders, named specific administrative bodies and even specific bureaucrats, stating that they would be 'held responsible' in case of non-compliance with the order. Theoretically, the Court could punish officials that ignore its orders for contempt. However, the Court hardly uses this power.[138] Still, it has been observed that officials generally 'do pay heed to the Court'.[139] Robinson quotes one state-level Right to Food commissioner who believes that officials 'are afraid they will get negative remarks in the record and it will effect [*sic*] their promotions if they cross the Court'.[140] The power to punish for contempt of court in itself thus seems to have 'more of a symbolic value', with officials mainly fearing negative effects on their reputation rather than the punishment itself.[141]

The developments around the *Right to food* case also show that civil society may play an important role in furthering rights, also beyond merely initiating legal proceedings by filing a petition. While the original petition was filed by PUCL, later, a whole network of organizations, the 'Right to Food Campaign', was formed around the case.[142] The Campaign is a decentralized association of organizations that coordinates its efforts with a small steering group at the national level.[143]

137 Birchfield and Corsi, 'Between Starvation and Globalization', 730.

138 Robinson, 'Closing the Implementation Gap', 343.

139 Robinson, 'Closing the Implementation Gap', 343.

140 Robinson, 'Closing the Implementation Gap', 343.

141 Sathe, *Judicial Activism in India*, 288.

142 See http://www.righttofoodcampaign.in/about, accessed on 15 August 2018.

143 Birchfield and Corsi, 'Between Starvation and Globalization', 719. The decentralization may actually be too strong for some tasks—the authors note that the 'Campaign must find a way to better represent itself, demonstrate a unified strength, and speak with a single, collectively supported voice. [...] [D]ecentralization has also meant that the Campaign is often unable to make quick political decisions or statements' (see Birchfield and Corsi, 'Between Starvation and Globalization', 726).

In many ways, the Campaign has played a similar role as the Commission. The Campaign has asked for specific measures of implementation, modifications, and expansions of social security schemes through Interlocutory Applications.[144] Some of the Court's orders are based on these applications, adopting specific recommendations, such as, for instance, definitions of calories and protein contents for child nutrition schemes.[145] Furthermore, the Campaign has helped in identifying specific officials responsible for inadequate implementation through its applications.[146]

The Campaign has also provided important data to the Commission itself.[147] Thus, the Campaign and Commission complement each other, with the Commission responding to demands made by civil society, but also itself relying on data collected by civil society for its reports.[148]

The Campaign has also directly worked with government officials. In doing so, members of the Campaign's steering group cooperated with the central government's Planning Commissions.[149] In order to further on-the-ground implementation, it has also educated citizens about their entitlements and mobilized them to exert more pressure on the State,[150] focusing on such issues that the Court has passed orders on.[151] Such on-the-ground measures also include public hearings performed by the Campaign itself,[152]

144 See Birchfield and Corsi, 'Between Starvation and Globalization', 720.

145 Birchfield and Corsi refer to the orders dated 28 November 2001; 2 May 2003; 20 April 2004; 7 October 2004 (see Birchfield and Corsi, 'Between Starvation and Globalization', 722).

146 See Birchfield and Corsi, 'Between Starvation and Globalization', 721.

147 See Birchfield and Corsi, 'Between Starvation and Globalization', 722–3.

148 Birchfield and Corsi, 'Between Starvation and Globalization', 730–1.

149 See Birchfield and Corsi, 'Between Starvation and Globalization', 725.

150 Birchfield and Corsi, 'Between Starvation and Globalization', 723. The media has also played an important role in spreading awareness, as noted by Robinson, 'Closing the Implementation Gap', 343.

151 Birchfield and Corsi, 'Between Starvation and Globalization', 731.

152 Birchfield and Corsi, 'Between Starvation and Globalization', 724.

similar to the ones organized by politicians and the Karnataka State Child Rights Commission, as described in Chapter 5.[153] The Campaign can, of course, not pass any 'judgments' after hearing a case, but uses the hearings to inform the poor about their entitlements under government food schemes, potentially creating a common demand for government accountability.[154]

The Campaign has also cooperated with other movements in order to strengthen its cause, for instance, with the Right to Information Campaign. The Right to Information Act ultimately helped the Right to Food Campaign in accessing more information to frame its Interlocutory Applications.[155]

Similar to the story of the right to information campaign eventually succeeding in convincing the legislature to create the Right to Information Act, the Right to Food Campaign's work (and, of course, the litigation in the *Right to food* case) led to the passage of the National Food Security Act, 2013.[156] The Act, among other things, defines concrete entitlements for citizens and for households, for children, and for pregnant and lactating women (Sections 3, 4, 5), aims to improve the performance of the PDS (Section 12), includes provisions to improve transparency (Chapter XI/Sections 27–9), and defines obligations for governments and local authorities (for example, Chapters VII-X/Sections 22–6). It also creates a grievance redress mechanisms similar to the one under the Right to Education Act (Chapter VII/Section 14 et seq.), also including provisions for the constitution of State Food Commissions, which shall be part of the grievance redress system, but shall also monitor and evaluate the implementation of the Act (Section 16(6)). These Commissions have not yet been constituted in many states.[157]

[153] 'Lack of Implementation', in the previous chapter.

[154] Birchfield and Corsi, 'Between Starvation and Globalization', 724.

[155] Birchfield and Corsi, 'Between Starvation and Globalization', 724.

[156] For a summary of the contents of the Act, also see Jean Drèze, 'Summary of the National Food Security Bill 2013', *Tehelka*, 22 March 2013, http://old.tehelka.com/exclusive-summary-of-the-national-food-security-bill-2013/, accessed on 19 August 2018.

[157] An overview at http://www.righttofoodcampaign.in/food-act/state-information, accessed on 24 February 2019, only names the Food Commission of Haryana. Other states seem to at least be in the process of

Since the passage of the Act, there have been no additional orders in the *Right to food* case. The Supreme Court Commissioners have also not released any reports since 2012.[158] In February 2017, the Supreme Court dismissed the petition, stating that after the passage of the Food Security Act, 'nothing further survives in this petition'.[159] However, in spite of this assessment, a new petition could be filed in the future, now focusing on the implementation of the Act. The Court even stated in its 2017 order that 'in case the petitioner has any grievance with regard to the implementation or otherwise of the National Food Security Act, 2013, he may file a fresh petition'.[160] In such a new petition, the Right to Food Campaign could continue with similar efforts and the State Food Commissions could take over the roles of the Supreme Court Commission (or of the nodal officers with the Supreme Court Commission remaining as a national institution). The Court could, depending on how activist it would decide to be, also test the Act's shortcomings in future orders or judgments.[161]

---

setting up their commissions; see, for instance, *Times of India*, 'Ranglal Jamuda Appointed Odisha Food Commission Chairperson', 9 May 2016, http://timesofindia.indiatimes.com/city/bhubaneswar/Ranglal-Jamuda-appointed-Odisha-food-commission-chairperson/articleshow/52193346.cms (Odisha), accessed on 19 August 2018; *The Hindu*, 'Karnataka to Set Up Food Commission', 14 June 2016, http://www.thehindu.com/todays-paper/tp-national/karnataka-to-set-up-food-commission/article8725862.ece (Karnataka), accessed on 19 August 2018.

[158] https://web.archive.org/web/20171007030111/http://www.sccommissioners.org/Reports/commissioners.html, accessed on 15 August 2018. As of August 2018, the original website was not available anymore, with some private party having taken over the domain sccommissioners.org.

[159] See the order dated 10 February 2017, available at https://www.sci.gov.in/jonew/ropor/rop/all/901064.pdf, accessed on 18 August 2018.

[160] See the order dated 10 February 2017, available at https://www.sci.gov.in/jonew/ropor/rop/all/901064.pdf, accessed on 18 August 2018.

[161] Such shortcomings have been highlighted by, for instance, Surendranath, who notes how the Court 'was in the process of developing a robust food security regime that accounted for various structural factors, rather than just ensuring that people received foodgrains', while

## PIL and Grievance Redress for 'Micromanagement and Macromanagement'

While the judiciary may or may not decide to assess the adequacy of statutory provisions defining entitlements under the right to food as read into Article 21 of the Constitution, it is clearly empowered to (and, if such questions are raised in court, also obliged to) measure the Right to Education Act against Article 21A, as explained above and in Chapter 3. It may also test the entirety of the State's implementation measures against the Act, as well as against Article 21A itself.

Obviously, the judiciary could also decide individual cases raised by aggrieved individuals, if it were more accessible in practice. As this is not the case, 'adjudication' (understood in a broad sense, including formal adjudication in courts as well as grievance redress in other forums) of the right to education will realistically be performed at several levels, at least in the foreseeable future.

Grievance redress to the local authorities and Child Rights Commissions would take place at the 'lower' level, and petitions to the high courts and the Supreme Court, mostly as PILs, would take place at the 'upper' level. In such a system, one can recognize a division of responsibilities between 'micromanagement' at the lower and 'macromanagement' at the upper level. While grievance redress authorities would deal with individual cases, larger policy and implementation issues would be decided by the higher judiciary.[162]

---

the National Food Security Act does just that—concentrat[e] only on food entitlements and ignoring integral aspects of food security such as the non-food elements of nutrition, security of small farmers, protection of livelihoods, control of resources by people, etc.' (see Anup Surendranath, 'Life and Personal Liberty', in *The Oxford Handbook of the Indian Constitution*, ed. Sujit Choudhry, Madhav Khosla, and Pratap B. Mehta [Oxford, New York: Oxford University Press, 2016], 771).

[162] Bilchitz has suggested a similar approach for 'division of labour' for the South African context (see David Bilchitz, 'Expanding Access to Justice for Socio-Economic Rights Complaints in South Africa: Which Direction Should We Head in?', https://voelkerrechtsblog.org/expanding-access-to-justice-for-socio-economic-rights-complaints-in-south-africa/, accessed on 12 August 2018).

Courts may thus be the forum in which claimants can 'challenge the soundness, legality, or constitutionality' of policies, while grievance redress bodies may rule on the implementation of these policies in a given case. The latter may also eventually lead to a change in policy, as the sum of grievances raised and resolved will lead to additional expenses that may then most easily be avoided by changing or adapting to existing policies.[163]

If the grievance redress system worked as desired, based on clearer provisions calling for specific remedies, it could provide relatively fast and effective relief for a wide range of grievances. Grievance redress bodies, called upon by parents, could order admission of children in government schools (as well as private schools under the 'Section 12 quota'), order that schools allow the transfer of a child from one school to the other, threaten disciplinary measures against government school teachers or impose fines against private schools if discrimination against individual children or groups of children in a school persists, order disciplinary measures or fines against a teacher not fulfilling their duties, or order that parents are given effective access to SMCs.

If a grievance redress body had powers to give orders that have budgetary implications, it could also order that additional teachers have to be assigned to a school, that a school's infrastructure has to be upgraded, or even that a new school has to be established in a neighbourhood. Even if the lower grievance redress bodies lack such powers (and therefore cannot provide immediate relief themselves), they can still fulfil their 'fire alarm' function by drawing the government's attention to implementation deficiencies. The Child Rights Commissions' tasks as monitoring bodies could also be supported in this way. The grievance redress mechanisms would also provide detailed information concerning how widespread those deficiencies are in terms of quantity and quality as well as possible regional differences.

In addition to such information, the grievances themselves could also be channelled upwards. Firstly, of course, after being decided

163 Varun Gauri, 'Redressing Grievances and Complaints Regarding Basic Service Delivery', Policy Research Working Paper, World Bank, http://elibrary.worldbank.org/doi/pdf/10.1596/1813-9450-5699, accessed on 19 August 2018, 6, 19 et seq.

upon by the grievance redress bodies, they would be handed to the state child rights commissions by way of appeal. Depending on how far-reaching their competences to give binding orders would be, they could then redress such grievances themselves, or start litigation in the respective high court or the Supreme Court. The higher judiciary would then also be competent to test larger, more abstract policy questions connected to these cases.[164]

Generally, at the upper level, meaning the courts, the national, and state child rights commissions could play a similar role as the Supreme Court Commission, as its state nodal officers did in the *Right to food* case. As bodies charged with the function of monitoring the implementation the right to education, they were created for a similar purpose. The fact that the Supreme Court, in the *Right to food* case, saw the need to appoint commissioners and persons in the states to assist them shows that it recognizes that it struggles with monitoring rights implementation itself, even when it has given specific orders. The Child Rights Commissions and the entire grievance redress system, with 'eyes and ears' at a low level of the administration hierarchy, could fulfil this function effectively. The Commissions could gather data through the workings of the grievance redress system and provide data and advice to the courts in right to education cases, either initiated by the Commissions themselves or by the civil society as PILs.[165]

With individual grievances being redressed at the lower local authority and Commissions level, the courts would be able to focus their attention on 'macromanagement'. Macromanagement would involve larger policy and implementation questions that could then be addressed with 'structural injunctions'.

[164] This system of 'channelling' broader questions 'upwards' could work similarly to the German institution of 'concrete judicial review' (see Article 100(1) of the Basic Law).

[165] The Supreme Court Commission in the *Right to food* case was also charged with grievance redress functions, but was not able to effectively fulfil this function because of lack of personnel and financial constraints (see Birchfield and Corsi, 'Between Starvation and Globalization: Realizing the Right to Food in India', 730; Robinson, 'Closing the Implementation Gap', 343).

Civil society organizations could participate in 'micromanaging' by aiding individuals with their grievance redress efforts at the lower level (with such cases that can be decided in the grievance redress system). They could also participate in macromanagement at the upper level, where they would focus their litigation efforts on broader questions.

Focusing on fewer, but broader policy cases at the upper level, especially such that are strategically important, could make litigation more efficient.[166] Cases of 'strategic importance' could include such that improve the grievance redress system in order to facilitate on-the-ground measures that would allow for bottom-up implementation of the right to education. They could also include petitions aiming for clearer definitions of individual claims that could then be brought to the grievance redress system, for example, the question whether or not grievance redress authorities or state child rights commissions may order that school facilities be upgraded or more teachers appointed to meet the minimum standards set by the Right to Education Act. If such individual claims had previously been denied at the lower level because of budgetary constraints, the courts may test to what extend this 'defence' is permissible, and potentially even order the allocation or re-distribution of additional funds. The lower grievance redress bodies may then also decide upon the allocation of these funds. In addition to civil society organizations, the Child Rights Commissions could act as an 'interface' between the 'micromanagement and macromanagement' efforts, basing recommendations for improvements of the grievance redress system and/or for defining individual claims on the on-the-ground data that they collect through their monitoring efforts and as an appellate body in the grievance redress system.

166 Currently, many groups shy away from litigation as it is costly and time-consuming, with some groups having made the experience of 'they realiz[ing] they do not have the capacity to adequately represent an issue only after they have brought a case' to the courts (see Robinson, 'Expanding Judiciaries', 57). For the perceptions of (non)effectiveness of litigation for social society groups, also see Jayanth K. Krishnan, 'Social Policy Advocacy and the Role of the Courts in India', *American Asian Review* XXI, no. 2 (2003), and Chapter 4.

Human rights advocates, NGOs, and other civil society groups should therefore follow the example of the Right to Food Campaign and work at all levels. Importantly, they should not just lobby for the delivery of education to all children, but work towards empowering parents so that they can ask for it themselves in grievance redress systems that need to be strengthened progressively. Strengthening these systems must, in turn, become an important issue in civil society groups' lobbying efforts as well as their litigation efforts.

In this set-up, there would also be different degrees of judicial activism that may be more or less acceptable to other branches of power and also to civil society. In spite of the benefits of structural injunctions and the justification for awarding strong remedies arising out of Article 21A, also in PIL cases, a certain degree of judicial self-restraint, or rather, cooperating with other parties might be beneficial. Even a court that sees itself as a strong political player should primarily focus on facilitating sound policy decisions rather than always taking them themselves, and therefore avoid decreeing matters finally and employing 'command-and-control' methods.[167] This way, the court could be 'an ally to strong civil society groups and movements in their attempt to make the process of Indian democracy more participatory, inclusive, and effective'.[168]

Furthering access to justice in the alternative fora 'on the ground' would in itself be a step in this direction. In this system, in spite of taking up macromanagement functions, the higher judiciary could still refrain from taking a directly confrontational stance against the other branches of power. The *Right to food* case has shown how

[167] Thiruvengadam quotes Fredman, who, writing about PIL in India, argues that the court should be 'a vehicle for social conversation between co-equal citizens', facilitating democratic interaction between judges, the government, and social and political groups, which would be more desirable than a mere transfer of hierarchical power to the court (see Sandra Fredman, *Human Rights Transformed: Positive Rights and Positive Duties* [Oxford, New York: Oxford University Press, 2008], 125, 133, quoted in Thiruvengadam, 'Revisiting the Role of the Judiciary in Plural Societies', 363 et seq.).

[168] Thiruvengadam, 'Revisiting the Role of the Judiciary in Plural Societies', 365.

this may be achieved. For instance, as described above, the Court did not directly order budgetary allocations, but instead asked officials to file affidavits concerning such allocations. Such a strategy may then spark a dialogue between the branches of power and the civil society concerning priorities for budgeting. The Court's 'command and control' powers could remain as a last resort.

* * *

As described in Chapter 4, the Constitution only provides for claiming fundamental rights from the state through the high courts and the Supreme Court. The grievance redress system may act as an alternative to this system, at least partly compensating for lack of access to the higher judiciary.

If the system is equipped in a manner that it may provide that individual cases are resolved effectively at the lower level to the extent that this is possible, with the higher judiciary mainly focusing on macromanagement cases brought as PIL, it might actually be a superior alternative for adjudication of the right to education.

This 'superiority' becomes apparent when (once again) considering the workings of the system from the perspective of the rights-bearers. Importantly, adjudication of socio-economic rights must provide tangible, swift results for citizens claiming their rights in order for socio-economic rights to be successful or even legitimate. If adjudication is incapable of producing tangible benefits to the right-bearers, 'then these rights [...] have largely failed'.[169]

[169] Marius Pieterse, 'Eating Socioeconomic Rights: The Usefulness of Rights Talk in Alleviating Social Hardship Revisited', *Human Rights Quarterly* 29, no. 3 (2007): 804. The author criticizes an 'abstract and conceptually empty articulation of socioeconomic rights' by courts, naming several cases of the South African Constitutional Court as examples—amongst them, once again, the *Grootboom* case, in which the court restricted its assessment of a possible rights violation to whether or not the State had taken 'reasonable measures', meaning that ultimately, the decision 'did not result in the alleviation of the housing needs of the successful litigants', who were successful only in so far as that the Court saw a violation, but not a concrete benefit that they could claim because of it, only to a 'reasonable' procedure through which the state shall attempt to

Considering the mixed results of socio-economic rights adjudication in different jurisdictions, it has been argued that instead of 'rights-talk', the debate around socio-economic services to be provided by the government should focus on the fact that 'people need food and shelter right now', with the most important issue being whether or not those needs be satisfied, regardless of characterizing this satisfaction as enforcing a right.[170] However, articulating such needs as 'rights' does have value, as merely articulating a need in itself does not compel a society to fulfil that need.[171] Importantly, through rights terminology, needs may be 'reconceptualized' as entitlements.[172] However, if socio-economic rights are applied as rights, then there must be a tangible positive effect on factual circumstances.[173] For right-bearers, such tangible results are the top priority, and, therefore, one may only expect them to rely on the legal process for claiming their socio-economic rights if they believe that they can receive such benefits.[174]

In the South African example, one may summarize the Constitutional Court's answer to the question: 'What are socio-economic rights [...] for?' as 'the assurance that government, in attempting to alleviate poverty and hardship, will act in a manner consistent with good governance, and only that'.[175] In such

---

provide such benefits (see Pieterse, 'Eating Socioeconomic Rights', 799, 807–9, 811).

[170] Mark Tushnet, 'An Essay on Right', *Texas Law Review* 62, no. 8 (1984): 1394, quoted at Pieterse, 'Eating Socioeconomic Rights', 801.

[171] Pieterse, 'Eating Socioeconomic Rights', 801.

[172] Pieterse, 'Eating Socioeconomic Rights', 802–3.

[173] Pieterse, 'Eating Socioeconomic Rights', 803–4.

[174] Pieterse, 'Eating Socioeconomic Rights', 804.

[175] Danie Brand, 'The Proceduralisation of South African Socio-Economic Rights Jurisprudence, or "What are Socio-Economic Rights For?"', in *Rights and Democracy in a Transformative Constitution*, ed. Henk Botha, A.J. Van der Walt, J.C. Van der Walt, 1st edition (Stellenbosch, South Africa: SUN Press, 2003), 36–7, quoted at Pieterse, 'Eating Socioeconomic Rights', 811.

cases in which it has shied away from giving strong remedies, as described in Chapter 3, the stance of the Indian Supreme Court, may also be described similarly. For instance, as highlighted by Khosla for the *Olga Tellis* case, citizens for whom the Court solemnly declared that they have a right to housing were essentially only given a right that the state implement housing schemes non-arbitrarily. But they were not given an actual, unconditional right *to housing* in a sense that the State will actually provide housing to them.[176] Such somewhat abstract conceptualization and definition of rights does have value in itself and may further the provision of socio-economic rights,[177] but is 'at most of indirect and secondary importance to the beneficiaries'.[178]

If, in India, there were a functioning and effective grievance redress system for enforcing the right to education, at least some tangible benefits that do not require that the State first take broader policy decisions could be claimed relatively easily and quickly, giving right-bearers actual incentives to use these systems in order to improve their (or, rather, their children's) situation.[179] Further definition of concrete entitlements that could be claimed at the 'lower end' could be, as described above, promoted by the courts.

176 See Chapter 3.

177 'Whereas this doubtlessly has positive consequences for the progressive realization of socioeconomic rights generally, it is more often than not of little use to people in urgent need of access to particular social goods', Pieterse, 'Eating Socioeconomic Rights', 812.

178 Pieterse, 'Eating Socioeconomic Rights', 804.

179 Consequently, Pieterse as well states that '[i]n addition to a substantively articulated legal right, it will be necessary that mechanisms through which this right may be enforced are readily accessible and that they are practicably capable of tangibly delivering the content of the right'. He also calls for legislation defining concrete benefits of a given right in order to facilitate such a process, which, for the right to education in India, already exists in the form of the Right to Education Act (albeit with shortcomings) (see Pieterse, 'Eating Socioeconomic Rights', 820).

As for the more 'abstract' questions are concerned (such as the reasonableness of government policies, an obligation to consider redrafting them, sharing of financial responsibilities between the centre and the state, and so on), they do play an important role in the provisioning of the right. But they do not provide *direct* tangible benefits for right-bearers. Therefore, it seems adequate to not expect them to raise these questions in court themselves, even if the courts were more accessible than they are now. Considering the far-reaching deficiencies in the Indian education system, as described in Chapter 1, there are pressing, immediate issues causing grievances for them, such as teacher absence, an unacceptable teacher/pupil ratio, or private schools refusing to admit their children under the 'Section 12 quota', that require swift and direct action.

Still, more broad, abstract questions may be decisive for implementing socio-economic rights. But such questions are, to an extent, detached from such individual grievances. Therefore, it might be more adequate that they be raised in court independent of individual cases. In other words, PILs filed by civil society organizations might be the most adequate means for raising broader implementation issues in court.

This would be the case even if the higher judiciary were easily accessible. If PIL as an institution did not exist, civil society groups or human rights advocates would have to 'use' individual right-bearers as litigants for petitions raising such abstract questions, perhaps as class-action lawsuits to draw more attention to them, meaning that many individuals would have to 'join' these efforts as petitioners, even though a positive outcome of the case might benefit them very indirectly and with a long delay. Allowing such civil society groups to act as petitioners might therefore be more adequate. One could also say that it would be more honest, as 'using' individuals' grievances for 'strategic litigation' is only a strategy in order to achieve the same results that one can achieve through PIL. Perhaps an institution such as PIL might therefore be a role model even for other jurisdictions, and not just in developing countries.[180]

[180] The famous 2010 *Hartz IV* case of the German Federal Constitutional Court demonstrates that strategic litigation can be frustrating for right-bearers whose cases are 'channelled upwards', even if they ultimately win. In this case, families who were recipients of welfare (*Arbeitslosengeld II/Hartz IV*) attempted to claim additional benefits, also for their children, in German social courts (*Sozialgerichte*). The social courts were convinced that the existing statutory welfare provisions did not fulfil the constitutional obligation under Articles 1(1) and 20(1) of the Basic Law. They therefore referred the case to the Federal Constitutional Court. The Constitutional Court then decided that the manner in which welfare benefits for children to be provided to each family were calculated according to the statutory provisions in question were arbitrary, calling on the legislature to re-draft these provisions (see 'Hartz IV' BVerfGE 125 (Bundesverfassungsgericht, 9 February 2010), 175–260, http://www.bundesverfassungsgericht.de/SharedDocs/Entscheidungen/DE/2010/02/ls20100209_1bvl000109.html, accessed on 19 August 2018). However, the Constitutional Court refrained from deciding whether or not the actual sum that resulted from application of the unconstitutional law itself infringed the beneficiaries' rights. Instead, the sum might have even been less, as long as it would not have been calculated arbitrarily. In the aftermath, the legislature applied a new, non-arbitrary method, but did not raise the benefits to be paid for children by a single Euro. While it is positive that the State ceased to calculate the benefits arbitrarily, the result was hardly satisfying for those who had brought their grievance to the courts.

# Conclusion and Outlook

This study has shown that the right to education holds a unique position amongst socio-economic rights in Indian constitutional law. Its singularity goes beyond merely being included in the constitutional text. Even though Article 21A as such has received very little scholarly and judicial attention, its existence has far-reaching consequences.

First of all, legislation that seeks to implement it may and must be measured against the contents of that Article. The legislature is, therefore, not free to choose the degree to which the State shall provide benefits to its citizens, and the State can thus be held accountable for more than just implementation of statutory law.

In addition to that, the Article's position in the fundamental rights catalogue has important consequences for the manner in which the State must provide for the Right. It has an obligation to provide a functioning education system to all children without discrimination, with a certain standard of quality, and to ensure that private schools fulfil the duties that the State assigns to them by law. In addition to that, it must also provide mechanisms through which right-bearers can enforce the Right against the State and through which they can initiate proceedings that will remedy any instance in which the State did not provide the Right to them in the manner that it is obliged to do. This promise is made by the Constitution itself, by guaranteeing that fundamental rights be enforceable in the Supreme Court and high courts.

As the members of the parts of society whom the right to education is aimed at are not currently able to access the higher judiciary in practice, the State is obligated to provide alternative enforcement mechanisms that may compensate for this lack of accessibility. The grievance redress system created by the Right to Education Act currently offers such compensation only to a very limited extent, meaning that there is an obligation on the State to act accordingly and to improve that system. The higher judiciary may order such improvements when adjudicating Article 21A. For this to happen in practice, the question whether the grievance redress mechanisms are adequate should be raised by rights advocacy groups through PIL.

Of course, it remains to be seen whether grievance redress systems, as part of a rights-based 'bottom-up' implementation approach to the education system, will actually lead to better results. The debate whether or not justiciability of socio-economic rights is desirable is still ongoing, and there are still good arguments against courts' strong involvement in policy decisions. These concern not only their legitimacy to do so but also the question whether they are actually capable of doing so. Thus, one may still argue that it is more adequate for the executive and, especially, the legislature to make policy decisions concerning service delivery. It is also clear that the judiciary will be reliant on the other branches of power's activity to further the implementation of the right to education. Consequently, Article 21A itself calls for implementing legislation.

However, concerning the right to education, the Constitution explicitly empowers and obligates the judiciary to be active in the implementation process and it gives a corresponding promise to the society that citizens may participate in that process by being able to rectify wrongs through mechanisms provided for by the State. Solemnly declaring that education is every child's right, without them actually having any means to experience it as their entitlement and not just a service that the State benevolently decides to provide to them, clearly falls short of that promise.

Also, past experience with the provision of an education system by the State 'from above', with elections being the only measure of exerting pressure 'from below', shows that this mechanism has only worked to a very limited extent. At the same time, one must also note that many of the advances made in the field of education were caused by developments that started even before the inclusion of Article 21A in the constitutional text. Most notably, the 'top-down' programme *Sarva Shiksha Abhiyan*, which started already in 2000, improved the education system to a considerable extent.

Still, as was argued by this study, a combination of a better functioning grievance redress system dealing with 'simpler' cases quickly and effectively at the 'bottom', allowing the judiciary at the 'top' to focus on larger policy issues would function in ways that give reasons to expect positive results for the education system as a whole.

If this expectation is fulfilled in practice, then the State could also use the example of the right to education and its enforcement mechanisms for other benefits that it provides to its citizens. It has been shown that the State is *legally* obligated to create effective and accessible enforcement mechanisms for the right to education. For other 'rights', such as the right to information, the right to employment, and the right to food, this is not the case, at least not as clearly, as the Constitution does not explicitly promise them as justiciable fundamental rights. But if the State chooses to employ a 'rights-based approach' for a larger variety of rights, even without also adding them to the constitutional text, then, merely by calling them 'rights', it is creating an expectation that they be enforceable as well.

Therefore, it would be adequate for it to bring enforcement mechanisms concerning these rights in line with the right to education. As has been shown, some of the mechanisms provided by the other rights' regimes are actually currently more powerful than the right to education's grievance-redress regime, particularly the one created by the Right to Information Act.

Importantly, rights-advocacy groups should, therefore, also go beyond speaking of 'rights' and 'empowerment' and exerting political pressure on the State and beyond merely calling for the implementation of schemes for service delivery. They should instead focus part of their attention on calling for improvements of such mechanisms that will progressively allow right-bearers to take matters concerning the delivery of these services into their own hands, without having to hope that these groups will fight for their causes. Public Interest Litigation may be an important tool to raise the issue of accessible enforcement mechanisms at the highest level.

Of course, the infrastructure created for the enforcement of one right could also be used for other rights. Therefore, perhaps it would be sensible to assign service delivery grievance redress for a wider range of rights to the same independent institutions, including rights commissions, rather than creating separate systems for different rights with different commissions at the top. Perhaps such systems could then even be used for the enforcement of civil and political rights. This way, the State could generally provide for fundamental rights 'adjudication' at the lowest, locally accessible level.

More generally, even at the international level, the discussion concerning the 'rights-based approach' and 'legal empowerment' could focus more on the question of how tangible results for right-bearers may be achieved, and how *they* may hold bureaucrats in their countries accountable and initiate proceedings that will guarantee the delivery of their rights to them. The 'legal empowerment' approach is still somewhat new and, so far, it also names the Indian example of PIL as a means of providing access to justice. Therefore, currently, the discussion at this level also focuses too much on whether or not poor right-bearer's issues are brought to court, rather than questioning *who* actually raises these issues.

Ultimately, this shift in focus has been the core idea of this study. The State's efforts concerning justiciable rights, as well as the discussion around them, must put right-bearers at the centre of attention and must examine what means they have to enforce their rights. The State must also ensure that the right (however broadly it is defined, however strongly it is being lobbied for politically) is not just promised to the right-bearers or given to them merely because of the State's benevolence. Rather, for them, a service being a 'right' must have the tangible consequence of them being able to actually effectively and swiftly claim benefits themselves. At least for the right to education in India, making this a reality is a constitutional duty.

# Bibliography

'Maastricht Guidelines on Violations of Economic, Social and Cultural Rights'. 1997. https://www1.umn.edu/humanrts/instree/Maastricht guidelines_.html (accessed, 19 August 2018).

Ackerman, Bruce. 'The New Separation of Powers'. *Harvard Law Review* 113, no. 3 (2000): 633–725.

Afridi, Farzana. 'The Impact of School Meals on School Participation: Evidence from Rural India'. https://web.archive.org/web/20170707221925/http://www.cid.harvard.edu/neudc07/docs/neudc07_s6_p01_afridi.pdf (accessed, 19 August 2018).

Aggarwal, Shobha. 'The Public Interest Litigation Hoax in India: Its Adverse Impact on the Poor and Working Class'. *South Asia Citizens Web*, 23 April 2015. http://sacw.net/article11105.html (accessed, 19 August 2018).

Ahmad, Nesar, Mahendra S. Rao, and Hariom Soni. 'Community Monitoring of Right to Education: A Case of Udaipur District'. In *Right to Education in India: Resources, Institutions and Public Policy*. Edited by Praveen K. Jha and P.G. Rani, 305–27. Abingdon, New York: Routledge, 2016.

Aiyar, Yamini and Bala Posani. 'State of Accountability: Evolution, Practice and Emerging Questions in Public Accountability in India'. 2009. http://accountabilityindia.in/sites/default/files/working-paper/34_1244199435.pdf (accessed, 19 August 2018).

Alkema, Evert Albert. 'The Third-Party Applicability or "Drittwirkung" of the European Convention on Human Rights'. In *Protecting Human Rights: The European Dimension: Studies in Honour of Gérard J. Wiarda = Protection des droits de l'homme: la dimension européenne*. Edited by Franz Matscher and Herbert Petzold, 33–45. Köln: Heymanns, 1988.

Allahabad High Court. *Buddhu* vs. *Municipal Board and Ors* MANU/UP/0297/1952, 18 March 1952.

Alston, Philip, and Gerard Quinn. 'The Nature and Scope of States Parties' Obligations under the International Covenant on Economic, Social and Cultural Rights'. *Human Rights Quarterly* 9, no. 2 (1987): 156–229.

Alston, Philip, and Nehal Bhuta. 'Human Rights and Public Goods: Education as a Fundamental Right in India'. In *Human Rights and Development: Towards Mutual Reinforcement*. Edited by Philip Alston, 242–65. Oxford: Oxford University Press, 2005.

Andhyarujina, T.R. 'The Age of Judicial Reform'. *The Hindu*, 1 September 2012. http://www.thehindu.com/opinion/lead/the-age-of-judicial-reform/article3845041.ece (accessed, 19 August 2018).

Andhyarujina, T.R. 'The Evolution of Due Process of Law by the Supreme Court'. In *Supreme but not Infallible: Essays in Honour of the Supreme Court of India*. Edited by B.N. Kirpal, 193–213. New Delhi, New York: Oxford University Press, 2000.

Andreassen, Bård-Anders, Alan G. Smith, and Hugo Stokke. 'Compliance with Economic and Social Human Rights: Realistic Evaluations and Monitoring in the Light of Immediate Obligations'. In *Human Rights in Perspective: A Global Assessment*. Edited by Asbjørn Eide. 252–67. Oxford: Blackwell Business, 1993[1992].

ASER Centre. 'Annual Status of Education Report (Rural) 2013'. ASER Centre, New Delhi, 2013.

ASER Centre. 'Annual Status of Education Report (Rural) 2014: Provisional'. 13 January 2015. http://img.asercentre.org/docs/Publications/ASER%20Reports/ASER%202014/fullaser2014mainreport_1.pdf(accessed, 2 March 2019).

ASER Centre. 'Annual Status of Education Report (Rural) 2016: Provisional'. 18 January 2017. http://img.asercentre.org/docs/Publications/ASER%20Reports/ASER%202016/aser_2016.pdf (accessed, 2 March 2019).

*Assam Times*. 'Legal Awareness Campaign'. 11 May 2016. http://www.assamtimes.org/node/16854 (accessed, 19 August 2018).

Austin, Granville. *The Indian Constitution: Cornerstone of a Nation*. Oxford, New York: Oxford University Press, 1999.

Austin, Granville. *Working a Democratic Constitution: A History of the Indian Experience*. Delhi, Oxford: Oxford University Press, 2003.

Azam, Mehtabul, Aimee Chin, and Nishith Prakash. 'The Returns to English-Language Skills in India'. April 2011. http://www.

uh.edu/~achin/research/azam_chin_prakash.pdf (accessed, 2 March 2019).

Bandyopadhyay, D. 'Singur: What Happened, What Next and Time to Pay the Cost'. *Economic & Political Weekly* XLIII, no. 48 (2008): 13–16.

Banik, Dan, ed. *Rights and Legal Empowerment in Eradicating Poverty.* Farnham, England, Burlington, VT: Ashgate Publishing, 2008.

Banik, Dan. 'Introduction'. In *Rights and Legal Empowerment in Eradicating Poverty*, 1–8.

Banik, Dan. 'Rights, Legal Empowerment and Poverty: An Overview of the Issues'. In *Rights and Legal Empowerment in Eradicating Poverty*, 11–30.

Bansal, Samarth. 'What does the 7th Pay Panel Mean for govt. Employees?', *The Hindu*, 30 June 2016. http://www.thehindu.com/news/national/7th-pay-commission-benefits-to-government-employees/article8791800.ece (accessed, 19 August 2018).

Basham, A.L. *Wonder that was India: Survey of the History and Culture of the Indian Sub-Continent before the Coming of the Muslims*. 3rd edition (London: Sidgwick & Jackson, 1967).

Baxi, Upendra, and Marc Galanter. 'Panchayat Justice: An Indian Experiment in Legal Accesss'. In *Access to Justice*. Edited by Bryant Garth and Mauro Cappelletti, 341–85. Alphen aan den Rijn: Sijthoff and Noordhoff, 1978. http://upendrabaxi.in/documents/Panchayat%20justice_%20an%20indian%20experiment%20in%20legal%20access.pdf (accessed, 9 December 2016).

Baxi, Upendra. '"The Little Done, the Vast Undone" - Some Reflections on Reading Granville Austin's "The Indian Constitution"'. *Journal of the Indian Law Institute* 9, no. 3 (1967): 323–430.

Baxi, Upendra. 'Directive Principles and Sociology of Indian Law: A Reply to Dr. Jagat Narain'. *Journal of the Indian Law Institute* 11, no. 3 (1969): 245–72.

Baxi, Upendra. 'From Takrar to Karar: The Lok Adalat at Ragpur - A Preliminary Study'. *Journal of Constitutional and Parliamentary Studies* 10, no. 52 (1976). http://upendrabaxi.in/documents/From%20takrar%20to%20karar_%20the%20lok%20adalat%20at%20rangpur%20a%20preliminary%20st.pdf (accessed, 19 August 2018).

Baxi, Upendra. 'Judicial Discourse: Dialectics of the Face and the Mask'. *Journal of the Indian Law Institute* 35, no. 1 and 2 (1993): 1–12.

Baxi, Upendra. 'Taking Suffering Seriously: Social Action Litigation in the Supreme Court of India'. *Third World Legal Studies* (1985): 107–32.

Baxi, Upendra. 'Taking Suffering Seriously'. In *Law and Poverty: Critical Essays*. Edited by Upendra Baxi. Bombay: N.M. Tripathi, 1988.

Baxi, Upendra. 'The Avatars of Indian Judicial Activism: Explorations in the Geographies of (In)Justice'. In *Fifty Years of the Supreme Court of India*.

BBC. 'Indian PM Plea on Justice Backlog'. 17 September 2009. http://news.bbc.co.uk/2/hi/south_asia/8204607.stm (accessed, 19 August 2018).

Bedi, Aneesha. 'Denied Recognition, Several Schools Continue to Function'. *Hindustan Times*, 23 September 2015. http://www.hindustantimes.com/chandigarh/denied-recognition-several-schools-continue-to-function/story-FaxqCjuGMvXW68qYsj1i1I.html (accessed, 19 August 2018).

Beeckman, Katrien. 'Measuring the Implementation of the Right to Education: Educational Versus Human Rights Indicators'. *The International Journal of Children's Rights* 12, no. 1 (2004): 71–84.

Beiter, Klaus Dieter. *The Protection of the Right to Education by International Law: Including a Systematic Analysis of Article 13 of the International Covenant on Economic, Social, and Cultural Rights*, Vol. 82. Leiden, Boston: Martinus Nijhoff Publishers, 2006.

Bellenoit, H.J.A. *Missionary Education and Empire in Late Colonial India, 1860–1920*. London: Pickering & Chatto, 2007.

Berlin, Isaiah. *Four Essays on Liberty*. London, New York: Oxford University Press, 1969.

Béteille, André. 'Record of Rights: The Marie-Antoinette Solution'. *Times of India*, 28 January 1999.

Bharatiya Janata Party. 'Ek Bharat Shreshtha Bharat. Election Manifesto 2014'. 7 April 2014. http://www.bjp.org/images/pdf_2014/full_manifesto_english_07.04.2014.pdf (accessed, 3 March 2019).

Bhatnager, Gaurav Vivek. 'Norms for Delhi Schools Relaxed'. *The Hindu*, 27 March 2013. http://www.thehindu.com/news/cities/Delhi/norms-for-delhi-schools-relaxed/article4554032.ece (accessed, 19 August 2018).

Bhattacharjee, Malini, and Dolashree Mysoor. '"Unredressed" Grievances under RTE: Navigating the State Labyrinth'. *Governance: An International Journal of Policy, Administration, and Institutions* 29, no. 1 (2016): 31–45.

Bhattacharjee, Malini, Dolashree Mysoor, and Arun Sivaramakrishnan. 'RTE Grievance Redress in Karnataka'. *Economic & Political Weekly* XLIX, no. 23 (2014): 37–41.

Bhatty, Kiran. 'Educational Deprivation in India. A Survey of Field Investigations'. *Economic & Political Weekly* XXXIII, no. 27 (1998): 1731–40.

Bhatty, Kiran. 'Hobsons (School) Choice'. *Indian Express*, 28 May 2009. http://indianexpress.com/article/opinion/columns/hobsons-school-choice/ (accessed, 19 August 2018).

Bhuwania, Anuj. *Courting the People: Public Interest Litigation in Post-Emergency India*. Cambridge: Cambridge University Press, 2017.

Biju, C.M., and Amirtha Jothi. 'The Paradigm and Practice of Pollution in Caste System in Malabar'. *International Journal of Scientific & Engineering Research* 3, no. 12 (2012). http://www.ijser.org/researchpaper%5CThe-Paradigm-and-Practice-of-Pollution-in-Caste-System-in-Malabar.pdf (accessed, 19 August 2018).

Bilchitz, David. 'Expanding Access to Justice for Socio-Economic Rights Complaints in South Africa: Which Direction Should We Head in?'. 2017. https://voelkerrechtsblog.org/expanding-access-to-justice-for-socio-economic-rights-complaints-in-south-africa/ (accessed, 12 August 2018).

Bilchitz, David. *Poverty and Fundamental Rights: The Justification and Enforcement of Socio-Economic Rights*. Oxford, New York: Oxford University Press, 2007.

Birchfield, Lauren, and Jessica Corsi. 'Between Starvation and Globalization: Realizing the Right to Food in India'. *Michigan Journal of International Law* 31, no. 4 (2010): 691–764.

Biswas, A. *Development of Education in India: A Historical Survey of Educational Documents Before and After Independence*. Reprinted. New Delhi: Concept Publishing Company, 1994[1986].

Bloch, Frank. S., and Iqbal S. Ishar. 'Legal Aid, Public Service and Clinical Legal Education: Future Directions from India and the United States'. *Michigan Journal of International Law* 12, no. 1 (1992): 92–120.

Brand, Danie. 'The Proceduralisation of South African Socio-Economic Rights Jurisprudence, or "What are Socio-Economic Rights For?"'. In *Rights and Democracy in a Transformative Constitution*. Edited by Henk Botha, Andre Van der Walt, and J.C. Van der Walt 1st edition, 57–66. Stellenbosch: SUN Press, 2003.

Bruce, John W., Omar Garcia-Bolivar, Tim Hanstad, Michael Roth, Robin Nielsen, Anna Knox, and Jon Schmidt. 'Legal Empowerment of the Poor: From Concepts to Assessment'. March 2007. http://pdf.usaid.gov/pdf_docs/Pnadm500.pdf (accessed, 19 August 2018).

Bundesverfassungsgericht. BVerfGE 7, 198 – 'Lüth', 15 January 1958.

Bundesverfassungsgericht. BVerfGE 81, 242 – 'Handelsvertreter', 7 February 1990.

Bundesverfassungsgericht. BVerfGE 114, 1–72 – 'Bestandsübertragung', 26 July 2005.

Bundesverfassungsgericht. BVerfGE 125, 175–260 – 'Hartz IV', 9 February 2010. http://www.bundesverfassungsgericht.de/SharedDocs/Entscheidungen/DE/2010/02/ls20100209_1bvl000109.html (accessed, 19 August 2018).

*Business Standard*. 'Govt Extends Provisional Recognition to Pvt Schools for 5th Time'. 28 April 2016. http://www.business-standard.com/article/pti-stories/govt-extends-provisional-recognition-to-pvt-schools-for-5th-time-116042801191_1.html (accessed, 19 August 2018).

Canaris, Claus-Wilhelm. 'Grundrechte und Privatrecht'. *Archiv für die civilistische Praxis (AcP)* 184 (1984): 201–46.

Canaris, Claus-Wilhelm. 'Grundrechtswirkungen und Verhältnismäßigkeitsprinzip in der richterlichen Anwendung und Fortbildung des Privatrechts'. *Juristische Schulung (JuS)* 29, no. 3 (1989): 161–72.

Carothers, Thomas. 'The Rule of Law Revival'. *Foreign Affairs* 77, no. 2 (1998): 95–106.

Cassels, Jamie. 'Judicial Activism and Public Interest Litigation in India: Attempting the Impossible?', *The American Journal of Comparative Law* 37, no. 3 (1989): 495–519.

Chandra, Aparna. 'India and International Law: Formal Dualism, Functional Monism'. *Indian Journal of International Law* 57, no. 1–2 (2017): 25–45.

Chandra, Sushant, and Nityash Solanki. 'Legal Aid in India: Returning Philosophical Chords'. *BRICS Law Journal* 2, no. 2 (2015): 68–85. https://web.archive.org/web/20160508190124/http://www.bricslawjournal.com/data/documents/Chandra-iz-BLG_2_2015.pdf (accessed, 19 August 2018).

Chandrachud, Abhinav. 'Supreme Court's Seniority Norms. Historical Origins'. *Economic & Political Weekly* XLVII, no. 8 (2012): 26–30.

Chari, Mridula. 'Why Bangalore Schools are Rushing for Minority Certificates'. *Scroll.in*, 19 May 2014. http://scroll.in/article/664538/why-bangalore-schools-are-rushing-for-minority-certificates (accessed, 19 August 2018).

Chatterjee, Partha. *The Politics of the Governed: Reflections on Popular Politics in Most of the World*. New York: Columbia University Press, 2004.

Cherednychenko, Olha O. 'Fundamental Rights and Private Law: A Relationship of Subordination or Complementarity?', *Utrecht Law Review* 3, no. 2 (2007): 1–25.

Chin, Aimee. 'Can Redistributing Teachers Across Schools Raise Educational Attainment? Evidence from Operation Blackboard in India'. *Journal of Development Economics* 78, no. 2 (2005): 384–405.

Chopra, Pran, ed. *The Supreme Court Versus the Constitution: A Challenge to Federalism*. New Delhi, Thousand Oaks: SAGE, 2006. http://

site.ebrary.com/lib/alltitles/docDetail.action?docID=10313102 (accessed, 2 March 2019).

Chossudovsky, Michel. 'India under IMF Rule'. *Economic & Political Weekly* 28, no. 10 (1993): 385–7.

Choudharil, Abhishek. 'States, UTs may be Allowed to Formulate Their Own No-Detention Policy Soon'. *Times of India*, 26 October 2016. http://timesofindia.indiatimes.com/city/nagpur/States-UTs-may-be-allowed-to-formulate-their-own-no-detention-policy-soon/articleshow/55058260.cms (accessed, 19 August 2018).

Choudhry, Sujit, Madhav Khosla, and Pratap Bhanu Mehta, eds. *The Oxford Handbook of the Indian Constitution*. Oxford, New York: Oxford University Press, 2016.

Clapham, Andrew. 'The "Drittwirkung" of the Convention'. In *The European System for the Protection of Human Rights*. Edited by Ronald J. St. Macdonald, Franz Matscher, and Herbert Petzold, 163–206. Dordrecht, Boston: M. Nijhoff, 1993.

Committee for the Review of National Policy on Education. 'Report of the Committee for the Review of National Policy on Education, 1986'. 1990. https://web.archive.org/web/20120131104621/http://www.education.nic.in/cd50years/g/t/v/Toc.htm (accessed, 19 August 2018).

Committee on Economic, Social and Cultural Rights. 'General Comment 1, Reporting by States parties (Third session, 1989)'. U.N. Doc. E/1989/22.

Committee on Economic, Social and Cultural Rights. 'General Comment 11: Plans of Action for Primary Education (Twentieth session, 1999)'. U.N. Doc. E/1992/23.

Committee on Economic, Social and Cultural Rights. 'General Comment 12, Right to Adequate Food (Twentieth session, 1999)'. U.N. Doc. E/C.12/1999/5.

Committee on Economic, Social and Cultural Rights. 'General Comment 3, The Nature of States Parties' Obligations (Fifth session, 1990)'. U.N. Doc. E/1991/23.

Committee on Economic, Social and Cultural Rights. 'General Comment 13, The Right to Education (Twenty-first session, 1999)'. U.N. Doc. E/C.12/1999/10.

Committee on Economic, Social and Cultural Rights. 'Substantive Issues Arising in the Implementation of the International Covenant on Economic, Social and Cultural Rights: Day of General Discussion Organized in Cooperation with the World Intellectual Property Organization (WIPO)'. 2000. https://web.archive.org/

web/20151004182847/http://www.unhchr.ch/tbs/doc.nsf/898586b1dc7b4043c1256a450044f331/6b748989d76d2bb8c125699700500e17/$FILE/G0044704.pdf (accessed, 19 August 2018).

Conrad, Dieter, ed. *Zwischen den Traditionen: Probleme des Verfassungsrechts und der Rechtskultur in Indien und Pakistan gesammelte Aufsätze aus den Jahren 1970-1990*. Stuttgart: Steiner, 1999.

Conrad, Dieter. ‚Die Zukunft des indischen Rechtsstaates'. In *Zwischen den Traditionen: Probleme des Verfassungsrechts und der Rechtskultur in Indien und Pakistan gesammelte Aufsätze aus den Jahren 1970–1990*. Edited by Dieter Conrad, 135–47. Stuttgart: Steiner, 1999.

Constitutional Court of Colombia. Sentencia T-025/04, 22 January 2004. http://www.corteconstitucional.gov.co/relatoria/2004/t%2D025%2D04.htm (accessed, 17 November 2015).

Constitutional Court of Colombia. Sentencia T-760/08, 31 July 2008. http://www.corteconstitucional.gov.co/relatoria/2008/t%2D760%2D08.htm (accessed, 17 November 2015).

Coomans, Fons. 'Identifying the Key Elements of the Right to Education: A Focus on Its Core Content'. 2007, 1–10. https://www.crin.org/en/docs/Coomans-CoreContent-Right%20to%20EducationCRC.pdf (accessed, 19 August 2018).

Coomans, Fons. 'Justiciability of the Right to Education'. *Erasmus Law Review* 2, no. 4 (2009): 427–43.

Craig, P.P., and S.L. Deshpande. 'Rights, Autonomy and Process: Public Interest Litigation in India'. *Oxford Journal of Legal Studies* 9, no. 3 (1989): 356–73.

Craven, Matthew C.R. *The International Covenant on Economic, Social, and Cultural Rights: A Perspective on its Development*. Oxford: Clarendon, 1995.

Craven, Matthew. 'Towards an Unofficial Petition Procedure: A Review on the Role of the UN Committee on Economic, Social and Cultural Rights'. In *Social Rights as Human Rights: A European Challenge*. Edited by Krzysztof Drzewicki, Catarina Krause, and Allan Rosas, 91–113. Turku/Åbo, Finland: Institute for Human Rights, Åbo Akademi University, 1994.

Cross, Frank B. 'The Error of Positive Rights'. *UCLA Law Review* 48 (2001): 857–924.

Dam, Shubhankar. 'Right to Education in India: Horizontal Implications'. *The Law Quarterly Review* 128, Part 4 (2012): 507–11.

Dann, Philipp. 'Federal Democracy in India and the European Union: Towards Transcontinental Comparison of Constitutional Law'. *Law and Politics in Africa, Asia, Latin America (VRU)* 44, no. 2 (2011): 160–76. https://www.nomos-elibrary.de/10.5771/0506-7286-2011-2-160/federal-democracy-in-india-and-the-european-union-towards-transcontinental-comparison-of-constitutional-law-jahrgang-44-2011-heft-2?page=0 (accessed, 19 August 2018).

Daruwala, Maja, Venkatesh Nayak, and Amikar Parwar. 'A Rapid Study of Information Commissions Established Under the Right to Information Laws in India'. May 2012. http://humanrightsinitiative.org/old/publications/rti/ICs-compstudy-final-Delhi-May12-VenkatN&AmikarP.pdf (accessed, 19 August 2018).

Datar, Arvind P. 'The Case that Saved Indian Democracy'. *The Hindu*, 24 April 2013. http://www.thehindu.com/opinion/op-ed/the-case-that-saved-indian-democracy/article4647800.ece (accessed, 19 August 2018).

De, Anuradha. *Probe Revisited: A Report on Elementary Education in India*. New Delhi: Oxford University Press, 2011.

Delhi High Court. *Abul Hassan* v. *Delhi Vidyut Board* MANU/DE/0011/1999, 15 January 1999.

Delhi High Court. *Birndavan Sharma* v. *State* MANU/DE/2524/2007, 24 August 2007.

Delhi High Court. *Jatin Singh* v. *Kendriya Vidyalaya Sangathan* MANU/DE/5469/2012, 9 November 2012.

Delhi High Court. *Laxmi Mandal* v. *Deen Dayal Harinagar Hospital* MANU/DE/1268/2010, 4 June 2010.

Delhi High Court. *Master Mohd. Abdullah (Minor)* v. *Govt. Of Nct Of Delhi And Ors* MANU/DE/2807/2011, 23 May 2011.

Delhi High Court. *Master Singham* v. *Directorate of Education and Ors* MANU/DE/2625/2018, 2 July 2018.

Delhi High Court. *Mohd. Ahmed (Minor)* v. *Union of India* MANU/DE/0915/2014, 17 April 2014.

Delhi High Court. *Naz Foundation* v. *Government of NCT of Delhi* MANU/DE/0869/2009, 2 July 2009.

Delhi High Court. *Shishti Solkar & Ors* v. *Mahavir Sr. Model School & Ors* MANU/DE/7010/2011, 23 December 2011.

Delhi High Court. *Siddharth International Public School* v. *Motor Accident Claim Tribunal and Ors* MANU/DE/2218/2016, 26 August 2016.

Delhi High Court. *Social Jurist a Civil Rights Group* v. *Govt. of NCT of Delhi and Ors* MANU/DE/1647/2015, 7 May 2015.

Delhi High Court. *Social Jurist* v. *GNCT and Ors* MANU/DE/0203/2008, 8 February 2008.

Desai, Sonalde, and Veena Kulkarni. 'Changing Educational Inequalities in India in the Context of Affirmative Action'. *Demography* 45, no. 2 (2008): 245–70. http://www.ncbi.nlm.nih.gov/pmc/articles/PMC2474466/ (accessed, 19 August 2018).

Deva, Surya. 'Human Rights Realization in an Era of Globalization: The Indian Experience'. *Buffalo Human Rights Law Review* 12 (2006): 93–138.

Dhamija, Ashok. 'Empowering District Courts to enforce Fundamental Rights'. 3 May 2012. http://tilakmarg.com/opinion/empowering-district-courts-to-enforce-fundamental-rights/ (accessed, 19 August 2018).

Dhavan, Rajeev. 'Law as Struggle: Public Interest Law in India'. *Journal of the Indian Law Institute* 36, no. 3 (1994): 302–38.

Dhawan, Payal. 'RTE: "Closed" Schools Function without Problem'. *Times of India*, 31 January 2014. http://timesofindia.indiatimes.com/city/ludhiana/RTE-Closed-schools-function-without-problem/articleshow/29622330.cms (accessed, 19 August 2018).

DiBona, Joseph. *One Teacher, One School: The Adam Reports on Indigenous Education in 19th Century India*. New Delhi: Biblia Impex, 1983.

Dicey, A.V. *Introduction to the Study of the Law of the Constitution*. Indianapolis: Liberty/Classics, 1982.

*DNA India*. 'Maharashtra to Raise Government Staffers' Salaries, Pensions'. 30 June 2016. http://www.dnaindia.com/mumbai/report-maharashtra-to-raise-government-staffers-salaries-pensions-2229526 (accessed, 19 August 2018).

Dohrman, Jona Aravind. *Directive Principles of State Policy in der indischen Verfassung unter Berücksichtigung der Staatszielbestimmungen des deutschen Grundgesetzes*. Würzburg: Ergon, 2002.

Drèze, Jean, and Amartya Kumar Sen. *India: Development and Participation*. 2nd edition. Oxford, New York: Oxford University Press, 2002.

Drèze, Jean, and Amartya Sen, eds. *Indian Development: Selected Regional Perspectives*. Delhi, New York: Oxford University Press, 1997.

Drèze, Jean, and Amartya Sen. *An Uncertain Glory: India and Its Contradictions*. London: Penguin Books, 2013.

Drèze, Jean, and Aparajita Goyal. 'Future of Mid-Day Meals'. *Economic & Political Weekly* XXXVIII, no. 44 (2003): 4673–83.

Drèze, Jean, and Geeta Gandhi Kingdon. 'School Participation in Rural India'. 2007. http://sticerd.lse.ac.uk/dps/de/dedps18.pdf (accessed, 19 August 2018).

Drèze, Jean, and Haris Gazdar. 'Uttar Pradesh: The Burden of Inertia'. In *Indian Development*, 33–128.

Drèze, Jean. 'Summary of the National Food Security Bill 2013'. *Tehelka*, 22 March 2013. http://old.tehelka.com/exclusive-summary-of-the-national-food-security-bill-2013/ (accessed, 19 August 2018).

*Economic Times*. 'Centre to Give Rs 148 Crore to National Legal Services Authority'. 31 January 2016. https://economictimes.indiatimes.com/news/politics-and-nation/centre-to-give-rs-148-crore-to-national-legal-services-authority/articleshow/50795255.cms (accessed, 19 August 2018).

*Economic Times*. 'States Criticise the "No-Detention" and "Continuous Evaluation" Provisions of RTE'. 7 June 2012. https://economictimes.indiatimes.com/industry/services/education/states-criticise-the-no-detention-and-continuous-evaluation-provisions-of-rte/articleshow/13885701.cms (accessed, 19 August 2018).

Eide, Asbjørn, Catarina Krause, and Allan Rosas, eds. *Economic, Social and Cultural Rights: A Textbook*. 2nd edition. Dordrecht: Martinus Nijhoff, 2001.

Eide, Asbjørn. 'Economic, Social and Cultural Rights as Human Rights'. In *Economic, Social and Cultural Rights*, 9–28.

Eide, Asbjørn. 'State Obligations Revisited'. In *Food and Human Rights in Development*. Edited by Wenche B. Eide, 137–58. Antwerpen: Intersentia, 2007.

Endicott, Timothy A.O. 'The Impossibility of the Rule of Law'. *Oxford Journal of Legal Studies* 19, no. 1 (1999): 1–18.

Engle, Eric. 'Third Party Effect of Fundamental Rights (Drittwirkung)'. *Hanse Law Review* 5, no. 2 (2009): 165–73. https://papers.ssrn.com/sol3/papers.cfm?abstract_id=1481552 (accessed, 19 August 2018).

Epp, Charles R. *The Rights Revolution: Lawyers, Activists, and Supreme Courts in Comparative Perspective*. Chicago: University of Chicago Press, 1998.

European Commission for the Efficiency of Justice. 'European Judicial Systems: Efficiency and Quality of Justice. An Overview'. 2014. https://web.archive.org/web/20160625050701/http://www.coe.int/t/dghl/cooperation/cepej/evaluation/2014/synthese2014_en.pdf (accessed, 2 March 2019).

European Court of Human Rights. *Campell and Cosans* v. *The United Kingdom*, 25 February 1982.

European Court of Human Rights. Relating to Certain Aspects of the Laws on the Use of Languages in Education in Belgium, 9 February 1967.

European Court of Justice. *Andrea Francovich and Danila Bonifaci and others* v. *Italian Republic*, 19 November 1991.

European Court of Justice. *Case of Airey* v. *Ireland*, 9 October 1979. http://hudoc.echr.coe.int/eng?i=001-57420#{"itemid":["001-57420"]} (accessed, 19 August 2018).

Evans, Stephen. 'Macaulay's Minute Revisited: Colonial Language Policy in Nineteenth-Century India'. *Journal of Multilingual and Multicultural Development* 23, no. 4 (2002): 260–81.

Fabre, Cécile. *Social Rights under the Constitution: Government and the Decent Life*. Oxford, New York: Clarendon Press; Oxford University Press, 2000.

Fernandes, Walter. 'Singur and the Displacement Scenario'. *Economic & Political Weekly* XLII, no. 3 (2007): 203–6.

*Financial Express*. 'How Delhi Government Schools Performed Better than Private Schools in CBSE 12th Exams'. 28 March 2018. https://www.financialexpress.com/india-news/how-delhi-government-schools-performed-better-than-private-schools-in-cbse-12th-exams/1183001/ (accessed, 12 August 2018).

*Financial Express*. "Tat' Pulls Out of Singur, Blames Trinamool Stir'. 4 October 2008. http://www.financialexpress.com/archive/Tata-pulls-out-of-Singur-blames-Trinamool-stir/369241/ (accessed, 19 August 2018).

Francis, Alys. 'Why India's Landmark Education Law is Shutting Down Schools'. BBC, 6 March 2014. http://www.bbc.com/news/world-asia-india-26333713 (accessed, 19 August 2018).

Frank, Katherine. *Indira: The Life of Indira Nehru Gandhi*. New Delhi: HarperCollins, 2005.

Fredman, Sandra. *Human Rights Transformed: Positive Rights and Positive Duties*. Oxford, New York: Oxford University Press, 2008.

Fried, Charles. *Right and Wrong*. Cambridge, Mass.: Harvard University Press, 1978.

Fuller, Lon L. 'The Forms and Limits of Adjudication'. *Harvard Law Review* 92, no. 2 (1978): 353–409.

Galanter, Marc, and Jayanth K. Krishnan. '"Bread for the Poor": Access to Justice and the Rights of the Needy in India'. *Hastings Law Journal* 55, no. 4 (2004): 789–834.

Galanter, Marc, and Nick Robinson. 'India's Grand Advocates: A Legal Elite Flourishing in the Era of Globalization'. 2013. http://ssrn.com/abstract=2348699 (accessed, 19 August 2018).

Galanter, Marc. 'Snakes and Ladders: Suo Moto Intervention and the Indian Judiciary'. *FIU Law Review* (2014): 69–83.

Ganz, Kian. 'SH Kapadia, End of an Era: India's Greatest Ever CJI or Missed Opportunity? How will You Remember the Legacy?', *Legally India*, 28 September 2012. http://www.legallyindia.com/interviews/sh-kapadia-end-of-an-era-indias-greatest-ever-cji-or-missed-opportunity-how-will-you-remember-the-legacy (accessed, 19 August 2018).

Ganz, Kian. 'Supreme Court's Battle Against Backlog in Cases'. *Live Mint*, 7 June 2012. http://www.livemint.com/Politics/ziffwni3N64eFBcaWZobtL/Supreme-Court8217s-battle-against-backlog-in-cases.html (accessed, 19 August 2018).

Gardbaum, Stephen. 'The "Horizontal Effect" of Constitutional Rights'. *Michigan Law Review* 102, no. 3 (2003): 387–459.

Gauri, Varun. 'Fundamental Rights and Public Interest Litigation in India: Overreaching or Underachieving?', *Indian Journal of Law & Economics* 1, no. 1 (2010): 71–93.

Gauri, Varun. 'Redressing Grievances and Complaints Regarding Basic Service Delivery'. 2011. http://elibrary.worldbank.org/doi/pdf/10.1596/1813-9450-5699 (accessed, 19 August 2018).

Ghai, Yash, and Jill Cottrell. 'The Rule of Law and Access to Justice'. In *Marginalized Communities and Access to Justice*. Edited by Yash P. Ghai and Jill Cottrell, 1–22. Abingdon [England], New York: Routledge, 2010.

Global Initiative to End All Corporal Punishment of Children. 'Corporal Punishment of Children in India'. 2015. https://web.archive.org/web/20160122194628/http://www.endcorporalpunishment.org/assets/pdfs/states-reports/India.pdf (accessed, 2 March 2019).

Golub, Stephen. 'Beyond Rule of Law Orthodoxy. The Legal Empowerment Alternative'. http://carnegieendowment.org/files/wp41.pdf (accessed, 19 August 2018).

Golub, Stephen. 'Beyond the Rule of Law Orthodoxy: The Legal Empowerment Alternative'. Carnegie Endowment for International Peace, Washington, DC. 2003. http://carnegieendowment.org/files/wp41.pdf (accessed, 24 February 2019).

Gough, Kathleen. 'Literacy in Kerala'. In *Literacy in Traditional Societies*. Edited by Jack Goody, 133–60. Cambridge: Cambridge University Press, 1968.

Government of India - Ministry of Human Resource Development - Department of School Education & Literacy. 'Sarva Shiksha Abhiyan - Framework for Implementation: Based on the Right of Children to Free and Compulsory Education Act, 2009'. 2011. http://mhrd.gov.in/sites/upload_files/mhrd/files/upload_document/SSA-Framework.pdf (accessed, 19 August 2018).

Government of India - Ministry of Human Resource Development. 'Education for All: Towards Quality with Equity'. 1st edition, New Delhi, August 2014. http://mhrd.gov.in/sites/upload_files/mhrd/files/upload_document/EFA-Review-Report-final.pdf (accessed, 2 March 2019).

Government of India - Ministry of Human Resource Development. 'Some Inputs for Draft National Education Policy 2016'. New Delhi, 2016. http://mhrd.gov.in/sites/upload_files/mhrd/files/Inputs_Draft_NEP_2016_1.pdf (accessed, 2 March 2019).

Government of India - Ministry of Women and Child Development. 'India: Third and Fourth Combined Periodic Report on the Convention on the Rights of the Child'. New Delhi, 2011. http://tbinternet.ohchr.org/_layouts/treatybodyexternal/Download.aspx?symbolno=CRC%2fC%2fIND%2f3-4&Lang=en (accessed, 2 March 2019).

Government of India, Planning Commission of India. *Eleventh Five Year Plan, 2007–2012: Social Sector. Volume II*. New Delhi: Oxford University Press, 2008. http://planningcommission.nic.in/plans/planrel/fiveyr/11th/11_v2/11th_vol2.pdf (accessed, 19 August 2018).

Government of India, Planning Commission of India. *Twelfth Five Year Plan (2012–2017): Social Sectors. Volume III*. New Delhi: SAGE. http://planningcommission.gov.in/plans/planrel/fiveyr/12th/pdf/12fyp_vol3.pdf (accessed, 19 August 2018).

Government of India. *National Policy on Education, 1986. As Modified in 1992*. 1992. http://mhrd.gov.in/sites/upload_files/mhrd/files/document-reports/NPE86-mod92.pdf (accessed, 19 August 2018).

Goyal, Sangeeta, and Priyanka Pandey. 'How Do Government and Private Schools Differ?', *Economic & Political Weekly* XLVII, no. 22 (2012): 67–76.

Guha, Ramachandra. *India after Gandhi: The History of the World's Largest Democracy*. New York: Harper Perennial, 2007.

Gupta, Amita. *Early Childhood Education, Postcolonial Theory, and Teaching Practices and Policies in India: Balancing Vygotsky and the Veda*. New York, Basingstoke: Palgrave Macmillan, 2013.

Gupta, Vikas. 'Politics of the Guarded Agenda of National Education Policy 2015–16'. *Economic & Political Weekly* LI, no. 42 (2016): 59–69.

Guruswamy, Menaka, and Bipin Aspatwar. 'Access to Justice in India: The Jurisprudence (and Self-Perception) of the Supreme Court'. 2013. http://ssrn.com/abstract=2498459 (accessed, 19 August 2018).

*Hans India*. '105 Unrecognised Schools Continue to Exist in Krishna'. 12 January 2016. http://www.thehansindia.com/posts/index/Andhra-

Pradesh/2016-06-12/105-unrecognised-schools-continue-to-exist-in-Krishna/234588 (accessed, 19 August 2018).

Hart, Henry C. 'The Indian Constitution: Political Development and Decay'. *Asian Survey* 20, no. 4 (1980): 428–51.

Hartog, Philip. *Some Aspects of Indian Education Past and Present*. London: Oxford University Press, 1939.

Hidayatullah, M. 'Highways and Bylanes of Justice'. *Supreme Court Cases (Journal)*, no. 2 (1984): 1–7.

Hirschl, Ran. *Towards Juristocracy: The Origins and Consequences of the New Constitutionalism*. Cambridge, Mass.: Harvard University Press, 2004.

Hoffmann, Florian F., and Fernando R.N.M Bentes. 'Accountability for Social and Economic Rights in Brazil'. In *Courting Social Justice: Judicial Enforcement of Social and Economic Rights in the Developing World*. Edited by Varun Gauri and Daniel M. Brinks, 100–45. Cambridge, New York: Cambridge University Press, 2008.

Holmes, Stephen, and Cass R. Sunstein. *The Cost of Rights: Why Liberty Depends on Taxes*. 1st edition. New York: W.W. Norton, 1999.

Human Rights Committee. *Gonzalez del Rio* v. *Peru* U.N. Doc. CCPR/C/46/D/263/1987 (1992), 2 November 1992.

Human Rights Committee. *Karttunen* v. *Finland*, Communication No. 387/1989, 5 November 1992.

IDFC Foundation. 'India Infrastructure Report 2012: Private Sector in Education'. 2013. http://www.idfc.com/pdf/report/iir-2012.pdf (accessed, 2 March 2019).

*India Today*. 'Schools Follow RTE Act: Says MHRD'. 25 October 2016. http://indiatoday.intoday.in/education/story/schools-follows-rte-act-says-mhrd/1/794821.html (accessed, 19 August 2018).

*Indian Express*. '7th Pay Commission: Govt "By and Large" Accepts Recommendations, Minimum Salary Raised to Rs 18,000'. 30 June 2016. http://indianexpress.com/article/business/business-others/7th-pay-commission-cabinet-meeting-latest-updates-today-2882835/ (accessed, 19 August 2018).

*Indian Express*. 'Government Schools Adhering to RTE Act Norms: Centre to HC'. 24 October 2016. http://indianexpress.com/article/education/government-schools-adhering-to-rte-act-norms-centre-to-hc-3100815/ (accessed, 19 August 2018).

*Indian Express*. 'Gujarat Government to Implement 7th Pay Commission from August 1'. 31 July 2016. http://indianexpress.com/article/business/7th-pay-commission-gujarat-government-to-implement-7th-pay-commission-from-august-1-2946531/ (accessed, 19 August 2018).

*Indian Express*. 'RTE Admissions: Dismal Response Forces Authorities to Start 2nd Round of Online Applications'. 9 October 2016. http://indianexpress.com/article/pune/rte-admissions-dismal-response-forces-authorities-to-start-2nd-round-of-online-applications-3072792/ (accessed, 19 August 2018).

*Indian Express*. 'Unrecognised Delhi Schools Face Threat of Closure'. 8 February 2018. https://indianexpress.com/article/education/unrecognised-delhi-schools-face-threat-of-closure-5055594/ (accessed, 12 August 2018).

International Law Commission. 'Report of the International Law Commission on Its Twenty Ninth Session: Yearbook of the International Law Commission, Vol. 2 (1977)'. International Law Commission, 1977. http://legal.un.org/ilc/documentation/english/reports/a_32_10.pdf (accessed, 9 March 2019).

Jain, Mahabir Prashad, Ruma Pal, and Samaraditya Pal. *Indian Constitutional Law*. 6th edition. Gurgaon: LexisNexis Butterworths Wadhwa Nagpur, 2010.

Jain, Mahabir Prashad. 'The Supreme Court and Fundamental Rights'. In *Fifty Years of the Supreme Court of India*, 1–100.

Jain, Pankaj S., and Ravindra H. Dholakia. 'Feasibility of Implementation of Right to Education Act'. *Economic & Political Weekly* XLIV, no. 25 (2009): 38–43.

Jain, Pankaj S., and Ravindra H. Dholakia. 'Right to Education Act and Public-Private Partnership'. *Economic & Political Weekly* XLV, no. 8 (2010): 78–80.

Jain, Purvi. '70% RTE Quota Seats not Filled in MP'. *Hindustan Times*, 14 October 2016. http://www.hindustantimes.com/education/70-rte-quota-seats-not-filled-in-mp/story-5S1UTCB3f1Ras3w5GaGsLI.html (accessed, 19 August 2018).

Jeffrey, Robin. 'Governments and Culture: How Women Made Kerala Literate'. *Pacific Affairs* 60, no. 3 (1987): 447–72. http://www.jstor.org/stable/2758883 (accessed, 19 August 2018).

Jha, Praveen K. *Public Provisioning for Elementary Education in India*. New Delhi, Thousand Oaks: SAGE, 2008.

Jha, Praveen K., and P. Geetha Rani, eds. *Right to Education in India. Resources, Institutions and Public Policy*. Abingdon, New York: Routledge, 2016.

K.S., Vidya, and Padma M. Sarangapani. 'Is Education News?', *Economic & Political Weekly* XLVI, no. 42 (2011): 69–76.

Kabir, Altamas. 'Bringing Legal Aid a Step Closer Home'. *The Hindu*, 9 November 2011. http://www.thehindu.com/opinion/lead/bringing-legal-aid-a-step-closer-home/article2609718.ece (accessed, 19 August 2018).

Kalantry, Sital, Jocelyn E. Getgen, and Steven Arrigg Koh. 'Enhancing Enforcement of Economic, Social, and Cultural Rights Using Indicators: A Focus on the Right to Education in the ICESCR'. *Human Rights Quarterly* 32, no. 2 (2010): 253–310.

Karnam, Murali, and Trijeeb Nanda. 'Conditions of Undertrials in India: Problems and Solutions'. *Economic & Political Weekly* LI, no. 13 (2016): 14–16.

Keay, F.E. *Ancient Indian Education: An Inquiry into its Origin, Development, and Ideals*. New Delhi: Cosmo Publications, 1992.

Khera, Reetika. 'Mid-Day Meals in Primary Schools. Achievements and Challenges'. *Economic & Political Weekly* XLI, no. 46 (2006): 4742–50.

Khosla, Madhav. 'Making Social Rights Conditional: Lessons from India'. *ICON* 8, no. 4 (2010): 739–65.

Khosla, Madhav. *The Indian Constitution*. New Delhi: Oxford University Press, 2012.

Kingdon, Geeta Gandhi, and Mohd Muzammil. 'A Political Economy of Education in India–II: The Case of UP'. *Economic & Political Weekly* XXXVI, no. 33 (2001): 3178–85.

Kingdon, Geeta Gandhi. 'The Progress of School Education in India'. 2007. https://web.archive.org/web/20130421051641/http://economics.ouls.ox.ac.uk/12991/1/gprg-wps-071.pdf (accessed, 19 August 2018).

Kingdon, Geeta. 'Schooling without Learning: How the RTE Act Destroys Private Schools and Destroys Standards in Public Schools'. *Times of India*, 26 August 2015. http://blogs.timesofindia.indiatimes.com/toi-edit-page/schooling-without-learning-how-the-rte-act-destroys-private-schools-and-destroys-standards-in-public-schools/ (accessed, 19 August 2018).

Klein, Hans Hugo. 'Grundrechte am Beginn des 21. Jahrhunderts'. In Merten; Papier, *Handbuch der Grundrechte in Deutschland und Europa*, 269–312.

Kothari, Jayna, and Aparna Ravi. 'A Battle of Rights: The Right to Education of Children Versus Rights of Minority Schools'. *Oxford University Commonwealth Law Journal* 16, no. 2 (2017): 195–218.

Kothari, Jayna. 'Social Rights and the Indian Constitution'. *Social Justice & Global Development Journal* 2 (2004).

Kothari, Jayna. 'Social Rights Litigation in India: Developments of the Last Decade'. In *Exploring Social Rights: Between Theory and Practice*.

Edited by Daphne Barak-Erez and Aeyal M. Gross, 171–92. Oxford, Portland, Or: Hart Publishing, 2007.

Kothari, Rita. *Translating India*. Hoboken: Taylor and Francis, 2014.

Kremer, Michael, Karthik Muralidharan, Nazmul Chaudhury, Jeffrey Hammer, and F. Halsey Rogers. 'Teacher Absence in India: A Snapshot'. *Journal of the European Economic Association* 3, no. 2–3 (2005): 658–67.

Krings, Günter. *Grund und Grenzen grundrechtlicher Schutzansprüche: Die subjektiv-rechtliche Rekonstruktion der grundrechtlichen Schutzpflichten und ihre Auswirkung auf die verfassungsrechtliche Fundierung des Verbrauchervertragsrechts*. Berlin: Duncker & Humblot, 2003.

Krishna Kumar, Joachim Oesterheld, and Sonia Amin, eds. *Education and Social Change in South Asia*. New Delhi: Orient Longman, 2007.

Krishnan, Jayanth K. 'Social Policy Advocacy and the Role of the Courts in India'. *American Asian Review* XXI, no. 2 (2003): 91–124.

Krishnan, Jayanth K., Shirish N. Kavadi, Azima Girach, Dhanaji Khupkar, Kalindi Kokal, Satyajeet Mazumdar, Nupur, Gayatri Panday, Aatreyee Sen, Aqseer Sodhi, and Bharati Takale Shukla. 'Grappling at the Grassroots: Access to Justice in India's Lower Tier'. *Harvard Human Rights Journal* 27, no. 1 (2014): 501–39.

Krishnaswamy, Sudhir. 'Horizontal Application of Fundamental Rights and State Action in India'. In *Human Rights, Justice, and Constitutional Empowerment*, 47.

Krishnaswamy, Sudhir. *Democracy and Constitutionalism in India: A Study of the Basic Structure Doctrine*. New Delhi: Oxford University Press, 2009.

Krueger, Anne O. *Economic Policy Reforms and the Indian Economy*. Chicago: University of Chicago Press, 2002.

Kumar, C. Raj, K. Chockalingam, and V.R. Krishna Iyer, eds. *Human Rights, Justice, and Constitutional Empowerment*. 2nd edition. New Delhi: Oxford University Press, 2010.

LaDousa, Chaise. *Hindi is Our Ground, English is Our Sky: Education, Language, and Social Class in Contemporary India*. New York: Berghahn Books, 2014.

Landau, David. 'The Reality of Social Rights Enforcement'. *Harvard International Law Journal* 53, no. 1 (2012): 189–247.

Langford, Malcolm, and Jeff A. King. 'Committee on Economic, Social and Cultural Rights'. In *Social Rights Jurisprudence*, 477–516.

Langford, Malcolm, ed. *Social Rights Jurisprudence: Emerging Trends in International and Comparative Law*. Cambridge, New York: Cambridge University Press, 2008.

Langford, Malcolm. 'The Justiciability of Social Rights: From Practice to Theory'. In *Social Rights Jurisprudence*, 3–45.

Lashkari, Milind R. 'Delay in RTE Admissions in Second Round Worries Parents in Indore'. *Hindustan Times*, 13 October 2016. http://www.hindustantimes.com/indore/delay-in-rte-admissions-in-second-round-worries-parents-in-indore/story-JMITGZdpZbqFZEWIMS9p-gL.html (accessed, 19 August 2018).

Law Commission of India. 'One Hundred Twentieth Report on Manpower Planning in Judiciary: A Blueprint'. 1987. http://lawcommissionofindia.nic.in/101-169/report120.pdf (accessed, 2 March 2019).

Leftwich, Adrian. 'Governance, Democracy and Development in the Third World'. *Third World Quarterly* 14, no. 3 (2007): 605–24.

Liebau, Heike. '"Indianisation" and Education: Reaction from Protestant Christians of the Madras Presidency to the Lindsay Commission Report'. In *Education and Social Change in South Asia*, 44–73.

Mashaw, Jerry Louis. 'Accountability and Institutional Design: Some Thoughts on the Grammar of Governance'. 2006. http://papers.ssrn.com/sol3/papers.cfm?abstract_id=924879 (accessed, 19 August 2018).

Masing, Johannes. *Die Mobilisierung des Bürgers für die Durchsetzung des Rechts: Europäische Impulse für eine Revision der Lehre vom subjektiv-öffentlichen Recht*. Berlin: Duncker & Humblot, 1997.

Matthey-Prakash, Florian. 'School Management Committees as a Means for Bottom-Up Implementation of the Right to Education in India'. *Law and Politics in Africa, Asia, Latin America (VRU)* 49, no. 2 (2016): 193–215. https://www.nomos-elibrary.de/10.5771/0506-7286-2016-2-193/school-management-committees-as-a-means-for-bottom-up-implementation-of-the-right-to-education-in-india-jahrgang-49-2016-heft-2?page=1 (accessed, 19 August 2018).

Maurer, Hartmut. *Allgemeines Verwaltungsrecht*. 18th edition. München: Beck, C.H., 2011.

Mehendale, Archana, Rahul Mukhopadyay, and Annie Namala. 'Right to Education and Inclusion in Private Unaided Schools. An Exploratory Study in Bengaluru and Delhi'. *Economic & Political Weekly* L, no. 7 (2015): 43–51.

Mehendale, Archana. 'Right to Education and Constitutional Amendment. A Case of India'. Currently not available online, On file with the author.

Mehra, Ajay K. '"Due Process" or "Procedure Established by Law?"', In *The Supreme Court Versus the Constitution*, 114–30.

Mehta, Pratap Bhanu. 'India's Judiciary: The Promise of Uncertainty'. In *The Supreme Court Versus the Constitution*, 155–77.

Mehta, Pratap Bhanu. *The Burden of Democracy*. New Delhi, New York: Penguin Books, 2003.

Meleisea, Ellie. *Promising EFA Practices in the Asia-Pacific Region: Sarva Shiksha Abhiyan Case Study*. Paris: The United Nations Educational, Scientific and Cultural Organization, 2015.

Merten, Detlef, and Hans-Jürgen Papier, eds. *Handbuch der Grundrechte in Deutschland und Europa*. Heidelberg: C. F. Müller, 2006.

Ministry of Women and Child Development. 'Report of the Working Group on Child Rights for the 12th Five Year Plan (2012–2017)'. 2011. https://web.archive.org/web/20140922134717/http://wcd.nic.in/reportwgdtd01032012.pdf (accessed, 19 August 2018).

*Morung Express*. 'Awareness Programme Held in Zunheboto'. 3 June 2016. http://morungexpress.com/awareness-programme-held-zunheboto/ (accessed, 19 August 2018).

*Morung Express*. 'NSLSA Holds State Level Training for PLVs'. 22 May 2016. http://morungexpress.com/nslsa-holds-state-level-training-for-plvs/ (accessed, 19 August 2018).

Motta Ferraz, Octavio L. 'Brazil: Health Inequalities, Rights, and Courts: The Social Impact of the Judicialization of Health'. In *Litigating Health Rights: Can Courts Bring More Justice to Health?* Edited by Alicia E. Yamin and Siri Gloppen, 76–102. Cambridge, MA: Human Rights Program, Harvard Law School; Harvard University Press, 2011.

Moudgil, Rajesh. 'Lapses in SSA: Long Delays in Providing Books, Uniforms'. *Hindustan Times*, 16 July 2014. https://www.hindustantimes.com/chandigarh/lapses-in-ssa-long-delays-in-providing-books-uniforms/story-6APSM3tSw7HaOf3PptFyiM.html (accessed, 19 August 2018).

Mukherjee, Mithi. *India in the Shadows of Empire: A Legal and Political History; 1774–1950*. 3rd edition. New Delhi: Oxford University Press, 2011.

Müller, Amrei. *The Relationship between Economic, Social and Cultural Rights and International Humanitarian Law: An Analysis of Health-Related Issues in Non-International Armed Conflicts*. Leiden, Boston: Martinus Nijhoff Publishers, 2013.

Muralidhar, S. *Law, Poverty and Legal Aid: Access to Criminal Justice*. New Delhi: LexisNexis Butterworth, 2004.

Muralidharan, Karthik, and Michael Kremer. 'Public and Private Schools in Rural India'. 2006. http://citeseerx.ist.psu.edu/viewdoc/download?doi=10.1.1.168.3057&rep=rep1&type=pdf (accessed, 19 August 2018).

Muralidharan, Karthik, and Michael Kremer. 'Public and Private Schools in Rural India'. 2007. http://scholar.harvard.edu/files/kremer/files/public_and_private_schools_in_rural_india_final_pre-publication.pdf (accessed, 19 August 2018).

Muralidharan, Karthik. 'Public-Private Partnerships for Quality Education in India'. Seminar, no. 565 (2006): 1. http://econweb.ucsd.edu/~kamurali/papers/Other%20Writing/public%20private%20partnerships%20for%20quality%20education%20in%20india.pdf (accessed, 19 August 2018).

Murswiek, Dietrich. 'Zu den Grenzen der Abänderbarkeit von Grundrechten'. In *Handbuch der Grundrechte in Deutschland und Europa*, 157–219.

Nagarajan, Rema. 'Those Who Speak English Fluently Earn Up to 34% More than Others: Study'. *Economic Times*, 5 January 2014. http://economictimes.indiatimes.com/jobs/those-who-speak-english-fluently-earn-up-to-34-more-than-others-study/articleshow/28426329.cms (accessed, 19 August 2018).

Nair, Preetu. 'Get Affiliation or Face Action, CBSE Schools Told'. *Times of India*, 8 April 2015. http://timesofindia.indiatimes.com/city/kochi/Get-affiliation-or-face-action-CBSE-schools-told/articleshow/46843140.cms (accessed, 19 August 2018).

Nambissan, Geeta B. 'The Indian Middle Classes and Educational Advantage. Family Strategies and Practices'. In *The Routledge International Handbook of the Sociology of Education*. Edited by Michael W. Apple, 285–95. London: Routledge, 2009.

Nanda, Prashant K. 'CBSE Class X Board Exam to Return, No-Fail Policy to Go'. *Live Mint*, 25 October 2016. http://www.livemint.com/Education/SR6AToBI1jzo4Vaffn2YWO/Govt-may-bring-back-CBSE-Class-X-board-exam-amend-nofail-p.html (accessed, 19 August 2018).

National Council for Teacher Education. 'Notification F. No. 61-03/20/2010/NCTE/(N&S)'. https://web.archive.org/web/20150412072603/http://www.ncte-india.org:80/Norms/RTE-3.pdf (accessed, 19 August 2018).

Nawani, Disha. 'Reflections on "Annual Status of Educational Research 2012"'. *Economic & Political Weekly* XLVIII, no. 12 (2013): 19–22.

Nelken, David. 'Introduction'. In *Beyond Law in Context*. Edited by David Nelken, xi–xxviii. London: Routledge, 2009.

Neuborne, Burt. 'The Supreme Court of India'. *ICON* 1 (2003): 476–510.

*New Indian Express*. 'CBSE Disaffiliates Six National Public Schools in Karnataka'. 7 September 2016. http://www.newindianexpress.com/states/karnataka/CBSE-disaffiliates-six-National-Public-Schools-in-Karnataka/2016/09/07/article3614785.ece (accessed, 19 August 2018).

*New Indian Express*. 'RTE Seat Vacancies on the Rise in Karnataka'. 6 August 2018. http://www.newindianexpress.com/states/karnataka/2018/aug/06/rte-seat-vacancies-on-the-rise-in-karnataka-1853905.html (accessed, 12 August 2018).

*New Indian Express*. 'State Govt to Implement 7$^{th}$ Pay Commission Recommendations'. 28 October 2016. http://www.newindianexpress.com/states/odisha/2016/oct/28/state-govt-to-implement-7th-pay-commission-recommendations-1532809.html (accessed, 19 August 2018).

Nielsen, Kenneth. '"Not on Our Land!" Peasants' Struggle against Forced Land Acquisition in India's West Bengal'. In *Rights and Legal Empowerment in Eradicating Poverty*, 217–45.

Noorani, Abdul Gafoor Abdul Majeed. 'How the Political Class has Looted India'. *The Hindu*, 30 July 2012. http://www.thehindu.com/opinion/lead/how-the-political-class-has-looted-india/article3700211.ece (accessed, 19 August 2018).

Nowak, Manfred. 'The Right to Education: Its Meaning, Significance and Limitations'. *Netherlands Quarterly of Human Rights* 9, no. 4 (1991): 418–25.

Nowak, Manfred. 'The Right to Education'. In *Economic, Social and Cultural Rights*, 245–71.

Odhekar, Prachi Deshmukh. 'India'. *International Journal for Education Law and Policy* 7, no. 1 (2011): 131–42.

Office of the High Commissioner for Human Rights. *Human Rights in the Administration of Justice: A Manual on Human Rights for Judges, Prosecutors and Lawyers*. New York, Geneva: United Nations, 2003.

Ohara, Yuki. 'Examining the Legitimacy of Unrecognised Low-Fee Private Schools in India: Comparing Different Perspectives'. *Compare: A Journal of Comparative and International Education* 42, no. 1 (2012): 69–90.

Ojha, Pandit Gopesh Kumar. *Progress of Compulsory Education in India*. Delhi: Universal Book & Stationary Co., 1966.

*Orissa Diary*. 'Odisha: Mobile Lok Adalat & Legal Awareness'. 30 May 2016. http://orissadiary.com/CurrentNews.asp?id=67502 (accessed, 19 August 2018).

Oxfam India. 'Oxfam India Newsletter. May 2014'. https://www.oxfam-india.org/sites/default/files/Oxfam%20India%20Newsletter%20May%202014.pdf (accessed, 19 August 2018).

Padma Ramachandran, and Vasantha Ramkumar. *Education in India*. 1st edition. New Delhi: National Book Trust, India, 2005.

Palacio, Ana. 'Legal Empowerment of the Poor: An Action Agenda for the World Bank: To the attention of the World Bank'. December 2005. http://siteresources.worldbank.org/INTLAWJUSTINST/Resources/LegalEmpowermentofthePoor.pdf (accessed, 19 August 2018).

Panda, Prativa. 'Legal Aid in India - An Overview'. *Indian Journal of Applied Research* 6, no. 2 (2016): 748–9.

Pednekar, Puja. '4.8K RTE Seats Vacant in Marathi Schools as Parents Opt for Popular English Institutes'. *Hindustan Times*, 22 April 2017. https://www.hindustantimes.com/mumbai-news/4-8k-rte-seats-vacant-in-marathi-schools-as-parents-opt-for-popular-english-institutes/story-kOxZV6zUSxgaYqjSbpsGzH.html (accessed, 12 August 2018).

Peisakhin, Leonid, and Paul Pinto. 'Is Transparency an Effective Anti-Corruption Strategy? Evidence from a Field Experiment in India'. *Regulation & Governance* 4, no. 3 (2010): 261–80.

Phillipson, Garvin. 'The Human Rights Act, "Horizontal Effect" and the Common Law: a Bang or a Whimper?', *Modern Law Review* 62, no. 6 (1999): 824–49.

Pieterse, Marius. 'Eating Socioeconomic Rights: The Usefulness of Rights Talk in Alleviating Social Hardship Revisited'. *Human Rights Quarterly* 29, no. 3 (2007): 796–822.

Prefontaine, Daniel C., and Joanne Lee. 'The Rule of Law and the Independence of the Judiciary'. *Revue québécoise de droit international*, 1998, 163–86.

Rajagopal, Balakrishnan. 'Pro-Human Rights But Anti-Poor? A Critical Evaluation of the Indian Supreme Court from a Social Movement Perspective'. *Human Rights Review* (2007): 157–86.

Rajamani, Lacanya, and Arghya Sengupta. 'The Supreme Court'. In *The Oxford Companion to Politics in India*. Edited by Niraja G. Jayal and Pratap B. Mehta, 80–97. New Delhi: Oxford University Press, 2011.

Ramachandran, V.K. 'On Kerala's Development Achievements'. In *Indian Development*, 205–324.

Ramchandani, Urmi. 'Evaluation of Monitoring Mechanisms of DCPCR to Ensure the Implementation of RTE Act in Delhi'. Working paper no. 337. http://ccs.in/internship_papers/2015/337_evaluation-of-monitoring-mechanisms-of-dcpcr_urmi-ramchandani.pdf (accessed, 19 August 2018).

Ramnath, Kalyani. '"We the People": Seamless Webs and Social Revolution in India's Constituent Assembly Debates'. *South Asia Research* 32 (2012): 57–70.

Rao, Nirmala, Kai-Ming Cheng, and Kirti Narain. 'Primary Schooling in China and India: Understanding How Socio-Contextual Factors Moderate The Role Of The State'. *International Review of Education* 49, no. 1 and 2 (2003): 153–76.

Rao, Nitya. 'Total Literacy Campaigns: A Field Report'. *Economic & Political Weekly* XXVIII, no. 19 (1993): 914–18.

Rao, P.P. 'Fundamental Right to Education'. *Journal of the Indian Law Institute* 50, no. 4 (2008): 585–92.

Raphael, T. 'The Problem of Horizontal Effect'. *European Human Rights Law Review* (2000): 493.

Reddy, K. Vivek. 'Minority Educational Institutions'. In *The Oxford Handbook of the Indian Constitution*, 921–42.

Rizvi, Saiyid Athar Abbas, and A.L. Basham. *The Wonder that was India*. London: Sidgwick & Jackson, 1987.

Robinson, Nick, Anjana Agarwal, Vrinda Bhandari, Ankit Goel, Karishma Kakkar, Reeba Muthalay, Vivek Shivakumar, Meera Sreekumar, Surya Sreenivasan, and Shruti Viswanathan. 'Interpreting the Constitution: Supreme Court Constitution Benches since Independence'. *Economic & Political Weekly* XLIV, no. 9 (2011): 27–32.

Robinson, Nick. 'A Quantitative Analysis of the Indian Supreme Court's Workload'. 2012. http://papers.ssrn.com/sol3/papers.cfm?abstract_id=2189181 (accessed, 19 August 2018).

Robinson, Nick. 'Closing the Implementation Gap: Grievance Redress and India's Social Welfare Programs'. *Columbia Journal of Transnational Law* 53, no. 2 (2015): 321–62.

Robinson, Nick. 'Expanding Judiciaries: India and the Rise of the Good Governance Court'. *Washington University Global Studies Law Review* 8, no. 1 (2009): 1–70.

Robinson, Nick. 'Right to Public Service Acts in India: The Experience from Bihar and Madhya Pradesh'. 2012. http://accountabilityindia.in/sites/default/files/policy-brief/right_to_public_services_act_nick_robinson.pdf (accessed, 19 August 2018).

RTI Assessment & Analysis Group & National Campaign for People's Right to Information. 'Safeguarding the Right to Information. Report of the People's RTI Assessment 2008. Executive Summary'.

2009. http://freedominfo.org/documents/india-safeguarding-executivesummary.pdf (accessed, 19 August 2018).

Sadgopal, Anil. 'Right to Education vs. Right to Education Act'. *Social Scientist* 38, no. 9/12 (2010): 17–50.

Sankar, Deepa. 'Financing Elementary Education in India through Sarva Shiksha Abhiyan: Challenges in Recent Times'. 2007. http://siteresources.worldbank.org/INTINDIA/2132853119144401932 8/21507645/SankarFinancingEducation.pdf (accessed, 19 August 2018).

Sankaranarayanan, Gopal. 'The Fading Right to Property in India'. *Law and Politics in Africa, Asia, Latin America (VRU)* 44, no. 2 (2011): 220–33. https://www.nomos-elibrary.de/10.5771/0506-7286-2011-2-220/the-fading-right-to-property-in-india-jahrgang-44-2011-heft-2?page=0 (accessed, 19 August 2018).

Sarkari, Sumita. '900 Seats under RTE in Schools Yet to be Filled'. *Times of India*, 22 September 2016. http://timesofindia.indiatimes.com/city/nashik/900-seats-under-RTE-in-schools-yet-to-be-filled/articleshow/54457478.cms (accessed, 19 August 2018).

Sarker, Shuvro Prosun, ed. *Clinical Legal Education in Asia: Accessing Justice for the Underprivileged*. New York, s.l.: Palgrave Macmillan, 2015.

Sarker, Shuvro Prosun. 'Empowering the Underprivileged: The Social Justice Mission for Clinical Legal Education in India'. In *Clinical Legal Education in Asia: Accessing Justice for the Underprivileged*. Edited by Shuvro P. Sarker, 177–93. New York, s.l.: Palgrave Macmillan, 2015.

Sarker, Shuvro Prosun. 'Empowering the Underprivileged: The Social Justice Mission for Clinical Legal Education in India'. *International Journal of Clinical Legal Education* 19 (2013): 321–40.

Sathe, S.P. 'Supreme Court and NBA'. *Economic & Political Weekly* XXXV, no. 46 (2000): 3990–4.

Sathe, S.P. *Judicial Activism in India*. 2nd edition. Delhi, Oxford: Oxford University Press, 2003.

Scharfe, Hartmut. *Education in Ancient India*. Leiden, Boston, Köln: Brill, 2002.

Scheinin, Martin. 'Economic and Social Rights as Legal Rights'. In *Economic, Social and Cultural Rights*, 29–54.

Scheinin, Martin. 'Justiciability and the Indivisibility of Human Rights'. In *The Road to a Remedy: Current Issues in the Litigation of Economic, Social, and Cultural Rights*. Edited by John Squires, Malcolm Langford, and Bret Thiele, 17–26. Sydney, NSW, Geneva, Switzerland: Australian Human Rights Centre, University of New South Wales; Centre for Housing Rights and Evictions, 2005.

Scott, Craig. 'Interdependence and Permeability of Human Rights Norms: Towards a Partial Fusion of the International Covenants on Human Rights'. *Osgoode Hall Law Journal* 27, no. 3 (1989): 769–878. http://digitalcommons.osgoode.yorku.ca/cgi/viewcontent.cgi?article=1791&context=ohlj (accessed, 19 August 2018).

Seervai, H.M. *Constitutional Law of India: A Critical Commentary*. 4th edition, 3 vols. Mumbai, Delhi: N.M. Tripathi; F.H. Seervai; Distributors, Universal Law Pub. Co, 1991–6.

Sengupta, Ananya. 'Child Rights Panels Exist but on Paper'. *The Telegraph*, 6 January 2014. http://www.telegraphindia.com/1140106/jsp/nation/story_17756333.jsp#.V55QnGVwPws (accessed, 19 August 2018).

Sepúlveda Carmona, M. Magdalena. *The Nature of the Obligations under the International Covenant on Economic, Social, and Cultural Rights*, Vol. 18. Antwerpen, New York: Intersentia, 2003.

Seth, Sanjay. 'Secular Enlightenment and Christian Conversion: Missionaries and Education in Colonial India'. In *Education and Social Change in South Asia*, 27–43.

Seth, Sanjay. *Subject Lessons: The Western Education of Colonial India*. Durham, London: Duke University Press, 2007.

Seventh United Nations Congress on the Prevention of Crime and the Treatment of Offenders. 'Basic Principles on the Independence of the Judiciary: Endorsed by General Assembly resolutions 40/32 of 29 November 1985 and 40/146 of 13 December 1985'. 1985. http://www.ohchr.org/EN/ProfessionalInterest/Pages/IndependenceJudiciary.aspx (accessed, 2 March 2019).

Shah, Parth J. 'Where Private and Public Co-Exist'. *Pragati*, 1 March 2010. http://pragati.nationalinterest.in/2010/03/where-private-and-public-co-exist/ (accessed, 19 August 2018).

Shankar, Uday, and Divya Tyagi. 'Socio-Economic Rights in India: Democracy Taking Roots'. *Law and Politics in Africa, Asia, Latin America (VRU)* 42, no. 4 (2009): 527–51. https://www.nomos-elibrary.de/10.5771/0506-7286-2009-4-527/socio-economic-rights-in-india-democracy-taking-roots-jahrgang-42-2009-heft-4?page=0 (accessed, 19 August 2018).

Shariff, Abusaleh. *India, Human Development Report: A Profile of Indian States in the 1990s*. New Delhi: Oxford University Press, 1999. http://www.loc.gov/catdir/enhancements/fy0605/99939190-d.html (accessed, 2 March 2019).

Sharma, Shikha. 'Again, Govt Extends Provisional Recognition of Schools'. *Indian Express*, 7 January 2015. http://indianexpress.com/article/cities/delhi/again-govt-extends-provisional-recognition-of-schools/ (accessed, 19 August 2018).

Sharma, Shruti. 'An Assessment of Girls Education under Sarva Shiksha Abhiyaan'. *Mainstream Weekly*, 21 June 2014. http://www.mainstreamweekly.net/article5000.html (accessed, 19 August 2018).

Shaw, Malcolm N. *International Law*. 8th edition. Cambridge, United Kingdom, New York, NY, Port Melbourne, VIC, Delhi, Singapore: Cambridge University Press, 2017.

Shrinivasan, Rumini. 'Paper Power'. *Times of India. The Crest Edition*, 13 April 2013. https://web.archive.org/web/20160417132947/ http://www.timescrest.com/society/paper-power-10113 (accessed, 19 August 2018).

Shukla, Rakesh. 'Rights of the Poor: An Overview of Supreme Court'. *Economic & Political Weekly* XLI, no. 35 (2006): 3755–9.

Singh, Jai S. 'Expanding Horizons of Human Right to Education: Perspectives on Indian and International Vision'. *Journal of the Indian Law Institute* 52, no. 1 (2010): 34–59.

Singh, Mahendra Pal. 'Constitutionalization and Realization of Human Rights in India'. In *Human Rights, Justice, and Constitutional Empowerment*, 26–46.

Singh, Mahendra Pal. 'Fundamental Rights, State Action and Cricket in India'. *Asia Pacific Law Review* (2005): 203–13.

Singh, Mahendra Pal. 'The Statics and the Dynamics of the Fundamental Rights and the Directive Principles - A Human Right Perspective'. *SCC (J)*, no. 5 (2003): 1–14.

Singh, Mahendra Pal. *V.N. Shukla's Constitution of India*. 12th edition. Lucknow: Eastern Book Co., 2013.

Singh, Parmanand. 'Promises and Perils of Public Interest Litigation in India'. *Journal of the Indian Law Institute* 52, no. 2 (2010): 172–88.

Singh, Renu, and Sudipa Sarkar. 'Teaching Quality Counts: How Student Outcomes Relate to Quality of Teaching in Private and Public Schools in India'. Young Lives Working Paper 91, University of Oxford, Oxford, UK. 2012. http://www.younglives.org.uk/files/working-papers/wp91-singh-sarkar (accessed, 19 August 2018).

Siwachi, Sukhbir. 'Haryana to Implement 7th Pay Commission Report Soon'. *Times of India*, 3 October 2016. http://timesofindia.indiatimes.com/city/chandigarh/Haryana-to-implement-7th-pay-commission-report-soon/articleshow/54662265.cms (accessed, 19 August 2018).

Sonkamble, Yashpal. 'Half-Empty RTE Seats Call for Fresh Admission Round'. *Pune Mirror*, 10 October 2016. http://punemirror.indiatimes.com/pune/civic/Half-empty-RTE-seats-call-for-fresh-admission-round/articleshow/54769837.cms (accessed, 19 August 2018).

Srikrishna, B.N. 'Judicial Independence'. In *The Oxford Handbook of the Indian Constitution*, 349–66.

Sripati, Vijayashri, and Arun Thiruvengadam. 'Constitutional Amendment Making the Right to Education a Fundamental Right'. *ICON*, 2004, 148–58.

Sripati, Vijayashri. 'India's National Human Rights Commission: A Shackled Commission?', *Boston University International Law Journal* 18, no. 1 (2000): 1–46.

Steiner, Henry J., Philip Alston, and Ryan Goodman. *International Human Rights in Context: Law, Politics, Morals; Text and Materials*. 3rd edition. Oxford: Oxford University Press, 2008.

Stern, Klaus. *Allgemeine Lehren der Grundrechte*. München: Beck, 1988.

Supreme Court of India. *A.K. Gopalan* v. *The State of Madras* MANU/SC/0012/1950, 19 May 1950.

Supreme Court of India. *Additional District Magistrate, Jabalpur* v. *Shiv Kant Shukla Etc.* MANU/SC/0062/1976, 28 April 1976.

Supreme Court of India. *Ahmedabad Municipal Corporation* v. *Nawab Khan Gulab Khan and others* MANU/SC/0051/1997, 11 October 1996.

Supreme Court of India. *Ajay Hasia Etc.* v. *Khalid Mujib Sehravardi* MANU/SC/0498/1980, 13 November 1980.

Supreme Court of India. *Ashoka Kumar Thakur* v. *Union of India and Ors* MANU/SC/3169/2007, 17 May 2007.

Supreme Court of India. *Ashoka Kumar Thakur vs. Union of India and Ors* MANU/SC/1397/2008, April 10, 2008.

Supreme Court of India. *Avinash Mehrotra* v. *Union of India and Ors* MANU/SC/0555/2009, 13 April 2009.

Supreme Court of India. *Bachpan Bachao Andolan* v. *Union of India and Ors* MANU/SC/0431/2011, 18 April 2011.

Supreme Court of India. *Bandhua Mukti Morcha* v. *Union of India* MANU/SC/0051/1983, 16 December 1983.

Supreme Court of India. *Bhartiya Seva Samaj Trust Tr. Pres. and Anr.* v. *Yogeshbhai Ambalal Patel and Anr.* MANU/SC/0741/2012, 14 September 2012.

Supreme Court of India. *Bokaro And Ramgur Ltd.* v. *The State of Bihar and Another* MANU/SC/0404/1962, 14 March 1962.

Supreme Court of India. *Chaitanya Kumar and Ors* v. *State of Karnataka and Ors* MANU/SC/0297/1986, 9 April 1986.

Supreme Court of India. *Childline India Foundation and Anr.* v. *Allan John Waters and Ors.* MANU/SC/0254/2011, 18 March 2011.

Supreme Court of India. *Consumer Education and Research Center and others* v. *Union of India and others* MANU/SC/0175/1995, 27 January 1995.

Supreme Court of India. *Divisional Manager, Aravali Golf Club & Anr.* v. *Chander Hass & Anr.* MANU/SC/4463/2007, 6 December 2007.

Supreme Court of India. *Dr. Ashok* v. *Union Of India* MANU/SC/0577/1997, 2 May 1997.

Supreme Court of India. *Election Commission of India* v. *St. Mary's School and Ors* MANU/SC/4627/2007, 6 December 2007.

Supreme Court of India. *Environment and Consumer Protection Foundation* v. *Delhi Administration and Ors* MANU/SC/0821/2012, 3 October 2012.

Supreme Court of India. *Environmental and Consumer Protect. Found.* v. *Delhi Administration and Ors* MANU/SC/0822/2011, 29 March 2011.

Supreme Court of India. *Environmental and Consumer Protect. Found.* v. *Delhi Administration and Ors* MANU/SC/1366/2011, 29 April 2011.

Supreme Court of India. *Environmental and Consumer Protect. Found.* v. *Delhi Administration and Ors* MANU/SC/0393/2012, 12 March 2012.

Supreme Court of India. *Francis Coralie Mullin* v. *The Administrator, Union Territory of Delhi and Others* MANU/SC/0492/1981, 13 January 1981.

Supreme Court of India. *I.C. Golak Nath* v. *State of Punjab* MANU/SC/0029/1967, 27 February 1967.

Supreme Court of India. *In Re: The Kerala Education Bill* MANU/SC/0029/1958, 22 May 1958.

Supreme Court of India. *In the Supreme Court of India (In Re: Appointment & Transfer of Judges)* v. *Civil Advisory Jurisdiction* MANU/SC/1146/1998, 28 October 1998.

Supreme Court of India. *Indian Council for Enviro-Legal Action* v. *Union of India* MANU/SC/1112/1996, 13 February 1996.

Supreme Court of India. *J. K. Raju* v. *State Of Andhra Pradesh And Anr.* MANU/SCOR/30475/2015, 28 October 2015.

Supreme Court of India. *Jatya Pal Singh and Ors* v. *Union of India and Ors* MANU/SC/0401/2013, 17 April 2013.

Supreme Court of India. *Joint Secretary, Political Department, Government of Meghalya* v. *High Court of Meghalya* MANU/SC/0317/2016, 18 March 2016.

Supreme Court of India. *Jolly George Varghese and Ors* v. *The Bank of Cochin* MANU/SC/0014/1980, 4 February 1980.

Supreme Court of India. *K. Veeraswami* v. *Union Of India And Others* MANU/SC/0610/1991, 25 July 1991.

Supreme Court of India. *K.P. Gopalakrishna and Ors* v. *The State of Karnataka and Ors* MANU/KA/0778/2017, 5 April 2017.

Supreme Court of India. *Kedar Nath Yadav* v. *State of West Bengal & Ors* MANU/SC/0964/2016, 31 August 2016.

Supreme Court of India. *Kesavananda Bharati* v. *State of Kerala* MANU/SC/0445/1973, 24 April 1973.

Supreme Court of India. *Kharak Singh* v. *The State Of U. P. & Others* MANU/SC/0085/1962, 18 December 1962.

Supreme Court of India. *L. Chandra Kumar* v. *Union Of India* MANU/SC/0261/1997, 18 March 1997.

Supreme Court of India. *M.C. Mehta* v. *Union of India* MANU/SC/0092/1986, 20 December 1986.

Supreme Court of India. *M.C. Mehta* v. *Union of India* MANU/SC/0175/1997, 30 December 1996.

Supreme Court of India. *M.C. Mehta* v. *Union of India* MANU/SC/0586/1988, 12 January 1988.

Supreme Court of India. *M.C. Mehta* v. *Union of India* MANU/SC/0327/1999, 29 April 1999.

Supreme Court of India. *M.C. Mehta* v. *Union of India* MANU/SC/0570/1996, 8 July 1996.

Supreme Court of India. *Madhav Hayawadanrao Hoskot* v. *State Of Maharashtra* MANU/SC/0119/1978, 17 August 1978.

Supreme Court of India. *Maharshi Mahesh Yogi Vedic Vishwavidyalay* v. *State of M.P. and Ors* MANU/SC/0644/2013, 3 July 2013.

Supreme Court of India. *Malpe Vishwanath Acharya & Ors* v. *State Of Maharashtra & Anr.* MANU/SC/0905/1998, 19 December 1997.

Supreme Court of India. *Maneka Gandhi* v. *Union Of India* MANU/SC/0133/1978, 25 January 1978.

Supreme Court of India. *Minerva Mills Ltd. & Ors* v. *Union Of India & Ors* MANU/SC/0075/1980, 9 May 1980, 31 July 1980.

Supreme Court of India. *Miss Mohini Jain* v. *State of Karnataka and Ors* MANU/SC/0357/1992, 30 July 1992.

Supreme Court of India. *Municipal Council, Ratlam* v. *Vardhichan* MANU/SC/0171/1980, 29 July 1980.

Supreme Court of India. *N. Parthasarathy* v. *Controller of Capital issues and Anr.* MANU/SC/0592/1991, 16 April 1991.

Supreme Court of India. *Nand Kishoe Ojha* v. *Madan Mohan Jha* MANU/SC/7238/2007, 19 March 2007.

Supreme Court of India. *Narmada Bachao Adolan* v. *Union of India* MANU/SC/0640/2000, 18 October 2000.

Supreme Court of India. *Olga Tellis And Others* v. *Bombay Municipal Corporation And Others* MANU/SC/0039/1985, 10 July 1985.

Supreme Court of India. *P. N. Kumar And Another* v. *Municipal Corporation of Delhi* MANU/SC/0127/1987, 2 November 1987.

Supreme Court of India. *P.D. Shamdasani* v. *Central Bank Of India Ltd.* MANU/SC/0017/1951, 21 December 1951.

Supreme Court of India. *Paschim Banga Khet Mazdoor Samity* v. *State of West Bengal* MANU/SC/0611/1996, 6 May 1996.

Supreme Court of India. *People's Union for Civil Liberties* v. *Union of India and Others.*

Supreme Court of India. *People's Union for Democratic Rights* v. *Union of India* MANU/SC/0038/1982, 18 September 1982.

Supreme Court of India. *Practice & Procedure: A Handbook of Information.* 3rd (Revised) Edition. Self-published, 2010. http://164.100.107.37/handbook3rdedition.pdf (accessed, 3 March 2019).

Supreme Court of India. *Pradeep Krishen* v. *Union of India* MANU/SC/0505/1996, 10 May 1996.

Supreme Court of India. *Pramati Educational & Cultural Trust* v. *Union of India & Ors* MANU/SC/0419/2014, 6 May 2014.

Supreme Court of India. *R.D. Upadhyay* v. *State of A.P. and Ors* MANU/SC/2061/2006, 13 April 2006.

Supreme Court of India. *Rajasthan State Electricity Board* v. *Mohan Lal* MANU/SC/0360/1967, 3 April 1967.

Supreme Court of India. *Ram Kumar Misra* v. *State Of Bihar And Others* MANU/SC/0251/1983, 21 September 1983.

Supreme Court of India. *Ramana Dayaram Shetty* v. *The International Airport Authority* MANU/SC/0048/1979, 4 May 1979.

Supreme Court of India. *Re. Exploitation of Children in Orphanages in the State of Tamil Nadu* v. *Union of India* MANU/SC/1304/2013, 16 December 2013.

Supreme Court of India. *Rural Litigation and Environment Kendra Dehradun* v. *State of UP* MANU/SC/0043/1985, 12 March 1985.

Supreme Court of India. *S. P. Gupta* v. *Union of India and Ors.* MANU/SC/0080/1981, 30 December 1981.

Supreme Court of India. *Satwant Singh Sawhney* v. *D. Ramarathnam, Assistant Passport Officer* MANU/SC/0040/1967, 10 April 1967.

Supreme Court of India. *Secretary Mahatama Gandhi Mission and Ors* v. *Bhartiya Kamgar Sena and Ors* MANU/SC/0024/2017, 5 January 2017.

Supreme Court of India. *Shiv Sagar Tiwari* v. *Union of India and others* MANU/SC/0739/1997, 23 December 1996.

Supreme Court of India. *Shrimati Vidya Verma* v. *Dr. Shiv Narain Verma* MANU/SC/0072/1955, 11 November 1955.

Supreme Court of India. *Sindhi Education Society and Anr.* v. *The Chief Secretary, Govt. of NCT of Delhi and Ors* MANU/SC/0476/2010, 8 July 2010.

Supreme Court of India. *Society for Un-aided Private Schools of Rajasthan* v. *Union of India & Another* MANU/SC/0311/2012, 12 April 2012.

Supreme Court of India. *State of Bihar and Ors* v. *Project Uchcha Vidy, Sikshak Sangh and Ors* MANU/SC/0054/2006, 3 January 2006.

Supreme Court of India. *State of Madras* v. *Champakam Dorairajan and The State of Madras* v. *C.R. Srinivasan* MANU/SC/0007/1951, 9 April 1951.

Supreme Court of India. *State of Maharashtra* v. *Sant Dnyaneshwar Shikshan Shastra Mahavidyalaya and Ors* MANU/SC/1756/2006, 31 March 2006.

Supreme Court of India. *State of Orissa and Anr.* v. *Mamata Mohanty* MANU/SC/0110/2011, 9 February 2011.

Supreme Court of India. *State of Rajasthan and Anr.* v. *S. R. Hr. Sec. School and Ors.* MANU/SC/1264/2004, 15 September 2004.

Supreme Court of India. *State of U.P. and Ors* v. *Anand Kumar Yadav and Ors* MANU/SC/0897/2017, 25 July 2017.

Supreme Court of India. *State of U.P. and Ors* v. *Bhupendra Natz Tripathi and Ors* MANU/SC/0917/2010, 29 October 2010.

Supreme Court of India. *State of U.P. and Ors* v. *Shiv Kumar Pathak and Ors* MANU/SC/0898/2017, 25 July 2017.

Supreme Court of India. *State of U.P.* v. *Pawan Kumar Divedi* MANU/SC/0753/2014, 2 September 2014.

Supreme Court of India. *State of U.P.* v. *Shiv Kumar Pathak* MANU/SC/1241/2014, 17 December 2014.

Supreme Court of India. *Sub-Committee on Judicial Accountability* v. *Union of India* MANU/SC/0368/1991, 8 May 1991.

Supreme Court of India. *Suk Das* v. *Union Territory of Arunachal Pradesh* MANU/SC/0140/1986, 10 March 1986.

Supreme Court of India. *Sukhdev Singh, Oil & Natural Gas Commission* v. *Bhagat Ram* MANU/SC/0667/1975, 21 February 1975.

Supreme Court of India. *Sunil Batra (II)* v. *Delhi Administration* MANU/SC/0265/1979, 20 December1979.

Supreme Court of India. *Supreme Court Advocates-on-Record Association and another* v. *Union of India* MANU/SC/0073/1994, 6 October 1993.

Supreme Court of India. *Supreme Court Advocates-on-Record Association and another* v. *Union of India* MANU/SC/1183/2015, 16 October 2015.

Supreme Court of India. *Suresh Kumar Koushal & Anr.* v. *Naz Foundation & Ors* MANU/SC/1278/2013, 11 December 2013.

Supreme Court of India. *T.C. Basappa* vs. *T. Nagappa And Another* MANU/SC/0098/1954, 5 May 1954.

Supreme Court of India. *The State Of Bihar* v. *Maharajadhiraja Sir Kameshwar Singh* MANU/SC/0019/1952, 2 May 1952.

Supreme Court of India. *The State of West Bengal* v. *Subodh Gopal Bose and Ors* MANU/SC/0018/1953, 17 December 1953.

Supreme Court of India. *TK Rangarajan* v. *Government of Tamil Nadu* MANU/SC/0541/2003, 6 August 2003.

Supreme Court of India. *Union of India* v. *Delhi High Court* MANU/SC/0194/2002, 14 March 2002.

Supreme Court of India. *Union Of India* v. *Sankal Chand Himatlal Sheth* MANU/SC/0065/1977, 19 September 1977.

Supreme Court of India. *Unni Krishnan, J.P. and Ors* v. *State of Andhra Pradesh and Ors* MANU/SC/0333/1993, 4 February 1993.

Supreme Court of India. *Vikas Sankhala and Ors* v. *Vikas Kumar Agarwal and Ors* MANU/SC/1318/2016, 18 October 2016.

Supreme Court of India. *Virender Gaur* v. *State of Haryana* MANU/SC/0629/1995, 24 November 1994.

Supreme Court of India. *Vishaka & Ors* v. *State of Rajasthan & Ors* MANU/SC/0786/1997, 13 August 1997.

Supreme Court of India. *World Saviors* v. *Union of India* MANU/SC/1455/1998, 6 December 1996.

Supreme Court of India. *Zee Telefilms Ltd.* v. *Union of India* MANU/SC/0074/2005, 2 February 2005.

Supreme Court of India. 'Court News: Vol. X, Issue No. 3'. 2015. https://web.archive.org/web/20170428163330/http://supremecourtofindia.nic.in/courtnews/July,%202015-sept-2015.pdf (accessed, 19 August 2018).

Supreme Court of India. 'The Supreme Court of India. Annual Report 2014'. 2014. https://web.archive.org/web/20161225150946/http://supremecourtofindia.nic.in/annualreport/annualreport2014-15.pdf (accessed, 19 August 2018).

Surendranath, Anup. 'Life and Personal Liberty'. In *The Oxford Handbook of the Indian Constitution*, 756–76.

Tankha, Madhur. 'Lack of Toilets Keeps Girls Away from Schools'. *The Hindu*, 12 October 2013. http://www.thehindu.com/todays-paper/tp-national/tp-newdelhi/lack-of-toilets-keeps-girls-away-from-schools/article5227297.ece (accessed, 19 August 2018).

Thakur, Pradeep. 'India has 17 Judges for a Million People, 5,000 Posts Vacant'. *Times of India*, 17 April 2016. http://timesofindia.indiatimes.com/india/India-has-17-judges-for-a-million-people-5000-posts-vacant/articleshow/51860142.cms (accessed, 19 August 2018).

Tharakan, P.K. Michael. 'Socio-Economic Factors in Educational Development. Case of Nineteenth Century Travancore'. *Economic & Political Weekly* XIX, no. 10 (1984): 1913–28.

*The Economic Times*. 'Assembly Election 2011 West Bengal: Trinamool Congress Rises Like a Phoenix'. 13 May 2011. https://economictimes.indiatimes.com/news/politics-and-nation/assembly-election-2011-west-bengal-trinamool-congress-rises-like-phoenix/articleshow/8293363.cms (accessed, 19 August 2018).

*The Government of the Republic of South Africa and Others* v. *Irene Grootboom and Others* [2000] ZACC 19; 2001 (1) SA 46; 2000 (11) BCLR 1169. Constitutional Court of South Africa, 4 October 2000. http://www.saflii.org/za/cases/ZACC/2000/19.pdf (accessed, 16 November 2015).

*The Hindu*. 'Cabinet Defines What is a Minority Institution'. 7 July 2012. http://www.thehindu.com/news/national/karnataka/cabinet-defines-what-is-a-minority-institution/article3610611.ece (accessed, 19 August 2018).

*The Hindu*. 'High Court Initiates PIL on Out-Of-School Children'. 2 April 2013. http://www.thehindu.com/news/national/karnataka/high-court-initiates-pil-on-outofschool-children/article4570507.ece (accessed, 19 August 2018).

*The Hindu*. 'Karnataka to Set Up Food Commission'. 14 June 2016. http://www.thehindu.com/todays-paper/tp-national/karnataka-to-set-up-food-commission/article8725862.ece (accessed, 19 August 2018).

*The Hindu*. Educating India'. 4 April 2011. http://www.thehindu.com/opinion/editorial/educating-india/article1599783.ece (accessed, 19 August 2018).

The PROBE Team. *Public Report on Basic Education in India*. New Delhi: Oxford University Press, 1999.

*The Tribune*. 'Legal Awareness Camps for Teachers, Elderly in P'kula'. 27 May 2016. http://www.tribuneindia.com/news/chandigarh/community/legal-awareness-camps-for-teachers-elderly-in-p-kula/242801.html (accessed, 19 August 2018).

Thiruvengadam, Arun. 'Characterising and Evaluating Indian Social Rights Jurisprudence into the 21st Century'. In *Constitutional Rights to Welfare in India*. Edited by Sudhir Krishnaswamy and Malini Bhattacharjee. Oxford University Press, Forthcoming. https://azimpremjiuniversity.edu.in/SitePages/pdf/Characterising-and-evaluating-Indian-social-rights-jurisprudence-into-the-21st-century.pdf (accessed, 16 August 2018).

Thiruvengadam, Arun. 'Revisiting the Role of the Judiciary in Plural Societies (1987): A Quarter-Century Restrospective on Public Interest Litigation and the Global South'. In *Comparative Constitutionalism in South Asia*. Edited by Sunil Khilnani, 341–69. New Delhi: Oxford University Press, 2013.

Thiruvengadam, Arun. 'The Global Dialogue among Courts: Social Rights Jurisprudence of the Supreme Court of India From a Comparative Perspective'. In, *Human Rights, Justice, and Constitutional Empowerment*, 264–309.

*Times of India*. 'Fresh Move to Decrease Number of Tribunals'. 25 November 2015. http://timesofindia.indiatimes.com/india/Fresh-move-to-decrease-number-of-tribunals/articleshow/49918099.cms (accessed, 19 August 2018).

*Times of India*. 'Full Text of Letter: Four Senior Judges Say Situation in SC. Read more at: Full Text of Letter: Four Senior Judges Say Situation in SC "Not In Order"'. 12 January 2018. https://timesofindia.indiatimes.com/india/full-text-of-letter-four-senior-judges-say-situation-in-sc-not-in-order/articleshow/62472957.cms (accessed, 12 August 2018).

*Times of India*. 'Ranglal Jamuda appointed Odisha Food Commission Chairperson'. 9 May 2016. http://timesofindia.indiatimes.com/city/bhubaneswar/Ranglal-Jamuda-appointed-Odisha-food-commission-chairperson/articleshow/52193346.cms (accessed, 19 August 2018).

*Times of India*. 'Right to Education Admissions may be Delayed Again'. 21 December 2016. http://timesofindia.indiatimes.com/city/pune/RTE-admissions-may-be-delayed-again/articleshow/56091823.cms (accessed, 19 August 2018).

*Times of India*. 'Time to Roll Back Licence Raj in Education'. 18 October 2016. http://timesofindia.indiatimes.com/city/hyderabad/Time-to-roll-back-licence-raj-in-education/articleshow/54908232.cms (accessed, 19 August 2018).

*Times of India*. 'With RTE a Success, Govt to Shift Focus to Quality of Education'. 15 January 2014. http://timesofindia.indiatimes.com/india/With-RTE-a-success-govt-to-shift-focus-to-quality-of-education/articleshow/28811588.cms (accessed, 19 August 2018).

Tripathi, P.K. *Spotlights on Constitutional Interpretation*. Bombay: N.M. Tripathi, 1972.

Tushnet, M. 'The Issue of State Action/Horizontal Effect in Comparative Constitutional Law'. *International Journal of Constitutional Law* 1, no. 1 (2003): 79–98.

Tushnet, Mark V. *Weak Courts, Strong Rights: Judicial Review and Social Welfare Rights in Comparative Constitutional Law*. Princeton, N.J., Woodstock: Princeton University Press, 2009.

Tushnet, Mark. 'An Essay on Right'. *Texas Law Review* 62, no. 8 (1984): 1363–403.

Twining, William. *Law in Context. Enlarging a Discipline*. Oxford: Oxford University Press, 1997.

UNESCO. *Teaching and Learning: Achieving Quality for All*. EFA Global Monitoring Report 2013/4. 2014.

United Nations Committee on Economic, Social and Cultural Rights (CESCR), 'General Comment No. 3: The Nature of States Parties' Obligations (Art. 2, Para. 1, of the Covenant)', 14 December 1990, E/1991/23. http://www.refworld.org/docid/4538838e10.html (accessed, 3 March 2019).

United Nations General Assembly. 'Extreme Poverty and Human Rights: Note by the Secretary-General'. A/67/278, 9 August 2012.

United Nations. 'Committee on Economic Social and Cultural Rights: Report on the Forty Second and Forty Third Sessions (4-22 May 2009, 2-20 November 2009)'. 2010.

United Nations: Economic and Social Council. 'Preliminary Report of the Special Rapporteur on the Right to Education, Ms Katarina Tomasevski, submitted in accordance with Commission on Human Rights resolution 1998/33: Commission on Human Rights. Fifty-fifth session. Item 10 of the provisional agenda'. E/CN.4/1999/49, 13 January 1999.

United Nations: Economic and Social Council. 'Report of the Special Rapporteur on the Right of Everyone to the Enjoyment of the Highest Attainable Standard of Physical and Mental Health, Paul Hunt: Commission on Human Rights. Sixty-second session. Item 10 of the provisional agenda'. E/CN.4/2006/48, 3 March 2006.

Upendra Baxi, 'Demosprudence Versus Jurisprudence: The Indian Judicial Experience in the Context of Comparative Constitutional Studies', *Macquarie Law Journal* 14 (2014): 3–23.

US Supreme Court, *Munn* v. *Illinois*, 1 March 1877.

van de Meene, Ineke, and Benjamin van Rooij. *Access to Justice and Legal Empowerment: Making the Poor Central in Legal Development Co-Operation*. Leiden: Leiden University Press, 2008.

van Rooij, Benjamin. *Bringing Justice to the Poor: Bottom-up Legal Development Cooperation* (Amsterdam: Leiden University Press, 2008).

Verma, S.K., and K. Kusum, eds. *Fifty Years of the Supreme Court of India: Its Grasp and Reach*. New Delhi, New York: Oxford University Press, 2000.

Vierdag, E.W. 'The Legal Nature of the Rights Granted by the International Covenant on Economic, Social and Cultural Rights'. *Netherlands Yearbook of International Law* (1978): 69–105.

Vishnoi, Anubhuti. 'NCERT Asks Government Not to Scrap "No Detention"'. *Economic Times*, 10 October 2016. http://economictimes.indiatimes.com/news/politics-and-nation/ncert-asks-government-not-to-scrap-no-detention/articleshow/54770835.cms (accessed, 19 August 2018).

Walker, Maurice. 'PISA 2009 Plus Results: Performance of 15-Year-Olds in Reading, Mathematics and Science for 10 Additional Participants'. 2011. http://research.acer.edu.au/cgi/viewcontent.cgi?article=1000&context=pisa (accessed, 19 August 2018).

Ward, Michael. 'Aid to Education: The Case of Sarva Shiksha Abhiyan in India and the Role of Development Partners'. *Journal of Education Policy* 26, no. 4 (2011): 543–56.

# Index

# About the Author

**Florian Matthey-Prakash** studied law at the University of Freiburg, Germany, and The WB National University of Juridical Sciences, Kolkata, India. He has completed his PhD from the University of Giessen, Hesse, Germany. He remains particularly interested in socio-economic rights, comparative constitutional law, and education as an independent researcher. He now works as a judge in Germany. While working on his doctoral dissertation, he also wrote an article on School Management Committees in India, which was published in *Law and Politics in Africa, Asia and Latin America* in 2015. The author may be contacted at fmatthey@gmail.com.